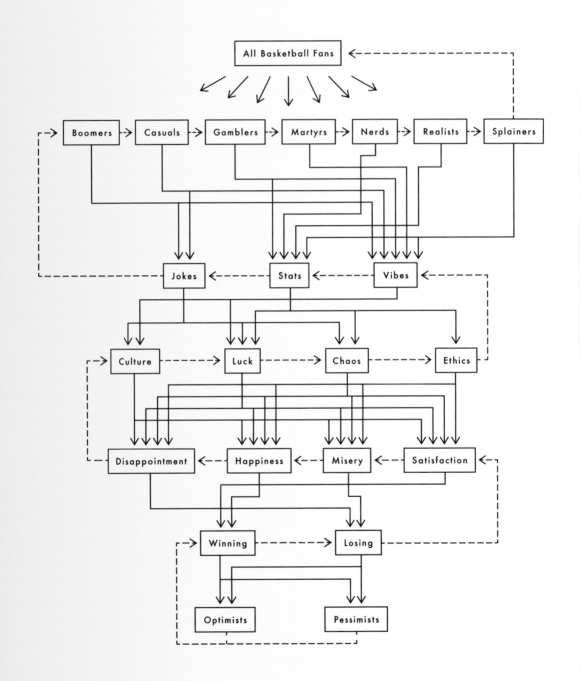

THE JOY OF BASKETBALL

BEN DETRICK &
ANDREW KUO

ABRAMS IMAGE, NEW YORK

1996

The Blizzard of '96.

General optimism/anxiety.

The Bulls are champions.

Allen Iverson is drafted.

Harry Potter is introduced.

Titanic premieres in theaters.

The Sopranos airs on HBO.

The Spurs are champions.

→ (CONT.)

Luka Dončić is born.

The Lakers are champions.

iTunes is launched.

9/11 happens.

Michael Jordan debuts for the Wizards

Yao Ming plays his first NBA game.

Myspace comes out.

The Pistons are champions.

Chris Paul is drafted.

Katrina hits New Orleans.

The Heat are champions.

Twitter is open for use.

"Umbrella" is a Billboard #1.

Kevin Durant debuts in Seattle.

The stock market crashes.

The Celtics are champions.

(CONT.)

Barack Obama is president.

Six teams pass on drafting Stephen Curry.

Ron Artest thanks his psychiatrist.

LeBron James makes a decision.

The Mavericks are champions.

The Social Network loses Best Film.

Osama Bin Laden is killed.

Jeremy Lin hits a winner in Toronto.

Sam Hinkie starts as Sixers GM.

Nikola Jokić is drafted #41 overall.

Becky Hammon becomes a Spurs coach.

The Yeezy Boost 750 is released.

The Warriors are champions.

Young Thug drops *Barter 6*.

American Apparel files for bankruptcy.

The Cavaliers are champions.

→ 2021

The Raptors are champions.

Billie Eilish releases her debut album.

Big Baller Brand opens for business.

Banksy's *Devolved Parliament* sells for $12.2M.

Kobe Bryant passes away.

Covid-19 upends the entire world.

George Floyd is murdered by the police.

LaMelo Ball enters the NBA.

CONTENTS

FOREWORD

Growing up in the Bronx, we had no basketball hoops. If you had one, someone would steal it. It wasn't always safe going to the park in the hood because of stray shots and shit. On my block, there was a sign on one of the buildings that said "Absolutely No Ball Playing." So, we decided that it would be the hoop—if the basketball hit that sign, it counted. We played 21 against it with full basketball rules and had a little tournament. That's the beauty of basketball. It doesn't take much to play. It's almost the perfect sport.

My house has always been a Knicks house. I've been going to games all my life with my sisters and my mom. You didn't really care if they won or lost. We've always gone for the atmosphere. There might be a fight in the stands, or you got a chance to boo Isiah Thomas. It was a great way to get your New York frustrations out. Being a Knicks fan has given me a greater appreciation for basketball: you learn about the fundamentals, you learn about playmaking, you learn about the things that your team should be doing.

The most impressive thing I've seen was when Melo set the arena's scoring record. It was just a random night against the Charlotte Bobcats, but it was such a group experience. I stood up for every shot and you're high-fiving people you've never seen in your life (now that we've been through COVID, I figure that's how things spread). And then there were the bad days, like when J. R. Reid had the heavy foul on the virgin A. C. Green and knocked his front teeth out.

I've been in the same section since before *Desus & Mero*, before the podcast, before any of this. There are security guards that just know me as a very aggressive Knicks fan that loves to drink and eat steak sandwiches. But they're the ones who will say, low-key, "I saw what you did with Obama and I'm proud of you." You made my day. Going to Madison Square Garden is just a love affair. All the fans rock with us, the celebrities rock with us. I'm one of the few people who can get teary-eyed when I see Steve Schirripa. The fans have the same energy whether it's Red Panda kicking a ball off her head at halftime or a Game 7.

The last Knicks game I went to was the day Kobe died. It was one of the saddest games I've ever been to, but everyone at Madison Square Garden carried themselves with a sense of respect and reverence. We lost someone who did something here on the biggest stage. No other arena really feels like that. No shots fired, but you don't really have people dying to go to an arena in Memphis. We go so hard as Knicks fans because we love that place.

My favorite Knicks player of all-time is Latrell Sprewell. He played with such reckless abandon. And every time he came down the court, he looked like he was going to murder someone. He could jump so high and he had those braids. At the time, he looked like what people were telling us to be terrified of in the Central Park wilding and things like that. He was just the personification of anger in the NBA. And from a non-basketball perspective, the idea that he choked out his boss—we could all relate to that. He also had sneakers that had spinning rims and went on to be one of the biggest tax scofflaws. Just because he stopped playing, it doesn't mean he stopped being great.

That generation brought a new energy and new blood to the game. This sounds like the worst cliche from a *Rolling Stone* writer from 1991, but it felt like the Hip-Hop-ification of basketball. The underlying aspects of the culture changed and it just became cooler. When Allen Iverson came into the league, it was one of the first times you looked on the court and saw yourself. He looked like one of your homies that literally came off the corner and was lighting people up. He didn't change or anything, got the same outfit on. We carry ourselves the same.

Your heroes became human. They became accessible. They're not deities like Larry Bird, Magic Johnson, and Michael Jordan. But then you saw them on the court and they could *play*. Like the first time when A.I. crossed up Jordan—that was scientifically not supposed to happen. It changed how you rooted for teams and what it meant to be an NBA fan. It's similar to when you went from Nintendo to Xbox: same video games, but it was completely different.

I miss the physicality of the old games, but they were just straight-up having fistfights without fouls being called. It's wild to watch now. We remember it as majestic and poetic. We remember Magic Johnson doing this skyhook. But are these our actual memories or have they been carefully edited by the NBA and put over a beautiful score by John Tesh? If you look back, the games were ugly. The players were ugly. The outfits were ugly. It was a rougher sport for a rougher world—take an elbow to the face and keep it moving.

I don't want to say today's game is polished, but it's more fine-tuned. There's more precision. It's like someone playing the violin, lightly plucking the strings and just floating. I love the pacing and spacing. Anyone could hit a 3. Now you get the chance to see Damian Lillard shoot the ball from the opposite locker room and it's one that he regularly hits. But no player is completely unstoppable. The game kind of balances itself, like a physical game of chess. If you watch it enough, it turns into *The Queen's Gambit*—you see Xs and Os on the court. If an old, stodgy curmudgeon like myself can come around to it, anyone can.

In the past, players didn't have the power they have today. You never had Kyrie Irving saying, "Yo, I'm taking a personal day." If that had happened in the eighties, Ronald Reagan would have had his house bombed. You weren't allowed to be an individual. You were just a player with a number on your back and you did what the coach and the organization said. And now you see players actually picking their destiny, deciding where they're going, and who they're playing with. It's not a bad thing.

I was at a dinner with a player—I'm not going to use his name—and he said one of the reasons he didn't want to go somewhere was because of the travel time to the arena. You can get a Nike deal, unlimited groupies, fifty cars, and Drake as a side-kick, but no one wants to go to a job that they're miserable at. Trust me. The old heads say this new generation is soft. But in the back of their heads, they're thinking they should have been more aggressive about their happiness.

You would think NBA players are super-sensitive. But they love when we mention them on the show or the podcast, even if it's in a negative way. Me and Mero don't do that thing where we pretend to be sports analysts. We're going to joke about your goofy haircut, the clothes you wore when you were walking into the arena, or the person you're dating. It's nothing hurtful and we're funny. And that helps a lot, because these players are really tall and they're really scary. I do not want any problems with them.

Because of social media, we view today's NBA players as more well-rounded. We didn't see any of this stuff about Michael Jordan until last year, when *The Last Dance* came out. We never saw him going through it with Juanita, except in the *National Enquirer*. We never knew the details. If he had to deal with Twitter and *TMZ*, I don't know if Michael would have been Michael. You have to realize, these players are not that old. People have to stop and say, are we really bullying young people? We're clowning them if they show emotion? Why is that okay?

In the future, I'd like to see more representation in the league, with people of color in higher places. I'd like to see the league do more with the WNBA. When they started, they were a laughingstock— not because they were actually a laughingstock, but because we treated them like one. We were misogynistic. Like, there are broads playing basketball? But they're out there doing their thing. There's a whole new generation growing up falling in love with the sport. As much as it hurts my heart to say, there's a group of kids in Brooklyn who just saw the Nets go to the playoffs and they'll always remember that.

As a Knicks fan, I just want another playoff run. We almost burned down the city after winning one playoff game. If we win two in a row, they're gonna have to call the national guard in.

INTRODUCTION

BEN DETRICK & ANDREW KUO

Loving basketball is easy. It does not ask for too much, at first. Anyone can appreciate a twisting dunk or a parabolic shot hoisted from a great distance that settles into the bottom of the net. Scoring is constant and handily broken down into countable ones, twos, and threes. Athletes are extraordinary in size and skill, but they are not wearing hats, helmets, or bulky carapaces of protective gear. We can see their faces, their hair, their autobiographical tattoos, their expressions of happiness, despair, rage, or mockery. Early investment is not required.

But take warning: despite its easy accessibility, basketball can consume you—just as it has consumed us. You will realize you have crossed the Rubicon when your social media feeds are scrambled by NBA memes, quote-tweeted hot takes, and Instagram accounts dedicated to parsing whether a drive is a travel or a legal gather-step. A debate between drunken strangers about the defensive tendencies of a backup point guard becomes the only audible sound in a noisy Canal Street dive bar. Your phone automatically ushers you to the Basketball-Reference website, due to the number of times you have frantically needed to confirm who led the league in attempted 3-pointers in 2004. You dawdle momentarily at any playground pickup game, quickly noting which guy

playing in a Van Heusen dress shirt is unsuitable to operate as a primary distributor. If this has happened to you, just know that you are not alone.

One beautiful thing about basketball is that fans can interpret the game however they want. There are true believers who blindly trust whoever wears team colors and cynics who maintain the same faith that their heroes will inevitably turn into pumpkins when it matters the most. There are body language experts who practice phrenology over broadband, analytics dorks, games-watchers, and casuals. Some fans complain that the sport has become bloodless and homogeneous in the decades since they wore a Pistons Starter jacket. Others accept the sport as a snaking waterway and drift along for the ride. A few of us stare at the constellations in hopes of mapping out the direction where hoops might go next, aware that we are wrong all the time. In every case, we are rooting for weirdness.

Basketball is always changing. Over the last quarter century, ideas have spread from the brainstems of quirky visionaries to pervade every level of the sport as if part of one roundball mycelium network. Concepts about outside shooting, positional flexibility, floor spacing, and rim protection have gone from avant-garde to conventional to, maybe, boomer drivel. Offenses fueled by coal collectively turned to nuclear fission. But what if wind turbines are the energy source of the future? What if it is something else? What if it was coal all along?

As in every sport, basketball players keep getting stronger, faster, and more talented. The NBA's keystone species evolved from titanic centers to sculpted power forwards to lanky wings to ball-dominant guards to randomized combinations of those archetypes. Now there are big men who contribute as hybrid shot-blocker/perimeter shooters, mites who feast at the free-throw line, and bruisers who annually rank among the league's assists leaders. The divergent paths leading to versatility and specialization have split, crisscrossed, and intertwined like a bowl of soba noodles.

We respect innovative coaches and wily front office decision-makers, but the NBA revolves around a carousel of about 450 dudes who are the best on the planet at what they do. An infinitesimally tiny sliver of the population has ever set a screen, rolled to the basket, and mushed home a two-handed alley-oop on a regulation court. We cannot handle the ball like Kyrie Irving, shoot like Stephen Curry, or swat away shots at their apex like Anthony Davis. Yet we feel a sense of kinship when we chuck a lopsided Pizza Hut ball at a double-rim or play H.O.R.S.E on a slab of particleboard screwed to a garage. It is romantic to believe that basketball reveals the character of those on the court in a relatable sense, but we create those storylines while watching people who are a zillion times better at it than we are.

The power of narrative arcs—for teams, coaches, executives, and especially players—is obvious. The NBA is a serialized drama with recurrent characters, fresh faces, emerging villains, fallen angels, tragic losers, devious leprechauns, tales of betrayal, and sagas of redemption. We create mythologies and subscribe to religions that are based on arbitrary bounces. We attempt to explain the game with numbers, playbooks filled by squiggles and arrows, or high priests who bellow about the need to dominate. But we need to raze the temples that have been erected by previous generations and build our own.

Our priorities can be different from those of the past. We do not need to accept the idea that a playoff series, a seventh game, or a single shot at the buzzer will define a person's professional life. There are countless smaller wins and losses that are just as exhilarating and crushing, depending on your point of view. These are moments when we hug strangers in a sports bar, drop truth-bombs in a group chat, or weep in solitude over a pirated stream on a laptop. We are unable to feel exactly what players feel, in the same way we are unable to do what they do, but our emotional stakes are real. Their adrenalized successes and traumatic failures are deeply personal and truthfully unknowable, yet we collectively experience them in our own way. Ideally, we celebrate their victories and catch them when they fall.

History segregates athletes into winners and losers, but a meaningful basketball legacy can exist outside of that cruel binary arrangement. It could be a new way to shear a defender's ankles, a patented one-footed fall-away jumper, an undersized defensive genius who plays center, a pull-up jumper from the logo, a pregame talcum toss, a pair of exotic sneakers pulled from a vault, or the refusal to play after an unarmed man is shot by police. The cultural vocabulary of the NBA—on and off the court—is only translatable by those who pay attention. We get what we give.

There is growing awareness that basketball players, despite being very tall, are people. They deserve to be treated with kindness and respect, especially at a time when the membrane separating athletes and the public is more permeable than ever before. Everyone knows that players should not be physically spat upon, but dehumanization also occurs in less overtly phlegmy ways. The availability of professional-grade arcana like salary figures and Collective Bargaining Agreement rules has turned a generation of fans into econometric gurus who care more about cap hits than personalities. In some quarters, there is an inclination to describe an underpaid player as "being on a good contract," to side with management instead of labor, and to vilify players for missing a practice or spending their offseason doing anything besides pouring sweat in an empty gym. We should be more thoughtful about these dynamics.

Our game has never been better than it is today. We will say the same thing in a decade, then again in a hundred years. And it will be true. We are not advocating mindless optimism or the Panglossian belief that everything on the hardwood will turn out for the best. It will not. Your team will agonizingly lose. Your favorite player will brick a key jumper off the side of the backboard. You will be frustrated and miserable. But you should not get angry. You should not behave cruelly. You should not burn a jersey in your Big Green Egg while staring into the flames in wraparound shades.

Being a sports fan is inherently futile: we are wholly detached from what occurs on the court. Our cheers and curses and intricate superstitions mean nothing. It is a rain dance draped in ceremonial garb of Mitchell & Ness. We are accustomed to caring about things we cannot control—but basketball is a reliable hope-generating machine that always gives us another season, another game, another possession with the shot clock dwindling to double zeros. Life does not always grant do-overs, but basketball does.

AFRICA

In the 1994 comedy *The Air Up There*, Kevin Bacon plays an American basketball coach who travels to Kenya to recruit a prospect from the "Winabi" tribe. At the time, the NBA included only a handful of players from Africa, and there was a perception that undiscovered giants were waiting for Westerners to pull up with an unfamiliar orange object. Like diamonds, oil, or copper, height was a natural resource primed for exploitation. Twenty-five years later, the league's growing population of athletes from Africa reflects the league's spectrum: All-NBA superstars, journeymen, scrubs clinging to roster spots. The sport has been cultivated by developmental programs like Basketball Without Borders and Giants of Africa, which has hosted camps and clinics in sixteen nations. During the 2020 NBA Draft alone, eight players from Nigeria or with at least one Nigerian parent were selected.

It is easy to forget there was a time when the Motherland was represented by one towering figure. Hakeem Olajuwon, whose résumé includes two Finals Most Valuable Player awards, two Defensive Player of the Year awards, and two titles, was the first African to play in the NBA. He was the perfect ambassador, with his influence splashing both sides of the Atlantic. A quarter century after his prime, the 7-foot center's game is still shockingly modern. Nimble but detonative, Olajuwon was a defensive maestro who swatted more shots than anyone in history and led the league in rebounds several times. His repertoire included turnaround baseline jumpers, hooks, stutter-stepping drives, and the Dream Shake, a sequence of shoulder fakes with precise footwork that has been passed down to players such as Kobe Bryant and Joel Embiid like sterling silverware. "Hakeem was the best of the lot," rival center Vlade Divac told the *Times of India*. "He could play outside and inside, he could shoot and pass. It was very difficult to stop him, but you could learn a lot from him."

Despite Olajuwon's dignified brilliance, stereotypes and discrimination against Africans persisted. In 2014, Danny Ferry, then general manager of the Hawks, paraphrased an uncomplimentary scouting report about Luol Deng, a two-time All-Star from Sudan (today South Sudan). "He's a good guy overall, but he's not perfect," Ferry said on a conference call with Atlanta ownership about potential free agent signings. "He's got some African in him. He has a storefront out front that's beautiful and great, but he may be selling some counterfeit stuff behind you."

African players are often rumored to be older than their listed ages—an idea strengthened by incidents in which birth dates were fudged. In the case of Manute Bol, a 7-foot-7 center and humanitarian from South Sudan, the coach who brought him to the United States simply made one up. "I gave him his birthday because they didn't know how old he was," said Kevin Mackey. "He was probably forty, fifty years old when he was playing in the NBA." There have been whispers about Serge Ibaka, Bismack Biyombo, and Thon Maker, who was the subject of a Reddit investigation by internet gumshoes. "It really doesn't disturb me, but it hurts when your wife starts feeling uncomfortable about it," said Dikembe Mutombo, who entered the league at twenty-five and retired at forty-two, then the fourth-oldest player in NBA history. "Even my daughter says, 'Daddy, why are they talking about your age?'"

One of the leading advocates for African basketball is Masai Ujiri, a clever front office executive who was born in London and raised in Nigeria. He cofounded Giants of Africa in 2003. While some of his success is the result of routinely fleecing the Knicks in trades, he was the architect of the 2019 Raptors team that won the franchise's first championship. His Toronto squad included Ibaka (Republic of the Congo), Pascal Siakam (Cameroon), and OG Anunoby (parents from Nigeria). "People hear 'Africa' and they think about charitable commercials, or safari tours and animals," Ujiri said in *Sports Illustrated*. "It's our responsibility to help change that perspective. . . . It's time to start thinking of it as an investment."

Siakam exemplifies Ujiri's vision for a pipeline from Africa to the NBA. Like most kids in Cameroon, he was partial to soccer—until a trip to South Africa for a Basketball Without Borders camp that was hosted by Deng and Ibaka. Mentored as a teen by countryman Luc Mbah a Moute, a rugged forward who played for teams like the Bucks and Clippers, Siakam attended high school and college in the United States. He was scooped up by Toronto late in the first round of the 2016 draft, spent time in the G League as a rookie, won Most Improved Player in 2019, then was named All-NBA in 2020 after averaging 22.9 points and 7.3 rebounds a game. Only eight years after taking up basketball, Spicy P signed a contract extension worth nearly $130 million. The wiry forward's path from seminary bunk beds in the tiny village of Bafia to ripping spin moves in the NBA is not easily replicable—but it is increasingly, at least, possible.

AMAECHI, JOHN

A large Englishman who bounced between the NBA and European leagues, John Amaechi had the lowest field-goal percentage of any center who played real minutes during the 2001 season. But clunked jumpers were

never what made him memorable. "John is the smartest player I've met in this league," Orlando teammate Michael Doleac said to *Sports Illustrated*. "He's also the only player I know whose beverage of choice is Earl Grey." In that same article, Amaechi declared that his passion was child psychology and that he was not really a fan of basketball.

In 2007, three years after retirement, Amaechi became the first NBA player to publicly announce that he was gay. The response from members of the basketball community was mixed, with the general consensus being that it was cool—but might get awkward in the locker room, where heterosexual athletes diligently ignore the buffet of veiny, soap-slicked physiques. "As long as you don't bring your gayness on me, I'm fine," said Sixers forward Shavlik Randolph. In recent years, Amaechi has weighed in on topics like Black Lives Matter and white privilege. "You can't be a part-time man of principle," he told the *Guardian*. "You don't have a choice in being a role model—the only choice is whether to be a good or bad one."

ANALYTICS

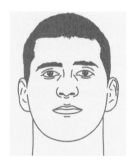

Without numbers, it would be difficult to tell who won a basketball game. We could declare champions based on dunks, vibes, or moistness of tunnel drip, but the world is not sophisticated enough. So we use points. While keeping track of the score, we added conventional, per-game "counting stats" like rebounds, assists, blocks, and steals.

The rise of analytics in the NBA trailed their use in baseball, but followed a similar trajectory: resistance, grudging adoption, extinction of deniers, public accessibility. In 2012, when Sixers coach Doug Collins was asked if he was an analytics guy, he reacted passionately. "I'd blow my brains out," he told the *Philadelphia Inquirer*. He resigned from the job within six months.

While analytics are seen as shorthand for one strategy—take 3s and free throws, avoid midrange jumpers—they are ways to glean more information about a sport with nearly infinite moving parts. Which lineups play well together? How do players affect the performance of teammates? What kinds of plays are most valuable? By now, fans can visit the NBA's website and dig through sortable data about pick-and-rolls, catch-and-shoot jumpers, post-ups, shot distance, proximity of defenders, running speed, and on-off splits organized over specific dates.

Much of the stigma attached to analytics is due to composite, all-in-one player ranking equations with inscrutable names like Win Shares, Player Efficiency Rating (PER), Value Over Replacement Player (VORP), or FiveThirtyEight's CARMELO and RAPTOR. These models are based on actual events—shots made, rebounds grabbed, steals racked up—but the weighted components reflect the biases of whoever cracked open the spreadsheet to create them.

There will always be animosity toward dorky acronyms that disgorge opaque numbers, but it really simmers when results do not jibe with widespread beliefs. In 2020, for example, Box Plus-Minus (BPM) ranked Devin Booker 40th among qualifying players, behind Hassan Whiteside, Ivica Zubac, Daniel Theis, and Jarrett Allen. At the same time, composite models identified the greatness of players like Nikola Jokić, who was pegged as having superstar production while coming off the bench for part of his second season in Denver.

Metric-haters often accuse metric-lovers of not watching games—as if people who care enough to sift through the minutiae of lineup data are not fans of the sport—but it is true that math is just part of the puzzle. "A lot of the analytics stuff can be very useful, but if you're using that in place of sitting down and watching film yourself and seeing what's going on, you're making a big mistake," coach Stan Van Gundy said at MIT's Sloan Sports Analytics Conference in 2014.

ANTETOKOUNMPO, GIANNIS

A physical Adonis, Giannis Antetokounmpo looks as if a nine-heads-high fashion croquis was penciled in with bulging shoulder muscles, then leapt from the sketchbook to dunk on everyone with mean-spirited glee. His proportions are staggering. The forward is 6-foot-11 with a wingspan four inches longer than his height. His hand measures a full foot from the tip of his pinky to the tip of his thumb. His strides are estimated at nine feet long. As if conjured by the Moirai—not to be confused with the Morrii—the Greek superstar has a 13.5-inch Achilles tendon, nearly twice the length of an average adult man's.

Those kinesiological edges have made Antetokounmpo the Most Improved Player, a Defensive Player of the Year, and a two-time Most Valuable Player. His greatness is based on a simple and powerful outlier skill: he is very good at putting the ball in the basket from a couple of inches away. The combination of his agility, strength, athleticism, wingspan, and hand size is not replicable—even in the NBA, where superhumans are normies—and it is nearly impossible to prevent him from mashing the rock through the rim without committing a foul. Still, he is a blunt object in a sport that respects fine craft.

Antetokounmpo was born in Sepolia, a dusty Athens neighborhood two miles from the Acropolis. The son of Nigerian immigrants, he helped his family survive in lean times by peddling watches and sunglasses on the street. "Sometimes, our fridge was empty," he told the *New York Times* in 2013. "Some days, we didn't sell the stuff and we didn't have money to feed ourselves." He and his brother, the only non-white kids in their school, shared a pair of basketball sneakers.

Unlike superstars who were hyped at prep academies, colleges, or overseas, Antetokounmpo was an unknown commodity before washing ashore in the 2013 NBA Draft. He averaged 9.5 points and 3.8 rebounds for Filathlitikos AO, a second-tier Greek franchise that signed him to its youth team when he was barely a teen. Back then, *SB Nation* described his floor and ceiling as, respectively, Thabo Sefolosha and Scottie Pippen, a pair of wings who are from a different basketball phylum from the current version of Antetokounmpo. Others spotted attributes that would later define his game: "He's the type of guy who looks like he can get from the half-court line to the rim with just two dribbles," wrote *Bleacher Report*.

Antetokounmpo was selected fifteenth by the Bucks, behind luminaries like Alex Len and Shabazz Muhammad. He sprouted two inches over the next year to stand at 6-foot-11, which altered his positional calculus. For a few seasons, Milwaukee wedged him into traditional lineups with post-dwelling centers. While Antetokounmpo blossomed into a star, the hiring of coach Mike

Budenholzer unleashed his optimized powers. The Bucks switched to an offensive system that spaced the floor with Brook Lopez, a 7-footer who took more 3s than any other center in 2019, and handed Antetokounmpo sole jurisdiction of the interior. He exploded, setting highs in scoring efficiency and points, rebounds, and assists per game.

When operating on the block, Antetokounmpo employs those meteorite shoulders to bludgeon defenders beneath the backboard. Then he dunks in their dumb faces. Other times, he uses a running start from the cusp of the arc and his long appendages to finish above or around opponents. If a victim passively drops back in the paint, Antetokounmpo has useful Euro-step counters that allow him to glide by without excessive contact. But power trumps grace. He is annually near the top of the NBA leaderboard in both free throws earned and offensive fouls committed. Part of his rise to megastardom was gaining more than fifty pounds since entering the league. "He's just gotten way stronger," teammate Khris Middleton told FiveThirtyEight in 2017. "He's been trying to do these things for years, but now he's finally able to put guys on his body and just push them backward instead of it being the other way around."

Antetokounmpo is petrifying in transition. His loping strides and the NBA's "gather rule" result in ruined orgasms where he jackhammers a dunk home with anticlimactic ease. For someone who is considered a primary ball-handler, Antetokounmpo doesn't do that much of it. He averaged only 2.18 dribbles and 3.35 seconds per possession in 2020 (in comparison, James Harden averaged 5.77 dribbles and 6.07 seconds). He's not here to fool around.

Like most parts of his game, Antetokounmpo's passing is a by-product of his unguardability around the hoop. The difficulty of stopping him one-on-one necessitates double-teams, and the Bucks have learned to keep four complementary shooters on the floor with him at all times. He is not a noticeably smooth or anticipatory passer, but is unselfish and capably reads the floor as his gravitational pull sucks defenders into his orbit. While he specializes in finding spotted-up shooters from unorthodox angles, he can make sneaky interior passes to baseline cutters and teammates around the basket who have been abandoned by overzealous helpers. In 2019, Antetokounmpo was twenty-first in the NBA in points per game created off assists, sandwiched between lead distributors Mike Conley and Luka Dončić.

Because Antetokounmpo is still regarded as an unfinished glob of Silly Putty with boundless talent, it can be tricky to disentangle the actual player from what people want him to become. With his humble backstory, reputation as a hard worker, and exponential early-career improvement, he is a Rorschach test for the beholder's view on basketball futurism. Depending on who you ask, Antetokounmpo is imagined as a taller-than-he-is point guard, a versatile Swiss Army knife of a defender, or a cultivator of imperiled skills (see: Lost Arts) with tradwife values toward midrange jumpers and respect for the game. No one seems content with his apex being Mobile Shaq. After a pair of second-round losses in MVP seasons, Antetokounmpo faced accusations from hooper-appreciators that he had no bag. "I wish I could just run and be 7 feet and just dunk," James Harden once scoffed. "Like, that takes no skill at all."

Modern basketball's hive mind has trouble accepting a superstar who cannot shoot. Antetokounmpo is a bricklayer from behind the 3-point stripe. He is a stonemason from midrange. And he is a flinger of crudely packed earthenware from the foul line. While Antetokounmpo makes more than 60 percent of his 2-point field-goal attempts—including almost 80 percent around the rim—he insists on launching a fusillade of 3-balls despite a career success rate of below 30 percent. Opponents rarely bother to contest his attempts from deep at all, collectively viewing them as a governor's reprieve from a fate of execution by electrifying dunk.

In 2021, Antetokounmpo was redeemed. He carried Milwaukee to a title by doing what he does better than anyone: getting to the rack, ripping down boards, and swatting shots as a helpside defender. Warts were visible—he shot 58.7 percent from the line and 18.6 percent from deep in the postseason—but his domination was irrefutable. In the clincher, Antetokounmpo dumped 50 points, 14 rebounds, and 5 blocks on Phoenix's helpless frontline. It looked as if the Suns were warding off an ax attack with bare hands.

We demand perfection from superstars until the moment it becomes clear that imperfection does not disqualify one from greatness. Fortunately, the type of people who wail about Antetokounmpo's lack of Jordan-esque skill usually subscribe to the idea that rings trump all else. "I could go to a superteam and just do my part to win a championship," he said after the win. "But this is the hard way to do it, and we did it."

A

ANTHONY, CARMELO

Introduced to basketball from a window of Brooklyn's Red Hook West housing projects, Carmelo Anthony is our King Tutankhamun: schoolboy nobility down in Baltimore, collegiate demigod at the University of Syracuse, divine ruler with the Nuggets, Knicks, Thunder, Rockets, Hawks, and Blazers. In many ways, Anthony is the last of a royal bloodline. Over a decade and a half, he has been both a beneficiary and a casualty of a league that shifted from glamorization of volume-scoring chuckers to an obsession with means-tested efficiency and staccato, popcorn-machine ball movement.

After deadlifting Syracuse to a national title on his rounded shoulders, Anthony was drafted third overall by Denver in the celebrated 2003 draft class that included LeBron James, Dwyane Wade, and Chris Bosh. Detroit took Darko Miličić with the second pick, a choice that may have affected Anthony more than the Pistons. For Detroit, the calamitous decision was papered over by the success of the second iteration of the Bad Boys, a bruising squad that made consecutive trips to the Finals. Had Anthony carried home an NCAA championship as a freshman and an NBA championship as a rookie, he would have been deified by the age of twenty as the ultimate winner. That was not to be.

Anthony and James were initially regarded as youthful peers, and Anthony's Nuggets won seven of their first nine encounters against the Cavaliers. But parallels diverged as James ascended toward the acme and Anthony plateaued as a polished bucket-maker who didn't possess many skills outside of making buckets. Still, Anthony's gifts were revered. He was a virtuoso who could drill 3s, jab-step into jumpers, or use his sturdy frame and impeccable footwork to trespass the lane by strength or guile. "I'm laid-back, I take my time, get the job done," Anthony said. "LeBron is high-flying, dunking, passing the ball well. He's getting the job done too. But we're different."

Early in his career, Anthony was criticized for appearing in a Baltimore street DVD titled *Stop Snitching*, in which he stood around in a luxuriant red fitted hat, red durag, and red polo shirt while alleged drug dealers roasted him for winning a bronze Olympic medal ("How he gonna tell a bitch he worth

$100 mil, and he chased a big penny for two months straight?"). Facts only!

Eventually, Anthony maneuvered his way out of Denver. Fearing he would leave in free agency, Nuggets general manager Masai Ujiri convinced the Knicks to bid against themselves in a midseason deal that returned a haul of four players along with draft picks that eventually became Jamal Murray and Dario Šarić. The blockbuster trade paired Anthony with Amar'e Stoudemire, giving the Knicks a frontcourt strapped with firepower but thin on body armor.

While Melo was greeted with fanfare befitting a native son, the trade disemboweled a promising roster and became representative of his own (supposed) misplaced priorities. Had he waited until the off-season, New York could have signed him as a free agent without sacrificing young talent or assets— but, due to restrictions in the collective bargaining agreement, his new contract would not have been as lucrative. For the remainder of his prime, Anthony was perceived as a man who valued money, top-billing status, and living in a city with a legitimate Fashion Week more than winning. In New York, Melo exorcised all challenges to his autonomy—namely, coach Mike D'Antoni and fleeting sensation Jeremy Lin—and, in 2013, led the Knicks to 54 wins, the franchise's best record since 1997.

With A$AP Rocky's "Fuckin' Problems" pulsing across the airwaves and Gothamites queueing up for ramen burgers and Cronuts, Anthony embraced the Dirk Nowitzki role on a team constructed to mimic the 2011 title-winning Mavericks. New York had nabbed two Dallas starters in free agency (Jason Kidd and Tyson Chandler) and preserved D'Antoni's offensive principles. Shaking off an organizational love of stodginess, the Knicks ranked third in offensive rating and led the NBA in made 3-pointers. After the elderly Dallas mercenaries ran out of gas, the team lost in the Eastern Conference Semifinals to the Pacers. Anthony finished third in MVP voting.

Though he has gravitas among NBA peers as a legend and all-around cool dude, Anthony did not age gracefully on the court. He was a poor defender whose declining efficiency and affection for midrange jumpers made him a tough fit for more limited roles. The cachet of scoring that had taken him from child prodigy to Hall of Famer became a distasteful addition to a contender's offensive stockpot. After being jettisoned by the Knicks, his insistence on remaining in the starting lineup for Oklahoma City was seen as evidence of vanity or delusion. He spent one season

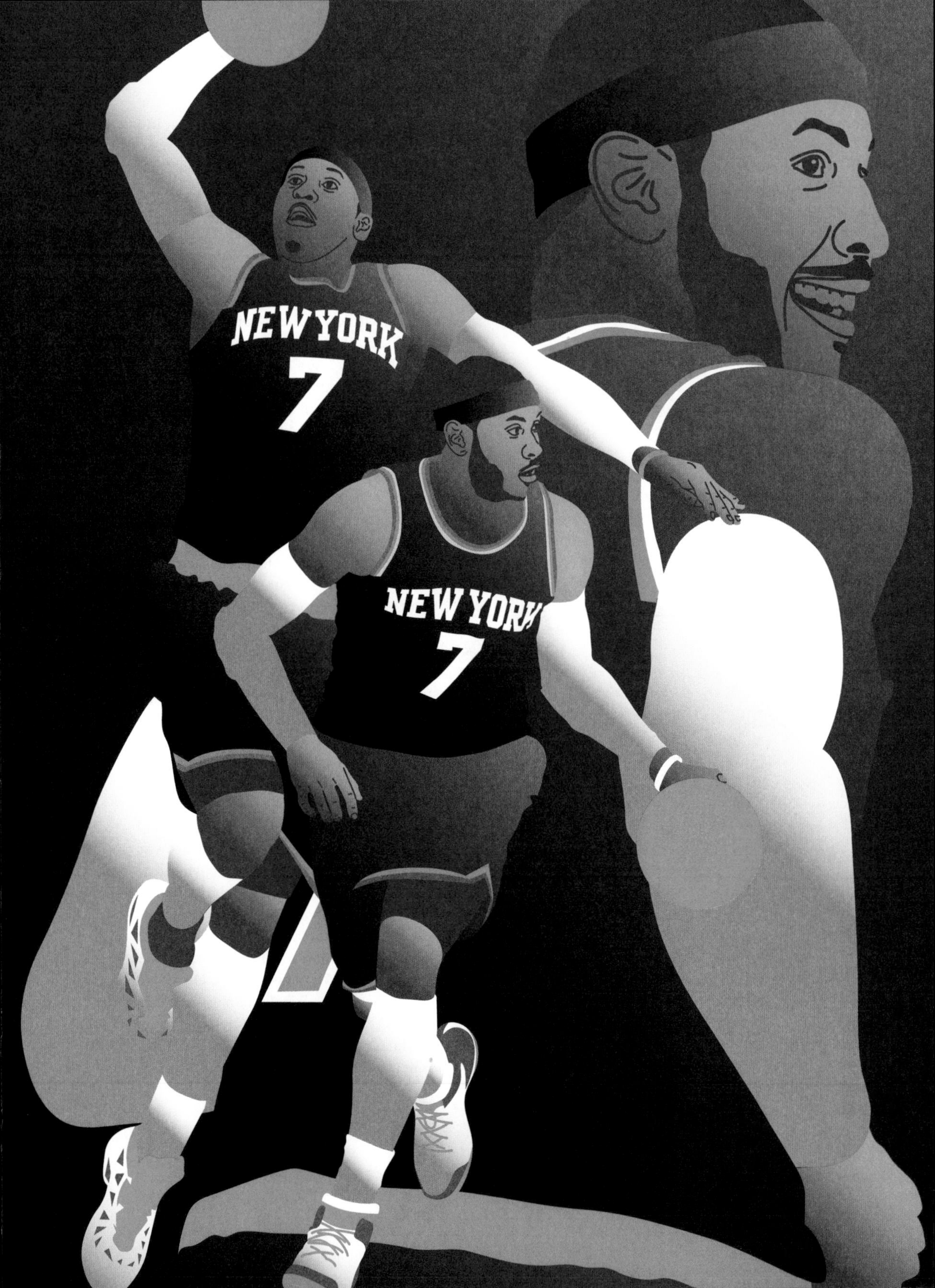
NEW YORK
7
NEW YORK
7

with the Thunder before being traded again. "I felt so belittled," Anthony said on JJ Redick's podcast. "Like, damn, is it me? Am I doing something wrong?"

He was exiled from the league during the early half of the 2020 season, and some contemporaries viewed his absence with suspicion, in part because of his progressive political stances. "Melo is absolutely being blackballed," said Royce White. "While a guy like LeBron is walking around like he's the face and the voice of the players, how is he letting his banana boat brother hang out there in the wings?" Later in the season, Anthony joined the Blazers, a turn of events that was undeniably joyful.

Off the court, Anthony has always been a powerful and enthusiastic advocate for hats. Newsboy hats. Fedoras. Borsalinos. Eastern European military chapeaus in olive drab with antelope fur linings. And hoodies (see: Hoodie Melo). In one memorable moment, he wore a bowler hat and a bowtie while eyeballing Rihanna in the background of a photo. It went viral on Twitter with the caption, "Melo off the Henny & a few pulls of sour, ready to jeopardize it all."

ART

As men with disposable income, professional basketball players are perfect for the art world. Not only can purchases be justified as investments that will accrue value, they also convey a sense of taste and refinement while looking nice on the walls of a Denver loft.

Early NBA athletes with an interest in art were Bernard King, a Hall of Famer who led the league in scoring in 1985 with the Knicks, and Darrell Walker, a Bullets guard whose collection includes artworks by Kehinde Wiley, Robert Colescott, Norman Lewis, and Lynette Yiadom-Boakye. Walker served as a mentor to Elliot Perry, a high-socked guard who spent ten years in the NBA before retiring in 2002. "This has been kind of a labor of love and passion," he told *The Undefeated* of a collection that focuses on "young, living, contemporary artists."

Collegiate rivals Chris Webber and Grant Hill are both collectors who specialize in African American art and have organized public exhibitions. Webber's collection includes artifacts like a postcard from Malcolm X to writer Alex Haley, an autographed program from a tribute to Martin Luther King Jr., and a book of poems from the 1700s by Phillis Wheatley, an enslaved woman. "I have read her book many times," he told the Warriors' website. "It's so beautifully written and it's so complex."

If an NBA player gets really into the scene, he can attend Art Basel Miami Beach and pose in front of a Picasso for a *Vogue* photo diary—as Amar'e Stoudemire has done. As a member of the mid-2000s Suns, the power forward was a 6-foot-10 stick of plastique. The precepts of Mike D'Antoni's Phoenix offense have been emulated for nearly two decades, but the pick-and-roll combo of Nash and Stoudemire is harder to copy: a divine passer whose shooting ability kept defenders wobbling in the lane and a diving archaeopteryx who lived to impale slow-footed centers with dunks.

The six-time All-Star is one of the league's most visible art buffs and a guy with varied interests (Stoudemire converted to Judaism and owns a 190-acre farm in Upstate New York). His collection includes works by Jean-Michel Basquiat and Hebru Brantley, he acts as an adviser to former teammates like Justise Winslow and Udonis Haslem, and he has considered working as a conduit between athletes and auction houses. Stoudemire prefers art that is not abstract. "Paintings that look very simple, I haven't really gotten into that yet," he told the *New York Times*. "It's tough. You're not sure. It seems like you can do it, anyone can create that painting."

That anyone might be Desmond Mason, who won the 2001 NBA Slam Dunk Contest while on the Sonics. A studio art major at Oklahoma State University, he became an abstract artist after seeing the movie *Pollock*. As a rookie, Mason was called to the office of NBA commissioner David Stern—who wanted to buy one of Mason's drawings. He told the *New York Post* that he was perplexed by Stern's choice: a portrait of Al Pacino in *Carlito's Way*. "Is he the consigliere of the Gambino family?" Mason wondered. "What is going on?"

A different cast of Bad Lads returned to Detroit in the early aughts. In 2002, the Pistons emerged as a 50-win team led by Ben Wallace, an undersized, psychotic center who led the league in rebounds and blocks per game. Resurrecting a working-class, General Motors assembly-line ethos, Detroit added pieces like Chauncey Billups, Rasheed Wallace, Richard Hamilton, and Tayshaun Prince. The team hired Larry Brown, a stodgy dogmatist of a coach, whose love of defense and bitter hatred of offense coincided with the Detroit way.

In 2004, the Pistons upset a favored Lakers team that featured Shaquille O'Neal and Kobe Bryant, along with ring-chasing veterans Karl Malone and Gary Payton. Winning in an unexpectedly breezy 4–1 gentleman's sweep, Detroit used smothering defense to limit every Laker starter except for O'Neal to under 40 percent shooting from the field. The Pistons returned to the Finals during the 2005 season, but lost to the Spurs in an excruciating (and widely loathed) series. Over seven unwatchable games between two of the thriftiest defenses in NBA history, the losing team averaged 78.6 points.

As the pace-and-space age approached, the Bad Boys 2 teetered from the bleeding edge to the brink of extinction. The empire toppled on May 13, 2007, when an unstoppable young maharajah, LeBron James, scored 25 consecutive points for the Cavaliers in an Eastern Conference Finals Game 5 victory over the Pistons. As with the original Bad Boys, their descendants were only keeping the throne warm for a new king.

BAD BOYS 2: MORE BAD BOYS

Before the NBA really existed, the Detroit Pistons won two championships with a feared "Bad Boys" cadre that included future New York Knicks coach Isiah Thomas and future New York Liberty coach Bill Laimbeer. They were famed for sharp elbows, flagrant fouls, and getting into shoving matches that periodically circulate through modern social media in blurry videos with captions like, "rmbr when men were men." If announcers wax nostalgic about the eighties and nineties over dead air, the original Bad Boys are always brought up as members of basketball's Greatest Generation and emblems of grit, heart, and physicality—regressive genes among today's Off-White-clad pansies. Merchandise for the Pistons featured a cracked skull and crossbones atop a basketball.

BALL FAMILY

"Play the game, don't let the game play you." It sounds like homespun wisdom, but is taken seriously in communities where basketball is a path to a better future. It acknowledges that organized sports provide opportunities—for higher education, for professional success, for escape—within a machine that devours bodies and bone like a woodchipper. LaVar Ball, the blustery patriarch of the Ball

CLASSIC NBA JOBS

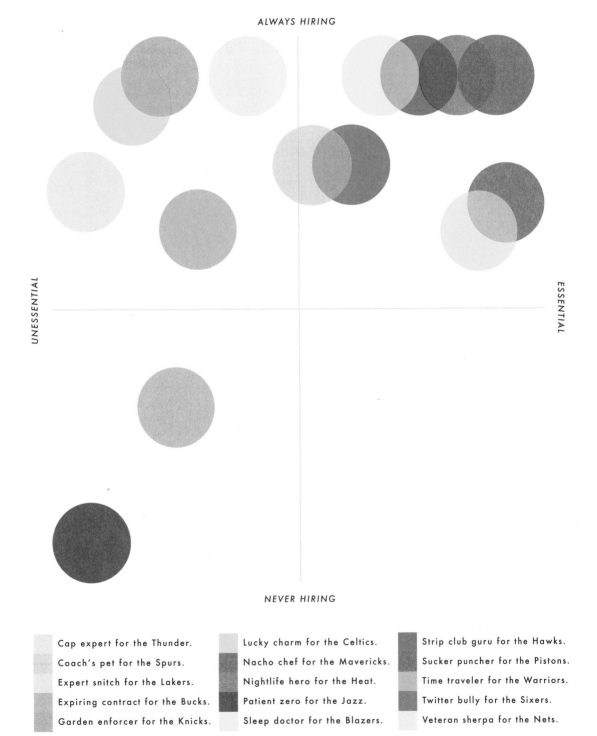

ALWAYS HIRING

UNESSENTIAL

ESSENTIAL

NEVER HIRING

Cap expert for the Thunder.

Coach's pet for the Spurs.

Expert snitch for the Lakers.

Expiring contract for the Bucks.

Garden enforcer for the Knicks.

Lucky charm for the Celtics.

Nacho chef for the Mavericks.

Nightlife hero for the Heat.

Patient zero for the Jazz.

Sleep doctor for the Blazers.

Strip club guru for the Hawks.

Sucker puncher for the Pistons.

Time traveler for the Warriors.

Twitter bully for the Sixers.

Veteran sherpa for the Nets.

brood, has this worldview. While he has been dismissed as a buffoon, he raised two sons who became top-three picks and he tried to upend established orders of the NCAA farm system, sports media, and apparel industry. He may be a hammy salesman, but he is a modern basketball folk hero.

The tip of the spear for his family's insertion into the NBA, Lonzo Ball was a UCLA star projected to be one of the top picks in the 2017 draft. At the time, LaVar's overbearing influence was viewed as a concern. He refused to let his son work out for any team besides his hometown Lakers, who owned the second pick. "Markelle Fultz is the perfect pick for [Boston]," Ball spouted. "He's the best player. Take him." Lonzo went to Los Angeles.

Emboldened by his eldest son's celebrity, LaVar created Big Baller Brand, an independent sportswear company that sold Lonzo's ZO2 signature sneakers for $495. He claimed that he could beat Michael Jordan in a game of one-on-one and was a fixture on television and sidelines. Later, he skirted the collegiate racket by sending younger sons, LaMelo and LiAngelo, to play professionally in Lithuania and Australia and created the Junior Basketball Association, a short-lived league that featured teams like the Atlanta Ballers, Dallas Ballers, and New York Ballers.

Despite being a sideshow, LaVar sired extraordinary basketball players. Winner of the 2021 Rookie of the Year award, LaMelo is a rising Zoomer king. LiAngelo was signed and then cut by the Pistons. And while Lonzo has not fully lived up to the hype, he is a brainy passer whose diagonal assists create transition dunks and open 3s. He was a poor shooter early in his career, due to a release that hoisted shots from the wrong shoulder like an imbalanced trebuchet, and a reputation for being a bricklayer has stuck around despite tangible improvements. In the summer of 2019, Lonzo was traded to the Pelicans in a blockbuster deal for Anthony Davis that LaVar characterized as "the worst move the Lakers ever did in their life and they will never win another championship."

BALL-HANDLING

The best current player from New York City, Kemba Walker, is a 6-foot lightning bug who grew up in the Sack Wern Houses in the Soundview section of the Bronx. He was a dancing enthusiast who

performed at Harlem's Apollo Theater, and the hobby is credited with developing the footwork and dexterity that would become hallmarks of the All-Star's game. Years later, Walker is one of the league's most bewitching ball-handlers. The point guard strings together crossovers, in-and-out-dribbles, and Euro steps like a featherweight popping a speed bag. "That guy finds space when there's no space," his teammate Marvin Williams told *Bleacher Report*. "He's the quickest dude I've ever seen on a basketball court, no question."

Few talents offer the enchanting functionality of gorgeous ball-handling. On a surface where the only rule governing mobility is that a player must bounce a basketball, the ability to explore the court's full 4700 square feet is the gift of freedom. For those with this skill, a rock-solid defense becomes as permeable as rain-dampened loam. Such a player can "get wherever he wants," as they say. In an empty gym or pick-up game, virtually any decent baller can pull off crossovers, shammgods, and the old in-and-out. But that privilege does not extend to NBA games, where self-regulating mores dictate which players are allowed to bring the ball up the court. For many of the league's largest men, the activity is restricted to a few clumsy dribbles in the post as they thrust their ass into a girded defender. In a sport that rewards height in so many ways, ball-handling is an equalizer.

In sepia-toned times, NBA players could not dribble. They bounced the ball with one hand and used their off-arm as a guardrail to keep defenders at bay. Bob Cousy of the Celtics was known as "Hardwood Houdini" because he was able to dribble in a circle without stumbling over his own feet and collapsing in a clammy heap of green mesh. As recently as the 1980s and early 1990s, even Hall of Famers like Isiah Thomas of the Pistons and Magic Johnson rarely demonstrated moves more advanced than staccato between-the-legs dribbles to change direction or sweeping behind-the-back carries to evade defenders in transition.

Rod Strickland and Kenny Anderson, two point guards strung from barbed wire, were anomalies. Both came from New York City, which has long been regarded as a breeding ground for spidery dribblers

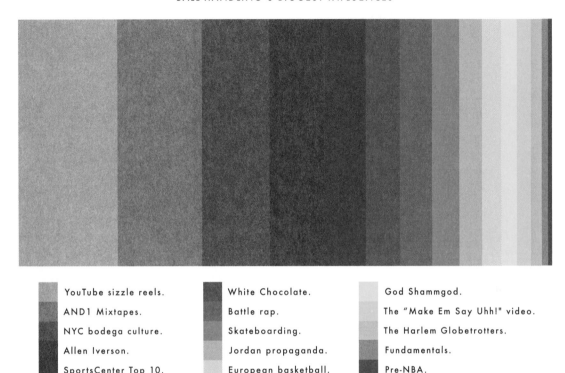

YouTube sizzle reels.
AND1 Mixtapes.
NYC bodega culture.
Allen Iverson.
SportsCenter Top 10.

White Chocolate.
Battle rap.
Skateboarding.
Jordan propaganda.
European basketball.

God Shammgod.
The "Make Em Say Uhh!" video.
The Harlem Globetrotters.
Fundamentals.
Pre-NBA.

and mediocre shooters. Public playgrounds are cold and rainy, asphalt is cracked and uneven, and baskets are positioned at inconsistent heights with dreaded "double rims." On these forlorn courts, tattered nets flutter in the wind like flags atop a campsite surrendered to wolves. "Jump shots weren't in style," said Strickland, on a 2019 episode of the podcast *Wizards Talk*. "A lot of times we went to the basket and you had to be creative—[we] spent a lot of time trying to figure out how to shake someone." Blazing a trail for local guards like Jamaal Tinsley and God Shammgod, Strickland lived up to the regional stereotype: he sparkled with the rock and led the NBA in assists in 1998, but shot only 28.2 percent from deep over his seventeen-year career. The way he sees it, ball-handling was less clinical in his era. "A lot of stuff back then was just natural," Strickland said. "It was reaction. I learned how to handle the ball. I didn't learn moves."

The rise of streetball in the late 1990s— popularized by the AND1 Mixtape Tour—elevated ball-handling to art. Optically, it was useless

showmanship that bordered on interpretive dance: bouncing the ball off the forehead of a defender, hiding the ball inside a caftan-like XXXXL T-shirt, shoulder-shimmying in place while ricocheting the ball off one's shins. Mixing the antics of the Harlem Globetrotters with the backdrop of hip-hop, street-ball was a short-lived cultural phenomenon. AND1, an apparel company, used street teams to promote highlight "mixtapes" as if releasing rap singles and put out shirts with slogans like "I'm the busdriver. I take everyone to school" and "yo mama" jokes. Larry Hughes, a stylish shooting guard who led the NBA in steals in 2005, had the brand's logo—a brolic but faceless basketball player—prominently tattooed on his right bicep. "I was looking for something that said, 'Playing ball is what I'm about,'" Hughes told the *New York Times*.

As unserious and subversive as streetball seemed to be, the new infatuation with dribbling improved one of basketball's fundamental tasks. For a younger generation, the ability to cook a defender off the bounce became a point of pride and an end unto itself—did a bucket even count if an opponent wasn't left staggering like a barfly at last call? As players with streetball skills rose into the professional ranks, it was not odd to see an NBA offense constructed around someone like Houston's Steve Francis, who would spend nine seconds trying to unbalance a defender with herky-jerky dribbles that mimicked the drum pattern of "Country Grammar."

Before long, those grainy VCR cassettes were swapped out for social media. "I was a typical high school kid when YouTube first came out," Kyrie Irving told *Bleacher Report*. "I was just watching a whole lot of videos of guys in the league I'm playing with now, guys that aren't in the league, and guys that came before me, just watching the moves that they do, and going out in my backyard and trying them. I did it almost every single day." Unlike groundbreaking ball-handlers such as Tim Hardaway Sr. and Allen Iverson, modern players including Irving, D'Angelo Russell, Trae Young, and Luka Dončić had the benefit of institutional knowledge one iPhone thumbprint away.

The ability to juke a defender off his feet as if yanking a throw rug out from under him is useful. But in the NBA, what occurs after the sleight of hand matters most. Do they use the newly opened fjord to generate a layup? Do they attract enough help defense to kick a pass out to the perimeter for an open 3? Or do they settle for a midrange floater, the type of shabby attempt available on every possession? Few activities on the hardwood allow for more expression than dribbling, and it can be tricky to separate the player from the puff of endorphins generated by a side-spun, fake-pass dribble that leaves an opponent cemented to the ground. Players like Jason "White Chocolate" Williams, Rafer Alston, Tyreke Evans, and Jamal Crawford (arguably the best ball-handler over 6-foot-3 in history), all were renowned for possessing excellent handles, but none exploited their gift in a way that transformed aesthetics into high-end results. Still, it looked insanely cool.

BARKLEY, CHARLES

A former player and civilian-facing basketball analyst, Charles "Chuck" Barkley is best known today as a host on the television comedy forum *Inside the NBA*. He is an eleven-time All-Star, a carnival barker who questions the manhood of modern big men without

post moves, and the human incarnation of vodka and luncheon meat. Despite being a notoriously lazy partier, Barkley hectors modern players about not wanting to win enough by his standards. His own career boasted one trip to the Finals and five losses in the opening round of the postseason. And while stat-based evaluation models present him as one of the greatest ballers in NBA history, Barkley taunts nerds who "never played the game" and "never got the girls in high school."

As a Rodney Dangerfield, 1980s-styled provocateur who lumpily tells it like it is, Barkley has been enmeshed in incidents involving "edgy" statements about gender and race. "I can be bought," he once said of returning to his former team, the Philadelphia 76ers. "If they paid me enough, I'd work for the Klan." Barkley made jokes about unattractive women in San Antonio and quipped that women should not be given watches as gifts because "there is a clock on the stove." In 2017, Barkley emceed a travel docuseries called *American Race* in which he attempted to end racism in America by starting a dialogue about race in America. After spending several hours with the Baltimore police department, he informed the congregation at a Black church that being a cop is tough. "We spend all of our time talking about the five-percent [who] screw up," said Barkley.

In fairness, Barkley's own interactions with the law did not result in him being murdered by the police. In 1997, he was arrested for throwing a 5-foot-1 man through a plateglass window in an Orlando nightclub. Then, in 2008, he was arrested in Scottsdale for driving under the influence (according to the arresting officer, Barkley said he rolled through a stop sign because he was in a rush to receive oral sex). As a basketball-adjacent personality, Barkley has repeatedly proven that being loud is far more important than being right.

BATTIER, SHANE

Shane Battier was a principled defender and a prudent shooter who was reliant on the blob of gray

matter twitching in his conical skull. His career averages of 8.6 points, 4.2 rebounds, and 1.8 assists per game do not tell the whole story—unless that story is about measuring on-court intangibles by making them tangible. "He can't dribble, he's slow, and hasn't got much body control," said Daryl Morey, former general manager of the Rockets. "When he's on the court, all the pieces start to fit together. And everything that leads to winning that you can get to through intellect instead of innate ability, Shane excels in."

With a solid 6-foot-8 frame and a wingspan three inches wider, Battier does not look like a human out of place in professional ranks. Nor does his hoops LinkedIn page: Mr. Basketball in Michigan, three-time state champion, 2001 NCAA tournament winner, Naismith College Player of the Year, lottery pick. This is the absurdity of the NBA. One of the most decorated amateur stars in modern history is, in part, exceptional because he could not have survived in the league without being a brainiac. The distant end of the basketball bell curve is threadbare.

Battier was always unique. As the child of a Black father and a Caucasian mother, he stuck out in Birmingham, Michigan, which he has described as "whitebread." He was larger than other children his age. Strangers mistakenly thought he had special needs because he was the size of a six-year-old when he was only three. Shane sought acceptance in organized sports, but even in an arena where he excelled, he bobbed awkwardly between his local team and Detroit AAU squads. "We all love our athletic heroes to be chiseled and have a steely will and a look and ice in their veins," Battier said of his lifelong dweebiness. "I was a skinny mixed kid from the suburbs who spoke well, wasn't super athletic. I was never going to be the cool kid or the smoothest basketball player."

After four years of accolades at Duke University, Battier was selected by Vancouver with the sixth overall pick in the 2001 NBA Draft. None of the first four prospects tabbed had played NCAA basketball, and traditionalists were scandalized by the league's infatuation with talent that glistened with amniotic sap. During summer league, Battier struck an imperious tone toward the youngsters drafted ahead of him. "I know what a municipal bond is," he said. "I know the value of a dollar today vs. a dollar a year from now. I can balance a checkbook. And I won't need Mom to live with me my rookie season." His classist haughtiness was not well-received. "He's disrespecting all us high school players," said Darius Miles of the Clippers. "He's disrespecting me, Kobe, and Garnett. I hate that."

After forgettable seasons with the Grizzlies, Battier was sent to the Rockets in a draft-day trade for just-selected Rudy Gay. The crowd assembled in Houston's Toyota Center hooted in disapproval. Like most fans, the grumpy Texans did not know Battier had been identified by the Rockets' front office as a player whose value was inaccurately reflected by box-score tallies. As it turned out, he was not just an unwitting test subject whose game coincidentally correlated positively with a regression analysis. Battier had already read *Moneyball* and was an eager pupil when Morey and understudy Sam Hinkie offered a crash course in Advanced Metrics 101. "Shane Battier is a lab rat who understood the experiment as much as the scientists," said Michael Lewis, the author of *Moneyball*, who wrote a feature for the *New York Times* magazine detailing Battier's hard-to-quantify talent.

As a player who relied on preparation, Battier viewed analytics as a cheat sheet for how to defend the NBA's most dangerous wings. Beyond discovering a player's tendencies, it was trustable math. "I knew exactly, to a tee, who Kobe Bryant was," Battier said after retirement, in a video for the website *Big Think*. "His worst-case scenario and my best-case scenario was to make him shoot a pull-up jumper going to his left hand." He explained that the average Laker possession generated 0.98 points and Bryant successfully made that specific shot at a 44 percent clip—or 0.88 points per possession. "All these tenths of a point add up," he said. "The margin between wins and losses is very, very thin. It's no different from playing the stock market."

Battier arrived in Miami in his early thirties, a season after the Heat had been upset in the Finals by Dirk Nowitzki's Mavericks. His offensive role was limited to standing behind the 3-point line and waiting for LeBron James or Dwyane Wade to pass him the ball. But that tight compartmentalization also made him the perfect coagulant for a top-heavy team. Miami won back-to-back titles as Battier irritated opponents with his trademark defensive

THE MOST ANNOYING PLAYERS

Austin Rivers
Bruce Bowen
Chandler Parsons
Dennis Rodman
Draymond Green
Dwight Howard
Grayson Allen
Isaiah Rider
Joakim Noah
J.R. Smith
J.J. Redick
Kevin Garnett
Kobe Bryant
Mark Madsen
Matt Geiger
Matthew Dellavedova
Metta World Peace
Michael Jordan
Nate Robinson
Nikola Mirotić
Patrick Beverley
Rajon Rondo
Reggie Jackson
Reggie Miller
Rick Fox
Scot Pollard
Scott Skiles
Shane Battier
Steve Blake
Trae Young
Tyler Hansbrough
Zaza Pachulia

Ball hog   Brainiac   Jerk   Prankster   Snob   Troll   Tyrant   Weirdo

tactic: sticking his hand in a shooter's face instead of trying to block the shot. "I absolutely hate it," Kevin Durant acknowledged in the 2012 Finals.

In South Beach, Battier became a nerd whisperer, feeding small but useful morsels of information to teammates that primed their palates to the gamey taste of dorkdom. After his retirement, the Heat hired him as director of Basketball Development and Analytics. "He's probably the number one smartest basketball player and person I've been around," said James. "He knows everything."

BIG 4

No team has ever been more celebrated for a single championship than Boston's Big Four. The Celtics quartet of Ray Allen, Kevin Garnett, Paul Pierce, and Rajon Rondo united before the 2008 season and promptly won 66 games and the organization's first title in more than twenty years. It was a striking reversal for a franchise that had slopped together the NBA's second-worst record the previous year—and a testament to general manager Danny Ainge's canniness. "It was definitely a low point," Pierce said of the 24–58 season. "I just thought I didn't have a future in Boston when I was looking at it."

In two trades, Boston dumped a trough of young players and draft assets to add Allen and Garnett, a pair of established studs who had combined for seventeen All-Star appearances before arriving in Beantown. Allen was already one of the greatest shooters ever, but the baby-faced two-guard was still more of a diverse scorer than the unitasker he would become in his late thirties (it is easy to forget he had enough bounce to compete in the 1997 NBA Slam Dunk Contest). In his final year in Seattle, he finished sixth in the NBA in points per game and led the league in 3-pointers made and attempted. Helmed by new general manager Sam Presti, the Sonics owned the second pick in the coming draft and intended to rebuild around Greg Oden or Kevin Durant. "The general consensus was that the 30-year-old Presti fleeced Celtics general manager Danny Ainge," wrote Tacoma's *The New Tribune*.

On the other hand, the Garnett acquisition reeked of collusion. One of the NBA's biggest superstars was traded to Boston for an unimpressive heap (the key components were a young Al Jefferson and two first-round picks—one of which became the sixth pick in 2009 and was squandered on Jonny Flynn instead of Stephen Curry) by Minnesota executive Kevin McHale, coincidentally a Celtics legend and former teammate of Ainge. "My NBA guide claims that McHale retired from the Celtics in 1993," wrote Bill Simmons, for ESPN, "but apparently that's a misprint."

The incoming talent was added to a roster that included Paul Pierce, a schlubby but versatile wing whose scoring methods resembled a midrange-oriented version of James Harden. He took tons of 3s, used "old man game" and change-of-speed instead of visible zip, and seduced infuriating amounts of fouls. In late 2000, he was stabbed multiple times and hit with a bottle in the head at a Boston nightspot called Buzz Club. While talking to some women, Pierce was confronted by a male partygoer and a melee broke out. "I didn't even know I was being stabbed," he recalled on *All the Smoke*. "I look up, my jacket is ripped, blood everywhere, leaking down my face. That night changed my life." He revealed that he carried a gun for the next two years, had 24-hour police surveillance, and avoided crowds. His attackers were reportedly associates of Ray Benzino, the infamous Boston rapper best known for warring with Eminem and seizing control of *The Source* magazine ("I can say that I had nothing to do with it," Benzino insisted).

The fourth member of the Big Four was Rajon Rondo, then a second-year point guard out of Kentucky who devoutly avoided shooting. He could be expressionless or volcanic, and his alien game included several seasons in which he averaged more assists than points. "He's a contrarian," said coach Doc Rivers of the four-time All-Star. "I figured that out early." Rondo was criticized for padding his assist numbers with needless unselfishness that became, in theory, selfish, but patented faking behind-the-back passes while slipping in for layups. He was brilliant at playing cards, could effortlessly call out opponents' inbound plays, and interned at men's fashion magazine *GQ*—yet was booted from the Mavericks during the Playoffs and called referee Bill Kennedy a vile homophobic slur, which led to the veteran official publicly coming out as gay. "He doesn't like to be told what to do," Ainge said of Rondo. "The question always was, 'Is he a good enough player to behave the way he does?'" The answer was: usually.

Under Rivers, who united the team under the Zulu concept of *ubuntu*—an idea described by Barack

Obama as "a oneness to humanity"—the Celtics boasted the league's best defense, record, and net rating. Aided by role players like Kendrick Perkins and James Posey, the suffocating defense allowed the lowest opponent field-goal percentage and created the highest rate of turnovers. Garnett was named Defensive Player of the Year and tallied the third-most Most Valuable Player votes. In the 2008 Finals, Boston crowded the lane and held Kobe Bryant to a 40.5 percent from the floor in a six-game win over the Lakers. In a memorable Game 1 performance, Pierce pooped his pants and slyly pretended to be injured. The Celtics would return to the Finals two seasons later, but lost to Los Angeles.

In contrast to the venom later spat at the Miami trio of LeBron James, Chris Bosh, and Dwyane Wade, the Boston superteam was embraced by the media. This is the Celtics, after all. While it was acceptable for Ainge to swindle his way to an instant contender— even by insider trading—it was a depraved upending of natural order when players conspired to join forces. Beyond all the obvious levers of race, class, and age, delineation of management and labor in front office decisions allows outsiders to engage in hot stove league fantasy that is more relatable when men in suits are calling the shots.

To that end, maybe the 2008 Celtics are worshipped, in part, as penance for their betrayal. Other than Allen, who joined the Heat via free agency, every other member of the Big Four was traded off by Ainge. Rather than ensuring that Pierce and Garnett retired as Celtics legends in the manner of McHale, Larry Bird, Bob Cousy, and Bill Russell, Ainge greedily squeezed out every last thimbleful of value from the aging All-Stars in a deal that sent them to Brooklyn in exchange for the Nets' entire future. Ainge's coldly transactional approach was repeated with both Rondo and short king Isaiah Thomas. "I loved it here," Pierce told *ESPN* magazine when he came back to play in Boston for the first time. "Never wanted to leave."

in powder form, mixed with water, and applied with a brush. Depending on its potency, a Bigen dye lasts between two and six weeks.

Bigen was worn in a 2012 game by Carlos Boozer, then a power forward on the Bulls, who was told by a barber that it would look like a "regular haircut" on his balding dome. "He just made myself look like shoe polish up there," he recounted on ESPN. "I tried to shampoo that thing seven or eight times, man."

An All-Star in Utah, Boozer was a muscled jump-shooter who hilariously conned blind Cavaliers owner Gordon Gund by signing with the Jazz after Cleveland released him from his contract with the expectation that he would reup with the team. He also rented his Beverly Hills house out to Prince—and sued the musical genius for remodeling alterations that included turning a bedroom into a hair salon, knocking down walls, and plastering the Prince symbol on the front gate. "He did some very specific things that were built for him and his lifestyle, which is very different from mine," Boozer said after reaching a settlement.

In 2017, Cleveland's Deron Williams had his head spackled the same way, but it is unknown if he used Bigen. The five-time All-Star point guard was Boozer's teammate for a few seasons with the Jazz, which may or may not be a coincidence. Once seen as a generational talent and the lodestone for a Brooklyn team hoping to attract eyeballs, Williams flamed out due to ankle injuries and, perhaps, the pressure of playing in a market that was not in the middle of the desert. "I think a lot of the pressure got to him sometimes," his Nets teammate Paul Pierce told ESPN. "The media in Utah is not the same as the media in New York, so that can wear on some people."

BIGEN

Pronounced "Beijing," Bigen is an inky, semipermanent dye meant to be applied to hair or beards. It is intended to create the impression of sharp edges and virile follicular health, but resembles a reflective coat of fresh paint. The product is packaged

BILLUPS, CHAUNCEY

Wise, patient, and strong, Chauncey Billups was an avuncular figure who shepherded young men with the calming powers of Gen X Tranquility. The 6-foot-3 guard was a five-time All-Star with Detroit

B

PYRAMID OF DEPENDABILITY

EVERY TIME

ALMOST NEVER

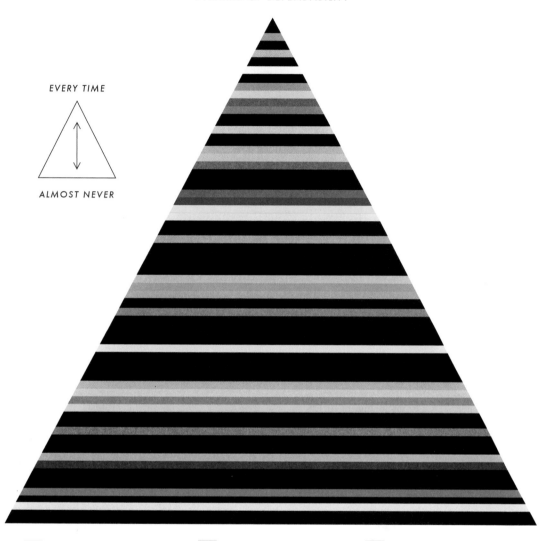

90s hip-hop fans as cops.
Aspirational millennials.
Believable UFO footage.
Ben Wallace denying jams.
Billups in a huge game.
Boomer BBQ nerds.
Cheese ravioli slices.
Chill Twitter replies.
Chocolate appetizers.
Darko being super Russian.

Delicious kale anything.
Drummond hunting stats.
Fashionable mixologists.
Food perfumed J trains.
Friendly Reggie Jackson.
Infinite Jest quitters.
Married pet influencers.
Mellow TicToc celebs.
NBA shorts + Wallabees.
Novelty socks energy.

Old rap tees under $50.
Rasheed being the best.
Richard Hamilton erasure.
Solid snacks at Barclays.
Stackhouse being a bully.
Stan Van breaking ankles.
Tech investor Deadheads.
Tolerable cardio sessions.
Vacationing couples on IG.
Wet noodle Tayshaun.

and Denver, the 2004 Finals MVP, and named to two NBA All-Defensive Teams. Over a seventeen-year career, he was one of basketball's greatest contributors of Steve Harvey–esque adulting energy.

Billups rarely dazzled, thriving on a cruiser-weight's combination of huskiness and hand-eye coordination. He backed down smaller guards and spun into one-footed fadeaways or angled drives. He didn't get to the basket much, but was capable of turning the corner and riding the rail of his shoulder to the rack. This coarse physicality rewarded him with trips to the foul line, where he shot 89.4 percent for his career—sixth-best in NBA history.

But Billups's forte was jumpers, specifically long ones, and the majority of those were 3-pointers. He loved pull-ups and step-backs out of pick-and-rolls, where he used choppy, crabbish horizontality to squiggle into safe crannies. The mix of deadeye free-throw shooting and a career percentage of 38.7 percent from deep made him devastatingly efficient, especially compared to the wanton chuckers of the early 2000s. His true shooting percentage in 2003 led all point guards, with Hall of Famers John Stockton and Steve Nash showing and placing.

On Detroit teams that went to the Finals in consecutive seasons, Billups was viewed as a reliable steward of proletariat hoops who rose to the occasion when necessary. Pistons announcer Rick Mahorn nicknamed him Mr. Big Shot. Numbers pulled up by the website *82Games* argue that the handle was a misnomer: over a seven-year stretch, Billups shot a miserable 6–37 from the floor in "clutch" situations. On the other hand, metrics that few people were aware of during his heyday portray him as a borderline superstar and the real engine of Detroit's wheezing offense.

Drafted by the Celtics with the third pick in the 1997 NBA Draft, Billups lasted only 51 games with the team. Despite his potential, Boston coach Rick Pitino craved a more experienced playmaker to distribute the ball among his army of former Kentucky players. Between the droning citywide clatter of Dropkick Murphys songs and the coach's antics, Billups did not enjoy the Celtics experience. "He was up on the court, screaming the whole game," he said of Pitino, in the *Deseret News*. "I was happy, actually, to get out of there."

The pattern repeated itself. By age twenty-four, Billups had speed-dated his way through four franchises and was close to being consigned to the bust bin. Teams were unsure if he was a traditional point guard or suited for playing off the ball. He found a home in Minnesota as Terrell Brandon's backup. Though Billups posted a modest 12.5 points and 5.5 assists during the Timberwolves' 50-win 2002 season, an injury to Brandon opened up a larger role down the stretch. Minnesota was trounced by the Mavericks in the first round, but Billups averaged 22 points a game. He was offered a sizable free agent contract from Detroit, where glory awaited.

In the *Players' Tribune*, Billups wrote a letter to his younger self. "Detroit is the *one* shot they're going to give you—this league, that almost spit you out, is going to give you—at greatness," he wrote. "At running your own show. This will be it, and then that will be that."

BLACK LIVES MATTER

 During the summer of 2020, untold millions of Americans took to the streets to protest police brutality, racism, and institutional inequality. The nationwide protests were sparked by the death of George Floyd, a forty-six-year-old Black man who was murdered by Caucasian Minneapolis police officers while handcuffed, and took place during the height of the COVID-19 pandemic. Floyd had been a close friend of former NBA player Stephen Jackson—they called each other "twin" due to a physical resemblance—and Captain Jack helped bring awareness to the incident. "I jumped up, screamed, scared my daughter and almost broke my hand punching stuff because I was so mad," Jackson said on the *Today Show*. "I'm the type of guy, I get a full face of tears when I see a homeless man on the street that I can't help. So let alone my best friend on TV for the world to see getting killed over a fraud charge."

Many NBA players took part in the protests that occurred during the COVID hiatus: Stephen Curry, Russell Westbrook, Tobias Harris, Malcolm Brogdon, Karl-Anthony Towns, and Enes Kanter—really, there is no end to the list. Jaylen Brown, a gifted shooting

guard on the Celtics, drove fifteen hours from Boston to Atlanta to participate in protests near his hometown of Marietta, Georgia. "Being a celebrity, being an NBA player, don't exclude me from no conversations at all," said Brown, who was once described by a league executive as being "too smart for the NBA." "First and foremost, I'm a Black man and I'm a member of this community. . . . As a young person, you've got to listen to our perspective. Our voices need to be heard."

As Black Lives Matter protests continued across the country, the NBA's plan to restart the season at Walt Disney World required players to sequester themselves in a resort instead of marching in the streets. The league claimed the athletes could have increased visibility by playing in the COVID Bubble and offered gestures such as emblazoned messaging on the Orlando hardwood ("Not every owner in the NBA was enthusiastic about having 'Black Lives Matter' on the court," reported ESPN's Adrian Wojnarowski). Players were issued an approved list of slogans that could be worn on the back of their jerseys that included Justice Now, Equality, How Many More, and Group Economics. Gordon Hayward of the Celtics donned an Education Reform jersey.

After the season restarted, playoff games were temporarily halted during a wildcat strike that was touched off when Jacob S. Blake, a Black man in Wisconsin, was shot seven times in the back by a Caucasian police officer. The moment crackled with unprecedented opportunity—"This is How A Revolution Starts" read a headline on *Mother Jones*—but former president Barack Obama coaxed the athletes back to work with a midnight phone call to Chris Paul, president of the Players Association. "My suggestion was that we use that platform to see if you can start asking for some specifics," Obama recounted on HBO's *The Shop*. As one concession, owners promised to turn NBA arenas into voting sites for the 2020 election.

BOOKER, DEVIN

Since entering the NBA as a teenager, cherub-faced Devin Booker has been viewed as a filament in basketball's bright future. He is a 6-foot-5 combo guard from Grand Rapids, Michigan, whose father played thirty-two NBA games in the mid-nineties. With a gorgeous shooting stroke, improving ball-handling skills, and the effortless ability to snowball buckets into avalanches, Devin is easy to love. He is a hooper's hooper, consistently more beloved by his peers than metrics dorks.

In a poll of NBA executives conducted before the 2018 season, he joined Curry and Klay Thompson as the only players to receive votes as the league's best pure shooter. "It means a lot," Booker said of the results. "Especially from GMs who are supposed to be the brains of basketball."

A three-level scorer whose efficiency has soared since his rookie season, Booker periodically ascends into god-mode. During a meaningless, late-season game in 2017, he dumped 70 points on the Celtics (who, nevertheless, won by 10). "You see special players come around this league and they all have *it*," teammate Tyson Chandler told *The Ringer*. "He has *it*."

There is mounting pressure for Booker to move beyond the role of a scoring machine on teams that have reliably stunk. Prior to a hot streak in the Bubble, he had not been part of a Phoenix squad that won more than 30 percent of its games. As a result of the Suns' putrid records, he has been a lightning rod for contentiousness between eye-test enthusiasts and metrics dorks. Depending on who you ask, Booker is either a rising star who has been sandbagged by inept teammates or a prom king whose lack of defensive chops waterlogs collective efforts (paltry numbers in categories like steals, blocks, and deflections back the perception that he is a pretty boy with the staunchness of gossamer).

Fortunately, Booker is now the recipient of the Kardashian blessing. During the COVID hiatus, he was spotted with Kendall Jenner when the pair pulled over at an Arizona rest stop in his Maybach. And, just like that, Book was dropping back-to-back 40-point games in the Finals.

BOSH, CHRIS

A nerdy and sensitive king, Chris Bosh was a bridge between big men of the past and present. There is no era where the lean, mobile, and cerebral big man with a wingspan of nearly 7-foot-4 would not have been marvelous. He could post up or face up, splash 3s, snatch rebounds, run the break like a terror bird, and glide between defensive assignments with ease. Not least of all, the eleven-time All-Star was selfless. Bosh went from the main attraction in Toronto to a third option in Miami next to LeBron James and Dwyane Wade. He switched positions from center to power forward, endured dips in his scoring and rebounding stats, moved back to center, and evolved into a prototypical stretch 5 years before they were in vogue. Despite all of it, Bosh was roasted.

The early 2010s were not long ago, but the treatment Bosh received after joining the Heat feels repulsively archaic. Due to his finesse style of play and goofy mannerisms, he was demeaned incessantly for being "soft." The word haunted him, spat as a defining adjective by adults who should have known better. It was not only used to describe traits that hoops heads have more specific vocabulary for today—like rim protection, points in the paint, or clutch scoring—it was about Bosh as a human. Shaquille O'Neal described him as the "RuPaul of big men." Podcast *The Basketball Jones* made a satirical song based on Lonely Island's satirical song "Like a Boss" and ended it with "No one loves me / no one loves me." He was dogged by rumors that he was gay. "What am I supposed to do?" Bosh asked, in an ESPN interview. "You want me to have cornrows and tats on my neck and just punch somebody in the face when they score on me?"

Attitudes changed, both in terms of barbaric jock masculinity and toward Bosh. After Miami's titles, his versatility on the court and quirky personality were appreciated. A willingness to look silly made him an early star in the social media meme economy, and his post-game photobombs turned into viral GIFs. Just when Bosh was finally accepted for who he was, a blood clot was discovered in his lungs and he was forced into early retirement. "I like to read," he told *Maxim*. "I like to play video games. I like technology. When other people see that you do the normal, weird, regular things that they do, I think they kinda appreciate it a little bit more."

BOSTON MEDIA MAFIA, AKA THE TINY GREEN HAND

From the row houses of Beacon Hill to the shillelagh-carrying warren of Southie, Boston has one civic goal: total domination of basketball media. New York is known for finance, art, publishing, fashion, and food; Los Angeles is known for movies about hitmen; Miami is known for pornography and Uruguayans in Maserati rentals. Boston exports Celtics propaganda. (Tied for distant second are Sam Adams Winter Lagers, Matt Damon, and vinyl-only singles from 7L & Esoteric.) The manipulation of national sports storylines and topics of frenzied debate—all of which benefit Beantown's interests—has functioned to keep the city relevant beyond Ben Affleck's beautiful dorsal tattoo. For the Boston Media Mafia, this is the leprechaun's bucket of bullion at the far end of the rainbow.

The BMM's strategy relies on disproportionate representation. They have polluted the groundwater of the information aquifers: New England–based cable networks, websites owned by Boston natives, advanced metrics portals doctored to boost the statistical profiles of Celtics players. Whether their operatives are pundits on television, podcast hosts, or journalists, the Beantown agenda is furthered at every step. In fact, it extends across all major professional sports. "Red Sox Nation? What a bunch of bullshit that is," said Hank Steinbrenner, the Yankees general partner, to the *New York Times* in 2008. "That was a creation of the Red Sox and ESPN, which is filled with Red Sox fans. Go anywhere in America and you won't see Red Sox hats and jackets, you'll see Yankee hats and jackets."

No one believes in the existence of Celtics Nation—as if there are gentlemen in the Ozarks wearing Realtree cargo shorts and Dino Radja jerseys—yet the BMM operates as if the team has global relevancy. It upstreams local bloggers to spawn on more influential and prestigious platforms. Former Boston players, no matter how wrong, bearded, or fecal-pantsed, are shunted into televised broadcasts. As if by decree, anyone who was a part of

B

Creating a solar system orbiting a tiny green sun.
Outfitting reporters with bright green top hats.
Broadcasting every draft pick as a pot o' gold.
Denying that Bird was a hard hat Rashard Lewis.
Pretending Ish Smith wouldn't cook Bob Cousy.
Showing undying patience for Gordon Hayward.
Keeping the Bonobros energy striving/thriving.

Pivoting back to Ray Allen's championship team.
Ripping Kyrie Irving, the best Celtics guard ever.
Dragging Sixers stars with "undisclosed sources."
Pushing the Dropkick Murphys as a top-3 band.
Establishing the criteria of "magically delicious."
Abandoning journalistic integrity during Poogate.
Ignoring a ten-year rebuild, aka the Re-Procedural.

the Celtics' championship team in 2008 is entitled to publicly share his muddled thoughts. This has included 60 percent of the starting lineup—Paul Pierce, Kevin Garnett, and Kendrick Perkins—as well as reserves like Brian Scalabrine and Eddie House. Though not celebrated for it, even pundits Shaquille O'Neal and Chauncey Billups are former Celtics. For the BMM, the only criteria that matter are if you once wore emerald and whether you committed a hate crime with Mark Wahlberg.

From a practical standpoint, the Bostonian echo chamber bolsters the historical prominence of former Celtics, raises the trade value of current players, and sows division among Eastern Conference Rivals. Bill Russell, a beta-test version of Ben Wallace, is considered a top-5 player of all time. Larry Bird is lauded as one of the finest marksmen in history, despite making fewer 3-pointers per game over the course of his career than Mike Muscala. And it is surely a coincidence that the 1980s Celtics, who won three titles before dunking was invented, are discussed far more than the 1980s Lakers, who won five titles and went 2–1 against Boston in the Finals.

In recent years, the BMM has focused its efforts on fabricating a glossy veneer of stardom around young forward Jayson Tatum. Despite averaging 12 points with a 36.4 field-goal percentage in a 2019 second-round postseason exit, the conventional swingman was propped up as a breakout talent. During the 2020 season, headlines from *The Ringer* included: "Jayson Tatum Is Everything the Celtics Need Him to Be," "Jayson Tatum Is Wreaking Havoc on the NBA," "Jayson Tatum Is Up to the Challenge," and "What We Learned by Watching Every Shot Jayson Tatum Has Taken This Season."

The BMM is notorious for conducting smear campaigns against its enemies. Philadelphia, who has been Boston's Eastern Conference nemesis for a half-century, has been subjected to decades of gaslighting, which has eroded the legacies of Wilt Chamberlain, Moses Malone, Julius Erving, Charles Barkley, and, most unforgivably, Allen Iverson. On ESPN's *NBA Countdown*, Pierce sputtered that LeBron James was not one of the top-5 players in NBA history. After Kyrie Irving left the Celtics in free agency, he was trashed endlessly by the Beantown-centric media for being a selfish team cancer. Later, during the COVID hiatus, Perkins slammed Irving, the vice president of the Players Association, for expressing reluctance about the league's Disney World bubble plan. "If you take Kyrie

Irving's brain and put it in a bird right now, guess what that bird is going to do?" Perkins said on ESPN. "It's going to fly backward, because Kyrie right now is confused." Beware the Tiny Green Hand!

BRAND, ELTON

Taken by Chicago with the first overall pick in 1999, Elton Brand was nicknamed Old School Chevy due to his girthy chassis, rumbling engine, and habit of leaking pools of radiator fluid on the hardwood. Going into the draft, Bulls GM Jerry Krause reportedly favored Brand because the player had a short neck, which allowed him to play bigger than his listed height. "He was analytics before it was on the computer," Brand later said of Krause. "He's basically talking about wingspan. And that's all we hear about today." Brand went on to play seventeen years in the pros, received two All-Star nods, and became a quiet superstar with the Clippers. While he was not a high-flyer, he used 7-foot-5.5-inch arms, agile footwork, and minotaur strength to place among the league leaders in scoring efficiency, rebounds, and blocks.

Prior to the 2008 season, Brand ruptured his Achilles tendon during a summer workout. He returned to play only eight games during the dregs of the season, but it was enough to convince Philadelphia to offer him a five-year, $82-million deal in free agency. Stripped of his pop, he never became the centerpiece the organization hoped it was acquiring. "That Achilles really changed the trajectory of my career," Brand later said on ESPN's *Hoop Collective* podcast. "That whole kinetic chain: once you get the calf, it's the ankle, the knee, the hips, the back. I wasn't the same guy."

Still, Philly could not stop paying him. In 2018, the Sixers hired Brand, who had virtually no executive experience, to the position of general manager. With Brand as the Sixers' meat shield, the team embarked on a multiyear quest to rid the roster of any player who could be considered a guard. It remains unclear if Brand harbored a goal of fielding a team composed solely of other Elton Brands or was

#1 PICKS

Allen Iverson.
Tim Duncan.
Michael Olowokandi.
Elton Brand.
Kenyon Martin.
Kwame Brown.

Yao Ming.
LeBron James.
Dwight Howard.
Andrew Bogut.
Andrea Bargnani.
Greg Oden.

Derrick Rose.
Blake Griffin.
John Wall.
Kyrie Irving.
Anthony Davis.
Anthony Bennett.

Andrew Wiggins.
Karl-Anthony Towns.
Ben Simmons.
Markelle Fultz.
DeAndre Ayton.
Zion Williamson.

simply a fleshy obstacle in a grander design. After the 2020 season, the organization hired Daryl Morey as the president of Basketball Operations, but left Brand in place as a respected and well-liked cheesesteak barricade.

BRANDON, TERRELL

Entombed within the ridgelines of your brain, next to AIM usernames and *Jazzmatazz* singles, is Terrell Brandon. The two-time All-Star is forgettable for many reasons, all understandable. He played on good (not great) teams in the NBA's fur-trading outposts, maintained a stony demeanor, and had his eleven-year career abbreviated by microfracture surgery. He had two first names. Even among his NBA peers, Brandon was a loner who rarely ventured from his hotel room while on the road. "This life is easy if you let it be," he told *Sports Illustrated*. "I won't complicate mine. I play the game, go home, wait for the next day." Brandon was the consummate professional introvert.

A 5-foot-11 point guard whose bounce and physicality outsized his frame, Brandon was lauded as a classical floor general. He mostly scored on jumpers, finding space by weaving around high screens or getting big men back on their heels. He was an unflappable passer who used no-look dimes and snappy one-handed passes with utility instead of showmanship. "I'm not just the leader of this team, I'm the guy with the ball in my hands," he told onetime understudy Chauncey Billups. "There isn't a moment that goes by during the game where I'm not thinking to myself, 'What am I doing to fulfill my responsibility as a point guard?'"

Brandon was born in North Portland, Oregon. His father was a ham-and-egger who moonlighted as an associate pastor. As a child, Terrell needed corrective boots. "My legs were like Forrest Gump," he said. Despite being a star at the University of Oregon and the eleventh pick in the 1991 draft, Brandon spent the first three years of his career backing up Mark Price—an unthinkable waste of time in the league today. "I wasn't depressed about not starting," he said in the *New York Times*. "The NBA isn't life, it's a fairy tale."

Even when Brandon finally got his chance, he was subjected to Cleveland coach Mike Fratello's painfully deliberate offense. The Cavs marched the court at the tempo of a funeral dirge—in fact, the slowest in league history—and the deflationary toll on Brandon's nightly statistics was profound. He was basically playing in snowshoes. In 1996, for example, he was an unremarkable twenty-sixth in the league in points per game. But when Cleveland's pace of 82.3 possessions a night is accounted for, Brandon surges to fifth in the NBA in scoring per 100 possessions. According to the rate-based metrics Box Plus/Minus and Win Shares per 48 Minutes, he was the third-best player in the league in 1996, behind only Michael Jordan and David Robinson.

Due to circumstances beyond his control and a personality that avoided rocking the boat, Brandon was a superstar hidden in *Plain Dealer* sight. Had he spent his prime under a less authoritarian regime, he would be remembered as a modernist scoring point guard—a precursor to short kings like Allen Iverson and Kemba Walker—instead of a diligent company man. But, being Terrell Brandon, he never complained about it.

BRAXTON, TONI

For decades, Toni Braxton, the R&B singer best known for the chart-topping ballad "Un-Break My Heart," has been blamed for splintering the Mavericks' young core of Jason Kidd, Jamal Mashburn, and Jimmy Jackson in the late nineties. The trio, dubbed "Triple J Ranch," was composed of collegiate studs who were top-4 lottery picks and represented the future of the Dallas franchise. According to the 1995 rumor mill, Braxton pulled up in a limo at the Mavericks' hotel in Atlanta to go on an arranged date with Kidd. Instead, Jackson jumped in. Braxton stoked the fire in media appearances, demurely saying, "Whether it's true or not, I can never kiss and tell."

Within two seasons, Mashburn was dealt to Miami and Kidd was traded to Phoenix. Although the young players had beefed about their roles in Dallas (and there were reportedly squabbles about other women), the Braxton myth became accepted lore. To this day, all three Js deny there was a love triangle involving Braxton. "I never met the woman and never thought I was going to meet the woman," Kidd told

ESPN. "But somehow this story came about and it just took off. Did not know her. No date." The real falsehood, however, might be that the young Mavericks core had untapped potential—during their two full seasons together, the team's record was 62–102.

BROTHERS

The presence of siblings in the NBA does not provide much insight into the algorithm of nature versus nurture. Should there be more players who sprung from the same loins and grew up under the same roof? Fewer? The Holiday family boasts three players in the league, Jrue, Justin, and Aaron, all of whom appeared in the same 2019 game. "It was cool," said Jrue. "I beat them and I got their jerseys, so I'll hang those up." Other brotherly trios have included the Barrys, Antetokounmpos, and Plumlees, an indistinguishable trio of tall white dudes who jumped higher than you would expect. In ancient times, four members of the Jones family all went from Albany State University to the NBA, overlapping each other from 1970 until 1998.

Duos are far more common. Notable pairs have included the Grants (Horace and Harvey), Wilkinses (Dominique and Gerald), Persons (Chuck and Wesley), Currys (Stephen and Seth), and Balls (Lonzo and LaMelo). Brook and Robin Lopez are twins who share goofy personalities and 7-foot builds but have experienced different levels of success. Brook averaged 18.6 points and made an All-Star team over nine seasons as a lurching post threat in Brooklyn—then morphed into a 3-point specialist and rim protector on Milwaukee teams with top-ranked defenses. Meanwhile, Robin was a chippy energy guy who has played for seven teams and is most famous for physically assaulting mascots. Whether on the same team or playing against

each other, they have a tradition of ignoring each other during games. Brook has a home on the grounds of Walt Disney World, the same site as the NBA's COVID Bubble. "They're unique and creative," Quincy Pondexter, a childhood friend who played in the NBA for Memphis, said in the *Chicago Tribune*. "They know how to draw. They know about art. They know everything about Disney."

Another pair of twins, Marcus and Markieff Morris, are spicier. The Morrii went to college at the University of Kansas, were inked with identical tattoos, and shared a bank account. One of the Morrii is slightly better than the other, but no one can remember which is which—perhaps by design. Early on, the pair were teammates on the Suns and signed a unique contract where they took millions less to stay on the same team. Not long afterward, Marcus was traded to Detroit. The separated twins were not happy. "My whole view of the millennial culture is that they have a tough time dealing with setbacks," owner Robert Sarver said of Markieff's anger. Marcus put it differently. "We're from North Philadelphia," he told *Bleacher Report*. "This isn't adversity. This is betrayal." In 2017, during the Eastern Conference Semifinals, it was suspected (but never proven) that the Morrii from an eliminated team subbed in for the Morrii who had gotten injured earlier in the series. Receiving two Morrii for the price of one Morrii is the Gift of the Morrii.

The greatest *hermanos* to play in the NBA are from the Gasol clan. Huge Catalonians, Pau and Marc were devastatingly skillful and smart players who combined for nine All-Star appearances and a handful of NBA titles. They were teammates on two Spanish silver-medal-winning teams in the Olympics. In an oddity, the brothers were traded for each other as components in a tasty blockbuster paella (though Marc was seen as a marginal prospect who was likely to play overseas at the time).

Pau was the first of the Gasol conquistadors to arrive on New World soil. Taken by Atlanta with the third pick of the 2001 draft and immediately shipped to Vancouver, he was skinny and agile enough to evoke comparisons to Toni Kukoč and viewed as a potential small forward. Even without much chorizo on his bones, Gasol thrived for the Grizzlies. He was deft with both hands, a double-digit rebounder, and a passer who could sling an occasional behind-the-back dish on a fast break.

In 2008, Gasol was traded to the Lakers in a deal that rescued the second act of Kobe Bryant's

career. Los Angeles went from a directionless team that had missed the playoffs and twice lost in the first round since Shaquille O'Neal's departure to three straight Finals appearances and two titles. As heretical as it sounds, Gasol may have been the best player on the Lakers for the second of those championships. While Bryant once told Gasol to put his "big boy pants on," the two were tight *compañeros*. "My first game in New Jersey, he was talking to me in Spanish," Gasol recalled. "All the play calls, all the coverages to gain my trust and to connect with me." Despite the team's success, the early 2000s were a time when willowy Europeans were still stereotyped as lacking physicality—and his scraggly, leaving-an-Ibiza-foam-party-at-6 a.m. appearance did not help. "Pau gasol is soft as fucc we need to get his bitch ass on the 1st thing smoking," tweeted Snoop Doog, in 2011. "Hes a fuccn weanie. this is comn from laker fan #1."

Slipping between forward and center, Gasol spent his prime in a league on the cusp of transformation. While he was a veteran on the Lakers, coach Mike D'Antoni encouraged him to take 3s, which caused Los Angeles fans to go batshit insane (his career mark of 36.8 percent from deep indicates that he should have shot a lot more of them). We may never have seen Gasol's creativity entirely unleashed—it is easy to imagine him as the bridge between Vlade Divac and Nikola Jokić—but he was moved by the ancient spirits. "When I was younger, some of the shots that are attempted today would have seen the coach send you to the bench as a punishment," Gasol told the Spanish newspaper *Marca*. "The fact is that the NBA likes this dynamism, this speed. This is how society and the world in general are evolving. Everything is like that, everything is more dynamic, faster."

His younger brother, Marc, was dynamic but not fast. Raised in Memphis as a fat kid, he grew into an appropriately ursine-shaped All-Star for the Grizzlies after Pau was dealt to the Lakers. For ten seasons, he was a load-bearing column at the middle of the Grit 'N' Grind defense. Though he seldom notched the same per-game points and rebounds as his sibling, he was a burly post presence who could initiate the offense from the elbow for a team whose personnel was better equipped for the other side of the ball. Later in his career, Gasol morphed into a 3-and-D starter for the title-winning Raptors and was instrumental in holding Sixers' center Joel Embiid to a paltry 37 percent field-goal percentage in a tightly fought Eastern Conference playoff series.

Off the floor, Gasol once joined a mission to help rescue refugees clinging to rafts in the Mediterranean. "It's not a jersey that you put on," he told ESPN of his life-changing experience with the humanitarian organization Proactiva Open Arms. "It's deeper than that, and you connect. You're so vulnerable out there: your feelings, emotions, where you're at. Everything is so real and pure. They have each other's back."

BRYANT, KOBE

As an exercise, imagine Kobe Bryant without the purple and gold uniform, without Shaquille O'Neal and Phil Jackson, without the five championship rings that validate his reputation for outworking and outwinning everyone else. Pretend he had been selected eighth in the 1996 NBA Draft by New Jersey—as the lowly Nets had reportedly planned, until coach John Calipari flinched and took Kerry Kittles (who went on to become an excellent and criminally underrated player).

Instead of being traded by Charlotte to the 53-win Lakers for Vlade Divac, Bryant enters the league vying for shots next to Kendall Gill and Jim Jackson, commuting to the Meadowlands from a 17th-floor condo in Hoboken. He finds comfort in Fiore's roast beef and mutz heroes, embraces Freestyle music, goes on to play for a few different franchises, manages to secure a title, leads the league in scoring a couple of times, and is celebrated as the best shooting guard of his generation. Is that *Kobe*? And would the elemental force of his ambition have permitted such a conventional fate?

Born in Philadelphia, Bryant was raised in Italy due to the career of his father, Joe "Jellybean" Bryant, a forward who spent eight seasons in the NBA before playing for teams like AMG Sebastiani Rieti and Olimpia Pistoia. The bambino was obsessed with hoops, acting as ball boy for his dad's teams and playing against adults. In Bryant's early teens, his family headed stateside and he became the nation's

B

top schoolboy prospect at Lower Merion. His prom date was R&B star Brandy. "He's not a stereotypical Black kid from an urban setting," Joe told the *New York Times*, when discussing whether Kobe would attend college or leap to the NBA. "We live in a five-bedroom house in a Philadelphia suburb . . . he has a kind of sophistication."

A sinewy, 6-foot-6 shooting guard who spoke fluent Italian, played for the Lakers, and jumped through the roof, Bryant was easy to adore. He won the NBA Slam Dunk Contest as a rookie and was named to the All-Star team in his second season, despite coming off the pine and averaging 15.4 points and 3.1 rebounds. "That little Laker boy's gonna take everyone one-on-one," Michael Jordan told Eastern Conference teammates in the All-Star Game locker room. "He don't let the game come to him. He just take it."

Jordan was gazing into a mirror. Despite the heights of his career, Bryant was a chiseled simulacrum of His Airness: the same unblockable fadeaways, immaculate footwork, leaning dunks, lupine defensive stance, and ability to pile up mountains of points. They shared the same revanchist worldview, sociopathic drive for legacy-building, and insistence that their success was due to mind-state and not athleticism. They inspired the same trembling fear in opponents. Even now, there is not even an identifiable Bryant archetype—instead, he was generational transmission of Jordan Originalism with baggier shorts. "Kobe was hell-bent on surpassing Jordan as the greatest player in the game," wrote Phil Jackson, who famously coached both, in his book *Eleven Rings*. "His obsession with Michael was striking. Not only had he mastered many of Jordan's moves, but he affected many of M.J.'s mannerisms as well."

Like Jordan, Bryant used competitiveness as a trompe l'oeil to create depth of personality and a marketable persona. Mamba Mentality—an orthodoxy derived from his self-supplied nickname of the Black Mamba—was not so much about striving for victory as about winning in the most self-aggrandizing way possible. It is an ethos of personal responsibility that presents not only work ethic and relentless effort as virtuous, but also jacking up the final shot. "It was his drive to win," said Nuggets point guard Jamal Murray. "It was his never-give-up on plays, his confidence level in himself and what he could do, his belief in his team, just everything." A lesser player could not have pulled it off, but Bryant was magnificent enough to win on his own terms.

Most famously, Bryant challenged Shaquille O'Neal for control of the Lakers during a stretch where the team went to four Finals in five seasons and won three titles. He grumbled about the big man's conditioning and groused that Jackson's triangle offense did not stretch a broad enough canvas to contain his artistry (Shaq's response was threatening to loaf: "If the big dog ain't me," he said, "then the house won't get guarded"). The center was soon postmarked for Miami. Bryant's coup was successful, but the Lakers went 34-48 the next season and failed to escape the first round of the playoffs until Pau Gasol joined the team four years later. He got the last laugh, however, winning two more chips as the Lakers' unchallenged alpha.

Bryant's five championships, two scoring titles, a Most Valuable Player award, 18 All-Star appearances, 81-point game, and 60-point career finale obscure the uglier moments. He publicly eviscerated Laker underlings like Kwame Brown and Smush Parker, and punched Samaki Walker in the face over an unpaid $100 bet ("It was his Beanie Sigel phase," teammate Jelani McCoy later told writer Jeff Pearlman. "Really fake.") Bryant was not shy about clipping opponents with mean-spirited elbows and, during one baffling stretch, hit several defenders in the grill with flailing strikes after releasing jumpers. According to Draymond Green, another guy accused of dirty play, Bryant once explained his attitude like this: "I never gave a fuck if they understood me, because I knew I was onto something so much bigger than they could even understand."

In 2003, Bryant was accused of felony sexual assault by a 19-year-old hotel employee while in Colorado to have knee surgery. Criminal charges were dropped after the victim refused to testify and a later civil case was settled out of court. "Although I truly believe this encounter between us was consensual, I recognize now that she did not and does not view this incident the same way I did," said Bryant in a statement. In 2018, he described himself as "too gritty" for the corporate sponsors who dropped him in the aftermath of his arrest.

Bryant's second act as a filmmaker, analyst, advocate for women's basketball, and father ended tragically in 2020 when a helicopter carrying him, his 13-year-old daughter, Gianna, and seven other passengers crashed in Calabasas. There were no survivors. It still feels surreal that a man whose presence consumed basketball for a quarter century—not only on the court but in the endless arguments he inspired from barbershops to message boards—was abruptly gone. "There aren't enough words to describe our pain right now," his wife, Vanessa Bryant, posted on Instagram. "I take comfort in knowing that Kobe and Gigi both knew that they were so deeply loved. We were so incredibly blessed to have them in our lives. I wish they were here with us forever."

BURNERGATE

Born into the NBA's most dynastic clan, Bryan Colangelo followed in his father's footsteps as a multiple-time winner of the league's Executive of the Year award. He was the architect of the offensive circus in Phoenix with Steve Nash, Shawn Marion, and Amar'e Stoudemire, then spent eight years in Toronto with mixed results (he acquired Kyle Lowry and DeMar DeRozan, but blew a number-one overall pick on Andrea Bargnani and spent $19.5 million on three seasons of Landry Fields). In 2016, after an exhaustive search that left no adult son unturned, his father brought him in to lead the Sixers from "Process 2 Progress."

While the Sixers had a shitty record, it was the NBA's most plum gig. Philadelphia had blooming young talent, an embarrassment of forthcoming draft picks, and cap space to make bold signings. But the charmed touch that Colangelo demonstrated with the Suns eluded him in Philadelphia. He overpaid veterans, paid a steep premium to move up in the draft for Markelle Fultz, and panic-flushed assets as if cops were breaking down the bathroom door.

In early 2018, an anonymous social media egg contacted Ben Detrick with a toothsome nugget: he believed that he had identified multiple "burner" accounts on Twitter that had ties to Colangelo. "I'm a fan of The Process and am absolutely disgusted at the moves Colangelo is making," wrote the tipster, who claimed to work in artificial intelligence. "I'm not Elon Musk, nor anyone like him."

Detrick shared the details with Andrew Kuo, his co-host on *Cookies Hoops*, the world's most

influential basketball podcast, and the pair began combing through thousands of tweets from accounts with names like Still Balling, Eric jr, and Honest Abe. It was clear that whoever was operating the accounts shared vectors with Colangelo: the University of Chicago basketball team (where his son played), an Arizona businessman who was president of a golf-related technology company that he had invested in, and a Toronto socialite who attended the same charity galas. Even more telling was the subject matter. Over and over, the accounts attacked Colangelo's perceived enemies while praising his record as a basketball executive. They even defended the dimensions of his shirts: "That is a normal collar," wrote Enoughunkownsources. "Move on, find a new slant."

The accounts had few followers and primarily acted as reply guys to Philadelphia beat reporters and bloggers. Had they stuck to insulting Sam Hinkie, the team's former general manager and a martyred hero, it might have resulted only in an embarrassing snafu. More troublingly, they appeared to leak sensitive information about players and goaded writers to interrogate members of the Sixers with specific questions. The accounts claimed a trade involving Jahlil Okafor fell through because of a failed physical, called Nerlens Noel a "selfish punk" who was "behaving like a vulture," and advocated trading star center Joel Embiid for Kristaps Porziņģis, then of the Knicks. "If I were mngt I would step on a ladder and kick his b#**," wrote Eric jr of Embiid.

When Markelle Fultz experienced mysterious issues with his shoulder, the accounts blamed the guard's longtime trainer. Even Joshua Harris, the most identifiable member of the team's ownership group, absorbed heat. "No other owner would have been conned the way Harris was by [Hinkie]," Still Balling tweeted. "He was able to get away with as much BS and Con job as he did because Harris was not able to stand up to him."

There were targets of ire outside of the Sixers organization. The burners loathed Masai Ujiri, who replaced Colangelo as general manager of the Raptors, Spurs coach Gregg Popovich, and ESPN's Adrian Wojnarowski. LeBron James was termed a "condescending bore." They described Rockets executive Daryl Morey as "my number one enemy" and implied that he played a role in preventing an eighteen-year-old boy—described by Still Balling as "someone I love"—from being accepted at the Sloan School of Management at the Massachusetts Institute of Technology. In a response to Morey, Still

PRETENDERS

Real.   Unreal.

Anonymous anti-Joel Embiid tweetstorms.
Kevin Durant's pro-Kevin Durant burners.
NYC bodegas with salad bars and no cats.
Believable plant-based substitutes for beef.
Toughguy defensive enforcers from the '80s.

Friends who live and eat clean every January.
Heiress, socialite and nightlife star Anna Delvey.
Semi-autobiographical storyteller JT Leroy.
The late Avril Lavigne's pop star stand-in.
The positive, mellow version of us on Twitter.

Balling wrote, "Do you have influence on the admission process at Sloan and MIT? And if so, have you even helped or more interesting [*sic*] blackballed a kid, just for spite and power trip?"

Immediately before the story broke, Detrick contacted the Sixers organization and inquired about two of the five accounts. Within hours of the phone call, the unmentioned three accounts all went private, including one that had recently been active and another that had been untouched for almost six months. Still Balling unfollowed thirty-seven accounts with ties to Colangelo. On May 29, the story was posted on *The Ringer* with the headline "The Curious Case of Bryan Colangelo and the Secret Twitter Account." It laid out the connections between the accounts and the executive but did not specifically say who operated them. As the story roared across social media, Embiid chimed in. "Fun night on Twitter lmao," he tweeted. "All jokes aside I don't believe the story. That would just be insane."

On June 7, Colangelo resigned from the Sixers. During the course of an investigation by New York legal firm Paul, Weiss, Rifkind, Wharton & Garrison LLP, his wife, Barbara Bottini, admitted to using the accounts. "We believe that Mr. Colangelo was careless and in some instances reckless in failing to properly safeguard sensitive, non-public, club-related information in communications with individuals outside the 76ers organization," said a statement from the lawyers.

After stepping down, Colangelo vanished from public view. In 2020, he bought a share of the Illawarra Hawks, a basketball team in Australia. "I have stayed very much under the radar on the topic because it's a sensitive topic, for a lot of reasons," Colangelo told the *Sydney Morning Herald*. "I have to say I was dealt a pretty big blow, personally and professionally. And it's been a difficult time dealing with the fallout. I was completely blindsided by the accusation and the storyline of the controversy."

BUSTS

Disappointing draft picks are called busts. The badge of dishonor is pinned on underperforming players who were selected in the lottery and conveys a depth of uselessness below mediocrity. Prototypes include schoolboy heroes who peaked early, unfortunates

who suffered terrible injuries, and athletic giants who discovered basketball through the arrival of a friendly missionary. Through no fault of their own, busts who went first overall in their respective draft classes are particularly infamous. Their ranks include Kwame Brown (bad), Andrea Bargnani (pretty bad), Greg Oden (injuries), Anthony Bennett (body-shamed), and Markelle Fultz (mystery, then maybe not a bust?).

The amount of scorn heaped on a bust can be proportional to the ability of alternative selections. Darko Miličić, taken second by Detroit in the stacked 2003 draft, was selected ahead of Carmelo Anthony, Chris Bosh, and Dwyane Wade. In 2009, Hasheem Thabeet, a 7-foot-3 stiff, was picked before James Harden and Stephen Curry. In the case of Oden, a hulking center from Ohio State with the visage of an Ent from *Lord of the Rings*, Portland's decision to take him ahead of Kevin Durant makes his broken knees even more painful. While Bennett was a dubious top pick to begin with, the only major talents in his 2013 class were Giannis Antetokounmpo (mined by the Bucks at fifteenth) and Rudy Gobert (who went twenty-seventh). For Cavaliers fans, there is no tantalizing Springfield-bound superstar reminding them of what might have been.

Now and then, a bust is vindicated, at least to an extent. Marvin Williams, who was notorious for being tabbed ahead of Deron Williams and Chris Paul—despite not even being a starter in college—morphed into a useful small-ball power forward and spent fifteen years in the NBA. "I've been very blessed," he said at his retirement. "God has been very, very good to me."

The quintessential bust, Michael Olowokandi, was selected first by the Clippers in the 1998 draft, ahead of Vince Carter, Paul Pierce, and Dirk Nowitzki. The Kandi Man was a Lagos-born, London-raised 7-footer who discovered basketball in his late teens. He attended the University of the Pacific after haphazardly picking the school from a list of American colleges and cold-calling the coach. "I went from London, trendy and sophisticated, to Stockton, which is pretty rural," Olowokandi said of

Just getting drafted by the NBA.

Being an apex playground GOAT.

Playing some college ball.

Living as a high school legend.

A. Start   B. End

"I am the master of this TV remote, gas grill, and universe."

"Barkley and Bird would average 35 and 15 in this NBA."

"You gotta at least attempt 3s to keep the defense honest."

"Ask for your bone-in ribeye well done, I'll ask you to leave."

"Passes and steals are great, but can Simmons get a bucket?"

"These sunglasses are tactical and eliminate 95% of glares."

"Harden cares more about strip clubs and Vegas than rings."

"Kobe's top-3 and Steph Curry's soft and smiles too much."

"Players demanding trades is a threat to our NBA way of life."

the California college. "You can imagine what that was like."

While scouts drooled over Olowokandi's size, mightiness, quick feet, and 4.55 speed in the 40-yard dash, he was accused of lacking drive. He was a decent defender and rebounder, but an abysmal offensive player at a time when feeding monsters on the block was standard policy. Over his first three seasons, Olowokandi had four times as many turnovers as assists. "Here's a guy who didn't seem all that interested in playing basketball, much less being a top player," Bill Walton, the stoner announcer suggested in 2002.

After retirement, Olowokandi still caught strays. Kareem Abdul-Jabbar, the Hall of Fame center who served as an assistant coach for the Clippers, called him out as an example of impertinence in a 2011 *ESPN* magazine op-ed. "At practice, I would attempt to point out Mr. Olowokandi's faults to him, ones he constantly repeated," Abdul-Jabbar wrote. "His reaction to my attempts to correct his bad habits was to take my input as a personal insult and embarrassment."

Even Olowokandi's ex-girlfriend, Suzie Ketchum of VH1's *Basketball Wives*, squatted atop the dogpile. "I had all this money and beautiful cars but felt so empty," she told *Essence* in 2010 about their ten-year relationship. Wait. Money? Beautiful cars? Reality television sweethearts? By any other standards, the life of an NBA bust qualifies as an outrageous success.

BUTLER, JIMMY

More of a rascal than a bad guy, Jimmy Butler does not shy away from his reputation for villainy. He has been criticized as selfish and disruptive, an egotistical try-hard whose idea of camaraderie is the emasculation of his teammates. He splintered several NBA locker rooms before opting for South Beach's retirement lifestyle of golf carts and ropa vieja at Versailles. But his chaotic neutrality is accompanied by mischievousness, joy, and steely competitiveness. Jimmy—which is not short for James—is a treasure.

Butler was raised in a fatherless household in Tomball, Texas. He was given the boot at age thirteen by his mother, received zero scholarships offers out of high school, and was taken by the Bulls with the thirtieth pick in 2011. "My whole life, people

have doubted me," Butler told ESPN before the draft. "People told me in high school I'm too short and not fast enough to play basketball. They didn't know my story." He carries a chip on his shoulder, to be sure, but there is also a gleeful sense of defying expectations that other people set for him. He acts as if he has already made it, because he has.

Butler plays with confrontational patience. He is bruising, intense, and rarely out of control. While his erratic long-range shooting and love for the midrange game appear antithetical to modern hoops, his versatility is cutting-edge. Butler pivots seamlessly from pass-first point guard to volume-scoring power forward, shapeshifting to the contours of a roster. He is good-to-excellent at most things: draining pull-up jumpers or curling off screens, bucking out into transition for easy dunks, gluing himself to ball-handlers, and disrupting passing lanes. The package is bound together by an uncanny ability to draw contact on drives or while ensnarled in the post. He has finished among the league's top-5 in total free-throw attempts twice.

At stops in Chicago, Minnesota, and Philadelphia, Butler acquired a reputation for prickliness. During an infamous Timberwolves practice, he reportedly led a third-string unit to victory against the starters—while taunting Karl-Anthony Towns and Andrew Wiggins. "I'm not the most talented player on the team," he told ESPN afterward. "Who is the most talented player on our team? KAT. Who is the most God-gifted player on our team? Wiggs. Who plays the hardest? Me!"

For Butler, who makes a habit of arriving at the gym at 3 a.m. to broadcast how much harder he works than everyone else, Miami was the perfect match: an organization whose commitment to industriousness was equally performative. In 2020, Butler topped the team in points, assists, and steals per game while stoking the Heat from room-temperature respectability to licking at contention. Though a five-seed in the Eastern Conference, the team scraped its way to the Finals in the COVID Bubble under the whipping flag of Heat Culture. Butler was magnificent in Miami's six-game loss to Los Angeles, averaging 26.2 points, 9.8 assists, and 2.2 steals a game. Even if his Joe Lunchpail routine is bluster, the results demand that we take him seriously.

a surge in double-pastry frontcourts around the NBA (the Knicks, for example, paired Patrick Ewing with Bill Cartwright). "Most people say it hindered me from scoring more points or getting more rebounds," said Sampson, who was 7-foot-4 and averaged 20.7 points and 10.9 rebounds and 2.0 blocks over his first three seasons, in a *Grantland* interview. "But every team had to adjust to two 7-footers playing every night." The Rockets made one Finals appearance before collapsing beneath the weight of injuries and drug issues.

The dual stromboli approach was more successful in San Antonio (David Robinson and Tim Duncan) and Los Angeles (Andrew Bynum, Pau Gasol, and, sort of, Lamar Odom), winning multiple championships for each franchise. In 2018, a short-lived beignet bundle in New Orleans that coupled Anthony Davis and DeMarcus Cousins looked promising, but was split apart after the latter ruptured his Achilles tendon. "It's fucked up," Cousins later told the *Athletic*. "It could've been something great, something special."

The late 1990s and early 2000s had odd culinary practices. Subway sandwiches were marketed as diet food. Epic bacon was for the win. The Timberwolves believed that Kevin Garnett could play small forward and the Magic thought it made sense to play Tracy McGrady for 95 percent of his minutes at shooting guard. The Mavericks blacked out in the bakery and woke up dusted with crumbs from a starting lineup that included 7-foot-6 Shawn Bradley, 7-foot Dirk Nowitzki, and 6-foot-11 Raef LaFrentz. At the time, teams believed there was an advantage to sizing up everywhere—which was a defendable policy, considering the history of the sport—and insisted that anyone who could run was a forward and anyone who could shoot was a guard. But there were consequences to bloating the court with focaccia slabs rolled up inside pancakes and orzo tacos. Offenses had the joyful spontaneity of a Soviet breadline and scoring cratered like a fallen cake.

In the whizzing pace-and-space era, most teams adhere to the Atkins diet. It is not a reluctance to put size on the court, exactly, but an emphasis on perimeter skills such as dribbling, shooting, defensive versatility, and the ability to dash in transition like a springbok—all attributes more commonly found in smaller players. While teams that embrace yeasty bully-ball may benefit in areas like rim protection, post play, and rebounding, lineups with too many behemoths experience clogged offensive arteries.

CARB ON CARB

Ravioli pizza, bagel burritos, pierogis stuffed inside a loaf of ciabatta, croissant nachos. These delicacies are the hallmarks of a carb-on-carb diet. The phrase is derived from "big on big," a colloquialism popularized by the rap group Migos to describe overdoing an activity to excess (but in a positive way). It refers to integrating carbohydrate-heavy foods with other carbohydrate foods. In basketball theory, going carb on carb means the same thing, except with big boys instead of pinto beans wedged into baguettes.

One time-honored example of carb-on-carb behavior is a twin breadsticks lineup that features two centers. This alignment was implemented by the 1980s Rockets when they drafted Hakeem Olajuwon and Ralph Sampson with consecutive number-one overall picks in the NBA Draft, a strategy that led to

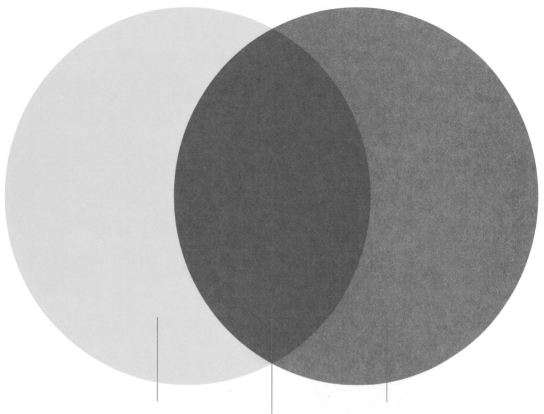

Pau Gasol.		Andrew Bynum.
Burritos.	A logical	Hash browns.
Dale Davis.	combination	Antonio Davis.
Macaroni.	satisfying all	Bread bowls.
Tim Duncan.	cravings and	David Robinson.
Pizza.	expectations.	Ravioli.
Dirk Nowitzki.		Raef LaFrentz.
Chips.		Sliced white.
Brook Lopez.		Giannis Antetokounmpo.
Croissants.		Donuts.
Joel Embiid.		Al Horford.
Oatmeal.		Granola.
Anthony Davis.		Dwight Howard.
Middle Big Mac buns.		Top/bottom Big Mac Buns.
Eddy Curry.		Tyson Chandler.

"Big guys are, like, bored to death," Spurs coach Gregg Popovich told the *San Antonio Express-News*. "They just sit on the bench and watch."

But basketball will never abandon height. Despite all the hype about "small ball," there are signs that flour-dusted appreciators are again on the rise, especially as it becomes easier to find at least one enormous man who can shoot from the perimeter. The Sixers attempted an ill-fated glucose experiment that crammed Tobias Harris, Al Horford, Ben Simmons, and Joe Embiid into the starting unit. In Milwaukee, Popovich disciple Mike Budenholzer constructed the NBA's top-ranked defense in 2019 and 2020 by funneling attacks toward two giant cannolis in the paint, Giannis Antetokounmpo and Brook Lopez. The COVID Bubble champion Lakers started both Anthony Davis and Dwight Howard, both of whom could be considered natural centers. A balanced diet will always leave room for carbs.

CARTER, VINCE

An incomparable dunker, Vince Carter was spectacular at every manner of mashing the ball through the hoop: during exhibition contests, amid the combat of a packed lane, over defenders, in the intimate moments of a fast-break when the encounter was reserved for him and an orange metal ring aching for debasement. He was 6-foot-6, normal-sized for the NBA, and big enough to challenge centers without looking like a bully yamming on a miniature basket. With long arms, huge hands, and a breathtaking vertical leap, Carter combined ferocity and sophistication like no other jammer. He could uncork an unnecessary windmill, twirl clockwise into a 360-degree slam in the half court, or crush a two-handed lob with his chest horizontally grazing the rim.

In the 2000 NBA Slam Dunk Contest, Carter trademarked a dunk in which he shoved his entire arm through the hoop and dangled, like a kid whose puffer jacket was caught on the chain-link fence. In the Olympic Games of the same year, he split his legs and cleared 7-foot-2 French center Frédéric Weis on a one-handed throwdown, which some call the greatest dunk in history. Carter's own personal favorite came in 2005, when he yoked one on the dome of the Heat's strongman center. "You see I tried to play it cool, but inside I was like a 7-year-old," he told *NBA.com*. "I was just thinking how that's

Alonzo Mourning, one of the best shot-blockers in the history of the game." It was not just the beauty and force of Carter's aerial strikes, it was the volume: he had hundreds of dunks that would top everyone else's top 5.

The rest of his legacy is trickier to pin down. In the same way Drake legitimized rappers from Toronto, Carter did it for the city's basketball team. An expansion franchise in 1996, the Raptors were a miserable squad with a name inspired by the *Jurassic Park* movie series in which Jeff Goldblum gapes at toothy CGI monsters. Carter arrived in 1999 via a draft day trade and "Vinsanity" gripped the T-Dot. He won Rookie of the Year, was named to six consecutive All-Star teams for the Raptors, and earned the nickname Half-Man, Half-Amazing.

Despite his wonderful play, Carter's reputation was smeared when he attended his own graduation ceremony at the University of North Carolina on the morning of Game 7 of the 2001 Eastern Conference Finals—and then missed a crucial jumper in the Raptors' loss to the Sixers. However preposterous, the feeling lingered that his love of mortarboards and scrolls superseded a passion for winning. A few seasons later, he was traded to New Jersey in a cloud of bad vibes resulting from knee injuries, the nickname Wince Carter, and criticism that he had quit on Toronto. Carter retired at forty-three after playing twenty-two years, ending the Odyssean journey of a man intent on exorcising the idea that he cared about anything in the world more than basketball.

CASSELL, SAM

With a bulby noggin, protruding ears, and prominent teeth swaddled by a towel on the sideline, Sam Cassell shared an uncanny resemblance to E.T. "Sam is losing his hair," said Ray Allen, his teammate on the Bucks. "He has peach fuzz on the side. He's not real tall. He's not muscular. He's not quick. He's not dunking on people." None of that mattered.

Cassell was a cheeky grifter who fit smoothly between the eras of teammates like Hakeem Olajuwon and Rajon Rondo, and bookended his fifteen-year career with two championships, one in Houston and another one in Boston. He went to the playoffs in seven of his first eight seasons and, overall, with five different teams. "I'm a winner, man," Cassell told the *New York Times*, while implying that his table-setting abilities could turn scrubs into stars. "When I played with Keith [Van Horn], people were mentioning Keith with Kevin Garnett and Tim Duncan. Now, people don't even mention Keith Van Horn at all." His best season came in 2004, when the 6-foot-3 distributor made his only All-Star team while posting 19.8 points and 7.3 assists per game for Minnesota.

As a scorer, Cassell dined on garbage. Like a goat nosing in the crabgrass for tin cans and old Lugz boots, he scrounged nourishment from the least arable pastures. Sixty-three percent of his career field-goal attempts were from the area between 10 feet and the 3-point line—with more than half of those coming from beyond 16 feet. It was a way to survive in an era of clogged lanes and clustro spacing. "I took advantage of the opportunity and I twisted it, like an old towel, got everything out of it," Cassell said near the end of his career.

Cassell was masterful at creating room without the benefit of an anato edge. He nudged defenders off balance with lowered shoulders that weren't quite powerful enough to earn charges. His elbow ended up wedged into someone's midsection. "That's all the space I need," he said during a midrange tutorial during a TNT broadcast. "Not a push off—a little bump. Step back, splash. No one in the world can jump backing up."

Referees were enmeshed in Cassell's bullshit. He leeched calls on both sides of the ball, whether collapsing like a Jenga tower after light contact or stepping in front of a big man plowing toward the rack. In 1998, he led all point guards in free-throw rate and was third among backcourt players (he trailed only Kobe Bryant and Jerry Stackhouse, both of whom were larger, high-flying swingmen). There are not available stats documenting how many offensive fouls Cassell drew early in his career, but rates from his twilight years are similar to those posted by Kyle Lowry, one of today's premier floppers.

Cassell's signature ruse was the midrange pump-fake. If a defender bit and left his feet—writhing and turning sideways in the air in a fruitless attempt to avoid contact, palms up like a suspect at gunpoint—he was at Cassell's mercy. When his midrange expertise was supplemented with frequent trips to the line (where he had a career free-throw percentage of 86.1), Cassell panhandled close to 20 points a game.

An infamous trash-talker, Cassell seized any competitive edge. In a *Players' Tribune* essay, Steve Francis described an evening when Cassell took him out to a club the night before his first pro game, regaling him with veteran wisdom until sunup. "This motherfucker has me hypnotized," Francis recalled. "Then around 5 a.m., the whole vibe changes. Now he's telling me how he's gonna whip my ass the next night." In his debut, Francis went 4–13 from the floor while Cassell torched him for 35 points. "I was so tired in the first quarter I thought I was about to pass out," said Francis.

Cassell introduced the NBA to the "Big Balls" dance, a celebration in which the participant mimics cradling enormous testicles with both arms after knocking down a crucial late-game shot. He drew inspiration from the movie *Major League II*, which includes a scene where a player punctuates a homer by clutching gigantic phantom nuts. As the exquisite method of nonverbal communication gained popularity—everyone from Julius Randle to Marco Belinelli to Kevin Martin has slung their paws around tremendous imaginary nads—the league began issuing fines for the "obscene and inappropriate gesture" that ranged from $15,000 to $25,000.

As a member of a 58-win Minnesota team, Cassell might have received the most severe punishment of all. After doing the Big Balls Dance in the 2004 Western Conference Semifinals, he aggravated a cartilage injury in his hip that limited his minutes and caused him to miss games against the Lakers in the next round. "I knew for a fact that if I was healthy, we would have won a championship," he said. "I know in my heart."

CASUALS

Do you even watch the games? Do you even have access to national broadcasts on monopolistic cable providers? Do you even use illegal streams with infuriating lag and scrolling comments by Lithuanians spouting racial epithets? Do you even sit in packed sports bars where you have to beg the waitstaff to flip one corner plasma screen away from the New York Rangers? Do you even attend live events at local arenas owned by foreclosure tycoons who donate millions of dollars to fascist politicians? Do you even pay $15 for a Bud Light tallboy while enjoying a relegated roster featuring the Morrii and Taj Gibson and a beautiful baby boy named Frankie Smokes? Do you even live in a COVID Bubble that requires a ten-day

A CASUAL WATCHING A GAME

START → 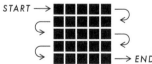 → END

"This will come down to who wants it more!"		"AD needs to dominate the offensive glass!"
"They live and die by their outside shot!"		"They've got to take the ball to the rack!"
"They have to stop the dribble penetration!"		"They're making a living at the 3-point arc!"
"Is it okay if I just pitch in for one slice?"		"All my LA Lakers day ones stand up!"

quarantine and your only sustenance is tiny bags of whole-grain Sun Chips? Do you even read blog posts about how Jayson Tatum is the reincarnation of Jesus Christ and Allah, but in the form of a conventional third-tier wing? Do you even listen to the perfect pod? Do you even waddle over to a neighborhood playground near your brownstone, call "winners," and get roasted by cruel teens when you tearfully insist that you could graze rim during the Clinton administration? Do you even lower the basket and do windmill jams with a novelty-size Charlotte Hornets Pizza Hut basketball? Do you even recognize the orange, bouncing object? Do you even exist?

CENTRISTS

In the political arena, moderates perpetuate the status quo. In the NBA, they are players who fit the game as it currently exists. They are not knee-deep in the primordial slurry where every drop-step pivot makes a rude sucking gulp. Nor are they a glimpse of a smooth, edgeless future where race, gender, and positionality merge into one iridescent cyborg who wears shorts made of wicking fabric no human has ever touched. It is not a description of talent, but philosophical fit.

Take, for example, Paul Millsap, the boxy forward who was named an All-Star four times while on the Hawks. After fourteen years, his career true shooting percentage rested almost precisely at the league's average over the same span. He spent most of his minutes at power forward, rarely dabbling in overgrown lineups or small-ball units. His unique ability to amass blocks and steals made him a tremendous defender, but not one who could be used to overhaul an existing system. As the league became more perimeter-based, he went from making two total 3-pointers over his first four seasons to canning an average of one a night. Instead of rocking the boat, Millsap dutifully swabbed the deck as it was buffeted by waves.

When centrists acquire new skills, it is in response to changes that are already underway. If a

big man who has spent his life chest-bumping in the paint like a sea lion begins taking 3-pointers, there is an urge to proclaim it as futuristic. After all, it dovetails with our vision of what basketball will look like in the years ahead. But that version of the future is the present. By definition, centrists evolve in lockstep with the expectations of their position.

When Utah's Mehmet Okur was the only full-time center flinging up shots from behind the arc in 2008, he was seen as avant-garde or quirky, not as a harbinger of radical change that could be replicated elsewhere. "There's not many guys 6-11, 7-foot that can shoot like that," said Utah guard Deron Williams, of the Turkish All-Star. By the time players like Nicola Vučević, Gorgui Dieng, and Aron Baynes began doing the same in the mid-2010s, they were updating their résumés with current job requirements: Slack, Keynote, above the break 3-ball as the trailer in transition. Centrists abide by the rules of Darwinism, but they are not the mutation.

CHANDLER, TYSON

Tyson Chandler was the king of thankless jobs. His checklist of responsibilities did not include dribbling, shooting, passing, or even scoring. But the slender center spent two decades as a threatening presence in the paint, where he guarded the basket, directed the flow of a game like a traffic cop, and dunked his way into the record books as one of the most efficient scorers ever. In a career that bent from disappointing prospect to injured journeyman to franchise anchor to emotional support vet, Chandler played for eight teams, won a championship with Dallas, and earned Defensive Player of the Year in New York.

Before centers developed 3-point range, Chandler was the ideal vertical spacer for the pace-and-space era. Traditionalists grumbled about his lack of a baby-hook or a tinny 12-footer, but his willingness to set picks and roll to the basket—over and over and over, on every possession, all game—collapsed defenses without him even touching the ball. Opponents were so fearful of giving up an easy lob (which Chandler would punctuate by pounding his chest and roaring at the crowd), that it created wide-open looks for perimeter shooters.

Chandler was listed at 7-foot but seemed taller. He entered the NBA as a skeletal bundle of limbs. Despite adding thirty pounds that seemed to migrate to his shoulders and biceps, he maintained the same poultry legs and knifing eruptiveness. When he soared to catch a lob at its apogee, it was as if he was swinging from the moon. He didn't block shots, he pulverized them. With mobility, springiness, and length, Chandler commanded airspace that was unreachable to beefier, terrestrial centers. "He is totally different, a big agile guy that anchors your defense and talks, chattering up the whole team," Knicks assistant coach Herb Williams told the *New York Times*.

As a child, Chandler slopped hogs with his grandfather on a family farm in California's Central Valley. By eleven, he was 6-foot-4 and drawing skepticism from neighbors when he showed up on their doorsteps to trick-or-treat. "All through elementary I got teased because everybody thought I flunked like four times," he said on *60 Minutes*, in a 1997 segment about how sneaker companies recruited young athletes through dubious channels. He relocated three hours away to San Bernardino and, by middle school, had been fed into the basketball meat-grinder. He was a sensation at Manuel-Dominguez High School, a Compton sports powerhouse that also produced NBA players Cedric Ceballos, Brandon Jennings, and Tayshaun Prince.

Chandler entered the 2001 draft straight from high school. He was selected by the Clippers with the second pick—and immediately traded to the Bulls. He and Eddy Curry, another large child taken fourth in the same draft, were cornerstones of a post-Jordan rebuild in Chicago that was dubbed the "Baby Bulls." Nothing grew to fruition in the Windy City, in part because of the impatience of coach Tim Floyd (career record: 93–231). "They tried to use them as whipping boys," said teammate Charles Oakley. "Blaming them for everything, losses, mistakes in games."

Chandler found his groove in New Orleans beside Chris Paul, a maestro of orchestrating the pick-and-roll. In 2008, the Hornets—who would later become the Pelicans—won 56 games, the most in franchise history. Wherever Chandler went, good things occurred. While he was in Charlotte, the team won more games than any other Bobcats squad. In Dallas, the Mavericks won their first championship. In New York, the Knicks won 54 games, the highest total since 1997.

Off the court, Chandler was a New York Fashion Week presence, especially during a phase where he wore black drop-crotch trousers, black draped cowl neck tees, black mesh, and black sleeveless sweaters. The Slenderman of VFILES patronized Alexander Wang, Rick Owens, and Ann Demeulemeester. "Probably the most dramatic pieces in my wardrobe would be capes," he told *Women's Wear Daily* in 2012. "I wouldn't consider myself goth, but I love gothic pieces."

Chandler was comfortable exploring his artistic side. He took art lessons at the Sofia Art Academy in Dallas. "When I paint, it's the best feeling in the world," he said. "I am calm, not stressed and am focused." Later, he befriended Ari Marcopoulos after learning that the acclaimed photographer had created a zine dedicated to him ("Chandler was the handsomest, coolest guy" in the 2011 Finals, according to Marcopoulos). Chandler exhibited his own photography in a show titled *A Year in a New York Minute*, hosted at a studio in Chelsea. It included portraits of Knicks teammates Jeremy Lin and Landry Fields.

A spiritual man with a beard befitting a biblical prophet, Chandler was a member of the Hillsong Church (along with Kyrie Irving and Kevin Durant). When singer Justin Bieber wanted to be baptized in New York City at 3 a.m. by celebrity pastor Carl Lentz, they used Chandler's Upper West Side bathtub. "It was specially made for a 7-footer," said Lentz, who was later fired from Hillsong for "moral failures" that included infidelity. "It was probably one of the most special things I've been a part of. We baptized him in that giant tub."

CHAOS ERA

It is difficult to glean meaning from the early 2010s. Frenzies of the past decade—September 11, the recession, war in Iraq, Hurricane Katrina, Gucci Mane's rivalry with Young Jeezy, Darfur, the death rattle of print media—were replaced by bland consumerism. The soundtrack was Drake, Skrillex, and, for some reason, a resurgence of Ginuwine's "Pony." Brunch became an occasion for ordering jeroboams of champagne and dancing on tables scattered with the remains of eggs Benedict. Collectors tossed wads of cash at Zombie Formalist artworks. Osama bin Laden's corpse was jettisoned into the North Arabian Sea and the Chilean miners were saved. We joined bacon-of-the-month clubs and Charlie Sheen boasted of his tiger blood. Families gathered around Rokus

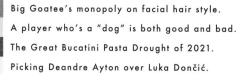

The puzzling popularity of J. Cole.

Seattle not having a basketball team.

95% of all sandwiches being too big.

Anyone who believes in "locals only."

Big Goatee's monopoly on facial hair style.

A player who's a "dog" is both good and bad.

The Great Bucatini Pasta Drought of 2021.

Picking Deandre Ayton over Luka Dončić.

to watch *Limitless*, the saga of a man who ingests pills that give him superhuman intelligence, which he uses to make a bunch of money on Wall Street. It was incomprehensible.

The NBA did not make sense either. There was no prevailing philosophy, epoch-defining team, or even a signature player. In 2010, Derrick Rose was Most Valuable Player, Kevin Durant led the league in scoring, and LeBron James had yet to win his first title. The back-to-back champion Lakers started a frontcourt with two 7-footers, neither of whom made a shot from behind the arc. Their opponent in the Finals that season was the Celtics, whose congregation of established stars presaged the rise of player mobility. While coach Mike D'Antoni had revealed the source code to the future of offense several years earlier in Phoenix, league-wide trends toward 3-point shooting and up-tempo play were stagnant (meanwhile, he was booed in New York by Knicks fans who considered his forward-thinking tenets as emasculating as a pink North Face Nuptse). A year later, James and Chris Bosh arrived in Miami, but were upset in the Finals by a Dirk Nowitzki–led Dallas unit that was quickly disassembled and never competitive again.

The woozy, disjointed feeling of the early 2010s is partly because it was the last time NBA basketball was not collectively experienced online. Fandom was Balkanized. Social media platforms like Facebook, Twitter, and Instagram were rising to compete with Myspace, blogs, and message boards, but had yet to reach critical mass. NBA Reddit was in its infancy. We were still getting acclimated to being enslaved by our cell phones, let alone watching games on them. Friends sent each other League Pass alerts via SMS text and the only people watching actually subscribed to League Pass (instead of a glitchy pirated stream that looks like *Virtua Fighter* once every five minutes). There was neither immediacy nor consensus. As crusty, numbskull journalism clashed with enlightened but uncredentialed voices, the phrase "hot take" gained traction as a way to dismiss anything you disagreed with. Fortunately, those days are long gone.

CHINA

At first, China was a destination for NBA players who wanted to pose for photos next to giant pandas or atop the Great Wall's endless squiggle. Then Yao Ming showed up. The son of two basketball players, he was

described at the age of fourteen as "a crane towering over a flock of chickens" by a Chinese newspaper. Seven-foot-5-and-change and a dominating presence for the Shanghai Sharks, Yao arrived at a time when there were lingering doubts about mysterious big men like Shawn Bradley and Michael Olowokandi. Though polished and mobile enough for a true giant, there were concerns that the Chinese government would meddle in his career. Still, he was selected first in the 2002 draft by the Rockets.

Over eight seasons, Yao was named an All-Star eight times—in part due to voting from the world's most populous nation—and averaged 23 points, 10.2 rebounds, and 1.9 blocks over the 2006–2008 span. He had legs like tree trunks, an unstoppable turnaround jumper, and a silken touch from the perimeter. Before the first eagerly anticipated duel between the two colossal centers, Shaquille O'Neal mocked him, saying, "Tell Yao Ming, 'Ching-chong-yang-wah-ah-soh'" (he quasi-apologized after blowback, and the two later became friends). Prematurely hobbled by foot and ankle issues, Yao was a dignified, warm-hearted, and humorous ambassador for Chinese basketball. "If I could get the fortune cookie I wanted, it would say: 'No more injuries,'" he once told *GQ*.

Besides Yao, there have been a handful of other Chinese NBA players, mostly of the tall variety. The first was Wang Zhizhi, a 7-foot center who debuted in 2001 for the Mavericks. Seldom-used reserves have included Zhou Qi, Mengke Bateer, and Sun Yue. Yi Jianlian, on the other hand, was drafted by the Bucks with the sixth pick of the 2007 draft and played for four teams over five seasons. The rubbery power forward from Shenzhen was nicknamed The Chairman due to (since debunked) claims that a pre-draft video showed him going one-on-one against an empty chair—a dog whistle for suspicion toward foreign prospects who had not proven themselves in the American amateur machine. Yi was marketed as a convergence of Chinese basketball, hip-hop culture, and the rising global popularity of the NBA. A Nike commercial depicted him playing against countrymen in durags who flexed AND1-style dribbling.

"Yao is the old school, Yi is new school," said ESPN's Fran Fraschilla. "He's hip-hop, he's 50 Cent."

Yi did not pan out—nor was there the anticipated wave of Chinese talent in the wake of Yao's success—but the Sleeping Giant has risen as an international market for the NBA. Business ties connected to television contracts, streaming rights, and merchandise are worth billions. In 2019, Joe Tsai, the Taiwanese-Canadian cofounder of technology company Alibaba, finalized his purchase of the Nets and their Brooklyn stadium for $3.38 billion. "In China, there's over 300 million people that play basketball, that watch NBA games," he said.

In late 2019, Daryl Morey, then general manager of the Rockets, tweeted an image showing support for uprisings in Hong Kong. The Chinese government's response was harsh and immediate. Morey was denounced, business deals were suspended, and broadcasts of an exhibition game in Beijing between the Lakers and the Nets were cancelled. As commissioner Adam Silver attempted to navigate a briar patch of issues that included free speech, human rights, billions in jeopardized revenue, and a testy authoritarian regime intent on making an example of the NBA, players like LeBron James were roasted for kowtowing to China. Everyone who opened their mouth regretted it. "We just came over here because it's our job to play the game, because the league wants to make money in the huge market," Jared Dudley of the Lakers wrote in his book *Inside the NBA Bubble: A Championship Season under Quarantine*. "Really, that trip was the prologue for a dark, challenging year."

CHUDS

Due to the demographics of NBA athletes—young, international, and three-quarters Black—the divisive politics that have turned the United States into a hissing instant cooker have not created schisms within the community of professional basketball players. A few voices, however, have added to the clatter of the right-wing noise machine.

Spencer Hawes, an early stretch 5 who averaged 8.7 points a game over ten seasons, was a climate change denialist who started a Facebook page for fans of grievance scarecrow Ann Coulter. When Sixers teammate Evan Turner visited Hawes's home, he found toilet paper printed with President Barack

Obama's face ("I refuse to use it though lol #mudbutt," Turner tweeted, presumably from the shitter). Dennis Rodman, the tortured rebounding dervish who visited North Korea on multiple occasions, called Donald Trump a "great friend" in 2016. "We don't need another politician, we need a businessman!" Rodman tweeted. And though Gordon Hayward, a swingman who has played for Utah, Boston, and Charlotte, spends most of his time eating breakfast cereal in front of a gaming rig, he followed alt-right pundits on social media and is married to a woman who donated twice to Trump's campaign.

Few players have plumbed the conspiratorial depths like Andrew Bogut, the first overall in the 2005 draft. The bruising 7-footer from Melbourne, Australia, started at center for the Golden State Warriors during two Finals runs and is notable for suffering a nauseating arm injury, mixing brutish physicality with deft passing, and leading the NBA in blocked shots in 2011. Bogut's flinty spirit was exemplified by his customized 2015 championship ring. "I've actually got my ring fitted for my middle finger so they can kiss that one," he told a San Francisco radio station.

While Bogut was a clever provocateur on the court—in 2016, his contemporaries voted him the third-dirtiest player—he is less witty elsewhere. Following his sophomore year at the University of Utah, he offered his thoughts on NBA athletes. "A lot of them get caught up in the hype and do video clips with rappers and all that crap," he told the *Washington Post*. "They want bling bling all over themselves and drive fast cars . . . a lot of NBA stars are arrogant and like to spend lots of money and have lots of girlfriends."

As Bogut increasingly logged on, brainworms nestled deeper into the hammy gutters of his noggin, devouring soft tissue and reproducing in a thrashing fuck-fest. The edgelord from Down Under groaned about "social justice warriors" and shitposted memes about feminists, GamerGate, and PizzaGate, the infantile pap that culminated with a crackpot firing an AR-15 inside a Washington, DC, pizzeria. "If only 1% of this #pizzagate scandal is true, all people

involved deserve life in prison (or worse)," Bogut tweeted.

When the COVID hiatus and nationwide Black Lives Matter protests inserted politics into the NBA on an unprecedented level, several players offered alternative perspectives. Michael Porter Jr., a young prom king on the Nuggets, earned derision for saying that he would pray for the police officers who murdered George Floyd. Later, he revealed himself as an anti-vaxxer, even as the globe was brought to a standstill by the pandemic. "Personally, I think the coronavirus is being used obviously for a bigger agenda," Porter Jr. said on Snapchat. "It's being used for population control."

Another gifted twenty-something, Jonathan Isaac of the Magic, was one of the few players who declined to kneel during the pregame rendition of the national anthem. A tantalizing defensive prospect whose combination of ranginess and mobility gives him the skittering upside of a 6-foot-11 tarantula, Isaac unconvincingly claimed that his refusal was based on religion, though his use of coded terms like "all lives matter" and "pointing fingers" led to a surge in jersey sales to right-wingers. Several days later, Isaac blew out his ACL.

CLOWNS

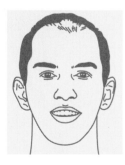

For professional athletes, blandness is a public relations strategy. Any soundbyte that deviates from cliché could become bulletin board material for an opponent. A photo of a player with bloodshot, weed-lidded eyes lasts forever. A suggestive DM to an Instagram wellness model-slash-creative director goes viral. Despite the population of handsome, famous, virile men in the prime of their lives, the NBA is a global, family-friendly corporation. With the exception of Kawhi Leonard, no player loses tens of millions of dollars because he was too boring. Stony facades and moats of banality are for self-defense.

Players who reveal more of their personality may benefit from cult celebrity and fan adoration, but risk turning into caricatures. When the ball is going in the basket, qualities like goofiness or being horny on main are celebrated as quirks. Hit a cold snap, though, and those characteristics reveal a lack of focus or misplaced priorities. Unlike other millionaires—owners, agents, hedge funders, real estate moguls, artists, actors, tech entrepreneurs—pro basketball players are treated like tall public servants. They are expected to be on the clock twenty-four hours a day. As an added wrinkle, they live on a schedule that demands they physically and mentally peak right around the time most people are eating dinner or getting ready for bed. For a basketball player, midnight might as well be happy hour.

Over the last decade, J. R. Smith has been the league's clown prince. The acrobatic shooting guard won Sixth Man of the Year in 2013, played roles of varying significance on two championship teams, and finished the 2020 season with the thirteenth-most career 3-pointers in NBA history. "I'd rather take a contested shot than an open shot any day," Smith once said (his percentages at the time showed that he made them at equal rates). "It's kind of boring when you take open shots."

His free-spirited approach to shot selection coincided with a reputation for swigging Hennessy and partying at New York's 1 OAK nightclub with Rihanna, social media forays in which he offered "the pipe," failing drug tests for marijuana multiple times, going shirtless for several months, and roughing up a vandal who damaged his car during the COVID hiatus. In the closing seconds of a tied Game 1 in the 2018 Finals, Smith appeared to forget the score (or the time) after grabbing an offensive rebound and dribbled out the clock instead of attempting a shot. "I knew we were tied," he claimed afterward, "I thought we were going to call timeout."

While Smith's shooting heroics and off-court antics made him a celebrity, he also became a tired punchline that allowed fans and the media to safely indulge in stereotypes within a Smith-size perimeter. It is impossible to know for certain if Smith's reputation for extracurricular hijinks sandbagged his career, but aging 3-point specialists with less baggage (like Kyle Korver, JJ Redick, and Wayne Ellington) had far less trouble gliding into roster spots in their twilight years. In fairness, Smith himself claimed that the bleak nightlife scene in Cleveland kept his mind on the game. "I think this is the best situation for me, 'cause there's nothing but basketball," he told NBA.com. "There's nothing, there's no going out,

there's no late nights." Players such as Dion Waiters, Michael Beasley, and Lance Stephenson fall into the same category as Smith: talented-but-flawed guys who have been reduced to cartoon characters.

JaVale McGee, an eruptive 7-foot journeyman who spent the most time with Washington and Denver, was infamous for on-court bumbling. Though a high-percentage scorer and shot-blocker who was viewed as a keystone for the Nuggets, he had a habit of attempting feats beyond his limitations. McGee's blooper reel included passes that sailed over the backboard, flagrant goaltends that smacked the ball into the stands, and disastrous attempts at dunking from the free-throw line on fast breaks.

McGee's errors were highlighted on a TNT segment called "Shaqtin' a Fool," in which host Shaquille O'Neal dubbed him "Tragic Bronson" and replayed the blunders with a soundtrack of guttural chuckles. In a 2013 on-air confrontation, McGee told O'Neal that he "didn't watch 'Shaqtin' a Coon'" and that the bullying Hall of Fame center was "old as dirt." A few years later, McGee said that the bit had harmful long-term effects. "Fans think it's real, like that's real life and they think I'm a dumb person," he told the Bay Area's *Mercury News*. "It's just really disappointing that grown men, 50-, 40-year-olds are having *America's Funniest Home Videos* of a player. And then making it a hashtag and really just trying to ruin someone's career over basketball mistakes." For all of the insults, McGee, like Smith, was part of multiple championship teams, winning two rings with the Warriors and one with the Lakers.

Some players are considered "funny" due to their appearance. By virtue of being even more giant than the other giants around them, 7-footers like Manute Bol, Gheorghe Mureșan, Boban Marjanovic, Sim Bhullar, and Tacko Fall have been deemed amusing. Other players are uproariously entertaining because they are Caucasian, like Brian Scalabrine. Perhaps the most riotous of all is Alex Caruso, a point guard on the Lakers who is (hilariously) white, balding, and able to dunk. "I don't know why they chose me," said Caruso, who has been given the nickname Bald Mamba. "I wish I had an easy answer, but the thing I like to tell people is that Lakers fans are like the seldom, few, sports fan-bases that actually understand the game they're rooting for." That must be it!

CLUTCH GENE

A player who repeatedly demonstrates the ability to score timely baskets is said to possess the clutch gene. While losers believe success in late-game scenarios is related to a relevant basketball skill set, schematic strategy, or the glimmer of coin-flip luck, real winners know that credit is owed to marrow-deep DNA. There is debate within the scientific community as to whether "wanting it more" is a product of the clutch gene or evidence against genetic basketball predestination. Still, it can be comforting to know that the difference between a shot clanking off the rim or swishing home is decided by entwined double helixes, as opposed to the ball slipping from your clammy palms, sailing out of bounds, and spilling Michael B. Jordan's vodka soda across celebrity row.

Few NBA players have exploited the clutch gene like Robert Horry, an early 3-and-D forward who mostly played for the Rockets, Lakers, and Spurs. While an excellent contributor, he was never an All-Star and averaged 7.0 points per game for his career. Yet, through fate, coincidence, and his own timely shooting, "Big Shot Bob" has seven championship rings—and drilled key shots in a number of high-leverage postseason moments. "If you have the confidence in yourself, and your team believes in you, you don't fear anything," Horry said. "You don't fear losing." This is the power of the clutch gene.

COLLINS, JASON

One of identical NBA twins, Jason Collins spent thirteen seasons as a defensive-oriented pugil stick. He frequently averaged more fouls per game than points, and his 2007 season was groundbreaking: he put up only 2.1 points (and 3.4 fouls) while starting 78 games for the Nets. After the 2013 season, Collins became the first active player in any of the four major sports to publicly announce that he was gay. "I wish

I wasn't the kid in the classroom raising his hand and saying, 'I'm different,'" he wrote in *Sports Illustrated*. "If I had my way, someone else would have already done this." The response was overwhelmingly positive, and included a supportive tweet from Kobe Bryant and a phone call from Barack Obama.

CONTINUITY

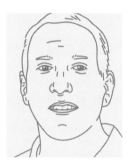

According to basketball folklore, teams that keep personnel together for multiple seasons are rewarded with success. This is called continuity. In theory, players gain deeper familiarity with each other and the coaching staff's system in a proportional relationship to the amount of time they spend in the same jersey. The idea is in harmony with our belief that relationships get stronger over time—in effect, teammates will finish each other's sentences like an old married couple who bicker harmlessly about whether to plant climbing hydrangea in their trellis. It is seductive to believe that young stars "learn to win" as part of an interpersonal journey.

The Spurs, who went to the postseason for twenty-two straight years and won five championships, are rightfully viewed as the paragon of stability. For most of that run, the franchise had the star trio of Tim Duncan, Manu Ginóbili, and Tony Parker (with sizable contributions from David Robinson and Kawhi Leonard), coach Gregg Popovich, and a front office helmed by R. C. Buford. The prolonged excellence was inseparable from Spurs Culture and the Spurs' Way of Doing Things, which, in turn, created a perception of institutional infallibility—any player drafted by San Antonio was hailed as an overlooked prospect that never should have slipped into their evil clutches. "They have done it really through savvy

maneuvering, great leadership, great organization, at all levels, continuity," said Golden State general manager Bob Myers.

But there is survivorship bias at work here. Barring the infusion of new personnel, teams improve because individual players get better, roles become defined, rotations are figured out, and parts adhere in more complementary ways. Personnel that a franchise deems cornerstones are less likely to be traded, waived, or allowed to leave in free agency. At the same time, clusters of inept players who fit together like a clanking, old-timey flying contraption are rarely left intact for long. Bad coaches and executive suckers get canned. Plenty of middling teams with middling talent play middling basketball middling year after middling year—that counts as continuity too. In the case of Shaquille O'Neal and Kobe Bryant, a long partnership bred only contempt and on-court friction, even as the Lakers won three consecutive titles.

In an era of increased player autonomy and movement, continuity could be more valuable—or meaningless. Coming into the 2020 COVID Bubble postseason, Milwaukee owned the best record in the NBA and a core of Giannis Antetokounmpo, Khris Middleton, and Eric Bledsoe that had spent three seasons in the starting lineup. "We talked about it a lot this summer, that our continuity, we thought, was one of the biggest things we had in our favor," coach Mike Budenholzer, a Popovich disciple, told the *Milwaukee Journal Sentinel* before the season. The Bucks caved in the second round. Yet the following season, after acquiring Jrue Holiday, Milwaukee escaped the same fate by the length of a Kevin Durant toenail and won a chip with two of their three studs and the same coach. It is comforting to believe that loyalty and persistence are rewarded, but evidence of continuity's importance has delicate margins.

COUSINS, DEMARCUS

Few injuries are death sentences in today's NBA. Players yawn at shredded ACLs and MCLs. Splintered bones—even the body horror suffered by Paul George and Andrew Bogut—are only setbacks. A torn Achilles tendon and its telltale calf quiver, however, remains an existential threat. Chauncey Billups and Kobe Bryant were never the same after

the injury. Wesley Matthews and Rudy Gay went from studs to role players. Kevin Durant missed the entire 2020 season and could be the best test case for whether a superstar can return to form—according to some statistical researchers, victims usually top out at 80 percent of their earlier productivity. In some ways, the injury can be crueler than career-ending trauma: it turns players into ghosts, husks of their former selves who wear the same headbands and have identical shooting form, but are different athletes altogether.

Before a 2018 Achilles injury, DeMarcus "Boogie" Cousins was a four-time All-Star and one of the league's only fire-breathing Godzillas. Listed at 6-foot-10 and 270 pounds, the gregarious Alabama native was a powerful and dexterous center, equipped with long reach, a tap dancer's footwork, and shoulders that forklifted defenders under the basket. Although Cousins was mobile enough to snatch a rebound and lead the break, he relied more on coordination and dad-strength than bouyancy. He was among league leaders in drawing charges and committing fouls, and had more of his shots blocked than any other player. "It's because I can't jump," Cousins told FiveThirtyEight. "It's really as simple as that."

While being a nightly 30/20 threat endeared him to grillmasters, Cousins evolved as the sport required. He became an excellent passer and a respectable perimeter scorer, going 3–18 from behind the arc as a rookie to hitting 36.1 percent on 363 3-point attempts in 2016. After almost seven seasons in Sacramento, where he became the second-leading scorer in modern franchise history, Cousins was traded to New Orleans for a package that included shooter Buddy Hield. "It was a coward move," he said of the Kings' dysfunctional front office (he learned about the deal in the middle of an All-Star Weekend press appearance).

On the verge of a free agent period where Cousins was expected to sign a max deal, the Achilles injury upturned his plans and, sadly, his career. He joined the Warriors, but suffered a torn quad. He joined the Lakers, but tore an ACL before playing a game. "I kind of feel like I was at the beginning of this so-called Achilles scare or wave that's been going on," said Cousins. "There's got to be something to it as to why it's happening so much more now."

COVID BUBBLE

When Rudy Gobert of the Jazz tested positive for COVID before a March 2020 game against the Thunder, viewers were treated to the unprecedented sight of teams being pulled off the floor moments prior to tip-off. Players were warming up, referees and coaches were conferring on the hardwood, the Oklahoma City hype-man was roaring encouragement to a packed audience of divorced oilmen. "The game has been postponed," a Thunder employee said to incredulous jeers. "You are all safe." Within hours, the NBA announced that the season was suspended.

Surreal scenes like the one at Chesapeake Energy Arena soon unfolded nationwide, as the United States bungled its way to more than half a million COVID-19 deaths over the following calendar year. Terms like social distancing, antibodies, and PCR tests were normalized. We scrubbed wine bottles, shamed joggers, joined Rancho Gordo's bean club, hoarded toilet paper, and allowed contaminated mail to pile up in horrifying stacks. During the NBA's hiatus—which went from Adam Silver's prediction of "at least thirty days" to more than the length of a typical off-season—the league's presence was minimized to a lethargic game of H-O-R-S-E between contestants like Mike Conley Jr. and Paul Pierce. Trae Young played on a slanted driveway hoop. "I gave it 5 min." tweeted JJ Redick. "Hard pass."

To complete the season, the NBA concocted a plan for a virus-free "bubble" at Walt Disney World, outside of Orlando. There was flimsy lip service about basketball's value to the American Way of Life, but no one was naive enough to believe that the league was motivated by anything except lost revenue and fulfilment of lucrative television contracts. When players balked at leaving their loved ones and being cloistered for months at a resort during a once-in-a-century global pandemic—not to mention at the height of Black Lives Matter civil rights protests—the NBA threatened to shred the existing Collective Bargaining Agreement. Many players were not

THERAPEUTIC ACTIVITIES

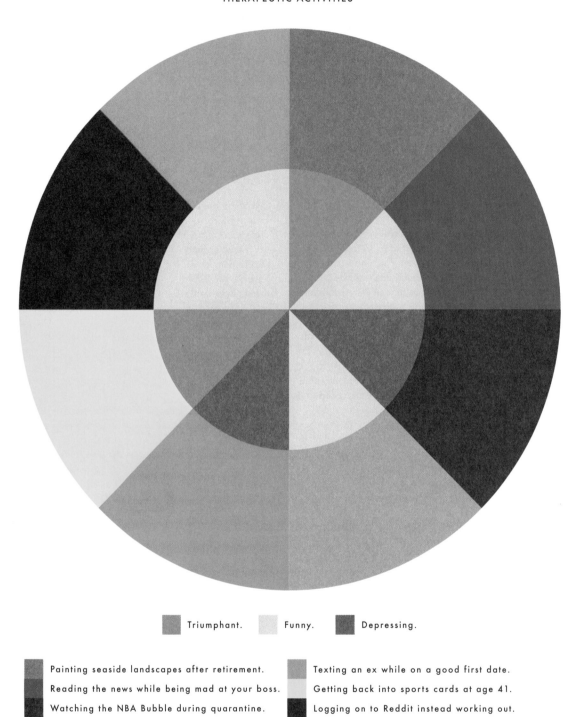

Triumphant.   Funny.   Depressing.

Painting seaside landscapes after retirement.

Reading the news while being mad at your boss.

Watching the NBA Bubble during quarantine.

Debating Hall of Fame qualifications anytime.

Texting an ex while on a good first date.

Getting back into sports cards at age 41.

Logging on to Reddit instead working out.

Dropping a fiery tweet before going to bed.

enthusiastic. "We don't know a lot of information," Carmelo Anthony of the Blazers told TNT's Ernie Johnson. "So until we have that, it's kind of hard to just commit to it 100 percent."

The agreed-upon plan sent 22 teams to the Disney campus, where they would play three scrimmages, eight "seeding games," and the postseason. Some players, such as Bradley Beal and Dāvis Bertāns of the Wizards, Willie Cauley-Stein of the Mavericks, and Avery Bradley of the Lakers, decided not to go; others, like LaMarcus Aldridge of the Spurs and Bojan Bogdanović of the Jazz, opted for surgery that excluded them from attending. "I think it's more important for me to be at home with my family," said Wilson Chandler of the Nets on Jameer Nelson's podcast *Court Vision*. "Then if you throw the whole social justice, everything that's going on with police brutality and with the government and all of that, it just makes it that more difficult."

If the COVID Bubble proved anything, it was that the spread of the virus could be curtailed—provided there was regular testing, mask-wearing, and social distancing (advantages that were not options for all Americans). When players arrived at Disney World, they were quarantined for two days and tested, before being released into the muggy, 9,000-acre playland of stocked fishing ponds and glass-encased barber shops. Inhabitants wore proximity alarms that beeped when they stood too close to another person for a few seconds.

Players griped about lackluster accommodations and Fyre Fest menus early on, but learned that fans, abandoned by the American government and left to forlornly cook shallot pasta, had little sympathy for rich people with jobs, accommodations, and food security. In truth, the players' disenchantment was really about the league compromising their autonomy. Incredibly successful and respected men were rounded up at a schlocky summer camp and bullied into playing basketball by their bosses.

Several players were outed for violating Bubble security protocols. The Clippers' Lou Williams left campus to attend a funeral and ended up at Magic City, a strip club in Atlanta. Bruno Caboclo ventured out of his room during the initial quarantine period, and Richaun Holmes crossed a boundary when picking up a food delivery. The most scandalous breach was committed by Danuel House, a shooting guard on the Rockets, who was booted from the Bubble after entertaining a female testing official in his room for several hours.

Considering the long hiatus and sedentary lockdown lifestyle, the quality of play in the COVID Bubble was of a stunning caliber. The main takeaway was that NBA athletes are phenomenally good at basketball. Games were played in a virtually empty arena surrounded by 17-foot screens that digitally superimposed the faces of fans and with pumped-in crowd noise (which qualified as home-cooking for Heat players). The endeavor was a success: There were no viral outbreaks, the Lakers seized the title, and the NBA reportedly recouped almost two billion dollars. Everyone wins?

CROUCH BIAS

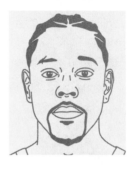

Players who hunch into low, menacing stances are often viewed as strong defensive players. This is crouch bias. Typical behavior includes gnashing teeth, slapping floorboards, and harrying a dribbler by poking and slapping at the ball. All the spitting and snarling appears annoying, so we assume it must be working. It is impressive when Jrue Holiday, a rugged guard who spent time with the Sixers, Pelicans, and Bucks, demonstrates the balance and intuition required to smoothly mirror a ball-handler for 46 feet from arc to arc. "He was picking me up full court," said Kevin Durant, of being guarded by Holiday in the 2018 playoffs. "Actually, it was tough to dribble on Jrue Holiday. He slides his feet so well, he's got good hands, he's strong, he's got good instincts." Still, Durant roughly matched his season averages in points per game and field-goal percentage, while turning the ball over only ten times in the five-game series.

At times, players who are celebrated as top-notch defenders do not measurably stack up to their reputations. Avery Bradley, a combo guard who was named to All-Defensive Teams in 2013 and 2016, was feared for hounding guards with stoic, Terminator-like determination. He was virtually unshakable, weaving around picks and attempting to pry the ball loose from unorthodox angles. When Bradley was excluded from the All-Defensive Team in 2017, NBA

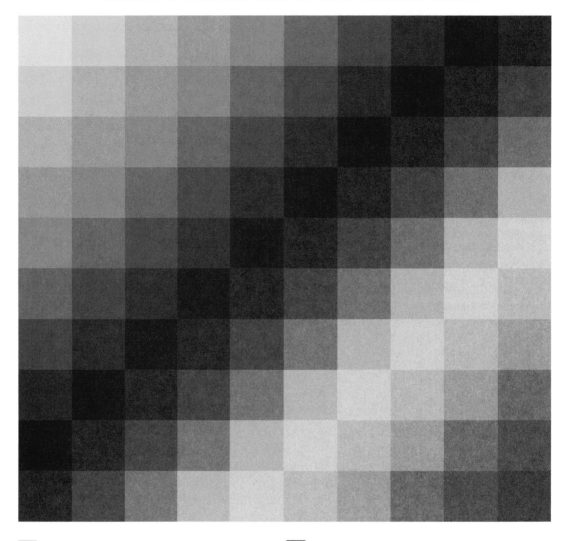

Coming out for warmups in full camo fatigues.

Taking down a seven-foot sub with four people.

Shoving Trae Young after being a nutmeg victim.

Yelling "fukouttahere" after a regular rebound.

Starting a Tuesday night with a shot and a beer.

Paying up front for a year's gym membership.

Slapping the floor in front of a superior player.

Diving for loose balls down twenty in the fourth.

Believing that good defense is wanting it more.

Saying you'll get it all done over the weekend.

Honing your game face as much as your game.

Bullying five bags of groceries with two hands.

Crediting effort and grit and not just being good.

Proving to your date that you enjoy spicy food.

Pretending that practice is an important thing.

Starting a ten-part crime miniseries at 12:18 A.M.

Trying to flip fifteen viral chicken sandwiches.

Thinking a player's lazy because they smile a lot.

Expecting Kyrie and KD to sign with the Knicks.

players erupted in disagreement. "Someone need slapped," tweeted Portland's C. J. McCollum. "Avery Bradley ain't make one team . . . fuxk outa heaaaa." Yet numbers suggest that Bradley was not a formidable defender, but an ordinary one: He did not rank among league leaders in categories like steals, deflections, or blocks, and Synergy Sports Technology statistics indicate that he gave up .992 points per possession on defense (putting him in the 44th percentile). The discordance is understandable. It was not that his peers fared poorly against Bradley—they just did not enjoy the experience of being parboiled by his hot breath for two hours.

When all the moving parts are considered, people cannot be faulted for trusting their own lying eyes. Measuring individual defense is challenging, not only for fans but also for scouts, coaches, and peers. There are tasks on and away from the ball, overlapping positional roles, a dearth of applicable box score statistics, and a slot machine of multiplayer lineups on both teams. While making a ball-handler uncomfortable is important, defense is more complicated than just being a gooey pest. It is harder to identify moments that speak to spatial awareness, basketball IQ, discipline, and motor. On a single possession, a weak-side defender might cut off a passing lane to a rolling big man, scramble out to the perimeter to prevent an open 3-point attempt, then slide into the paint to thwart a drive. But without lingering evidence, we are like moonshine-addled hayseeds recounting being zapped up into a UFO.

Crouch bias can work in reverse. James Harden, a zenith creator, has been roasted for his lapses on defense. A few seasons ago, a viral lowlight reel showed him waving feebly as opponents raced by or standing akimbo as backdoor cutters cruised in for layups. The video reinforced the perception that Harden was a lazy, distracted stoner and a liability on that side of the ball. But, according to Synergy, he is an excellent on-ball defender and among the league's best at smothering post-up attempts. In 2020, he led the NBA in total steals. "Take your worst 10 minutes from your job the last year and put them in a YouTube clip," former Rockets general manager Daryl Morey told *USA Today*. "I'm guessing it wouldn't come out very well for anybody. Without context, you can grab 10 minutes of anyone and make them look like shit. I think reality TV proves that."

CRUSTPUNKS

A high school phenom from Coney Island, Sebastian Telfair did not live up to his promise in the NBA (unless that fate was to be involved in a shootout with rapper and fellow Brooklynite Fabolous). He was rostered by eight teams and played 12,149 NBA minutes over a decade-long career—but not one second in the playoffs. Telfair's trail of misery included being a rookie on the Blazers the year after they traded Rasheed Wallace and joining the Timberwolves right after they dealt Kevin Garnett. He was on a Cavs team bound for the Eastern Conference Semifinals, and stuck around for four games. He dropped in on a Thunder team with Kevin Durant and Russell Westbrook, but was cut loose after sixteen games. Telfair was a true crustpunk.

Traditional journeymen experience a full life. They traipse around the league, hunting for contracts and foraging for playing time from contenders and rebuilding franchises alike. Occasionally they wander into a starting role or even contribute on a title-winning team. With a banjo on their knee, they sing for their supper, spinning yarns about championship parades and winning culture to wide-eyed lottery picks around embers of a campfire. The youngsters curl into their bedrolls as graying Dwight Howards and Rajon Rondos play the harmonica over an orchestra of crickets and whippoorwills.

But crustpunks are different. They have facial piercings, leather vests with lots of patches, and play exclusively for the NBA's worst teams. Ramon Sessions was a crustpunk guard who had a freakish gift for drawing fouls, spent eleven seasons on eight teams, and went to the playoffs only twice. Another example is Omri Casspi, a unitasker shooter who has been on only two teams with a winning record over ten years and seven franchises. Right before the 2018 playoffs, he was waived by the Warriors, who went on to win the title. "It wasn't fun," said Warriors coach Steve Kerr, of cutting the injured Casspi. "But the main thing is that Omri is a pro and a great teammate. He handled everything beautifully last night."

MOST LIKELY TO HAVE A SLIPKNOT TAPESTRY

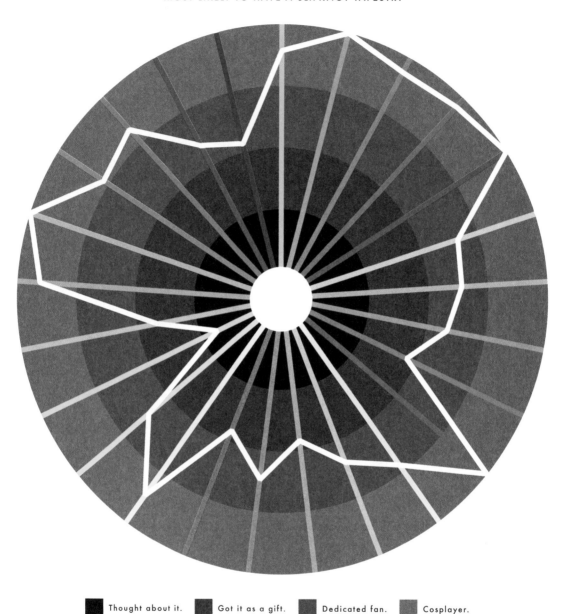

Thought about it.   Got it as a gift.   Dedicated fan.   Cosplayer.

Aron Baynes.
Cherokee Parks.
Chris Anderson.
Chris Kaman.
Dennis Rodman.

Derrick Rose.
DeShawn Stevenson.
J. R. Smith.
James Harden.
James Johnson.

Jason Williams.
Jayson Tatum.
Kelly Oubre Jr.
Kenyon Martin.
Kyle Kuzma.

Marcin Gortat.
Marcus Smart.
Mark Cuban.
Matt Barnes.
Mike Scott.

Robert Swift.
Russell Westbrook.
Steven Adams.
Tim Duncan.
Wilson Chandler.

Casspi was already on his way to St. Mark's Place with his German shepherd.

An interesting variety of crustpunks are the drifters who get rich. Somehow, they reap fruitful financial rewards while sleeping in a reefer on the way to Sacramento, slurping from a bowl of thin slumgullion in a hobo jungle outside of Phoenix, and, eventually, catching that highball train straight to Manhattan and Mister Dolan's Hooverville. They are not scrubs, per se, but the economics of the NBA creates a stratum of players who can earn market value only by signing with dismal franchises. While good teams use their cap space on stars and snag rotational veterans on the cheap, bad teams do not have either option. As a result, the NBA's underclass consistently overpays for mediocrity.

Drew Gooden, a bearded frontcourt player who looked like a Mennonite farmer, played for fourteen seasons and ten teams. He was a good shooter, a sturdy rebounder, and a temporary solution on the 2007 Cavaliers team that LeBron James yoked by the scruff of its neck and took to the Finals. After being traded away the next season, Gooden would go to the playoffs only three more times over nine years. Despite roaming from one shabby franchise to the next, starting sporadically, and averaging 9.9 points a game, he managed to make more than $45 million in salary.

There is nothing wrong with being a crustpunk. Making it to the NBA is unfathomably difficult and anyone who gets there has already scaled Big Rock Candy Mountain.

CURRY, STEPHEN

Stephen Curry is a two-time MVP, three-time NBA champion, and the greatest shooter who has ever lived. That singularly obscene talent bathes his career in a blinding white light. Attempting to scrutinize other components of his game, his role on championship-winning Golden State teams, and his position among the sport's historical luminaries is like squinting into the sun before walking into a movie theater.

Wardell Stephen Curry II was born in Akron, Ohio, but grew up in Charlotte, North Carolina, where his father spent ten years playing for the Hornets. Dell Curry was a 3-point specialist who won Most Improved Player in 1994 and passed along his long-range shooting abilities to Stephen (his younger brother, Seth, also became an NBA player). "He's

definitely better than I was," Dell Curry said of Steph, in a 2016 *GQ* interview. "But it's a different NBA. I would never take 35-foot 3-pointers with 17 seconds on the shot clock." On occasion, the Curry brothers would join their father's teammates in shooting contests, outgunning the team's big men. While there is a stereotype that most NBA players come from low-income backgrounds and broken homes, the opposite is true—athletes who make it to the highest level are more likely to have the same advantages in terms of class and stability that lead to success in other professional fields. A shooter of Steph's ability may not have been possible without extraordinarily rare vectors of genetics and opportunity.

Unheralded in high school, Curry was offered a walk-on slot at Virginia Tech, seemingly a gesture of politeness from his father's alma mater. Instead, he opted for Davidson, a small school in North Carolina—and became a sensation for his no-scope 3-balls. He entered the 2009 NBA Draft after his junior year, and many wondered if his boyish, raw-boned physique would be turned to pulp in the pros. There were doubts about his athleticism, defense, and ability to play lead guard. "All this analysis that people would put out there, all these scouting reports and whatever, that kept the focus on what I supposedly couldn't do," he said in the *Players' Tribune* in 2019. "'Undersized. Not a finisher. Extremely limited.' I can still reel them off to this day." Curry was selected by the Warriors with the seventh pick, behind fellow point guards Ricky Rubio and Jonny Flynn.

Early on, Curry did not exude the musk of an ascendant god. He struggled with ankle injuries and shared the Golden State backcourt with Monta Ellis, a lovable chucker. Curry's 3-point shooting was viewed as a mystical outlier, but there was little inkling that it could bend space and time like neutrinos spinning in reverse. In a 2013 preview, *Sports Illustrated* ranked him seventh among point guards, behind Rajon Rondo and Tony Parker. There were even grumbles from old heads about Curry's actual position. "You got shooting guards now that's playing point guard," said Gary Payton, the Sonics' Hall of Famer.

Those conversations ended in 2015, when Curry erupted into superstardom. Over the next five years, he would win back-to-back MVP awards (the second unanimously), lead the NBA in categories like scoring, free-throw percentage, and true shooting percentage, and amass three of the top four single-season totals for made 3-pointers in league history. The Warriors went to five straight Finals, winning three of them.

Defending Curry is like trying to trap swamp gas in a thermos. He seems holographic, a flickering wisp that momentarily appears, darts behind a hedgerow of tree-size men and respawns fifteen feet away. Fans would show up early to Golden State games to watch him shoot around, leading to an underground industry of phone-cam videos showing Curry knocking down successive half-court shots. Possibilities of perimeter scoring were redefined. Before Curry, a behind-the-back dribble into a sidestep into a moon-scraping hoist from 27 feet was a gamer's Mountain Dew Code Red fever dream. The mid-2000s Phoenix Suns, under coach Mike D'Antoni, were first to market with offensive innovation, but Curry was the god-mode hack that created disruption even after competitors had begun adapting.

Few players have benefited more from arriving at the optimal moment in league history than Curry. A master of both pace and space, he personified the rising primacy of shooting, ball movement, and up-tempo play across the NBA. It was an inflection point when glacial big men like Roy Hibbert and Greg Monroe were still playable and league-wide skill sets had not yet synchronized with the theoretical demands of modern basketball. The Warriors' knack for forcing switches that resulted in centers attempting to corral Curry beyond the arc caused rivals to reconsider the value of a defensive keystone that could be so sadistically exploited. He single-handedly sped up the doomsday clock for endangered big men.

But while Curry is the smiling avatar for the 3-point era—and his success with the Warriors validated a shot that troglodytes oinked at as gimmicky—the revolution was coming with or without him. From 2008 to 2012, the average number of 3-pointers attempted per game in the league was stagnant at slightly more than 18 a game. By 2020, it skyrocketed to 34.1. His true role was that of an accelerant. He popularized 3-pointers from locations beyond the arc without immunity to the diseases of the industrialized West. In 2014, Curry averaged 5.0 off-the-dribble 3s a game and no other player logged more than 3.5. By 2020, nine players took more than 5 pull-up 3s (with James Harden attempting a staggering 10.9).

It is difficult to know how a shooter of Curry's caliber would have been received in an earlier era. Had he come of age while the eyes of a nation were locked on *Daria*, the unanimous MVP-winning incarnation might not have existed. No matter how otherworldly his shooting, pro basketball's dawdling tempo and half-court structure did not allow players to take eleven 3-pointers a game until the 2010s. Curry's father led the NBA in 3-point percentage in 1999 at 47.6 percent (higher than any of Steph's annual averages), but managed to fire up only 3.5 attempts a game. Teams were using plutonium to power creaky windmills.

Curry was the most normal-sized MVP since Allen Iverson, but their brands could not have been more different. While Iverson was perceived as a societal menace, Curry sparkles with wholesomeness. He is clean-cut, religious, and married to a woman he met in a Charlotte church group as a teen. With a slight build and almost womanly features, he is pretty as shit. "I think most people looked at it like, 'Aw, man, this was a privileged kid growing up,'" said teammate Draymond Green in 2017, on his *Dray Day* podcast. "He ain't supposed to become this. It's supposed to be the guy from the hood that had nothing and had to grind for everything. And of course, Steph is light-skinned, so they want to make him out to be soft."

At times, Curry seems to lack the desire for self-aggrandizement and legacy-building exhibited by his contemporaries like LeBron James and Kobe Bryant. He plays with effervescent joy, which is frowned upon by basketball hard-asses who insist sports are as grim and laborious as forging a suit of armor on a hot anvil. But it cannot be ignored that Curry assisted in recruiting Kevin Durant to join a Warriors team that had appeared in consecutive Finals and set a record for the most wins in a regular season. It was an act of outreach and an admission of weakness that would be unthinkable coming from a sociopathic type-A personality. Instead of keeping an ugly Under Armour heel on a conquered rival's throat, Curry extended a hand. As a result of that alliance, Golden State's championships in 2017 and 2018 were drained bloodless, Durant made off with two Finals MVP awards that might have been earmarked for Curry, and the Warriors' dynasty became a story about competitive imbalance instead of basketball at its most gorgeous.

Curry's stardom is a mix of ethereal shooting with normalcy. He is handsome and charming, but in the nice-guy way of someone who should not wear leather. He has the height and proportions of a civilian. He is outrageously good at his job, but not a loony, driven overachiever like some of his peers. At his best, Curry is basketball's Spider-Man, exuberantly swinging from the Transamerica Pyramid on ropes of spider-ooze. Other times, he is Peter Parker.

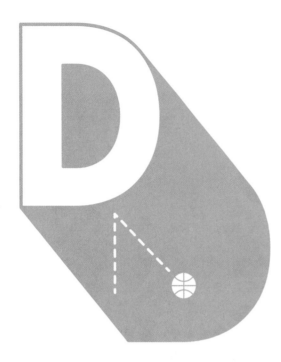

D

native was the model of unsexy reliability at point guard, taking care of the rock, munching on honeycombs, and jitterbugging into the paint to toss lobs for taller friends. "His height doesn't matter," said Stan Van Gundy, who coached Nelson in Orlando, to *Bleacher Report.* "Not because he's an unbelievable athlete—he plays bigger because he's so tough." In 2009, Nelson averaged a career-high 16.7 points, stole a league-leading number of windowsill pies, and was named to his lone All-Star team. Sadly, Nelson suffered a torn labrum and was scolded for disrupting the Magic's chemistry when he attempted to return during the Finals.

With a larger carriage, dancing bears run the risk of eating themselves out of the NBA by nibbling on too many raspberries and slabs of oil-rich sockeye salmon. The first overall pick in the 2013 draft, Toronto-born Anthony Bennett was a burly forward with nimble feet and enough bounce to evoke comparisons to Larry Johnson, another University of Nevada–Las Vegas export. Even before the draft, Bennett was body-shamed. He was rumored to have ballooned to 261 pounds after a shoulder injury prevented him from working out for prospective employers. He struggled in Cleveland, hitting only one of his first twenty-one shot attempts. "You came in overweight," said Gary Payton, rudely, on TV. "You look fat." Though Bennett repeatedly attempted to work his way back into the NBA, he has played only 1,905 total minutes in the league to date, spread between four teams over four seasons. He is the biggest bust in NBA history—but respect must always be paid to the dancing bear who helmed a draft class.

DANCING BEARS

Chunky players who move with surprising agility are dancing bears. In a sport that rewards physiques chipped from sandstone, rotund men who whirl and twinkle-toe through the lane are sources of joy. Dancing bears can inhabit any position. Guards include Raymond Felton and Khalid El-Amin, forwards include Luka Dončić and Julius Randle, and centers include Nicola Jokić and Jusuf Nurkić. Although Shaquille O'Neal transcended the category to become one of the most devastating weapons in NBA history, he possessed the convergence of ursine mass, incredible strength, and dainty footwork that would be appropriate for hunting sea cows atop a quavering sheet of ice.

While most dancing bears are big men, Jameer Nelson was 6-feet and built like an air-conditioning unit. For fourteen years, the stubbled Pennsylvania

DAVIS, ANTHONY

There is no denying that Anthony Davis is a wonderful player. It is not premature to suggest that the 6-foot-10 Laker is on pace to become one of the greatest big men in history. He is a fixture on All-Star teams, All-NBA teams, and All-Defensive teams, while repeatedly popping up among league leaders in categories like points, rebounds, and blocks (he has topped the NBA in swats multiple times). But unlike other megastars, Davis inspires neither fervor nor disdain. He has a beige personality and spent seven seasons on a mediocre team in a small market. He is Tim Duncan without the first-wave barista corduroys or immediate success.

One of the finest collegiate prospects in recent memory, Davis was taken by New Orleans with the first overall pick in the 2012 draft. He played guard for a dinky high school until a late growth spurt added eight inches in eighteen months but preserved his coordination and agility. Not only is the Chicago native's 7-foot-6 wingspan one of the widest in the NBA, but he wields his appendages like a mantis. He uses unparalleled mobility and elasticity to collect lobs from the stratosphere and mush opponents' doomed shots against the backboard. Reed thin as a rookie, he cladded his frame with thirty-plus pounds after his private chef introduced him to seafood.

Davis's preference has been for playing power forward—to avoid the stigma from when centers were enormous, lumpy turds—but it took him several years to develop the shooting and passing skills to operate dynamically away from the basket. In some ways, he is a magnificent amphibian, trapped between land and sea. There can be a bit too much cute finesse to his game, but it is reflective of his diverse gifts. "We got the best player in the NBA not named LeBron James," said Alvin Gentry, who coached Davis in New Orleans for several years. Still, Davis was a member of playoff teams only twice in his first seven seasons. It was not really his fault, yet complicates our perception of his ability to single-handedly push a squad to competitiveness.

During the 2019 season, Davis requested a trade from New Orleans, despite a year and a half remaining on his contract. It was a naked attempt by Klutch Sports Group to maneuver a superstar to Los Angeles to play beside James. The Pelicans refused to deal Davis and protected him in bubble wrap—he played in only fifteen of the team's final thirty-five games. Even with his bland persona, Davis was bathed in boos and temporarily became the avatar for the evils of player autonomy. "When you sign on that dotted line, you owe your effort and your play to that team, to that city, to the fans," said Warriors coach Steve Kerr. "The Davis stuff was really kind of groundbreaking and hopefully not a trend, because it's bad for the league." The next off-season, Davis landed in Los Angeles via a blockbuster trade—just as he, James, and the agency had planned.

In the COVID Bubble, Davis won a championship as, arguably, James's greatest Robin. He was majestic in the Finals, but the anticlimactic series and an injury to Bam Adebayo, Miami's most challenging frontcourt adversary, made the title feel perfunctory. There was no stress-test or baptism by fire to teach us more about Davis's melting point. To an extent, the difficulty in gauging his true impact as a superstar and the tepid response to his undeniable excellence are connected. In today's game, there is a ceiling, both on the floor and in our imaginations, that tamps the importance of traditional big men—even one as updated as Davis. While the NBA's greatest players appear to control their own fates, he seems destined to travel where waters carry him.

DEAD BALL ERA

For those who love frictionless basketball, the period surrounding the twist of the millennium felt like rug-burn. By league averages, the late 1990s and early 2000s featured the lowest points per game, field-goal percentages, and offensive ratings in modern history. The game was played at the slowest pace. Defenses thrived—if that was your kink—with the highest block and rebound rates in recent memory. Fouls and turnovers were rampant. One factor was reinstitution of the original (and longer) 3-point line before the 1998 season, which immediately lopped overall attempts by about 25 percent and siphoned accuracy from 36 to 34.6 percent. The sense of gloom was exaggerated by the second retirement of Michael Jordan, whose wattage had kept the league's aesthetic shortcomings in the shadows. TV ratings and attendance numbers dipped.

For teams at the time, a reasonable strategy was turning games into exhausting hatchet fights, preferably waged in a bog. In 2000, five of the six teams who played at the slowest pace had 50 or more wins, including the Heat and Knicks, who led the Atlantic Division despite sputtering offenses. That Jordan-sized vacuum was filled by post players such as Shaquille O'Neal and Alonzo Mourning and isolation scorers like Stephon Marbury, Jerry Stackhouse, and Grant Hill. With teams focused on exploiting one-on-one mismatches in the half court and hustling back on defense, the game quivered to a halt.

The NBA's solution seemed counterproductive. Going into the 2002 season, longstanding "illegal

defense" rules were scrapped, freeing teams to play zone. In theory, allowing defenses to load up against ball-dominant stars would encourage more passing and shooting, while incentivizing fast breaks. The measure was controversial. "The NBA is for men, and a grown man doesn't need to play zone," Shaquille O'Neal told *Sports Illustrated*. "Why do you think they call it man-to-man?" Others disagreed with the changes, but saw the bigger picture. "This is the game of the 21st Century," Miami coach Pat Riley told the *Chicago Tribune*. "I think the philosophy now is about versatility, quickness, mobility, stretching the game. The philosophy has transcended getting a big man."

At first, the new rules did not achieve the desired effect. While straight-up zones like those employed at the amateur level were unpopular and ineffective, it was much easier for defenses to adapt schematically than it was for offenses to find new personnel or for NBA players to develop perimeter shooting. Defenders were free to crowd the paint and cheat off the league's poor shooters—especially vestigial power forwards—openly daring them to knock down jumpers. O'Neal and Tim Duncan continued to win championships. In 2004, the Pistons, empowered by the second-best defensive rating in history, upset the Lakers in the Finals. The only team with a better defense? The 2004 Spurs.

Today, with league-wide scoring efficiency geysering to unprecedented heights, it is easy to ridicule the volume scorers of the early 2000s as sloppy chuckers. Guards like Stackhouse, Latrell Sprewell, Jason Richardson, Cuttino Mobley, and Nick Van Exel were erratic by modern statistical standards. But it is important to acknowledge that the average true shooting percentage in 2001 was 51.8 percent. By 2021, it had spiked to 57.2 percent. For slashing perimeter players who were asked to create buckets off the dribble, the early 2000s were a drag. Lanes were plugged with waiting defenders, teammates were brick-heavers, and elite scorers like Allen Iverson and Kobe Bryant were not comfortable taking many 3s. In 2002, Bryant took 20 shots a game, with only 1.6 coming from deep—and hit a laughable 25 percent.

Even our definition of "good shots" has changed. In an era when the average possession was worth about a point, players who shot 33 percent from downtown were justified in letting it fly. As the worst shots—specifically long 2s—were stripped from offenses, the overall accuracy of 2-pointers exploded. In 2002, the league shot 46.5 percent on 2-point shots. In 2021, it was 53 percent. As much as

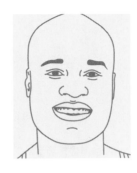

the 3-ball changed the sport, its real impact was a 2-ball revolution.

At any rate, we should not criticize scorers of the early millennium for hoisting up shots they were supposed to be taking. Have some sympathy for Antoine Walker, a meaty, shoulder-shimmying power forward who had his best years in Boston. From 2000 to 2004, he took 2,420 3-pointers—leading the league three times in attempts—despite making only 32.5 percent of them. When asked why he flung up so many 3s, Walker gave the perfect response: "Because there are no 4s."

A pair of underappreciated stars from the Dead Ball Era are Steve Francis and Baron Davis. They were selected second and third, respectively, in the 1999 draft, although Francis caused a dustup by refusing to play for Vancouver and forcing a trade to Houston: "I damn near cried when I got taken by the Grizzlies at No. 2," he wrote in the *Players' Tribune*. "I was not about to go up to freezing-ass Canada, so far away from my family, when they were about to move the franchise anyway."

Otherwise, the pair had many similarities. They were both 6-foot-3, spectacular athletes who could jump out of the gym, and part of a wave of NBA guards influenced by Iverson's stardom and AND1 streetball culture. The intersection of ball-domination, playground showmanship, dunk contest-worthy springs, and pedestrian shooting was scintillating—but did not lead to clinical efficiency that looks impressive on paper today. At the risk of sounding ageist, you had to be there.

DEFLECTIONS

When a defensive player gets a paw on the ball during a non–shot attempt, it is considered a deflection. Catalogued internally at many levels of basketball, deflection numbers for the NBA were unveiled to the public in the late 2010s. Unsurprisingly, the same kind of disruptors who rack up steals annually place among league leaders in deflections: Kawhi Leonard, Paul George, Draymond Green, Kris Dunn,

COMMON VICTIMS OF DEFLECTION

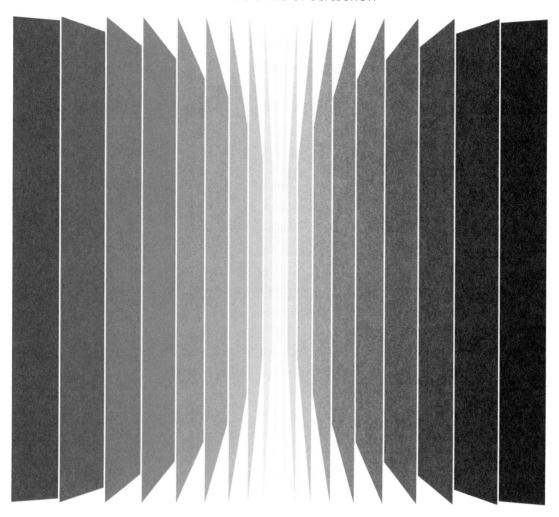

 Not true. ■ True.

The coach when the best player is Kanter.

Paul George when you can't beat Denver.

Ben Simmons when you hire Elton Brand.

Kawhi Leonard when San Antonio rebuilds.

The closest person when you drop a beer.

Friday night during a Saturday hangover.

Coworkers when you're underproducing.

Cab drivers when you're late for everything.

Dogs when there's a faint, haunting odor.

Bad luck after getting dumped three times in a year.

Jeans for your short legs and oddly shaped wagon.

Google when you get the serial killer's name wrong.

Big tech when you lose followers after a tweetstorm.

The internet after sending a passive-aggressive email.

Parents for the lack of ambition and professionalism.

Sandwiches when you pad on a few extra belly stats.

Work schedules when you forget a crucial birthday.

Hackers when you post a picture of your business.

SHOOTING ZONES

The Buzzer District.

Dame's Purgatory.

Larry Johnstown.

Curry's Rage Cage.

The Casual's Corner.

Kawhi's Wingstop.

The Nerd Inferno.

DeMar DeRozland.

Ray Ray's Room.

Numbers Jail.

The Devil's Interval.

Ethical Paradise.

Matisse Thybulle, and De'Anthony Melton. While it is an uncomplicated stat that can be skewed by the aggressiveness of a team's defensive scheme, high deflection rates indicate the presence of desirable qualities like a high motor, precognitive instincts, and off-ball activity. Research has shown that recovery of deflections appears to be based on luck.

Robert Covington, a forward who was named to the All-Defensive First Team in 2018, is annually among the NBA leaders in deflections. He is unremarkable when guarding the ball, but among the best at brewing pandemonium as a helper. Covington's signature might be chase-down strips where he slaps the ball loose and often sends it caroming off the offensive player's own leg. The challenge of scouting nontraditional areas of excellence—like deflections—could be the reason he went undrafted and labored in the developmental league before turning into a prized role player for squads like Philadelphia, Houston, and Portland. "His hands are incredible," Ben Falk, a former member of the Sixers front office, told *The Ringer*. "There's something about his quickness, his hand-eye coordination, his anticipation. He's able to get those deflections and be disruptive in a way that many players aren't."

DEVIL'S INTERVAL

The semicircular ribbon of space on a court that separates shots at the basket from those in the mid-range area, the Devil's Interval seduces players into tricky attempts. While only a few feet away from the rim, it is too far away for finger-rolls, dunks, or layups, and too close for standard jumpers. Instead, the region requires contorted, unorthodox shots like gliding hooks and short-armed pushes of the rock. These Sisyphean attempts are always contested by a defender—otherwise, players would mosey in for a wide-open dunk.

In terms of success rate, shots taken from the sulfurous crescent are low quality—just as the Father

of Lies intended—and only marginally better than shots from significantly farther away. "When you look at league-wide shooting numbers between 6 and 25 feet, the league is strangely consistent," Kirk Goldsberry wrote of data spanning 2014 to 2018 on the website FiveThirtyEight. "The effect of shot distance is pretty minor."

One salvation in this zone of perdition is the floater. Also known as a runner or teardrop, it is an arrhythmic one-handed attempt in which the attacker lofts the ball over earthbound defenders. Floaters require a downy touch and are powered by the momentum of a player's body, as opposed to a traditional shooting stroke or follow-through. While the offbeat timing makes them nearly unblockable, they are treacherous shots that efficiency cops disapprove of.

Traditionally, floaters have been used most frequently by smaller guards like Chris Paul, D'Angelo Russell, Tony Parker, Steve Nash, and Mike Conley. The reigning king is E'Twaun Moore, a wing who has played for teams like the Magic, Pelicans, and Suns. In recent years, big men who operate from the perimeter (like Joel Embiid, Anthony Davis, and Nikola Jokić) have supplemented old head pivot techniques with delicate runners.

With modern defenses geared toward rim protection, chasing shooters off the 3-point line, and "drop coverage" schemes where centers cede midrange turf, younger NBA players are bringing the floater back into vogue. "It keeps the defenders who are guarding me off their balance," Hawks guard Trae Young told the website HoopsHype. "They do not necessarily know if I'm going to shoot a floater or throw a lob or continue to try to get a layup." When the infuriating elf was learning the game, his father had him practice teardrops over an extended broom while dribbling at full speed. Like Young, recent draftees such as LaMelo Ball, Immanuel Quickley, and Tyrese Maxey all have floaters in their offensive bag—an angelic shot for a hellish area of the floor.

DIAW, BORIS

As a boon to uncultured and boorish Americans, there are self-help guides that instruct readers how to handle any situation like a French girl: entertaining, spending a day at the beach, styling bangs, going on a balmy summer date. Boris Diaw, the Cormeilles-en-Parisis–born forward and 2006 Most Improved

Player, could easily write the same about living, laughing, and loving in the NBA. Whether on the court or lazing on the banks of the Seine with a glass of cloudy pastis, he is the ultimate lifestyle guru.

"Bobo" was known for eccentricities that included keeping a small espresso machine in his locker, crashing a bachelorette party by swimming from his boat to the bride-to-be's vessel on a Texas lake, and filming a web series called *Sea the World* in which he sailed the coast of Africa. "His worst day is many times better than most of our best days," said Manu Ginóbili, his teammate on the Spurs. "He lives in a different place."

Diaw grew up in Bordeaux, the son of a mother who was a superstar on the French national basketball team. According to legend, she was the nation's first mademoiselle to shoot a jumper—yet did not pressure young Bobo to embrace the sport (though he did anyway). "Boris Diaw is literally a basketball savant," said former Suns executive Amin Elhassan on the *Dan Le Batard Show*. "It's like if you grew up in a household and Einstein was your parent. You were born to understand basketball in a way a lot of people don't."

Over a fourteen-year career that spanned 2004 to 2017, Diaw was a pudgy creator whose best moments came as a reserve on contending teams. An apex dancing bear, he had a girthy, 6-foot-8, 250-pound frame but thrived on his tiptoes. Diaw loved faking a 3 to get a defender off his feet, oozing into the soft midsection of the lane, and then spinning to the basket or dishing the ball to a cutting teammate. He was a capable shooter but better around the rim, where he potently mixed heft and misdirection. In 2016, Diaw shot 62.8 percent from the floor on post-up attempts—tops in the NBA out of anyone who did it with any frequency.

Diaw's ability to defend multiple positions and provide playmaking from the power forward slot was vital in the Spurs' 2014 Finals victory over LeBron James and the Miami Heat. His per-game numbers were typically oddball: 6.2 points on 36.4 percent shooting, 8.6 rebounds, and 5.8 assists. "He understands spatial relationships on the court," said Spurs coach Gregg Popovich, who referred to lineups that included Diaw as "Medium Ball." "He can find open people, he can post up for us. He allows us to stay big when the other team goes small."

Before his Finals redemption, Diaw was notorious for several forgettable seasons in Charlotte where he ballooned in weight and withered under expectations. The Bobcats imagined him as a point-center, which was a progressive way to utilize his size, 7-foot wingspan, and deft passing. But a year later, Paul Silas, the team's head coach, expressed frustration—a true boomer's lament—about Diaw's unwillingness to embrace volume scoring. "Some of the things that would go on, like not shooting the ball, passing all of the time, that doesn't help us," he said, shortly before Diaw was bought out and waived. "I needed hoops and he could put the ball in the hoop. When that wouldn't happen, it was very disturbing."

It was not the first time people grew irked at Diaw's reluctance to shoot—he averaged only 8.6 points a game for his career. Steve Nash, his teammate on Phoenix, recalled team-wide irritation when Diaw would burrow deep in the paint but kick the ball out to a perimeter shooter. "Just fucking lay it in!" Nash recalled yelling. "It was infuriating at the time. But when you watch him play, you realize that he sees things other people don't see. Such a smart, smart player."

For many years, Diaw was a victim of body-shaming. In San Antonio, there was a "weight clause" in his contract that kicked in up to $500,000 in bonuses if he remained below 254 pounds at various dates. Before the 2015 season, Popovich was asked by the media if he knew what Diaw had been up to over the summer. "Boris is having piña coladas," he said. "We have a pool where you guess his weight. You have to start at 275." In a response from overseas, Diaw posted a photo with a distinctively Gallic smirk and a raised glass of *vin*. "No worries, Pop, only one glass of wine and daily workouts!" he wrote.

There is a temptation to attribute Diaw's success solely to his philosophical approach to the game. It could be that the intellectual aspect was simply what he found interesting. "He was probably the fastest guy on the team from end to end," Todd Quinter, a member of the Suns' front office when Diaw was on the roster, told *ESPN* magazine. "He could also really leap. Yet somehow he doesn't rely on his athleticism to get things done. It's almost like he uses it as a last resort."

DISRUPTORS

If basketball is Nu-metal, certain players have the effect of a stink bomb flung onstage at a Slipknot

concert. They turn the bebopping improvisation of the beautiful game into a scramble for the exits over crushed cans of Rockstar energy beverages. This effect is not limited to any caste of baller. Prestigious studs like Ben Wallace, Draymond Green, and Ben Simmons possess it, but so do guys like Metta World Peace and Tony Allen. Disruptors include pickpockets (Mookie Blaylock, Brevin Knight, and Darrell Armstrong), undersized swatters (Dwyane Wade and Jerami Grant), oddball "stocks" accumulators of both steals and blocks (Jonathan Isaac, Jusuf Nurkić, and Matisse Thybulle), and charge-takers (Kyle Lowry, Anderson Varejão, and Ersan İlyasova). There are plenty of ways to ugly shit up.

The NBA's introduction of Hustle Stats during the 2016 season made it easier to identify undercover agents of mayhem. These metrics, captured by the SportVU motion tracking cameras installed in the rafters of every arena, include deflections, loose balls recovered, contested shots, and screen assists. According to a 2017 FiveThirtyEight story, obscure, undrafted Sacramento forward Anthony Tolliver led the NBA in whistle-drawing collisions that were proportionally ruled charges instead of blocks. "If you launch yourself backwards as soon as the contact hits you, the ref can see you getting hit without you having to take the full brunt of it," he explained of shifting into chaotic neutral. "Guys mess up because they start falling before they get hit."

Some disruptors are recognized for their ability to turn basketball into roller derby. Joakim Noah, for one, was a messy king. The son of a professional tennis player who won the 1973 French Open and a mother named Miss Sweden in 1978, he was born in New York City but spent his childhood racing the cobblestones of Paris with a fresh baguette tucked under his arm like an aromatic lance. That cosmopolitan upbringing molded his opinion of Cleveland, the blue-collar burg he dissed as a member of the Bulls. "I don't know about this place," Noah said on TNT. "It's pretty depressing here, man. It's bad. It's all factories."

With his black beard, a scraggle of hair knotted above his head, and exaggerated crouches, Noah

resembled a buccaneer preparing for a cutlass fight. Or he looked like the kind of guy who would propose to a Victoria's Secret model at Burning Man, which he did in 2019. He could be found at a New York Fashion Week rave or photographed buying a bong at a Chicago headshop. But on the court, Noah was the keystone of Tom Thibodeau's mighty defense, a group that gave up the fewest points per game in 2012 and 2014. The latter was Noah's masterpiece: he averaged 12.6 points, 11.3 rebounds, and an artful 5.4 assists, while winning Defensive Player of the Year. Along with his frenzied motor, he was a wonderful troll who barked at refs, sarcastically clapped in opponents' faces, and yelled "You're still a bitch, though!" at LeBron James—after getting dunked on by James.

Other disruptors are cult heroes. Nothing but fangs, claws, and armored hide, Marcus Smart is one of basketball's most beloved toughs. The boxy, 6-foot-3 Texan has a workmanlike, "bout it, bout it" demeanor and thrives on physical contact. He goes chest-to-chest with darting guards and accepts match-ups where he gives up eight inches and forty pounds in the post. "It's kind of like that little Pandora box, little mystery box, you never know what you're going to get from me and what position," Smart told reporters before a 2020 game. He led the league in steal percentage in 2019, was named to two All-Defensive teams, and won the 2018 NBA Hustle Award, which began in 2017 and no one cares about (or likely even heard of until reading this sentence).

The league's most shameless and unrepentant flopper, Smart slingshots himself into the stands after being grazed by a waft of hot breath. His encounters with spectators have not always been friendly. While at Oklahoma State, he shoved a Texas Tech fan who insulted him after he crashed into baseline seating, and as a member of the Celtics, he was involved in a verbal altercation with a spectator who told him to "Get on your knees" while he was entangled in the legs of a courtside chair. "We're going to end up protecting ourselves eventually," Smart said afterward. "And it's not going to be pretty for those fans and we don't want that. The league doesn't want that."

Being a Loki-tier disruptor does not even guarantee a stable job. At 6-foot-11 and 220 pounds, Nerlens Noel resembles cracks in a shattered windshield. The defensive savant has been typecast as a backup center throughout several stops in the NBA—potentially the result of a league-wide conspiracy to prevent Noel from reaching his unbridled power as an emissary of global pandemonium. While

his offensive toolbox is geared toward shoveling in zillions of alley-oops, his 68.4 field-goal percentage in 2020 would have been the seventh-best in history had he played enough minutes to qualify (just topping Wilt Chamberlain's 1967 mark). Noel is a capable passer and an improved free-throw shooter, but is hampered by hands that can seem as if he is corralling the ball with a pair of snowshoes.

Noel makes his bones on defense. He is a 6-foot-11 grasshopper who annually ranks among per possession leaders in disruptive categories. His peers in the Venn diagram of stocks are curiosities like Andrei Kirilenko, Hakeem Olajuwon, and David Robinson. From 2017 through 2020, Noel finished first or second in the league in deflections per minute each season. After reportedly turning down a long-term contract extension with Dallas and ending up in coach Rick Carlisle's doghouse, Noel caused a mild stir by eating a frankfurter in the Dallas media room during a game. "I needed some energy for the second half," he told *SB Nation*, despite not playing in the second half.

DONČIĆ, LUKA

An offensive polymath, Luka Dončić is one of the few young NBA players without a visible ceiling. It is up there, because it must be, among stratocumulus cottonballs and winking satellites. Born in Ljubljana, Slovenia, Luka was the son of a coach and professional basketball player. He entered a national basketball program at eight, was a sensation by thirteen, and earned the nickname Wonder Boy. He idolized LeBron James.

By the time the 2018 NBA Draft rolled around, Dončić had been named the youngest EuroLeague MVP in history. According to ESPN's Kevin Pelton, he had the highest projected "wins over replacement player" (WARP) for any prospect since numbers became accessible in 2006. Still, Dončić was selected third by Atlanta, with the intention of shipping him to Dallas for Trae Young and a first-round pick. Within two years, general managers in Phoenix and Sacramento who let him slip through their fingers were jobless.

By his second season in the NBA, Dončić was an All-Star who averaged an eye-popping 28.8 points, 9.4 rebounds, and 8.8 assists, while conducting the top-ranked offense in league history. He is James

Harden in the guise of James Corden: an iso-scorer who abuses defenders with a lightning first step and stuttering step-back 3s, a passing savant who whizzes skip-passes around the perimeter and leads cutters to unseen layups like a truffle pig. He plays with slovenly physicality around the basket, using heft and balance to create contact or dipping his speed to a near standstill. Dončić is guilty of the basketball crimes that Harden allegedly commits—flopping to draw fouls, inaccurately chucking too many 3s, ignoring defense, wailing to the refs—but absorbs little of the same criticism.

The better Luka gets, the more his whiteness rises creamily to the surface. In 2020, he was the only white player among the league's top twenty-three scorers (his teammate Kristaps Porziņģis was twenty-fourth). Although Dirk Nowitzki, Steve Nash, and Nikola Jokić have won MVPs, no white man has credibly laid claim to the title of the game's best player in roughly thirty-five years. Since Dončić's ascension theoretically coincides with the end of James's reign, that scenario appears possible. For fans and pundits who crave genetic relatability from their heroes, he seems like a knowable Slovene. He speaks with an accent, but he does not have the severe features or polygonic haircuts of Eastern European imports like Alexey Shved, Nenad Krstić, or Marcin Gortat. He has a nice smile and resembles Chris Farley with access to a Peloton. His first name is unique but not weird, a breezy mononym. Unlike Manu Ginóbili, Drazen Petrovic, or even Ricky Rubio, Dončić does not play with the offbeat regional time signature of an athlete from a basketball universe where mulleted fans pelt fifteen-year athletes with Żywiec bottles in a haze of cigarette smoke.

There is little about Luka's game that reads specifically as white. His craftiness and lack of observable pop are shared by non-white stars like Harden, Kyrie Irving, Trae Young, Devin Booker, and Kyle Lowry. But race is an unavoidable electrical rail, both in the giddy marveling about his performances and in how Dončić is perceived by his peers. During the 2020 Playoffs, Montrezl Harrell of the Clippers called Dončić a "bitch-ass whiteboy" during a skirmish. ("Nothing but respect for Luka," Harrell tweeted later. "He understood the heat of the battle and he said it didn't bother him.")

In the modern NBA, there are three prototypes for white stardom: Nash (small passer), Nowitzki (tall shooter), and Larry Bird (Boston arch-deity who magically represents all attributes of Caucasian basketball greatness). With Dončić blooming into a franchise player, comparisons have already shifted toward that paragon of porcelain-hued excellence. Outside of stature and seer-like passing, their games are not particularly similar. Dončić has been an erratic shooter from deep who lives at the line; Bird worked from the post or elbow and dribbled the ball as if it was a pork shoulder. But, beyond Bird, a white avatar of apex superstardom did not exist in the current NBA. Until now. As millions of European immigrants learned, long before Dončić stepped foot on the shores of the United States, this is a country that bestows the mantle of belonging as it sees fit.

DRUGS

Back in antediluvian times, the NBA was supposedly flooded with narcotics. A 1980 story in the *Washington Post* claimed that the majority of the league's players were sniffing cocaine and that 10 percent were smoking crack. A former player was quoted anonymously: "Coke is rampant in the league, man," he said. "I mean, 75 percent use it. It's like drinking water. You hit the blow to be sociable." In 1983, the league and the players union hashed out a policy that permanently banished any player who tested positive for using cocaine or heroin. "We felt the stigma of drug use has hurt our sport and we had to find a way to eliminate it," said Junior Bridgeman, an executive with the Bucks, to the *New York Times*.

In 1986, Maryland star Len Bias died of a cocaine overdose two days after being drafted second overall by the defending champion Celtics. The national scandal coincided with Reagan-era fearmongering about drugs and violence in inner-city America, and Bias became a postmortem tentpole to prop up bipartisan paternalism. As fate would have it, Tip O'Neill, the Speaker of the House, was a Democrat from Boston. "They want blood," he said of local newspapers at the time.

Bias's death generated momentum for the 1986 Anti-Drug Abuse Act, a barge of howlingly racist legislation with draconian sentencing and the infamous

"100-1" punishment disparity between crack (mostly used by poor people of color) and cocaine (mostly used by affluent white people). The laws would disproportionately decimate Black America for generations. "Hundreds of thousands of people would never have gone to jail if Len Bias had not died," said Eric Sterling, counsel to the House committee that designed the act. "The world would be completely different."

For decades, NBA policies toward harder drugs have seemed trapped in retrograde hysteria about ballers doing key-bumps in the locker room. In the 1980s and 1990s, players like Chris Washburn, Richard Dumas, Roy Tarpley, and Stanley Roberts were banned from the league (although some were reinstated). More recently, Chris "Birdman" Anderson, the mohawked center who won a title with the Heat, was punished with a two-year suspension for using "drugs of abuse," as were O. J. Mayo, the third overall pick in 2008, and Tyreke Evans, the 2010 Rookie of the Year. Not only did the players lose millions of dollars in voided contracts, the NBA's de facto monopoly on professional basketball in America made it impossible for them to earn a living in the United States. "Taking the game away is probably the closest thing to jail that I'll get to," Mayo told *Sports Illustrated*. He admitted smoking weed and popping prescription painkillers, but denied taking anything harder. "That was the lowest point in my entire life. All my peers are playing and I'm not because of boneheaded mistakes. Take the ball away, what is there to do?"

There is no shortage of players who struggled with substance abuse while remaining in the NBA. A Cottagecore traditionalist in the post, Vin Baker was a 6-foot-11 lug who used his shoulders and long arms to mudslide over defenders. He was named to three consecutive All-Star teams as a member of the Bucks and one with the Sonics, while averaging 19.7 points and 9.6 rebounds over that stretch. Baker was a basketball version of an "innings eater"—he was not great at any one thing, but missed only a total of four games over his first five NBA seasons and finished among the league's leaders in minutes per game three times. Half the job is showing up, as they say.

Before a 1996 game, Baker smoked marijuana while getting a haircut at teammate Glenn Robinson's house and played stoned for the first time. "Went to the game feeling kind of disoriented," he later told Boston station WBUR. "It was the anxiety of, 'Am I going to be walking on air? Am I going to pass out?'" Instead, while zooted off Big Dog's

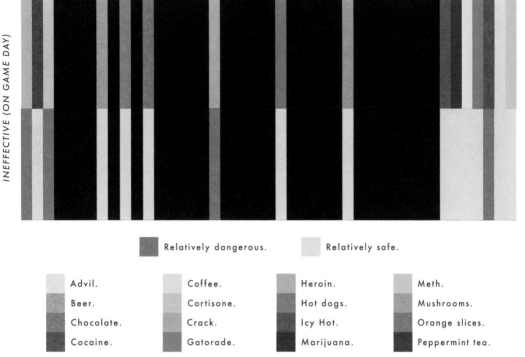

INEFFECTIVE (ON GAME DAY)

EFFECTIVE (ON GAME DAY)

Relatively dangerous.	Relatively safe.

Advil.	Coffee.	Heroin.	Meth.
Beer.	Cortisone.	Hot dogs.	Mushrooms.
Chocolate.	Crack.	Icy Hot.	Orange slices.
Cocaine.	Gatorade.	Marijuana.	Peppermint tea.

dirt weed, Baker scored another high: 41 points. "Statistically, it was my best game ever as a pro," he said. "It was a weird coming-out party for me."

After Baker was traded to Seattle, he began drinking during games and poured booze in his water bottle. Later, in Boston, he was suspended when coach Jim O'Brien caught a whiff of alcohol on his breath. Baker has claimed that surprise drug testers hired by the league offered to give him advance warnings for $100,000. Eventually he hit rock bottom: out of the league, untold millions of dollars invested in strippers and gambling, trudging around his house in a robe drinking cognac. "I wanted to get to the NBA, and I got there, but success came very fast for me," Baker told *SLAM* magazine. "Once I experienced it, I think I kind of lost my lust for it."

Baker's post-NBA salvation began when he embraced sobriety, religion, and Howard Schultz (former Starbucks chairman, onetime owner of the Sonics, and ignored 2020 presidential candidate). The coffee salesman gave Baker a barista job at Starbucks, where Baker arrived at 3:45 in the

morning to prepare peppermint mocha frappuccinos for commuters looking for their morning fix.

DUKE SCOURGE

A horned embodiment of all that is demonic about college basketball, Duke University has unleashed a soulless army of hellhounds into the NBA. The menagerie includes Austin Rivers, JJ Redick, Luol Deng, and the three-headed Cerberus of Marshall, Mason, and Miles Plumlee. Fiendishly, the collegiate powerhouse has used smug self-righteousness, waves of blue-chip prospects, and the foul mouth of coach Mike Krzyzewski to deceive the masses into believing that it is a respectable

D

SOME ALLEGEDLY DIFFICULT PERSONALITIES

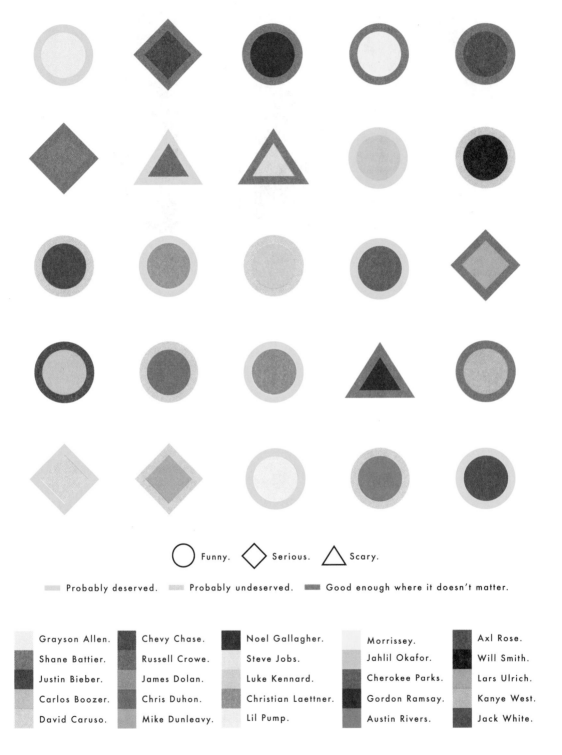

○ Funny. ◇ Serious. △ Scary.

▬ Probably deserved. ▬ Probably undeserved. ▬ Good enough where it doesn't matter.

Grayson Allen.	Chevy Chase.	Noel Gallagher.	Morrissey.	Axl Rose.
Shane Battier.	Russell Crowe.	Steve Jobs.	Jahlil Okafor.	Will Smith.
Justin Bieber.	James Dolan.	Luke Kennard.	Cherokee Parks.	Lars Ulrich.
Carlos Boozer.	Chris Duhon.	Christian Laettner.	Gordon Ramsay.	Kanye West.
David Caruso.	Mike Dunleavy.	Lil Pump.	Austin Rivers.	Jack White.

institution of higher learning (as opposed to a moral sinkhole). "I hated everything I felt Duke stood for," said Jalen Rose, whose Michigan team lost to the Blue Devils in the 1992 NCAA championship game. "Schools like Duke didn't recruit players like me. I felt like they only recruited Black players that were Uncle Toms."

Christian Laettner was a two-time NCAA champion at Duke who personified the school's heinous character. The 6-foot-11 center was sneering and handsome, a hardwood Stan Gable who oozed privilege and generational wealth (although he grew up on a farm in Upstate New York). In the documentary *I Hate Christian Laettner*, journalist Gene Wojciechowski called him the "number one asshole of all time." Despite being the leading scorer in NCAA tournament history, Laettner was not regarded as a guaranteed professional ubermensch. He objected to pre-draft critiques that compared him to disappointing Duke first-round picks like Danny Ferry and Mark Alarie. "I think it's a victim of being white and they don't think you're tough enough," said Laettner, who was taken third by Minnesota. He made the All-Star team in 1997 as a member of the Hawks, but was an unremarkable pro.

Perhaps the greatest trick the Blue Devils ever played was the creation of Grant Hill, a multifaceted incubus conjured for global domination. "Grant was the most talented player we've coached at Duke," said Krzyzewski. "Really, he could be president of the U.S." Hill's mother was a Washington consultant who was a dorm-mate of Hillary Clinton's; his father was an All-Pro running back in the NFL. Drafted by the Pistons, the 6-foot-8 small forward was named to five All-NBA teams from 1996 to 2000. He was graceful but coiled, an early "point forward" prototype who could score, rebound, pass, and defend.

When combined with wholesome charisma and his Duke pedigree, Hill was viewed as the heir apparent to Michael Jordan's throne. After a 34-point triple double against the Lakers, he embraced all the comparisons. "First, at the tip-off, Shaq wouldn't shake hands," he said of a moment when he *took it personal*. "Then Kobe Bryant got three baskets off me and started trash-talking. Kobe Bryant! High-school guy! So I did a Michael." Late in 2000, Hill worsened an ankle injury by attempting to play through pain—in part to ward off accusations that he was concerned about impending free agency—and he logged only forty-seven games over the next four seasons. Armageddon was averted.

While lottery picks such as Jahlil Okafor, Jayson Tatum, and Marvin Bagley III left Duke's notorious "one-and-done bust factory" after a single season, the practice is recent. For many years, no Duke player entered the NBA Draft as an underclassman. This grotesque ritual cost impressionable young men incalculable millions of dollars. In 1999, Elton Brand broke with exploitive tradition by turning pro after two seasons with the Blue Devils. When a Duke graduate sent him an email expressing disgust, Brand clapped back. "I'm sure daddy worked very hard to send your rich self to college," he typed. "Never being considered a part of your posh group of yuppies really hurts me to the heart. Yeah, right."

Although Krzyzewski has announced that he will retire in 2022, it is unclear if his unholy empire will fall with him.

DUNCAN, TIM

For nearly two decades, Tim Duncan ruled basketball with a clenched fist of blandness. He was the first pick in the 1997 draft and boringly spent all of his nineteen seasons with the San Antonio Spurs, sandbagging the All-Star game with tiresome excellence fifteen times. With a public persona that was quiet, humble, hardworking, and dedicated to the pursuit of titles, the 6-foot-11 big man was favorably juxtaposed by arbiters of sportsmanship to charismatic stars like Allen Iverson, Shaquille O'Neal, Kevin Garnett, and LeBron James. "He's the most real, consistent, and true person I've ever met in my life," said Spurs coach Gregg Popovich.

Duncan is adored by the kind of basketball fan who believes college athletes play for the love of the game. Or that wearing compression sleeves should be punishable by stoning. Due to a career that extended until middle age, five championships, and anti-fashion taste for Mudhoney flannel, polite basketball society collectively pretends that he was beloved during his prime (as opposed to widely disliked). As with Dirk Nowitzki of the Mavericks, the revisionism surrounding Duncan's image is linked to squaring off against James's reviled Miami Heat in the Finals.

When Duncan left Wake Forest University, he was described by NBA Scouting Director Marty Blake as arguably "the most complete player to enter the NBA in the last ten years." NBA teams courtesy-flushed the 1997 season in hopes of ping-ponging

their way to a brighter future through the draft lottery. The Celtics finished a franchise-worst 15–67, which coach M. L. Carr later told the *Boston Herald* was "part of the orchestration." Despite its terrible efforts, Beantown ended up with the third pick and the sixth pick, as Mighty Mighty Bosstones saxophones wailed into the Southie night.

San Antonio, regarded as the avatar of basketball rectitude, brazenly tanked as well, winning only 20 games after averaging 60.5 victories the prior two seasons. As a reward for intentionally sucking, the Spurs earned the opportunity to pair Duncan with David Robinson, another one of the finest centers in history. The cheating paid immediate dividends, as the "Twin Towers" duo won a title in only their second year together (1999's lockout-shortened season, which Phil Jackson, then coaching the Lakers, said required an asterisk).

A power forward in name only, Duncan was a traditional center, despite many pointless arguments between Gen Xers (when they weren't pining for Winona Ryder or listening to Hiero-affiliated rap CDs). He was an offensive superstar for the earlier portion of his career, averaging 22.5 points a game over his first eight seasons. O'Neal dubbed him The Big Fundamental as a nod to his flavorless, porridge-like diet of midrange banks, minor-arc hooks, and put-backs where he corralled the ball into the hoop with his mitts extended straight overhead. As time went on, the Spurs' brain trust surveyed the buckling plates of the NBA landscape and decided to fork scoring responsibilities more evenly between Duncan and teammates Tony Parker, Manu Ginóbili, and Kawhi Leonard.

Even as an old man, Duncan was a defensive force. Owing heavily to his craftsmanship, the Spurs were miserly for nearly two decades, finishing among the league's top three in defensive rating fifteen times during his career. Patrolling the middle, Duncan was an impermeable stone golem with the functional strength to keep opposing centers from bullying their way to the hoop and the surprisingly agile footwork to smother pick-and-rolls. He perennially landed among the league's top 5 in rebounds and top 10 in blocked shots.

As his physical skills eroded, Duncan made up for it with effort, intuition, intelligence, and the durability of a human cast-iron skillet. He lost weight in the early 2010s, which may have helped spare his thirty-something knees. "When we would go out to eat, Tim would split the bill and we had a big plethora of food out for us," his former teammate Bruce Bowen once said. "But now, he's starting to eat wheat bread and chicken only, no mayonnaise, no mustard, none of that." Duncan retired as the greatest Spur in history and an adored anti-star, but it is unclear how younger generations will translate the TikTok highlights of a superstar who excelled at plinking 14-footers off the glass and averaged only 14.1 points a game for his last six seasons.

Duncan has an enormous tattoo running down the right side of his back that he has described as "car part yin-yang, mechanical meets spiritual." Showing a taste for technocrats as well as technology, he was the only person to support Michael Bloomberg's doomed 2020 presidential campaign. These glimpses of Duncan's personality hint that decades of stoicism may all have been a competitive ruse. "You absolutely destroy them," Duncan told *Sports Illustrated*. "They can't get inside your head. They're talking to you, and there's no response other than to make this shot, make this play, get this rebound, and go the other way. People hate that."

DUNKS

 Anyone who has touched a basketball has dreamed of dunking. That fantasy may not have consumed your junior and senior years of high school, left welts and calluses on the upper ridge of your palm, or caused you to consider buying "strength shoes" that looked like alien clogs, but even the shortest of kings imagined flushing one home with authority and swinging from the rim with lightning bug-ass LA Gears splayed in the sky.

The modern NBA Slam Dunk Contest began at the All-Star Weekend in 1984, and dunk technology has followed the trajectory of cell phones and personal computers. The top-scoring dunks from professionals of thirty years ago—a nice reverse jam or flicking the ball off the backboard—are now casually done by high school players during games. It is like comparing a T-Mobile Sidekick to an iPhone 15.

Since the legendary 1988 duel between Michael Jordan and Dominique Wilkins, interest in the contest has waxed and waned depending on the presence of stars who are extraordinary in-game dunkers. That list is just Vince Carter and Blake Griffin. Outside of celebrated young players like Kobe Bryant and John Wall, contestants fall into several categories: flying rugrats (Spud Webb, Nate Robinson, Robert Pack), big dudes who look unimpressive because of their size (Shawn Kemp, Dwight Howard, Amar'e Stoudemire), and obscure bench leapers (Fred Jones, Jeremy Evans, Hamidou Diallo, Derrick Jones Jr.).

The contest's culture of jamming has grown to include endless theatrical stunts, most of which detract from the dunks themselves. Howard wore a Superman cape, Victor Oladipo donned a Black Panther mask, and Cedric Ceballos wore a blindfold that many suspected he could see through (he continues to deny it). Griffin jumped over a Kia Optima and JaVale McGee dunked two balls on side-by-side rims. "To me, the gimmicky thing is kind of overrated," Carter told *The Undefeated*. "Show them what you're cooking with. Don't put the onus on a guy to have to use a prop or a teammate."

Some dunk champions demure on repeat performances, citing a wish to be known as "more than a dunker." Zach LaVine, a gaunt shooting guard who was drafted by the Timberwolves and traded to Chicago in a deal for Jimmy Butler, proved this binary is nonsensical. By winning the NBA Slam Dunk Contest in 2015 and 2016 with crisply executed feats like a between-the-legs jam in which he went airborne from the free-throw stripe, LaVine matched Jordan, Robinson, and Jason Richardson as the NBA's only back-to-back champs. At the time, he was not famed for his jams, but excoriated as a mindless young chucker. In the coming years, however, he developed into one of the league's more dangerous perimeter scorers—and remained a guy who can immaculately pull off a 360-degree dunk on a breakaway.

Uncontested slams are fun, but powerfully yoking on an opponent is what gets teammates and fans fired up. Whether they really change momentum is debatable, but facials and posterizations are the true currency of the NBA dunker. A player who excelled at instigating midair incidents was Kenyon Martin, a forward taken by the Nets with the first overall pick in 2000. Though he rarely flooded the box score with crooked numbers, he pulsed with misanthropy and promise of grievous bodily harm. In the second of his four seasons spent in New Jersey, Martin was united with Jason Kidd, a passing virtuoso who became his muse. Aided by Kidd's arcing lobs and dimes that ricocheted off the backboard, he hammered down 459 jams over three years and the Nets made back-to-back Finals appearances. Martin was a master of an underrated aspect of jamming—sticking the landing—and added flourishes like swinging knees, backboard slaps, malevolent air punches, and threatening straddles.

Late in his career, Martin assumed his natural role as a Garden Protector with the Knicks. After retiring, he staked out terrain as a sourpuss who mourned the lack of physicality in the modern game. "Steph [Curry] ain't hit the ground enough," he said on New York's Power 105.1, while discussing the Finals. "I ain't saying take him out, or hurt him, or nothing. But make him know it's a contact sport, man."

DURANT, KEVIN

In oceanography circles, a rogue wave appears out of the cobalt expanse, taller and more destructive than other waves. It is a phenomenon swaddled in mythology, yet an explainable rarity. This is Kevin Durant. We cannot deny the existence of a reedy 6-foot-10 man who is able to bring the ball up the floor, shake a defender with a sweeping crossover at the top of the arc, and splash a line-drive jumper that barely stirs the net. We have seen him do it. We know that the confluence of height, hand-eye coordination, and speed are physiologically possible. That does not make Durant any less extraordinary, or less capable of capsizing the hull of a clipper ship.

Nicknamed the Slim Reaper because of his build and scythe-like 7-foot-5 wingspan—a handle he deemed too fiendish, while suggesting the nonsecular alias of the Servant—Durant is the most unstoppable scorer the modern NBA has ever seen. He does not require the optimization of a choreographed system or a shot chart that unearths his sweetest spots. Instead, Durant is boringly great at everything: scoring in the paint or from the post, scoring on pull-up jumpers or catch-and-shoot 3s, scoring in isolation, or scoring by drawing fouls by whipping his pipe-cleaner limbs into defenders. From 2017 to 2019, he shot 52.3 percent on 2-pointers over 16 feet, which are the same attempts every defense is trying to encourage. "Who the fuck wants to look at graphs while having a hoop convo?" Durant said in a Twitter debate about midrange jumpers—conveniently neglecting the fact that the math is different for him. Bad shots are for the rest of us.

Durant might be the best forward ever, if we stick him at whichever slot LeBron James does not play. He has led the NBA in scoring several times, and has topped the league in categories like free-throw percentage, value over replacement player, and win shares. He blocks shots, plucks rebounds, and, over the course of his career, more than doubled his assists per game without suffering a corresponding spike in turnovers. He has won an MVP Award and two championships, snaring the Finals MVP both times as a late addition to the Warriors' dynasty.

Despite unfurling a list of accomplishments the length of a CVS receipt, Durant has never been the best player on the planet due to the unlucky overlap of his career with that of LeBron James, who is the better creator and defender. It gnaws at him. "I've been second my whole life," he said in a 2013 *Sports Illustrated* story. "I was the second-best player in high school. I was the second pick in the draft. . . . I'm tired of being second. I'm not going to settle for that. I'm done with it." While on the Warriors, Durant hit Game 3 daggers against James in back-to-back Finals wins—and, still, few were convinced that the crown had moved from one head with hints of male pattern baldness to another.

Durant grew up in Seat Pleasant, a small Maryland town east of Washington, DC. His mother was a postal worker and his father was absent for much of Kevin's early childhood. "I felt like basketball was the only way I could get out of that wreckage," he said of his neighborhood, in a 2018 letter to his hometown published by *ESPN* magazine. He slept at the rec center and sprinted up steep Hunt's Hill until his legs collapsed.

After a year at the University of Texas, he was selected second overall in the 2007 NBA Draft by the Seattle SuperSonics (who greasily absconded to Oklahoma City a year later). Durant was the centerpiece of a rising Thunder powerhouse that soon included Russell Westbrook, James Harden, and Serge Ibaka. When the Thunder lost to James's Heat in the 2012 Finals, it was dismissed with a shrug befitting the spillage of exactly one beer—they would surely be back, many times.

Early on, Durant was celebrated for his goofy innocence. He kept a Bible in the backpack that he wore after games (the look was influenced by *The College Dropout*–era Kanye West: "His style is only something that he can pull off, the leather pants, the kilts," Durant once said). When he re-upped a long-term extension to stay in Oklahoma City in 2010, he was propped up as an example of an athlete who was untarnished by the trappings of wealth, celebrity, and professional autonomy. Even as he became the NBA's leading scorer, his image was that of a wholesome, sinless naif. "Just had a bad dream," he tweeted in 2012. "Wish I could go sleep in my mommy bed but I forgot that I'm 23."

The veneer cracked in 2014, when a headline in the *Oklahoman* dubbed Durant "Mr. Unreliable" during a playoff series that the Thunder ultimately won. He felt betrayed. His disillusionment grew worse after he was talked into abandoning the Thunder to join the Hamptons 5 in Golden State, a move that upended the league's competitive balance for three years. Criticism rained down from fans, pundits, and even other players. "I'm not a guy who goes into the neighborhood, gets beat up by the bully's gang, and then now I want to join their gang," said former Celtic and Instagram livestreamer Paul Pierce.

A bitter, testy Durant emerged from the crucible. He now racks up technical fouls and jaws with opponents, like calling Jerami Grant of the Thunder a "bitch-ass nigga" and a "pussy." He has been caught using anonymous burner accounts on social media to defend his honor. He confronts dweeby beat writers at press conferences and online with unnecessary but entertaining hostility. He called actor Michael Rapaport a "pale cock sucker" in a DM and suggested fighting at a steakhouse in Manhattan's meatpacking district. Alternatively irked, bored, and mopey, Durant exudes the millennial energy of a human "when you're trying to love people but you're also an introvert and have boundaries" meme.

After rupturing his right Achilles tendon during the 2019 Finals, Durant conspired with Kyrie Irving to join the Brooklyn Nets as free agents. He returned in 2021 looking as fearsome as ever, setting career highs in scoring efficiency and 3-point percentage, while nearly carrying a depleted Brooklyn team to victory over the title-winning Bucks. As usual, Durant continued to wage war against his critics in the media. "They wanna bully me and they feel like they found a little crackle or crease in my armor," he said on *All the Smoke*. "And when I call it out, I guess I'm a sensitive guy."

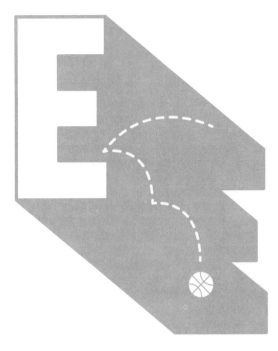

for 3-pointers being worth 3 points. Despite its simplicity, eFG% is infrequently cited because it carries the whiff of an "advanced" metric but doesn't include free throws. With nearly 40 percent of all field-goal attempts coming now from behind the arc, traditional FG% is virtually worthless: Steph Curry's career FG% of 43.5 on 3-pointers (1.3 points per possession) is superior to Enes Kanter's 55.0 percent field-goal percentage on 2-pointers (1.1 points per possession). Yet because FG% is included in the canon of box-score stats that we all grew up reading in newspapers, grillmasters cling to it like stainless steel tongs around a juicy tomahawk steak.

EMBIID, JOEL

The end of Joel Embiid's learning curve winks from afar like the signal mirror of a pilot downed in dense vegetation. This steep incline has applied to the 7-foot center's vacuum-like absorption of hoops, pop culture, and social media. He was fifteen when he picked up a basketball for the first time in Yaoundé, the capital of Cameroon. Within a year, he had moved to the United States to play at a prep school in Florida, where his awkwardness drew mockery from teammates. "Laugh all you want," said his coach. "But in five years you're going to be asking him for a loan, because he's going to be worth about $50 million."

Embiid was the consensus top talent in the 2014 class, but a stress fracture to the navicular bone in his right foot caused him to slip to the third pick, where he was plucked by the Sixers. Despite the risk, econometric guru Sam Hinkie believed the University of Kansas freshman was the crown jewel of a slashing rebuild dubbed "the Process." In part because Embiid was unable to play for his first two NBA seasons, Hinkie was bullied into resigning. Embiid later adopted the nickname the Process for himself and named his pet goldendoodle Klaus Hinkie De Paula Embiid.

His love of trolling extends to Twitter and Instagram, where he has taunted rivals, used an image of himself crying as an avatar, and publicly courted Rihanna. "When I was five or six years old, I had to go into the jungle to kill a lion," he convincingly lied to NBC's Dan Patrick. "I carried the lion on my back, back to the village. I think it was an easy job."

In an era when centers are increasingly as aerodynamic as balsa gliders, Embiid is an abnormality.

EDDIE

In 1996, wisecracking New York limo driver Edwina "Eddie" Franklin became coach of the Knicks after winning a halftime contest. Her spunky attitude gave life to the moribund franchise and she earned the respect of players like Rick Fox, Dwayne Schintzius, and Malik Sealy. "Actually, hiring Eddie was my idea from the beginning," said failed businessman Donald Trump, one of many New Yorkers who supported Franklin, despite her lack of coaching experience and insistence on running the obsolete Triangle Offense. Eventually, she thwarted a plot by Knicks ownership to move the team to St. Louis, a relocation that would have saved New Yorkers decades of incalculable pain.

EFFECTIVE FIELD-GOAL PERCENTAGE

Effective field-goal percentage is the socket wrench of statistics, useful but unsexy. Abbreviated as eFG%, it adjusts field-goal percentage (FG%) to account

He weighs 280 pounds and has a 7-foot-6 wingspan. He is not overly fast or spry or coordinated for a basketball player—unless that player is the size of an oil tanker, which he is. While he has been touted as a "unicorn," Embiid's combination of girthiness and skill is what makes him a true rarity: the two-way center who can anchor a team on either side of the ball. "When I look at myself, I'm not a big man," Embiid said. "I can do everything on the basketball court. You can name it—pass, post up, shoot the ball, bring the ball up, being a playmaker."

Embiid is annually among the league's leading scorers on post-ups, has a feathery touch on step-back jumpers, and can capably shoot from deep ("I don't like shooting 3s," he has said. "I only do it because of the spacing that we have"). His signature move is an up-fake from the top of the arc that sets an avalanche of flesh rumbling toward the basket and ends with unpredictable results. His nimble footwork leads to jaw-dropping Euro-step dunks—and sometimes an excruciating pivot drag, travel, and topple. Even then, he has become better than anyone at baiting fouls and is among the league leaders in free throw attempts per game. Defensively he is a constant. Embiid's ability to rebound, swat away shots, and make transgressors in the lane reconsider their lives is nearly unparalleled. He finished second in Defensive Player of the Year voting in 2018 and fourth in 2019. Even as an unfinished canvas, Embiid is a breathtaking work of art.

Still, there are good explanations for why so few NBA teams run their offense through the post in the 2020s. It is a tedious way to score. A paint protector needs to scramble back 94 feet in an up-tempo game, double-teams materialize from still air like popcorn thunderstorms, and the presence of a large lad in the paint clogs up driving lanes. But in a league trending smaller and lighter, few teams have an answer for a hyper-skilled giant—and there is only one Joel Embiid.

EMOTIONAL SUPPORT VETS

During a practice during his rookie season in Seattle, Gary Payton made the mistake of challenging older teammate Xavier McDaniel, one of the NBA's most feared tough guys and a known choking enthusiast. Sure enough, Payton ended up in a sleeper hold, on the verge of losing consciousness. "That shit was a wake-up call," Payton said in a *Players' Tribune* essay.

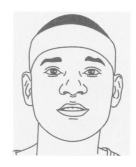

"After that, I did everything he said. Honest to God, no lie, my career wouldn't have been the same if I had got drafted by a team with all kids my same age."

In every profession, the act of mentorship is regarded as sacred. Just as long-toothed oldsters take greenhorns under their wings to teach them the hobo code while riding the rails, intergenerational relationships are cherished in the NBA. Most declining players prefer to spend their final days hobbling around on a contending roster in pursuit of an undeserved championship ring, but some are tasked with a different role: emotional support vet.

Rebuilding teams are full of young guys—recent lottery picks, desperados on ten-day contracts, undrafted free agents, assorted journeymen avoiding their destiny in Istanbul—and traditionalists cite the importance of a guiding hand from the league's graying statesmen. Advantages of a veteran presence are said to include passage of tricks of the trade, an oral history of cautionary tales about life on the road (and the Fashion Nova–sheathed predators who sink their talons into naive millionaires), and osmosis of professionalism by example. For now, we will ignore the reality that older players are competing for their livelihood against draft classes of poreless teens that annually flood the NBA with sweet adrenochrome.

Jared Dudley, a wing who has played for seven teams and is one of the few NBA players whose build could be described as "plumber-adjacent," logged a total of three minutes on the Lakers' title-winning team in the COVID Bubble. But his role was different from that of teammates like point guard Alex Caruso or wing Kentavious Caldwell-Pope. "We used to tell him all the time, there's 450 players in the league and you're 451 in athleticism," said former Suns executive Amin Elhassan, on the *Dan Le Batard Show*. "But brilliant basketball mind. Really smart, high IQ . . . great work ethic, great locker room guy, great energy and good dude."

Despite conventional wisdom, there is not much proof that emotional support vets necessarily improve a young player's long-term outlook. NBA organizations include a legion of coaches, psychologists, biomechanists, video coordinators, nutritionists, trainers, and other personnel. Players make true strides by investing off-season hours in the gym, lifting weights, and getting up shots. It is hard to quantify the impact of sage musings from a taxidermied small forward with two kids and three mortgages. Players who attribute their success to the influence of older teammates might just be experiencing survivorship bias.

In one example, star forward Karl-Anthony Towns was mentored by legendary big man Kevin Garnett while the two were briefly teammates on the Timberwolves. "Whenever I have questions, I always know he's on speed dial," Towns said later. "He always answers the phone." Towns's warm feelings aside, it is difficult to tell if Garnett turned him into a better player. Towns was the top college prospect in the country and the consensus number-one pick in the draft before the pair ever met. Garnett is one of the greatest defenders of all time, but Towns has continued to struggle on that side of the ball. On the other hand, Garnett's influence may not be as much about basketball as about being a basketball player.

"When it comes to off-the-court stuff and dealing with family and finances and the lifestyle of the league, you need veterans," Garnett told the *New York Times*. "Veterans sit around during dinners and plane rides and talk about people who have come before you: players that fought for mid-level exceptions and Bird rights. The franchise is not going to teach the players this. The players are exchanging the information you need to go up against a machine like the league."

EUROPEAN KINGS

Roundball archaeologists tracking the NBA's evolution from a hooting muck into a cosmos of spinning bodies always identify Steve Nash's "Seven Seconds or Less" Suns and Stephen Curry's "Death Lineup" Warriors as inflection points. But Sacramento teams of the early 2000s deserve to be mentioned as well, even if their importance is akin to that of the Neanderthal: Were

the early hominids an evolutionary dead end or were they absorbed into our gene pool?

The Kings never won a championship or went to the Finals, but their DNA sequence is found in the modern game. Hailed as "The Greatest Show on Court" by a *Sports Illustrated* cover story, Sacramento scrambled down the hardwood faster than any other team, moved the rock with flair and precision, and gorgeously wed the finesse of international basketball with homegrown sauciness. To some, the squad was less a glimpse of the futuristic than a flashback to the fluidity of the 1980s at a time when the sport was thigh-high in molasses. "The Kings are a reminder of better days in the NBA," wrote Bob Ryan of the *Boston Globe*. "Someone should send their game tapes to places where all the life and fun have been strangled out of the game."

Chris Webber, regarded as an underachiever at stops in Golden State and Washington, was the Kings' nobility. He arrived in 1998, via a trade for franchise anchor Mitch Richmond. "I did not want to go to Sacramento," Webber remembered on *The Lowe Post* podcast. "They were bottom-dwellers, terrible, they didn't put money into the team, they were a laughingstock." But the charismatic power forward was a box-score-stuffing showman, and his exuberance and creativity took root. From 2001 to 2005, the Kings averaged 56 wins a season under coach Rick Adelman.

Webber's supporting cast looked like a season of *Chef's Table*. Peja Stojaković was a three-time All-Star from Croatia who led the league in made 3-pointers and free-throw percentage in 2004. A wholly modern player, the 6-foot-10 forward was one of the NBA's only hyper-efficient scorers of the Dead Ball Era, raining trifectas after curling off screens, repositioning along the arc to create passing lanes, and side-stepping into open looks. The rest of the lads included young Turk Hedo Türkoğlu, another remarkably tall and adept foreigner; Doug Christie, an early 3-and-D prototype who was named to the All-Defensive Team for four consecutive seasons; Bobby Jackson, a combo guard who wore the largest shorts anyone has ever seen; and flashy point guard Jason "White Chocolate" Williams, who was soon replaced in the lineup by playmaker Mike Bibby.

The team's shaman was Vlade Divac. An early overseas import, he introduced American basketball to graceful treachery from the center position and seductive Balkan "This guy bones on yachts" energy. Over sixteen seasons spread between Los

Angeles, Charlotte, and Sacramento, he matched the anatomical gifts of a long-armed, 7-foot-1 frame with mobility, coordination, vision, and flair. "He's an artist," said fellow big man Bill Walton, during a broadcast. "He sees the game in a different way."

Divac grew up in Prijepolje, a town in Serbia. He turned pro at sixteen. He was national teammates with Yugoslavian stars like Dražen Petrović and Toni Kukoč, but ethnic strife and bloodshed splintered the world's best team outside of the States. "I was persona non grata in Croatia because I never said one side was bad or good," Divac said. "I was always saying it's a civil war and there were people killing each other on many sides." The documentary *Once Brothers* focused on Divac's lost friendship with Petrović, a feisty Nets shooting guard who died in a 1993 Autobahn accident.

Divac fell to the Lakers late in the first round of the 1989 draft, reportedly because teams were concerned by his casual attitude toward vices like alcohol and tobacco. He acknowledged smoking cigarettes, but said his habit was limited to ten butts a day. "That's what I knew Vlade for: smoking, drinking, and flopping," said center Tyson Chandler. Hollywood embraced the large Serb and he had cameos in productions like *Married . . . with Children*, *Space Jam*, and *Eddie*.

Next to genius playmaker Magic Johnson, Divac added stagecraft and basketball IQ to a Lake Show team that went to the Finals in his second season. A maestro when operating from the high post, he was adept at feeding cutters, weathervaning into scoop shots, and curling to the rim after faux handoffs. Divac was a charming ham who howled with incredulity at calls and flopped around like an inflatable tubeman in a used-car lot. In Sacramento, the frontcourt of Divac and Webber was a Rube Goldberg device that ended up with men in purple jerseys darting in for backdoor layups. "Vlade's the one," said Webber. "Vlade is a great man. I'd rather be a quiet leader."

By the mid-2000s, the curtain was drawn on the circus in Sacramento. Webber suffered a knee injury and was traded to Philadelphia. After going 44–38 and losing in the first round of the 2006 playoffs, the franchise would embark on a 15-season playoff drought that continued through the 2021 Play-In Tournament. Along the way, Divac was hired as general manager of the Kings. His major claim was passing on Luka Dončić in the 2018 draft in favor of Marvin Bagley III. One rumor was that

Divac did not like Dončić's father, who had played on the Yugoslavian national cadet team. "We all get heavier as we get older because there's a lot more information in our heads," Divac once said.

EWING, PATRICK

Described by *Sports Illustrated* as "the most recognized athlete ever to enter a major professional league," Patrick Ewing was chauffeured to the Knicks by the NBA's first lottery—an event shrouded in conspiracy theories—and proceeded to do everything except win a championship. "The only regret I have is that I didn't bring a title to New York," Ewing said in the local *Daily News*. "I'll carry that regret with me the rest of my life." That failure, if we consider it one, has acted as a velvet rope preventing his entry into the VIP room reserved for history's greatest big men, a place where Shaquille O'Neal, David Robinson, and Hakeem Olajuwon prance on the couches. Ewing belongs there too.

The Jamaica-born and Massachusetts-raised 7-footer was no stranger to indignity. He was subjected to racist taunts from fans in high school and from Georgetown opponents, which included horrors like thrown banana peels and a bedsheet scrawled with "Ewing is an ape." In New York, even after making eleven All-Star teams and averaging 20.6 points, 10.5 rebounds, and 2.2 blocks in 135 postseason games, he was criticized as a choker who let the team down when it mattered most. Discussion of Ewing's legacy always includes being outplayed by Olajuwon in the 1994 Finals, bricking a finger-roll at the buzzer in an elimination game against Indiana, and getting dunked on, straddled, and emasculated by Scottie Pippen. The "Ewing Theory" popularized by writer Bill Simmons suggested that Ewing's teams performed better when he did not play.

Younger basketball fans might see Ewing as a lumbering colossus, legs mummified in thick knee-braces and hobbled by an Achilles tear, moving across the lane as slowly as a freighter to toss up his running hook. While there is regality in his final role as a doomed warrior, Ewing should be remembered as a basketball god. He was herculean and everywhere: smacking away shots, protecting rebounds with elbows extended to the width of a minivan, tossing in soft 16-footers, flying diagonally for trailing dunks

on fast breaks. Not only did he pull double-duty as the Knicks' leading scorer and bulwark of top-ranked defenses, he defined the franchise and created the imposing team identity that the organization and its fans still crave today.

Ewing saved basketball in New York—and the city has not experienced sustained NBA success without him. "I never thought I'd end my career somewhere else," he told his college coach on *The John Thompson Show*, after being traded to the Sonics after 15 seasons in New York. "I've been stunned for two days, walking around."

EYE TEST

Other than physical freaks like Steve Nash, no one is born to play basketball. Muscle memory comes from repetition. Jumpers are taught, deconstructed, and rebuilt. Hours are spent on defensive slides and hip pivots, closing out on shooters without fouling and boxing out. And yet, despite the clinical aspects of the game, some players look like naturals. Conventionally known as the eye test, basketball phrenology idealizes players who are tall, chopstick-legged, and straight out of casting for *Above the Rim*.

Even in warmups, certain players move with a smooth, lackadaisical shimmy. It is almost as if they are bored by the prospect of wasting their talents on the game they are about to play in. If you were picking teams at the playground, they are the ones who would get chosen before they touched a basketball. They usually wear a compression sleeve.

It is advantageous for a player to exhibit on-court attributes that fall under existing paradigms of basketball stardom. Namely, do you look like Michael Jordan? Or, for larger lads, do you look like Hakeem Olajuwon? We expect buttery spin moves and graceful, arabesque footwork. Jab-steps into fadeaways. Dunks that come screaming across the sky. The connection of visual cues and stereotypes transforms any short white dude into a heady, gritty, coach's son gym-rat who makes up for his

fourteen-inch vertical by covering 98 percent of his body with third-degree floor-burns.

It is a long-running cliché that prospects are inevitably compared to established stars that resemble them. For NBA executives, it is not just the appeal of familiarity, it is self-preservation. Gravitating toward conventional wisdom is rarely grounds for criticism—when in doubt, just draft Jabari Parker, a smooth 6-foot-8 forward whose pedigree included being a South Side of Chicago native, the consensus top high school player in America, and a star at Duke. Taking Joel Embiid and his fractured foot might get you canned.

In Knicks' lore, the 1999 selection of Frédéric Weis, a 7-foot-2 French center, remains a blight on the House of Dolan. Unknown, European, and drafted one slot ahead of hometown favorite Ron Artest, Weis never played in an NBA game for New York and was memorably decapitated by a Vince Carter dunk in the 2000 Olympics. For two decades, Knicks fans have jeered every draft pick that superficially shares Weis-esque qualities (notably Danilo Gallinari and Kristaps Porziņ́gis)—yet conventional flameouts like Trajan Langdon, William Avery, Cal Bowdler, and Quincy Lewis were also top-20 picks in 1999.

As Michael Lewis detailed in *Moneyball*, his book about Athletics executive Billy Bean and the rise of Sabermetrics in baseball, there is untapped value in players who flunk the eye test. In 2010, the Rockets used 6-foot-6 Chuck Hayes at center as a fill-in for Yao Ming. Hayes had gone undrafted, stuck around in Houston after signing a ten-day contract, and used an unorthodox free-throw form in which he froze at the point of release and held the ball for an extra, late-term pregnant pause. But he had quick hands and used his lower center of gravity to plant himself like a fencepost in front of bigger and more high-flying players. "We don't put enough premium as scouts, as organizations, on people that do whatever it takes to win," coach Mike D'Antoni said of Hayes in the *New York Times*. "He's got big heart, plays hard, smart basketball-wise. We don't put a premium on that. We put a premium on guys shooting or jumping."

CELEBRITY FANS

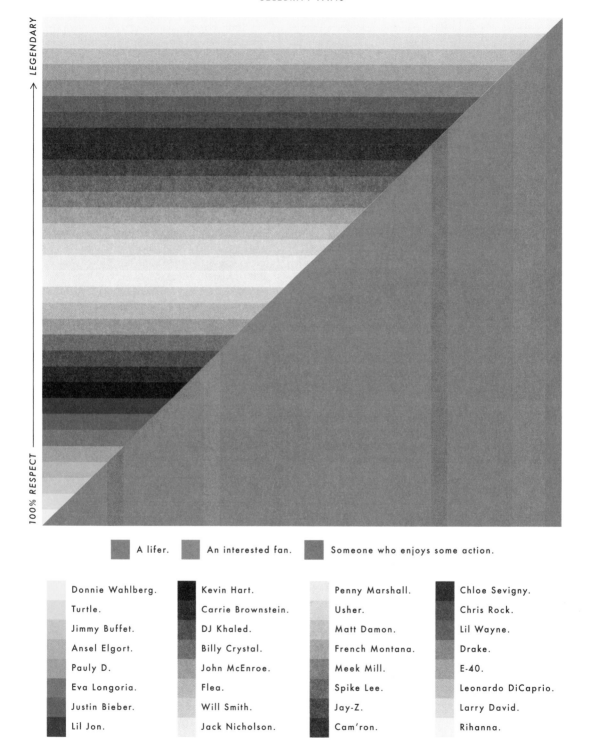

LEGENDARY →

100% RESPECT →

A lifer.   An interested fan.   Someone who enjoys some action.

Donnie Wahlberg.   Kevin Hart.   Penny Marshall.   Chloe Sevigny.
Turtle.   Carrie Brownstein.   Usher.   Chris Rock.
Jimmy Buffet.   DJ Khaled.   Matt Damon.   Lil Wayne.
Ansel Elgort.   Billy Crystal.   French Montana.   Drake.
Pauly D.   John McEnroe.   Meek Mill.   E-40.
Eva Longoria.   Flea.   Spike Lee.   Leonardo DiCaprio.
Justin Bieber.   Will Smith.   Jay-Z.   Larry David.
Lil Jon.   Jack Nicholson.   Cam'ron.   Rihanna.

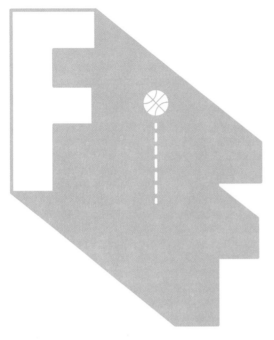

FANS

Due to proximity to the court, NBA fans are more tangible than spectators at other sporting events (like in hockey, where the savages on ice are separated from the savages in the crowd by thick plexiglass). This is not always a great thing— such as during the Malice at the Palace brawl or confrontations between fans and players like Russell Westbrook, Joakim Noah, or Isaiah Thomas. When Kyle Lowry tumbled into the stands during the 2019 Finals, he was pushed and cursed at by a Warriors minority owner who is a billionaire venture capitalist.

"Realize that we're still people at the end of the day," guard Fred VanVleet told Tyler R. Tynes of *The Ringer*. "It's not the zoo. And when you go to the zoo, you don't jump over the fence and taunt the tigers and shit like that. It's real consequences behind stuff like that."

But, overwhelmingly, the relationship between NBA players and fans is not so fraught. In larger markets, courtside seats at games—sitting wood, celebrity row, you could trip a referee—are a status symbol. At Madison Square Garden, one will inevitably spot Spike Lee prancing around like an orange-and-blue leprechaun, John McEnroe, Tracy Morgan, someone from an HBO show (usually Turtle, Johnny Drama, or Chris Moltisanti), or CC Sabathia. Over at Lakers games, bold-faced names on the sideline include Jack Nicholson, Flea, Ice Cube, Snoop Dogg and Will Ferrell. In Brooklyn, keen-eyed observers will identify the drywall king of Bensonhurst and the owner of the greatest beverage distributor in Borough Park.

With apologies to James Goldstein, who loves Saint Laurent and snakeskin, no one who serves courtside looks like Rihanna. She can be found in bucket hats, DKNY x Opening Ceremony collabs, and Céline dresses with plunging necklines. During the 2015 Finals, RiRi managed to roust Golden State executive Joe Lacob from his seat by loudly rooting for Cleveland's LeBron James. "I was getting irritated and said, 'I'm the owner of the Warriors,'" Lacob told *Chat Sports*. "She didn't care. Finally, I just said, 'That's it,' and moved a few seats away."

One megafan who blurred the lines between viewer and participant was Drake. As a Raptors loyalist who became an official team ambassador, the rapper was courtside during Toronto's title run in 2019, yapping at opponents, taunting Giannis Antetokounmpo after he fouled out, and giving coach Nick Nurse an impromptu shoulder massage. At various times, Drake has jawed with opposing players like Draymond Green and Kendrick Perkins. "I heard someone talking in the background with this soft voice," Perkins said later on *The Jump*. "It's a problem that you don't even want. At the end of the day, I don't have any beef with Drake."

After the COVID-19 outbreak, NBA games took place without fans in the Walt Disney World Bubble and, eventually, local arenas. While players acknowledged the absence of energy from home crowds, viewers at home were treated to cameras that lingered on the court and microphones that picked up more back-and-forth banter—as opposed to cutting away to Celtics fans wearing Jiří Welsch jerseys without a shirt underneath. Without Kiss Cams, children doing BlocBoy JB dances, and T-shirt cannons, all the family-friendly pomp was temporarily stripped bare, and our focus was fully on the players who make the product such a delight.

FERAL BIGS

Much like the invasive species of Eurasian boars that has swept across America, pillaging crops, gorging on native creatures, and occasionally killing humans, feral bigs are voracious frontcourt players who wreak havoc in hardwood biospheres. While related to stat hogs, feral bigs refuse to be tamed—they are unwilling and unable to be incorporated into contemporary NBA systems. Feral bigs are impressive in short bursts: they greedily root in the paint for points, forage for rebounds as if they were wild truffles, and provide a spike of activity from the center position that is initially mistaken as positive. But unlike lob-catching centers or stretch 5s, feral bigs are difficult to domesticate and rarely thrive in a structured offense or disciplined defense. Once they are liberated from the stockade, they return to roaming pastoral hillsides and lush glades, relentlessly oinking for the ball in the post, heaving up baby-hooks, and being hunted by pick-and-rollers. Examples of feral bigs include Enes Kanter, Al Jefferson, Greg Monroe, Bryant Reeves, and Eddy Curry.

FOURNIER, EVAN

A French national and a respectable combo-guard, Evan Fournier is best known for sharing his last name with a disease that can be described as dick gangrene. "By the way, NEVER google my last name," he once tweeted. "You don't wanna see that."

FOX, DE'AARON

Shooting can be improved by repetition. Thin frames can be freighted with muscle from kettlebells and wedges of ravioli-topped pizza. Film can be watched, cones can be dribbled around. Unusual quickness is more difficult to acquire. Double-time snappiness does not guarantee stardom—after all, it is a trait possessed by small men in a sport for mastodons. For every one Allen Iverson, John Wall, or Ja Morant there are scores of Tyronn Lues, Dennis Schröders, Ish Smiths, and Leandro Barbosas. Most speedsters eke out an existence scurrying for crumbs, not dashing to the top of the food chain. But players who move at a different tempo are X factors.

De'Aaron Fox pops. He was given the nickname of Swipa while playing elementary school basketball, a handle inspired by his knack for collecting steals and by the thieving fox from *Dora the Explorer*. When he has the ball, the 6-foot-3 lefty flits like a dragonfly, hovering momentarily then whizzing past flat-footed defenders. He chains jab steps and between-the-legs dribbles into sequences of misdirection, then bolts down the lane with the ball cuffed in the crook of his arm like a pigskin. Fox was among NBA leaders in drives per game in 2020, and defenders have learned to avoid being on the business end of his leaning throw-downs. He is one of the few players currently in the NBA who continues the tradition of showboating on breakaway dunks and is good for a windmill or a reverse jam.

Fox may not reach the open-court mileage per hour of long-legged sprinters like Ben Simmons or Giannis Antetokounmpo, but he is the speediest of men who are able to abruptly change direction. "I be watching film and I be looking at my feet and I be like, 'Man, there's no way people think I'm not the fastest person,'" he told *Yahoo Sports*. Drafted by Sacramento behind fellow point guard prospects Markelle Fultz and Lonzo Ball, Fox offered a combustible mix of bounce and haphazard shooting (he nailed only 24.6 percent of his 3-pointers during his single NCAA season). "When you're a point guard at Kentucky, I'm giving you the keys to the Maserati, man," said John Calipari, his college coach. "It's scary how fast he was."

GARNETT, KEVIN

A human Scotch bonnet pepper, Kevin Garnett had spiciness reserved for the Scoville scale. Sure, the first player to leap straight from high school to the NBA in the modern era was a champion, an MVP, a Defensive Player of the Year, and a fifteen-time All-Star. Of course, he finished his career within the NBA's top 20 in points, rebounds, steals, and blocks. And, yes, a case could be made that he was the most versatile basketball player ever.

But, unlike Hall of Fame–caliber peers such as Shaquille O'Neal, Tim Duncan, or Karl Malone, Garnett had an excellence that came with a wild-eyed, unhinged intensity. He was an abusive trash-talker whose antics included screaming in opponents' faces, crouching on all-fours to bark like a dog, and doing knuckle push-ups during games. Before Game 7 of the 2004 Western Conference Finals, he delved into an extended metaphor when describing his mindstate. "I'm loadin' up the pump," Garnett said on national television. "I'm loadin' up the Uzi. I got a couple M-16s, couple nines, got a couple joints with some silencers

on 'em. I'm just loadin' up clips. Got a couple grenades, couple missile launchers, with, you know, a couple missiles. I'm ready for war."

Garnett's exaggerated hostility baited detractors, who branded him as a fake thug, a studio gangster, and whatever other insults were popular in the early 2000s. He was seen as an instigator who would take refuge behind teammates instead of throwing hands. "Kevin Garnett was a porch puppy," his goony contemporary Kenyon Martin wrote in *Basketball News*. "A miniature chihuahua in a Dobermann's body." The Big Ticket also earned a reputation for doling out cheap-shots in the form of headbutts, over-aggressive picks, and blows to the groin. "I'm going to say it: He's a dirty player," said Joakim Noah of the Bulls. "I'm hurting right now because of an elbow he threw. It's one thing to be competitive and compete. But don't be a dirty player, man."

Although he was not a 7-footer, Garnett possessed every attribute advantageous in the sport of basketball: he was smart, fast, agile, coordinated, and indefatigable, able to score out of the post, pass from the elbow, and drill jumpers from 20 feet. While Garnett was not a victim of his era, it is easy to reimagine him as the greatest modern center had he been born a decade or so later. In the modern NBA, he would have been an effortlessly switchable, rim-protecting big man who thrived in transition and pushed his shooting range back a few feet—something he was oddly resistant to do. "When I walk around the streets, y'all can stop acting like you're shocked that I can shoot 3s," he said in 2012. "Everybody in Boston, everybody in the world, everybody in Minnesota, LA, wherever I'm at, Concord, Lexington, Burlington . . . I am here to do other things, not shoot 3s."

In retirement, Garnett played a magnetic version of himself in the Safdie brothers' film *Uncut Gems*. In the movie, which starred Adam Sandler, Lakeith Stanfield, and Julia Fox, his obsession with a hunk of Ethiopian black opal is tied into his performance in the 2012 playoff series between the Celtics and the Sixers. Other players considered for the role included Amar'e Stoudemire, Kobe Bryant, and Joel Embiid. "Because I'm a fucking disgusting, sick Knick fan, my instinct when I saw Kevin's name was, 'I hate him,'" co-director Josh Safdie told *The Ringer*. "I realized eventually that the reason why I hated him is because he's an incredible performer."

GENTLEMAN'S SWEEP

In comparison to a traditional sweep, a gentleman's sweep is completed with the losing team winning a single game. The sole victory theoretically provides a fig leaf of dignity to the otherwise exposed team. Not all solitary wins are equal: taking a game early in a series has greater psychological heft than when down 0–3 against a bored superior. For example, the Philadelphia 76ers' road victory in Game 1 of the 2001 NBA Finals (led by Allen Iverson's 48 points) was impressive during the Los Angeles Lakers' gentleman's sweep in Games 2–5.

GEORGE, PAUL

With an elegant bearing and a hairline unburdened by the passage of time, Paul George cuts a haughty profile on the hardwood. The blade-shaped wing plays with erudite detachment: preening with gooseneck follow-throughs after 3s, gliding into passing lanes for steals, and drilling step-back jumpers where he lunges away from defenders with the disgust of a midnight snacker encountering a waterbug. George's stylistic chilliness is warranted: he is a nearly flawless, annual All-Star who flirts with top-10 or even top-5 status. After spending the 2019 season on the Thunder, he finished third in voting for both Most Valuable Player and Defensive Player of the Year. Despite all this beauty, there are whispered suspicions of a latent ugly side: George might be a loser.

At 6-foot-8, George is a breezy plug-and-play solution at three positions, though he is most comfortable at small forward. Stick him somewhere and forget about it. He scores in isolation or as a spot-up shooter. He thrives in transition but can handle managerial duties as lead ball-handler in pick-and-rolls. He smothers guards on the perimeter while creating havoc all over the floor (he led the league in steals and deflections in 2019). "I feel like, say it is a LeBron or Carmelo, defensively I'm good enough to make him make turnovers or mistakes or bring him to reality," George told ESPN in 2013. "Offensively, I feel like I'm good enough to show what I got." A team might not necessarily be able to win a championship with the adolescently nicknamed PG-13 as its best player, but theoretically it is possible.

George hails from Palmdale, a dry Antelope Valley city of wide skies and deerbrush an hour north of Los Angeles. He is more country than his big-city airs indicate. "He's low-key as hell," his Thunder teammate Terrance Ferguson told *Bleacher Report*. "All he does is fish, which is kind of weird. If he had the chance to go fishing every day, he would be on that lake fishing." Paul's father was a carpenter who worked in a rim shop, his mother was a homemaker, and his two older sisters were high-level collegiate athletes. "I would beat him so bad sometimes, he would cry," said his sister Teiosha, who played basketball at Pepperdine.

George spent two seasons at Fresno State and was drafted by the Pacers with the tenth pick in the 2010 NBA Draft. Seldom used as a rookie, he rose to stardom amid a bitter Eastern Conference rivalry between Indiana and Miami—from which he emerged as a valorous but unsuccessful challenger to LeBron James. In 2014, George suffered a grisly leg injury while playing for Team USA that cost him all but six games of the following season.

While in the COVID Bubble as a member of the Clippers, George admitted the cloistered environment was punishing. "I underestimated mental health, honestly," he said. "I had anxiety. A little bit of depression. Just being locked in here. I just wasn't there. I checked out." After Los Angeles was upset in the second round by Denver—a wild series that included a seventh game where George went 4–16 from the floor with five turnovers and glanced a 3-pointer off the side of the backboard—his vulnerability was twisted against him like a stiletto. Despite Kawhi Leonard's 6–22 shooting performance in the final game, George took the brunt of the blame. The cawed refrain was that he lacked the mental toughness for the game's most defining moments. However unjustified the criticism, it did not help that he had once given himself the nickname of Playoff P.

GERALDS

The most athletic players in the NBA go by the name Gerald. It is unclear if they are twitchy superheroes as a result of being named Gerald or if they were named Gerald because their prodigious gifts required it. No one knows. Geralds include Gerald Green, Gerald Henderson, and Gerald Wilkins (brother of Hall of Famer and NBA Slam Dunk Contest

winner Dominique "the Human Highlight Reel" Wilkins).

A human catapult, Gerald Wallace earned the nickname Crash by launching himself across the basketball court with lovable recklessness. Born in Sylacauga, Alabama, he was a prized recruit as a teen. "Wallace runs the floor, hits the three, and plays every possession like it's his last," recruiting maven Brick Oettinger told *Sports Illustrated*. "Nobody has put on a show like him in nearly two decades." Lean, fast, and accessorized with flouncing braids, Wallace sprinted out on the break or hunted chase-down blocks with the resolve of a wolf pursuing an aging elk across unbroken snow. He was not a steady shooter, but excelled in areas that rewarded his raging motor: drawing fouls, snatching more rebounds than almost any wing, racking up defensive stats. The 6-foot-7 wing spent most of his prime on the Bobcats and, in 2010, made the All-Star team while anchoring the NBA's top-ranked defense. During that span, he suffered four concussions and had a lung punctured by a rib when he was flagrantly fouled by Andrew Bynum of the Lakers.

Jerry Stackhouse was almost a Gerald. An incendiary high-flyer who was a two-time All-Star with Detroit and the NBA's total points leader in 2001, Stack appears to have been given the name Jerry at birth. It is mind-blowing to conceive of the heights he could have reached had he been christened as a true Gerald.

GINÓBILI, MANU

Darting through mesquite trees and mesas of prickly pear cacti, Manu Ginóbili is the coyote, a trickster who outsmarts everyone else—and, sometimes, himself. Over a twenty-three-year professional career that spanned several continents, the Argentina-born swingman was a four-time NBA champion, Olympic gold medalist, EuroLeague titleholder, and one of the most influential spirit guides in modern NBA history.

Ginóbili played with unpredictable, oleaginous flair. He wheeled behind-the-back passes, flopped

unrepentantly, and imported the Euro step fifteen years before the footwork became part of every American kid's schoolyard repertoire. It felt familiar yet uncannily askew, as if basketball had been filtered through Google Translate and then raced back from the other direction. The 6-foot-6 lefty moved at a different tempo and saw angles from new perspectives. He played with eye-popping color but adhered to the limited modern palette of 3s, layups, and foul shots. In the *New York Times* magazine, writer Michael Lewis described Ginóbili as a "statistical freak" due to his weirdly balanced scoring. "He is equally efficient both off the dribble and off the pass, going left and right and from any spot on the floor," he wrote. There was no useful scouting report for Manu.

In an era before YouTube mixtapes and WhatsApp, Ginóbili was an unknown commodity while laboring in Argentinian and Italian leagues. His name was mispronounced during the 1999 NBA Draft, where San Antonio snagged him with the second-to-last selection. The Spurs were fresh off winning a championship and loathe to increase their immediate payroll. Financial motivations notwithstanding, the move would go down as the greatest late-draft coup ever and an inventive early use of the overseas "stash" gambit. "We got lucky as hell," Spurs general manager R. C. Buford would later tell ESPN.

The Spurs were already a thresher by the time Ginóbili arrived. He was a twenty-five-year-old rookie—ancient by NBA standards—in 2003, when the team won sixty games and another title. His fit was not seamless. Ginóbili initially rebelled against San Antonio's militaristic code of discipline and its lightless suppression of joy. But the team learned to live with his breaches of its somber ethos. "In the beginning, he would do some things that I thought were unnecessary," said head coach Gregg Popovich, before a 2017 game. "Until that point came when he came to me and said, 'I am Manu. This is what I do.'" In return for allowing an occasional indiscretion, the Spurs were rewarded with the ability to wage asymmetrical warfare.

Despite being the Spurs' best offensive player for a number of years, Ginóbili was part of the starting lineup for less than a third of his career NBA games. A devious playmaker and high-volume sniper who drained around 40 percent of his 3s, he swung between complementary and primary roles in the San Antonio offense. Yet Ginóbili was on the court whenever tension was as thick as carbonada criolla—he won Sixth Man of the Year in 2008 (and,

Real stars don't let the Red Rocket, aka the Sandwich Hunter, aka Matt Bonner, start over them.

The Spurs are allegedly boring, but this freak's playing like a crazed bat murderer on the run.

Every team should go to Argentina to pillage the Ginóbilis but not the Obertos and Herrmanns.

It's possible that this is the perfect shooting guard but with a schnoz and bald European energy.

This guy in New York would be in rap videos and have his jersey hanging in the 1OAK rafters.

truthfully, he could have won it almost every season). The stigma of coming off the bench didn't bother him, but he conceded that he was initially concerned that it would negatively affect his salary. "I understand when twenty- to twenty-three-year-old guys don't want to do it," Ginóbili told *USA Today*. "They want to [get] their numbers. They want to get paid."

Despite the Spurs' decades of success, it is tempting to wonder what Ginóbili could have done as the marquee attraction in a circus with fewer lion tamers and bearded women. In 2008, he ranked behind only LeBron James and Chris Paul by the metric of Box Plus/Minus. Was he ingeniously optimized or was the NBA deprived of a potential superstar who was hiding in plain sight? Popovich seems to ponder the same question. "I've always felt guilty about it," he said of bringing Ginóbili off the pine. "But I do it anyways." While Ginóbili was never pushed to reveal his true powers, there are clues. In 2010, he averaged 24.9 points and 5.6 assists on 63.9 true shooting percentage over a sixteen-game span in which starting guard Tony Parker was sidelined and the Spurs went 12–4.

On Halloween night of 2009, Ginóbili swatted down a confused bat that had disrupted a game between the Spurs and the Kings. There are mixed reports on whether the flying mammal survived the encounter. On a Facebook post, Ginóbili was rueful. "It wasn't a great idea," he wrote. "Not only for the fact that bats are [a] great part of the ecosystem, but also, because some carry rabies . . . avoid contact with bats, skunks, raccoons, rats and animals like that."

Ginóbili retired after the 2018 season, as the second-oldest player in the NBA. Two years later, he made news for carrying an elderly woman who had fallen on a sand dune to safety. An unorthodox hero to the end.

GOBERT, RUDY

Powerful, feared, and unloved, Rudy Gobert is an iron giant. The Frenchman, wonderfully nicknamed the Stifle Tower, is 7-foot-1 with a horizon-line wingspan. Since being drafted by the Nuggets late in the

FRANCE'S FINEST EXPORTS

Boris Diaw.
Rudy Gobert.
Tony Parker.
Baguettes.
Croissants.
Louise Bourgeois.

Nicolas Batum.
Evan Fournier.
Frank Ntilikina.
Ian Mahinmi.
Camembert.
Kevin Séraphin.

Champagne.
Joakim Noah's father.
Gérard Depardieu.
Guerschon Yabusele.
Mimes.
Quiche.

Perrier.
Bordeaux.
Striped sweaters.
Cigarettes.
Berets.
Frédéric Weis.

first round in 2013, and immediately traded to the Jazz, Gobert has been the league's most daunting interior presence: he has won Defensive Player of the Year twice and perennially ranks among the top 5 in blocks and rebounds. His career field-goal percentage places second in NBA history. Moored by the French Deflection and arms longer than the Thirty Years' War, Gobert has made Utah impossible to score on. But impact has not meant adoration.

Gobert has a demeanor that could be described as brusquely sensitive or sensitively brusque. "I understand that I'm annoying," he told ESPN, after clashing with teammate Donovan Mitchell. "I've been very demanding and maybe in not always a positive way." Gobert excels at underappreciated jobs. He fiercely protects the rim, slams lobs, and yanks down boards—but provides none of the inspiring je ne sais quoi we expect from a superstar.

Unlike the two other franchise centers of his generation, Joel Embiid and Nikola Jokić, the block-monsieur does not offer ballerino footwork, visionary passing, or the wonderment of seeing an enormous man do extraordinary things. Instead, he thwarts the artistry of others with the surliness of a car-burning Parisian yellow vest protester. To many, all the accolades cannot papier-mâché over his true nature: a stiff. "He is legitimately one of the best players in the league, but nearly none of the traditional ways of explaining it work," wrote Andy Larsen of the *Salt Lake Tribune*.

Few players are more disliked than Gobert. His hefty contract is mocked. Clips of him airballing two-foot shots go viral. He was taunted for an interview in which he grew teary after being snubbed from an All-Star team. The "screen assists" stat that he lords over is regarded as indicative of his illegitimate, nerdy stardom. He has been called disparaging names like Church of Latter-Day Ain'ts, French Bread Lohaus, Marc de Triomphe Eaton, Louis Vuittony Battie, Steak Frites Bill Wennington, Escargot Corie Blount, Samuel Camembert, Crepe LaFrentz, Eclair-y Sanders, Pâté Garrity, Coq au Vin Baker, and Marquiche Morris. Just horrible stuff.

After performatively rubbing a microphone during a press conference in defiance of COVID-19 safety protocols, he became the first NBA player to test positive for the coronavirus and caused the initial shutdown of the NBA in March 2020. Although science absolved him of being the league's Typhoid Mary, Gobert pledged $500,000 toward COVID relief in Utah, Oklahoma, and France. *J'adore!*

GOONS

Watch ten minutes of a televised NBA game and you will hear an old-school announcer complain about the lack of toughness in today's league. Following a preambulatory "Back in my day," they wheeze about how fouls that are now considered "flagrant"—physical contact deemed unnecessary or excessive— would have been mere caresses in decades past. This boomeristic claim is not inaccurate. There was a time when the league was more lenient in doling out fines and suspensions for body slams, elbows, and even fighting. In the 1987 postseason, for example, Celtics center Robert Parish clubbed Pistons forward Bill Laimbeer repeatedly in the face with a closed fist and was not called for a foul (after an outcry, he was suspended for one game and fined $7,500).

Players have gotten bigger, stronger, and more athletic, but rules have disincentivized chippy play. Committing two flagrant fouls in one game leads to an ejection, and an accumulation of violations over the course of the season or playoffs results in a suspension. Since the 2008 season, instant replay has been used to assess flagrant fouls (and, later, even potential flagrant fouls), meaning that justice was meted out immediately and with more accuracy.

Other measures dilute bad blood before emotions boil over. The seemingly useless "double technical foul," in which both players involved in a minor altercation are tagged with counterbalancing technicals, is intended to discourage retaliation without impacting the game in any meaningful way. Technical fouls for taunting, which have been on the books for ages, now include almost any kind of directed celebration: talking trash, pointing, staring down an opponent, even patting the top of one's skull to convey the message "on your head." In 2018, Lance Stephenson, the manic shooting guard, earned a technical for playing an air guitar. "He strummed right in front of a defender," said the announcer.

The curbing of violence has led to the near extinction of basketball's enforcer class. A willingness to lodge an elbow in an opponent's windpipe is no longer reason enough to keep a goon on the floor or even the roster. The decline of post play and the importance of offensive spacing create fewer interactions in the paint that can escalate into beef. Recent tough guys include Metta Sandiford-Artest (involved in Malice at the Palace chaos), Matt Barnes (chased Derek Fisher around a kitchen island because of a love triangle), James Johnson (a martial arts black belt), Jusuf Nurkić (an overgrown Nelson Muntz nicknamed "The Bosnian Beast"), Zaza Pachulia (more dirty than a brawler), Matthew Dellavedova (a small Aussie who loved rolling into opponents' ankles), and the Morrii (who categorically wanted all the smoke).

It is true that players like Charles Oakley, the rugged power forward who spent ten seasons on the Knicks, are rare today. Lionized in New York for his rapacious rebounding, contributions to league-best defenses, and enthusiasm for mixing it up, Oakley slapped Charles Barkley in the face and threw basketballs at the head of Tyrone Hill over gambling debts. Well into retirement, Oak was kicked out of Madison Square Garden during a 2017 game for heckling owner James Dolan. In an extraordinary scene that seemed normal only because it involved the Knicks, he tangled with a cadre of security personnel before being handcuffed and arrested. "I been jumped before," Oakley said later. "So my mind's automatically thinking, like, if you see seven, eight, nine, ten guys walking up on you, you have to brace yourself and be ready for the challenge."

One-dimensional goons are even more of a dying breed. Jamaal Magloire, a 6-foot-11 center who made his bones throwing bows, lasted until the early 2010s. With the exclusion of washed-up fan favorites, he was one of the least deserving All-Stars in modern history—although players like Chris Gatling or Kevin Duckworth could stake a convincing claim. Nicknamed Big Cat, Magloire was a terrible shooter, and a bad passer, and had an offensive repertoire limited to dunks and clunky baby-hooks. "Jamaal Magloire has a role and that role is to beat the hell out of people," said coach Stan Van Gundy.

A more contemporary ass-kicker was David West, an ethical king who patrolled the lane with righteous menace. He was a knotted 6-foot-9, with the countenance of a pissed-off undertaker. Despite winning two championships as a grouchy ring-chaser on Golden State, he was a throwback power forward from the Mondale era: brawny enough to rebound and defend the post, while cashing enough long 2s to give a center a wisp of oxygen around the basket.

West was an avid fan of boxing and trained in the ring. Once, when asked about his finest attribute off the hardwood, he reportedly answered, "My left hook." In 2012, he slap-boxed with Moondog, the Cleveland mascot, and dropped the anthropomorphic hound with a stiff right hand. After the encounter, the human inside the suit was taken to the hospital to get his eye examined. "I feel bad dude got hurt," West said after learning about the injury. "I thought I was just hitting the costume."

Despite the latticework of rules and draconian penalties created to prevent fighting on the court—a concern that is mysteriously absent from, say, baseball and hockey—professional basketball players are mocked for being uneager to exchange volleys of fisticuffs like inebriated pugilists. Even some of the league's more progressive figures perpetuate the idea that gargantuan, muscled, hypercompetitive athletes are, in actuality, soft as baby shit. "NBA fights are the silliest, namby-pambiest thing I've ever seen," scoffed Spurs coach Gregg Popovich.

GREEN, DRAYMOND

Draymond Green is a braying god of the forge who acted as the core of the Golden State Warriors' dynasty of the 2010s. His schizophrenic ingenuity on both sides of the ball, extrasensory intuition, and ability to thrive on the precipice of madness make him one of the most compelling superstars of his era. The 2017 NBA Defensive Player of the Year is also renowned for kicking other men in the balls.

After spending four years at Michigan State, Green entered the 2012 NBA Draft with some blemishes. He was seen as having less upside than younger underclassmen and being a pedestrian athlete, too small for power forward and too slow for small forward. "While his effort and aggressiveness will never be questioned, it is difficult to project him as an adequate NBA defender," wrote *DraftExpress*. Green was chosen in the second round, thirty-fifth overall, behind Arnett Moultrie and Fab Melo. He has made a vindictive parlor trick of reciting, in order, the name of every player selected ahead of him.

Coach Steve Kerr is lauded for turning Golden State's offense into a dynamo during the 2015 season, but the relationship between the Warriors' success and Green's expanded role is underestimated. Not only did Green's playing time soar in his third year

(from 21.9 minutes a game to 31.5), he was the fire-resistant sludge that cohered a title-winner around two elite perimeter shooters. Though a modest scorer who was erratic from beyond the arc, he became an archetypal hybrid of defensive specialist and playmaker—a long-tentacled menace capable of finishing each season among the league leaders in assists, rebounds, blocks, steals, and deflections.

The Warriors' fabled "Death Lineup," a dominant small-ball group during the team's 73-win 2016 season, was made possible by Green's ability to guard opposing centers. That year, Golden State's foes attempted to post him up 175 times, the second-most of any player in the NBA, and averaged a pathetic 0.66 points per possession on those plays (a mark that placed him in the 89.3 percentile of post defenders). It was a brutal double-whammy. Though Green's 6-foot-6 height lured teams into falsely believing their big men could overwhelm him in the paint, his strength, bandleader's timing, and 7-foot-1 wingspan were tools for basketball judo. Meanwhile, when the Warriors had the rock, unlucky centers were tasked with chasing a hyperactive creator who rumbled through the open court like a bowling ball careering down a stairwell.

In the 2016 Playoffs, Green went to war against the balls of his rivals—and potentially changed the course of NBA history with an accumulation of ball-strikes. In the Western Conference Finals, Green took on the Thunder center Steven Adams and repeatedly demolished his balls. In Adams's autobiography, *My Life, My Fight*, he described the balls-related incidents thusly: "The first kick was more to my shaft, but the second was straight to my balls . . . I was hunched over trying to breathe and not to cry . . . Draymond said it was accidental and I had no reason to believe any non-psychopath would deliberately kick another man there."

During the Finals, Green, still voraciously hunting for balls, ransacked LeBron James's balls. The amassment of flagrant fouls earned Green a suspension from Game 5, which allowed a Cavaliers team on the brink of elimination to pick up a critical win against the undermanned Warriors. The butterfly effect of ball abuse includes a Cleveland comeback, Kevin Durant signing with Golden State, James heading to Los Angeles, and the Warriors empire crumbling after winning only one reputable championship. Following his summer of ball-smashing, Draymond accidentally posted a photo of his dick on Snapchat.

GRIFFIN, BLAKE

A man who has done everything asked of him, Blake Griffin could never live up to his first impression. He has averaged more than 20 points a game, shot 50 percent from the floor, and made six All-Star teams. He is a wonderful passer who added a midrange jumper and, as the game shifted outward, developed a deep-ball reliable enough to cash as many 3s in 2019 as in the previous eight seasons combined. He won the NBA Slam Dunk Contest by hurtling a Kia, did stand-up comedy at the Laugh Factory, and dated Kendall Jenner (giving him the Kardashian blessing). Along the way, everyone soured on Blake Griffin.

Griffin went to the Clippers with the top pick in the 2009 draft, broke his kneecap in the pre-season, and returned a year later to win Rookie of the Year. One of the greatest in-game dunkers ever, the 6-foot-9 power forward was like an industrial refrigerator launched from a ballista. When Griffin was part of the Lob City trio along with Chris Paul and DeAndre Jordan, Clippers' games buzzed with the energy of a prizefight. Someone was getting dunked on.

At times, you saw it unfolding, as a lane sheared open during a pick-and-roll or Los Angeles flared into talon-like formation on a break. But it could also be abrupt, a drop-step into a pulverizing dunk or a putback where Griffin surfaced chest-high above a sea of players. He has short arms for a basketball player—his wingspan is only slightly above average—and some of his most celebrated dunks are really "throw ins," where he spiked the ball through the rim without touching it.

Besieged by injuries, Griffin is in his early thirties but seems like a remnant of a previous era. He is younger than Stephen Curry and Patrick Beverley. Griffin missed roughly 40 percent of his games from 2016 to 2020, and, more tragically, his seasonal dunk output crashed from a high of 214 as a rookie to only 39 rim-rocking slam-jams in seventy-five games of the 2019 season. And Griffin's cockiness turned into dickishness. While sitting on the bench during a 2015 game, he grabbed a kneeling trainer's head and yanked it toward his crotch. The following year, he broke his hand while punching the assistant equipment manager in the face multiple times during an incident in Toronto. In 2018, Griffin was traded to the Pistons and vanished from sight until joining the 2021 Nets as a rusty-framed buyout recipient.

GRIT 'N' GRIND

From 2013 to 2015, the Grizzlies had a beefcake reputation that was embraced by the organization, its players, and the city of Memphis. Known affectionately as Grit 'N' Grind, the era marked a new pinnacle for a franchise that had wallowed in the marshy lowlands since its birth as an expansion team in Vancouver. Prior to the arrival of this era, the Grizzlies had reached the playoffs only thrice in their fifteen-year history and were an embarrassing 0–12 after being swept each time.

Much like the championship-winning Spurs, the Grizzlies were a team that prized continuity and a yeoman work ethic. First coached by Lionel Hollins, who could have been a stunt double for actor John Witherspoon, Grit 'N' Grind was a four-wheeled monster truck: Marc Gasol (a Sierra Nevada–sized Spaniard who won Defensive Player of the Year in 2013), Mike Conley (took the floor in the 2015 Playoffs with three facial fractures), Zach Randolph (had a poster of Gangster Disciples founder Larry Hoover on his wall during an episode of *MTV Cribs*), and Tony Allen (a six-time member of the NBA All-Defensive Team). Memphis posted defensive rankings of second, seventh, and third in the league over a three-season stretch.

In 2014, the team's leading scorer and rebounder was Randolph, a coffee pot–shaped power forward nicknamed Z-Bo. Before Memphis, the two-time All Star from Marion, Indiana, had spent most of his career personifying the sins of other organizations. On the Portland squad dubbed the Jail Blazers, he punched teammate Ruben Patterson in the face and fractured his eye socket; in New York, he was another of executive Isiah Thomas's overpaid and underperforming acquisitions.

But with the Grizzlies, Randolph represented the team's salt-of-the-earth approach. The team's offense ran on whale oil—Memphis was last in the league in 3-pointers and free throws made—and he did most of his damage as a sturdy, low-altitude brawler in the short corner, using his elbows, shoulders, and hips to grease the skids for fall-away jumpers or running hooks. "This is us," Randolph said. "Scrappy, grit 'n' grind, hustling. We ain't fancy. We ain't running up and down the court throwing lobs and doing windmills. We in the mud."

The Memphis defense was anchored by Gasol, an unshaven man with a 7-foot-4 wingspan and the feet of a flamenco dancer. But the aesthetic representative was Allen, an indefatigable perimeter defender nicknamed the Grindfather who coined the "Grit 'N' Grind" motto. He tracked ball-handlers like a bounty hunter, slipping around screens to prod at the rock and jumping passing lanes for interceptions. In 2014 and 2015, he led the NBA in steals per 100 possessions. Kobe Bryant called Allen the toughest defender he faced, albeit in his self-aggrandizing way: "I could score 10 straight on him, he's not blinking," Bryant said at a promotional event in 2018. "He's still there, being physical. He's not backing down. . . . I finish playing with Tony Allen, I got scratch marks from here to here—and I love it."

In an era of sea change, Memphis was a school of prehistoric armored fish who snapped at anything that wriggled. The team routinely started three players—Gasol, Randolph, and Allen—who combined to average one 3-point attempt a game. In the 2015 Playoffs, a second-round clash between the top-seeded Warriors and underdog Grizzlies was elevated into an existential reckoning between coastal elite soy boys and real, barbeque-eating men. During a Game 2 victory in which Memphis defenders harried Stephen Curry into a 2–11 performance from deep, Allen lay on his stomach, slapping the floor and barking "first team all-defense!" Despite taking a 2–1 lead in the series, Memphis was eliminated in six games. As the Grit 'N' Grind window of contention faded, the team remained a gatekeeper in the manner of an aging prizefighter with a flattened nose and a granite chin—not good enough to win the belt, but a revealing tester of a rising fighter's mettle.

For years, Memphis resisted calls to slough off the roster's remaining talent for draft assets in hopes of jump-starting a rebuild. Through the reptilian eye of a bread-pricing McKinsey analyst, what is the econometric value of eking out forty-two wins and clawing for a seventh seed? But a zero-sum approach to team success ignores the sentimentality and love that a team, its players, and its fan base are supposed to share. Just as Magic Johnson's Lakers symbolized Los Angeles, Zach Randolph's Grizzlies spoke for Memphis, which even adopted the civic handle of Grind City. After being eliminated in the

playoffs by the Spurs, coach Dave Joerger broke down in tears at the postgame podium. "This season's been hard, really hard," he said. "They could have quit. Could have not made the playoffs. And every day they came out and fought like crazy." He went on. "So I hope as a community, and I know we do, we love our Grizzlies."

GUNS

Fortunately, America's bloody obsession with firearms has left the NBA relatively unstained by tragedy—but, this being America, guns are usually within arm's reach. Linguistic intersection between guns and basketball is natural: run-and-gun, shooters shoot, 3-point snipers, "Pistol" Pete Maravich, Chuck "The Rifleman" Person, Andrei "AK-47" Kirilenko. The Bullets had existed for more than three decades in Baltimore and Washington, but owner Abe Pollin was shaken by the 1995 assassination of Israeli prime minister Yitzhak Rabin. "My friend was shot in the back by bullets," he said. "The name 'Bullets' is no longer appropriate for a sports team." The team became the Wizards (which beat out names like the Sea Dogs and Express).

Players such as Scottie Pippen, Malik Beasley, Raymond Felton, Delonte West, and Kevin Porter Jr. were arrested for gun possession, as were former professionals like Sebastian Telfair, Corie Blount, and Oliver Miller. Robert Swift, who went 12th in the 2004 draft and spent five years with the Sonics franchise, was detained in a 2014 raid of a suspected drug house in Kirkland, Washington. Along with drug paraphernalia, authorities found a cache of nearly two dozen weapons that included pistols, shotguns, assault rifles, and a 4mm grenade launcher. The 7-foot-1 center was using heroin and, a few months later, was arrested in an attempted home invasion. "Don't make your entire life about basketball," Swift said in 2020, after cleaning up and joining a pro team in Spain. "Once I lost basketball, I had nothing."

In 2006, several members of the Pacers were involved in a melee outside of Club Rio, an Indianapolis strip club. As Stephen Jackson recounted on his talk show *All the Smoke*, he was leaving in his car when he saw teammate Jamaal Tinsley being accosted in the parking lot by men they had beefed with inside. Jackson got involved, and began the festivities with a pistol-whipping amuse-bouche. Then he started shooting. "I been in that position too many times," he said. "Before I get surrounded and stomped out, I'm gonna let off some warning shots: bow, bow." He was then hit by a moving car and thrown to the ground, knocking out his front teeth.

In the most tragic incident, Lorenzen Wright, a center who had played mostly for Atlanta and Memphis, was found shot to death in the Tennessee woods in 2010. The case remained a mystery for years, until the murder weapon was discovered in a lake and his ex-wife pleaded guilty to conspiring to kill Wright. He was thirty-four.

The oddest gun-related embroilment involved Gilbert Arenas, a three-time All-NBA guard on the Wizards. Nicknamed Hibachi, he was a gregarious futurist who ranked among league leaders in categories like points, steals, 3-pointers made, and free throws attempted. "There's ideology, and then there's Gilbertology," said Washington coach Eddie Jordan of Arenas's eccentricities, which included a habit for practical jokes and sleeping three hours a night.

During the 2010 season, a heated session of the card game Bourré on the Wizards' plane turned into an exchange of threats between Arenas and teammate Javaris Crittenton. "It was about me calling his bluff," Arenas told *The Action Network*, a sports gambling site. "You say you're going to shoot me? Fine, I'll bring you the guns to do it." And Arenas did, presenting four firearms in front of his Verizon Center locker—at which point Crittenton pulled out a semi-automatic handgun of his own and pointed it at Arenas's head (teammate Caron Butler gave a different account in which Arenas threatened to shoot Crittenton in the locker room).

After a league investigation, Arenas was suspended for fifty games, perhaps in part because he mocked the probe by shooting off finger guns during a pre-game dance routine. In an even more devastating epilogue, Crittenton was later sentenced to twenty-three years in prison after accidentally killing an innocent bystander in a gang-related drive-by shooting. According to prosecutors, he had joined the Mansfield Gangster Crips *after* being drafted as a first-round pick by the Lakers.

have had no time to reflect. I have not had time to look at my phone." The Popovich coaching tree is an oak, and Hammon should join the ranks of poached hires like Mike Budenholzer, James Borrego, and Monty Williams. "I look forward to the day where none of this is news," said Rudy Gay of the Spurs. "Just people accomplishing things and everybody having a chance and everybody having a shot at the same thing."

HAMPTONS 5

Few nicknames have ever been as appropriate as "the Hamptons 5." After the 73-win Warriors lost in miraculous form to LeBron James and the Cavaliers in the 2016 Finals, the organization launched a recruitment campaign aimed at seducing unrestricted free agent Kevin Durant. Their pitch, which drew scoffs of disbelief from the public, was that one of the greatest players in history should join one of the greatest teams in history. Golden State's pursuit began with a weepy postgame parking-lot phone call from Draymond Green to Durant, and peaked when four Warriors stars made an eastward pilgrimage to visit him over the summer in Long Island.

Durant's East Hampton estate was a five-bedroom, 7,400-square-foot manse on 3.2 acres that cost $100,000 for his ten-day vacay. There was a hot tub, two dishwashers, and a teak rooftop observation deck for admiring the ocean. He would pose in a sleeveless T-shirt on the cedar bridge near the gunite heated pool for a photo that accompanied the *Players' Tribune* article "My Next Chapter." In the editorial, he announced his decision to join the Warriors, citing a "potential for growth as a player" and "evolution as a man." So Durant signed with the 73-win squad.

The creation of the Hamptons 5, basketball's embodiment of late-stage capitalism, allowed the stupendously rich to get stupendously richer. It was birthed on the shores of one of the wealthiest places on the planet, as if Aphrodite had emerged from the seafoam strung with pearls and gulping fistfuls of caviar. With Durant lured into the fold, the Warriors seemed to fulfill the prophecy of principal owner Joe Lacob, a Silicon Valley archduke who invested in companies like Autotrader. "The great, great venture capitalists who built company

HAMMON, BECKY

Known as Big-Shot Becky for her timely buckets as a WNBA superstar, Becky Hammon joined the Spurs' coaching staff as an assistant in 2014. She was technically the league's second woman coach—Lisa Boyer was a part-time, volunteer assistant with Cleveland in the early 2000s—and proceeded to check off a number of historic NBA firsts. The South Dakota native was the first woman to coach in summer league, the first woman to coach in an All-Star game, and, after San Antonio coach Gregg Popovich was ejected during a matchup with the Lakers in late 2020, the first woman to coach an NBA team in a regular season game. "I try not to think of the huge picture and huge aspect of it because it can be overwhelming," she said after the game ended in a loss. "I really

after company, that's not an accident," he had said in the *New York Times* magazine. "We're light-years ahead of probably every other team in structure, in planning, in how we're going to go about things."

At any rate, there was little difference between the Hamptons 5 and the twenty-four-year-old Manhattan publicists who chip in on a summer house with visions of lounging by the pool and browning-out off watermelon margaritas at Ruschmeyer's: in the moment, the promise of boundless hedonism felt worth whatever it cost.

The Hamptons 5 immediately won a pair of championships with a cumulative Finals record of 8–1, but the victories were soulless. The quintet was omnipotent and unloved, like a tech disruptor whose hunger for monopoly poisons an established biome, and everyone was complicit: Durant, his Warriors teammates, the Golden State front office. With an unprecedented wealth of talent, the team turned from an orchestra of ball movement into dueling banjos. They grew sloppy. They shrugged on defense. Grumbles that Golden State had violated the competitive spirit of basketball followed the team like trash juice behind a garbage truck.

As a bored and irritated media stoked rumors of tension, the Warriors appeared to barely enjoy the experience themselves. In one vinegary post-game argument, Green called Durant "a bitch" and reminded him that the team was a champion before his arrival. After injuries to Durant and Thompson led to a loss in the 2019 Finals, the Hamptons 5 disbanded to a collective "good riddance" from the public and rest of the league. The greatest team ever assembled is remembered as a blip of inconvenience.

HARDAWAY JR., TIM

A pilot version of the point guards who would lay waste to the NBA decades later, Tim Hardaway Jr. was a shrew-sized offensive terror who made five All-Star teams with Golden State and Miami. Not only did he blur the lines between scorer and distributor—which at the time caused consternation over his "true" backcourt position—his snapping crossover and love of 3-pointers were futuristic. An ACL injury in 1993 cost Hardaway his unmatchable quickness, but, within four years' time, he had recovered enough to lead Miami to 61 wins and the Eastern Conference Finals. "He's a 6-foot Magic,

that's what he is," Heat coach Pat Riley told the *Orlando Sentinel*. "He's tough-minded. He's competitive. He challenges you."

Hardaway's signature move, the "UTEP two-step," named after his father's collegiate career at the University of Texas at El Paso, even predated the arrival of Allen Iverson and his own ankle-breaker. Hardaway has grumbled about a perceived lack of credit. "Iverson carried the ball," he said. "I had the original killer crossover and people are doing my move." However true, the underappreciated innovator was owned again by the GOAT's response: "I carried my crossover all the way into the Hall of Fame," said Iverson.

In 2007, Hardaway made a fool of himself on Dan Le Batard's radio show. "I hate gay people," he said. "I don't like gay people and I don't like to be around gay people. I am homophobic. It shouldn't be in the world or in the United States." He was banished from NBA All-Star weekend. After apologizing, Hardaway became an advocate for LGBTQ rights and was the first person to sign a petition to legalize gay marriage in Florida. He believes those comments have kept him out of the Hall of Fame—but his career postseason record of 21–35 does not provide the hull for an ironclad case.

HARDAWAY, PENNY

Like a drawer of old love letters, Anfernee "Penny" Hardaway evokes warm memories and an unsatisfiable pining to know what could have been. He was a supreme being sucked of divinity by knee injuries and part of a tandem with Shaquille O'Neal that was cleaved apart before either reached their mid-twenties. In only his second season in the league, the 6-foot-7 point guard was an All-Star and part of a 57-win Orlando team that reached the NBA Finals. "You never know what's going to happen," Hardaway said on the brink of Game 1 against the Rockets. "We could have injuries. There could be trades. This might be our only time we ever have to compete for it all."

Hardaway grew up in a three-room house on a dusty, dead-end road in Memphis. His grandmother nicknamed him Pretty but his friends engineered a remix. Between his freshman and sophomore years at the University of Memphis, he and several pals were robbed at gunpoint. One of the highwaymen

fired a gun at the ground and the bullet ricocheted off the pavement to break several of Hardaway's toes.

In the 1993 NBA Draft, Hardaway was selected by Golden State with the third pick and immediately shuffled to Orlando (along with three future first-round picks) for top selection Chris Webber. Magic fans jeered the deal, but ownership was giddy. "Penny was just dazzling," said Pat Williams, Orlando's general manager at the time. "In the very last workout, he hit a 3-pointer to win the game and walked off the court like, 'Is there anything else you want to see?'" When Hardaway was coupled with O'Neal, the top pick from the prior draft, the Magic became an expansion franchise that struck thick veins of lottery gold twice.

With narrow shoulders, long limbs, and angular features, Hardaway resembled a regal mink. His height, ball-handling, and passing abilities earned comparisons to Magic Johnson at a time when the ability to dribble was cuffed to the point guard position (today, he would be a much more elasticated Luka Dončić). Hardaway used his size advantage to post up smaller defenders and had an array of spins that created drop-step dunks or space for step-back jumpers. "It was deadly," he said of his signature ability to whirl in either direction. "Once you spun, you kinda spun into, like, freedom."

His hops, wingspan, and spatial awareness made him unstoppable in transition, and he seemed to float for an extra heartbeat in midair, calves tucked, before beheading a victim with a tomahawk or twisting to deliver a pass to a trailer. Hardaway made four consecutive All-Star Teams between 1995 and 1998, averaging 20.7 points and 6.5 assists over the span, and was the subject of a Nike campaign featuring a doll named Lil' Penny. "Move Over, Michael: It's Penny's League Now" screamed a headline in *Sporting News*.

But Hardaway's words about an unpromised future took on the gloom of Cassandra predicting the fall of Magic Kingdom. After a 60-win 1996 season, Orlando bungled negotiations with O'Neal and he decamped for Los Angeles. Then, in 1998, the killer: Hardaway suffered the first of a series of microfracture injuries to his knee. Within six years, he had undergone five operations and was a shell of himself. All we have left is unrequited love. "The age of the 6-foot-7 point guard is kind of a thing of the past," he has said.

HARDEN, JAMES

To some, the greatest offensive force in modern basketball represents everything that is wrong with an era and the sport. Here is James Harden, the 2018 Most Valuable Player, multiyear scoring champion, and reactor core for some of the most nuclear teams in league history. In the minds of his loud detractors, however, his grandmastery is deniable for reasons that are less about roundball than about aesthetics and the spirit of fair play. To them, Harden is the ultimate cheeser.

While the *New York Times* declared Golden State's Stephen Curry the "Player of the Decade" in 2019 (and offered an alternative case for LeBron James), the best candidate was Harden. He is not a bony extraterrestrial who arrived at the perfect moment for a paranormal shooter, nor a brawny Stan Lee superhero who would have manhandled the game in any epoch. Instead, the combo guard is the personification of an offensive evolution that has reshaped the NBA to the point of unrecognizability. He is a scorer-distributor hybrid who rejects mid-range jumpers, voraciously hunts free throws, and hoists up 3s with more of an emphasis on volume than accuracy. In 2019, he took 1,028 3-pointers—eight more than the 2010 Grizzlies attempted as an entire team. Harden is the bearded incarnation of contemporary basketball.

Harden was born in Los Angeles and raised by his mother in nearby Compton, a city that earned notoriety when DJ Yella made it a cappella. His first love was baseball. "I was a little Randy Johnson," he said. By high school he was a basketball star, and named to the McDonald's All-American team beside Derrick Rose and Kevin Love. After two years at Arizona State University, he declared for the 2009 draft. Scouts praised his "NBA-readiness," uncanny balance, and creativity as a facilitator, but there were doubts about his athleticism.

Selected third by Oklahoma City, Harden was the cherry atop a three-year run in which the Thunder also scooped up Kevin Durant, Russell Westbrook, and Serge Ibaka with first-round picks. It was an obscenity of talent. In the coming years, three of them would win MVP Awards. The team made the 2012 Finals in Harden's third season, almost as a lark. They were a crew of high school buddies on a humid summer night, wasted off Budweiser Lime-A-Ritas, and vowing eternal friendship as they inked each other with matching stick-and-pokes. The future was wide open.

Harden's initial job in Oklahoma was acting as connective tissue between the franchise's two established young superstars. He had the positional sponginess to complement the contours of their rigid games, but could massage bench units into usefulness by himself. At his best on the ball, he plays a game that is an infuriating jumble of jerking head-fakes, Euro steps, and drives that end in foul shots or layups or pratfalls. With glazed eyes and most of his lower face obscured by the bushy beard, Harden courts the rage of opposing players with the flat demeanor of a good internet troll.

In 2012, Harden won Sixth Man of the Year while Westbrook and Durant were named All-Stars for, respectively, the second and third times. "It took me three years to embrace that role," Harden said. But the snuggle party ended early. That summer, Harden and the Thunder could not reach an agreement on a contract extension—although the difference between the maximum deal he asked for and the team's offer was not chasmic. "That $4.5 million gap was symbolic: a test of Harden's commitment to the Thunder," wrote Sam Anderson in his book *Boom Town*, which wove the civic history of Oklahoma City with the short life cycle of the Thunder trio. Harden was aware of the criticism. "I heard that I was greedy, that I didn't care about winning," he said. "Heard the questioning of my loyalty."

Rather than let uncertainty linger through the final season of Harden's contract, the Thunder traded him to the Rockets. The bounty included Kevin Martin, a fine wet-noodle scorer, along with Jeremy Lamb and draft assets (one of the first-round picks became center Steven Adams). At the time, reactions were split between skeptics who were unsure if Harden deserved a monster contract and those who were aghast that Oklahoma City had cut the stem of a blooming dynasty. Daryl Morey, former general manager of the Rockets, fell into a slightly different camp. "I actually can't come up with any examples of a player of his caliber and age getting traded at the time he was traded," he said, gleefully. Years later, after the deal became viewed as a fleecing of the Thunder, Morey revealed that several other teams had passed on the chance to "easily" outbid the Rockets' offer.

Over the next seven seasons, Houston mutated to stay ahead of a league that adopted its principles of shooting, spacing, and pace—and Harden was as inseparable from the team's philosophy as Seth Grundle, the scientist in *The Fly* who melded with an insect between teleportation portals. From 2013 to 2020, his 3-point attempts per game doubled from 6.2 to 12.6.

While elevated usage almost always sandbags efficiency, Harden seems immune to that inverse relationship—his performance has been oddly impervious to an expanded workload. "They say if you put Michael Jordan on a team now he would do more than James Harden," said Morey. "That's possible. But if you're just saying: 'NBA history, if you give this guy the ball, how much does his team score after you give him the ball before the other team gets the ball?' It's James Harden. And I know that makes people mad, but it's literally a fact."

It is difficult to pinpoint why Harden is so unguardable one-on-one. He isn't mercury quick or a forceful finisher above the rim. While his handle has a hypnotic, staccato rhythm, his ball-handling isn't in the same category as Kyrie Irving's or Stephen Curry's. The conventional take was that he had sly, "old-man game." A few years ago, Harden visited the P3 sports science facility in Santa Barbara, California, and underwent a battery of tests designed to test physical attributes like vertical and lateral acceleration. He was average for an NBA athlete. But his "eccentric force" was in the 98th percentile. To put it simply, he has the best brakes in the NBA. His inexplicable ability to create space on step-backs or abruptly change direction made sense. "I didn't know before I was tested, but I can feel the difference," Harden told the *Wall Street Journal*. "I know what I'm great at and what I'm not great at—and I use it to my advantage."

Harden's knack for unearthing competitive edges makes people unhappy. Over his first eight years in Houston, he led the NBA in foul shots attempted seven times. He is a flopper who earns calls for going beyond the margins of traditional respectability: purposely entangling his arms with those of a defender, abruptly rising into an unnaturally awkward shot to induce contact, veering into opponents on drives. He draws more fouls on 3-point shot attempts than entire teams, due to his willingness to fire up shots with defenders in his face and a knack for subtly kicking both feet forward to create the illusion of an over-aggressive closeout. "They already let Harden travel on his step-back, and now he wants a foul too?" said Myron Brown,

who played a grand total of four games for the Timberwolves in 1991, in an *Undefeated* article titled "James Harden Is Disrespecting the Unwritten Rules of the Game." "I feel like the way these NBA guys expect calls today, if they came to the playground, I could give them the business right now."

Harden (reportedly) has more fans in the gentlemen's club industry. One Reddit user attempted to link his on-court play to the reputation of strip clubs in NBA cities. "I have proven, to a statistically significant degree, that James Harden's game performance declines in cities with higher-rated strip clubs," posted user AngryCentrist (real name Ryan Sullivan). The methodology came into question when it was revealed that the data ranked Salt Lake City's strip clubs ahead of those in Miami. Perhaps due to his stigmatization as a strip club connoisseur, Harden denied attending adult establishments during his successful, scorched-earth campaign to get traded from Houston to Brooklyn in 2021.

HEAT CHECK

After players make several consecutive jumpers, they are entitled to heave up a ridiculous, off-balance attempt from 40 feet away with defenders wrapped around their limbs. This is called a "heat check." In theory, this terrible shot is very wise: it is used to ascertain whether a player is simply shooting well or completely *en fuego*. If a player makes a heat check, he is allowed to take increasingly insane attempts until he misses. Jocks and nerds love to argue about the existence of the so-called "hot" hand, but neither side confronts the possibility that ritualistic heat checks might gum up data on streaky shooting. While the cosmic alignment of balance, propulsion, and touch can arrive with the rarity of a Great Conjunction, some players never leave that transcendent headspace. Dion Waiters, a shooting guard who has played for teams like the Cavaliers and the Heat, is famed for his belief—however accurate—that every shot he takes is going in. "I called it an irrational confidence, a

bravado to his game," said Miami coach Erik Spoelstra. "He has so much confidence in his own abilities that it becomes contagious to the rest of the team."

HEAT CULTURE

In the NBA, everyone wants to be a working stiff. "We're blue-collar players on a blue-collar team in a blue-collar town," said Ben Wallace, the rock-chewing center who starred for the 2000s Pistons. DeMarre Carroll, a 3-and-D wing who played for teams like Atlanta and Brooklyn, voiced similar proletarianism. "Blue-collar guys who play hard," he said, "you can tell that those guys have never had nothing handed to them." And when Milwaukee debuted new uniforms with a blue stripe on the collar, it was described by the team as a literal nod to the "blue-collar work ethic of not only the Bucks, but also of the city and state."

We get why franchises praise ham-and-egger values. Dogged effort, defensive focus, unselfishness, overachievement, smaller paychecks than they deserve, and so on. Every American city has a population of Joe Lunchpails who grouse in a regional lilt about the clowns in Congress while squinting at the carburetor of a rusted sedan. Adopting the vocabulary of class struggle is a nice way to pretend that billionaire owners, multimillionaire players, and ticket-purchasing proles are all on the same side. When the Sixers debuted an alternative uniform before the 2021 season, co-owner Chris Heck said the jersey design represented "New Philadelphia," a civic vision at odds with Yuengling-addled, battery-flinging fans. "We actually don't use the term 'Philly' because we think it's lazy and undersells the city," he said. "And sometimes I think 'blue collar' does the same thing." He apologized before his house was burned to the ground.

No team has harnessed plebeian energy more successfully than Miami. Despite playing in a city famed for cocaine, silicone implants, and bottle-popping debauchery, Heat Culture is an updated

Imposing. Slight. Not mean. Mean.

Armrests on benches.
Ben Wallaces.
Draymond Greens.
Emeka Okafors.

Jonathan Isaacs.
Patrick Beverleys.
Rocks under bridges.
Roy Hibberts.

Rudy Goberts.
Shawn Bradleys.
Skatestoppers.
Sloped windowsills.

Spiked handrails.
Studs on ledges.
Tony Allens.
Water sprinklers.

version of the ethos team president Pat Riley made famous with the Knicks of yesteryear: in his own words, "the hardest working, best conditioned, most professional, most unselfish, toughest, nastiest, most disliked team in the league." Back in 1997, the Heat won 61 games with the league's top-ranked defense and a core that included maulers like Alonzo Mourning and P. J. Brown—and the franchise has stuck to the mold.

Mourning, a Georgetown product in the bloodline of sentinels Patrick Ewing and Dikembe Mutombo, was a seven-time All-Star who won back-to-back Defensive Player of the Year awards in 1999 and 2000. He wore a goatee and a scowl, and vacillated between stoicism and molten rage like a vengeful samurai. After averaging 21.7 points a game and leading the league in blocks during the 2000 season, Mourning was diagnosed with focal glomerulosclerosis, a life-threatening kidney illness that would require a double transplant in 2003. He was cut down in his prime, missing a whole year and most of several others. But Mourning clawed his way back to health and the NBA, providing key reserve minutes behind Shaquille O'Neal on Miami's 2006 championship team and leading the league in postseason scoring efficiency. "There's no one on the face of this earth that's playing a sport at a highest level with a transplant," he said. "That alone continues to inspire me, because I realize throughout the whole world the struggles that people are going through."

In recent years, Mourning became the source of a treasured GIF that shows him on the sideline during a 30-point loss, shaking his head unhappily and then, after reconsideration, nodding in acceptance. "If you look at the score of the game, you can see why I had that facial expression," he said, when asked about the clip's popularity. "I'd like to think I was actually talking to myself."

Today, the Heat mystique includes grueling practices, weekly body-fat measurements, and, more recently, Jimmy Butler arriving at the gym at 3 a.m. and telling everyone about it. "If you have any ounce of soft in you, you're not gonna make it over there," said former shooting guard Josh Richardson. For seventeen years, the team's witch doctor was Udonis Haslem, a Miami native and accredited tough guy who helped acclimate younger teammates to the Heat. "Can't nothing happen in Miami without me knowing about it," he told *The Ringer*. "So whatever they're doing out there, I'm going to hear about it."

In fairness, most teams steep their identity in nostalgia. The Lakers forever yearn to recapture the Showtime era, with Magic Johnson tossing flashy passes as Jack Nicholson cackles on the sideline. The Celtics lust for a white star and a six-team league. The Knicks crave being respected as humorless goons who will protect Madison Square Garden by rocking you in the face with your nose bone.

HOODIE MELO

A late-career alter ego for Carmelo Anthony, Hoodie Melo was unveiled in the summer of 2017 as a figure whose passion for basketball was rivaled only by his love of playing the sport in a sweatshirt. In clips from workouts and pick-up games around New York City, Hoodie Melo was a monk-like figure with an obscured face. But that talent for bucketry was familiar. There were smooth running hooks from 15 feet, a dozen consecutive 3s from the top of the arc, vertical dunking drills, slithering drives around scrimmage partner LeBron James, endless spinning fadeaways, and late-night defensive slides in a Manhattan park.

"It started with a beanie," Hoodie Melo said at a media event after being traded to Oklahoma City (while wearing a Thunder jersey over a black hoodie). "I was just in the gym and I didn't have a haircut. I wanted to sweat. From there, it went to a hoodie and it got out. The phenomenon started." J. R. Smith, who was Anthony's teammate on both the Nuggets and the Knicks, detected a deeper change. "I think Hoodie Melo doesn't play with a conscience," said Smith, who has never been accused of playing with much restraint. "I like the Hoodie Melo better."

HOSTILE ARCHITECTURE

Hostile architecture (or defensive design) uses unfriendly physical elements to control behavior and deter unwanted interactions. Examples from

public spaces include armrests on park benches to prevent vagrants from sleeping, studs or brackets on smooth surfaces to keep rail-sliding skaters at bay, or bird spikes on windowsills to stymie defecating pigeons. These principles can be applied to hardwood real estate. Due to the relationship between shot value and the layout of the court, defenses need to make certain areas inhospitable. The emphasis is not only on making shooters miss—it is also aimed at preventing shots from being taken at all. If a shot is open, it doesn't matter if the nearest defender is a long-limbed wraith or a knob of butter. Like fencing off a street grate where an unhoused family could huddle for warmth on a subzero night, creating an environment of discomfort is a key to successful defense.

But not every great defender is visually intimidating. Shawn Bradley was 7-foot-6, played for the 76ers, and wore the jersey number 76. Despite being a zoodle-thin Mormon coming off missionary service in Australia, he was taken second in 1993 by Philadelphia—ahead of Anfernee "Penny" Hardaway. He lasted a little more than two seasons with the team and was widely regarded as a laughingstock, in part because opponents dunked on him repeatedly with barely contained glee.

While he is best known as a bony oddity who had a role in the original *Space Jam* film, Bradley led the NBA in block percentage six times and finished his career among the top 20 in career swats. From 1999 to 2001, the Mavericks' defense gave up, in successive years, 9.1 points, 11.0 points, and 13.1 points less per 100 possessions with the "Stormin' Mormon" on the floor. In that third season, his presence on the court was statistically the difference between the league's best-ranked defense and its worst.

Even as a gangly victim of violent posterizations, Bradley had the impact of a superstar on that side of the ball. "If you're in the NBA, you're going to be on the receiving and the giving end of that, by nature of being in the league," he said when accosted by TMZ during retirement. "I enjoy the challenge . . . it's okay to get dunked on. If you're shying away from the challenge, it's less effective." In 2021, Bradley suffered a serious spinal cord injury, which left him paralyzed, when he was struck by an automobile while biking near his Utah home.

HOWARD, DWIGHT

Can a sledgehammer be lovable? Dwight Howard tried. In his first incarnation, the top overall pick in the 2004 draft was a grinning, prank-playing menace with kettlebell shoulders for the Magic. He joined a franchise that had been scalded by the departure of Shaquille O'Neal and merrily wedged himself into that void, even appropriating O'Neal's Superman nickname and wearing a cape in the NBA Slam Dunk Contest (setting off a decade-long feud between the two centers). As Orlando's muscled linchpin, Howard led the NBA in categories like field-goal percentage, blocks, and rebounds.

While Howard came into the league as a teenager who hoped to use sports to introduce fans to Christianity, his wholesomeness was debatable. He had several children out of wedlock, reportedly showed his penis to adult-film actress Mary Carey, and dished out enough hard fouls to be called "Dwight Homicide" by the *Chicago Tribune*. Even after winning three Defensive Player of the Year awards and carrying Orlando to the 2009 Finals, he was seen as equally great and grating. When Howard was traded to the Lakers, former Magic teammate Glen Davis described him as "a great farter," elaborating with, "He can fart. He can fart loud. The loudest farts. Silent farts."

After disappointing stints in Los Angeles and Houston—perhaps due to complications from an injured back—Howard's star waned. He eventually returned to the Lakers as a backup in 2020, and contributed to the Bubble title by catching lobs and administering rib-cracking screens (he also was second in the NBA in fouls per minute among qualifying players). With greater ambitions replaced by self-awareness, Howard's zany bullying felt like a remnant of a bygone era and even nonbelievers were, at last, converted.

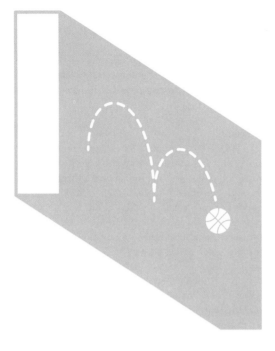

IGUODALA, ANDRE

An intellectual who excelled at clingy defense and unselfish aspects of offense, Andre Iguodala was underappreciated as a star but immortalized as a role player. His résumé includes three championships, the 2015 Finals MVP award, an All-Star appearance, two NBA All-Defensive Team listings, and an Olympic gold medal. "If I had to rank the smartest basketball players I've ever been around, I'd put him right there with Manu Ginóbili and Scottie Pippen," said Golden State coach Steve Kerr. "He's got that kind of basketball mind. He's brilliant."

When Iggy (as he hates to be called) joined Allen Iverson's Sixers as a rookie lottery pick in 2004, he naturally was dubbed "AI2." That coincidence only added to the feeling of primogeniture when the GOAT was traded in late 2006 and Iguodala inherited the estate. Despite posting excellent numbers—in 2008, Andre logged 19.9 points, 5.4 rebounds, 4.8 assists, and 2.1 steals per game—Philadelphia's media and fanbase groused that the best player on the team was not a legitimate "number-one option" and grew convinced that his standard mini-max contract had cinched the franchise purse strings.

Before the 2013 season, Iguodala was sent to Denver in the infamous Andrew Bynum trade. Though the Nuggets lacked big names, Iguodala—along with Ty Lawson, Danilo Gallinari, and Kenneth Faried—led the "star-less" cast to 57 wins, a 38–3 home record, and a 24–4 mark after the All-Star break. The team offered a glimpse of the blueprint general manager Masai Ujiri would later use to build the Raptors into a championship team. Paced by a hyper-aggressive assault, the Nuggets heaved themselves at the rim in transition, leading to copious points in the paint, free throws, and offensive rebounds. The dark-horse contender pulled up lame when Gallinari ruptured his anterior cruciate ligament and was lost for the playoffs. Without their second-leading scorer and most dangerous shooter, the Nuggets fell in six games to the Warriors in the first round.

That summer, in a move that eerily predated Kevin Durant's desertion from the Thunder to the Warriors, Iguodala signed with the team that had ousted him from the playoffs. While winning three titles in Golden State, he was corrupted by the immorality of Silicon Valley and became an investor in tech start-ups like Casper mattresses and Jumia, an e-commerce portal that hopes to become the Amazon of Africa. Despite his meaningful contributions to the Warriors, Iguodala was immortalized as the victim of a game-swinging, Game 7 chase-down block by LeBron James in 2016.

In the COVID Bubble, Iguodala played for the Heat in a jersey with "Group Economics" stitched on the back. "It's essentially how systemic oppression doesn't allow us to buy from our own communities, or get loans to build businesses so we can support ourselves and recycle our dollar," he told *USA Today*. "That's how you build your community, get better funding for schools, and how you invest in yourself and become landowners. The system is created for us not to be able to do those things."

INJURY GUYS

According to one adage, the greatest "ability" is "availability." Maybe! But a bad ironman does not

push a team closer to winning a title, and a fragile stud who gets healthy at an opportune time may elevate a franchise to new heights. It can be argued that staying healthy is a skill—like vertical leaping or spatial awareness—yet its presence is inconsistent and most visible in retrospect. Because basketball involves activities like running and jumping, the course of NBA history has been altered by injuries large and small. Title dreams have been dashed and would-be dynasties turned to castles in the sky.

We only glimpsed the sublime potential of players like Anfernee Hardaway or Grant Hill before injuries robbed them of their explosiveness—but at least they enjoyed long careers. Brandon Roy, a smoothly versatile wing from Seattle, did not get that. He was named to three consecutive All-Star games while averaging 21.1 points a game for the Blazers. By his mid-twenties, it was over, due to degenerative knee issues that left bone scraping on bone. "If I never play another game, I'll still be completely happy with my career," he said, after a failed comeback in Minnesota at the elderly age of twenty-eight. His injury luck did not improve after retirement: in 2017, Roy was shot in the leg—reportedly while shielding children after gunmen opened fire outside his grandmother's house in Los Angeles.

There is no greater symbol of grievous injury than Derrick Rose, a player ordained as Chicago's chosen one. The top overall pick in the 2008 draft, he grew up on the rugged South Side and returned as the Bulls' savior. He was a startling athlete, a contempo hybrid guard who placed among league leaders in scoring and assists. Although not much of a shooter, Rose had spasmic choppiness off the dribble, a galloping stride in the open court, and the ability to squat in midair while deciding how to scoop in a layup. His running floaters kissed high and softly off the glass. With Rose winning the 2011 Most Valuable Player award, it was presumed that he would challenge LeBron James for ownership of the Eastern Conference over the next decade.

Rose's dour attitude—which could be read as either stoic or sour—appealed to a reactionary subset of basketball fans. They were the type who disliked modern music, unless it was made by Talib Kweli. When Rose refused to dance during the 2012 All-Star Game introductions, grillmasters celebrated as if they had scored a new stainless-steel spatula. "Look at the disdain on Rose's face as LeBron goes into full shuck and jive mode," wrote a blog called *We Got This Covered*. "His passion is all about winning, and not clowning."

After three straight All-Star appearances, a series of devastating knee injuries kept Rose sidelined for all but 49 total games over a three-season span. By twenty-six, he was a shell of himself. Sapped of spectacular finishing abilities, his spotty perimeter game and average defense stuck out as unignorable liabilities. His reputation as a silent martyr took a darker turn in 2015, after a woman accused Rose and two of his friends of sexual assault. Although he was found innocent by a jury, his testimony included disturbing details, like unfamiliarity with the word "consent." The basketball world has grappled uncomfortably with the court case, viewing it alternatively as another hurdle that Rose has "overcome" or as indicative of a person that no one (except coach Tom Thibodeau) should want on their team.

Other players never even get a chance. Taken first overall by Portland in the 2007 draft, Greg Oden was a 7-footer whose incredible potential went fully unrealized due to cataclysmic knee trauma. He was subjected to mockery because of his weathered physical appearance and being selected ahead of Kevin Durant. Despite playing only 105 games and 2,028 minutes in the NBA, Oden showed glimpses of the talent that enticed the Blazers to scoop him up after his freshman year at Ohio State. He was wildly productive per 36 minutes in his abbreviated second season, averaging 16.7 points on 64.7 true shooting percentage, 12.8 rebounds, and 3.4 blocks (all rates that would have placed him among league leaders, had he played enough to qualify). A broken left kneecap ended his year and, for all purposes, his career.

Oden seemed unhappy. He carried a heavy spirit, both in his shuffling gait and a somber face carved out of a furrowed tree trunk. In 2010, he was photographed standing beside a young woman while wearing an orange shirt that read "Long story short, I F*CKED HER!" Soon after, a bathroom selfie that he had snapped of himself (and his penis) leaked online. He later admitted that he had locked himself in the house for three days after the photo went

Would've been: ■ Forgettable. □ One of the 30 top-15 players ever.

Allan Houston.
Amar'e Stoudemire.
Anfernee Hardaway.
Antonio McDyess.
Bobby Hurley.
Brandon Roy.
Bryant Reeves.
Dajuan Wagner.

Danny Granger.
Danny Manning.
Derrick Coleman.
Derrick Rose.
Emeka Okafor.
Gheorghe Mureșan.
Grant Hill.
Greg Oden.

Jabari Parker.
Jay Williams.
Jonathan Bender.
Kevin Johnson.
LaPhonso Ellis.
Larry Johnson.
Larry Sanders.
Markelle Fultz.

Royce White.
Shawn Bradley.
Steve Francis.
T.J. Ford.
Todd MacCulloch.
Tom Gugliotta.
Tracy McGrady.
Yao Ming.

viral, even as porn companies offered him movie deals. "I'm not going to apologize for it," he told Mark Titus of *Grantland*, a former AAU and Buckeye teammate. "After all, I'm human and there are worse things that 21-year-olds could do. When a girl sends me 100 pictures, I have to send something back every now and then. I'm not an asshole."

Thankfully, there are tales with more uplifting endings. Players like Shaun Livingston, Joel Embiid, and Zach LaVine recuperated from serious injuries early in their career. Caris LeVert, a crab-like combo guard whose stock dropped in the draft due to college injuries, has been plagued as a pro by maladies that include a frightening broken leg and ligament damage in his thumb—but keeps returning with strong results. In an odd twist, a cancerous growth in his kidney was uncovered only by a physical after LeVert was traded from Brooklyn to Indiana.

The story of Žydrūnas Ilgauskas would be a more instructive fable if he wasn't a giant by virtue of a genetic shell game, but it provides a lesson about the crooked path of destiny. Early in his career, the enormous Lithuanian with a velveteen shooting touch endured multiple operations on his feet, and suited up for an average of only 22 games a year during his first five seasons with the Cavaliers. "If you are going to make a mistake," Cleveland team president Wayne Embry told *Sports Illustrated*, "I always say make it a seven-foot-three mistake." And yet, after Ilgauskas's livelihood was jeopardized by the nightmarish sequence of injuries, he proved incredibly durable, missing only a total of 14 games over one five-season span. "Every time I walked off the court, it was a little victory for myself," Ilgauskas said.

IRVING, KYRIE

Kyrie Irving is a bundle of contradictions that everyone agrees upon. He has unrivaled basketball talent, but is rarely considered a top-10 player. He made one of the most clutch 3s in NBA history in the sensational 2016 Finals, but is viewed as a locker room virus who shrugs at losing. He is sensitive and thoughtful, but traffics in Prison Planet conspiracy theories. He is a marketing turbine with sneakers that fly off the shelves in Asia, but comes off as a boyish millennial loner. He deems sportswriters "pawns" who are unworthy of his interviews

but donates millions of dollars to charitable causes. All these qualities peacefully coexist.

Irving is a shade under 6-foot-2 in stocking feet and built like a cyclist. While dazzlingly quick, he is not in the NBA tradition of guys who can graze their teeth on the rim. Instead, Irving's stardom is a victory for low-altitude excellence. He is a daring scuttler who thrives amid the bulging roots and detritus of the forest floor, zipping across a shaded realm that is inhospitable to those squawking in the canopy above. Descriptions of Irving's game require qualifications. It is possible that he is the most skilled player ever, if we limit the definition to elements of basketball that require coordination, balance, quickness, and precision.

With the rock, Irving is a winking sleight-of-hand artist who understands that a trick relies on how it is unveiled. He uses a variety of pitter-patter crossovers to create room for jumpers or to shift direction, spins through crannies on a foot-wide turning radius, and maneuvers defenders into ball-screen tar pits. While not overtly a showboat, Irving does relish toying with foes, yanking them off their feet like strung marionettes or leaving them spinning in his wake. He was in a series of lovable Pepsi commercials (and an eponymous 2018 feature film) in which he roasted ballplayers on tri-state playgrounds in the guise of an elderly man named Uncle Drew. "Kyrie has the best handle of all time," shooting guard Eric Gordon told *The Undefeated*.

The NBA has an extraordinary number of shot-makers—players with the ability to put the ball through the basket regardless of circumstances—but Irving's knack for canning shots with a gnarly degree of difficulty is peerless. His layup package includes leaning scoop shots, looping one-handed jelly reverses, and Euro steps into lefty floaters. He attributes his mastery of angles and English off the glass to a childhood spent playing on a broken hoop that he and his father had assembled. "A corner of the backboard came out," Irving told *Bleacher Report* in 2017. "I had two choices, I could change my direction and only go left, or I can learn how to spin the basketball on my backboard so I can use it to my benefit."

Before shoddily assembling backboards, Irving's father was a professional basketball player on the Bulleen Boomers in Australia. Kyrie was born in Melbourne but his family moved to West Orange, New Jersey, while he was a toddler. As a schoolboy star, he was ranked third in the class of 2010. He attended Duke University, but was limited to eleven games due to a ligament injury in his toe—which saved Irving from being sickened by the toxic aquifers of Durham.

Irving was selected by Cleveland with the top pick in the 2011 NBA Draft, drawing comparisons to smallish, student-of-the-game point guards like Chris Paul and Mike Conley. Hometown icon LeBron James had departed for Miami the season before, leaving behind him a trail of charcoaled Cavaliers jerseys and a 19-win campaign. To lottery conspiracy theorists, Irving was the consolation prize for an embittered franchise that had been ghosted by the league's greatest superstar.

Despite winning Rookie of the Year, Irving did not earn a sterling reputation in Cleveland. The Cavs averaged only 26 wins over his first three seasons and he was reportedly accused by then-teammate Dion Waiters of passing only to his friends, being permitted to take bad shots, and playing slovenly defense. When James returned to Cleveland in 2014, he sounded like a man who had come home to discover that Airbnb guests had smeared feces on the wallpaper and peed on the plush carpeting. "A lot of bad habits been built up the past couple years," he told the media after a post-loss locker room discussion with Irving. "When you play that style of basketball, it takes a lot to get it up out of you."

Back then, the enigma of Kyrie being Kyrie was attributed to immaturity or the plague of losing that had infected Cleveland during James's hiatus at Club LIV. But even after three trips to the Finals—which included a 7-game victory over the 73–9 Warriors— his weeded-out version of ambition or wanderlust kicked in. Tired of laboring in James's shadow, he requested a trade and was dealt to the Celtics before the 2017 season. Later, when thrust into a mentor role in Boston, he called James to apologize for his youthful behavior. "I wanted to be the guy that led us to a championship," Irving said of his relationship with Celtics like Jayson Tatum and Jaylen Brown. "I did a poor job of setting an example for these young guys."

Despite a pre-season press event where Irving vowed to play out his career in Boston, his love for New England clam chowder curdled. The team underperformed and seemed to play with more verve when he was injured. Younger players rolled their eyes at his veteran routine. The little green hand of the Beantown Media Mafia went from gently caressing Irving's ego to smacking his ass. "Kyrie needs to stop talking about leadership," Bill Simmons tweeted in February 2019. "He's terrible at it. He's incredibly fun to watch, but if they traded him within the next 6 days . . . I'd honestly be fine with it." That summer, Irving fled Boston and teamed up with fellow free agent Kevin Durant in Brooklyn.

Irving's opaque motivations confound traditionalists. He does not appear driven by money, winning championships, or erecting a house of worship dedicated to his own greatness. In some ways he is the millennial Iverson, a representative of his generation who swapped baggy Girbaud jeans and hip-hop aesthetics for emotional sensitivity and inscrutable trolling.

Irving has received wads of attention for an appearance on Richard Jefferson's *Road Trippin'* podcast in which he expressed skepticism about the conventionally accepted shape of the earth. It is unclear whether he arrived at this moment of ambivalence by tumbling down a YouTube wormhole of *Ancient Aliens* videos while baked-as-hell or by virtue of his own curiosity. "Can you openly admit that you know the Earth is constitutionally round?" he asked the *New York Times*. "Our educational system is flawed. History has been changed throughout so much time. I literally got that from what they did to Nikola Tesla." While Irving was in on the joke—he carried a hardcover copy of *National Geographic Family Reference Atlas of the World* while boarding the Boston team plane during the 2019 Playoffs—his resistance to being pinned down on his precise beliefs is what makes him captivating.

Unfortunately, the perception of Irving as a conspiratorial goofball—rather than, say, a mischievous or sensitive soul—has caused people to take him less seriously on subjects of real-life importance. Although he was vice president of the NBA Players Association, his concern that playing in the COVID Bubble would detract from nationwide civil rights protests was brushed off as disruptive and misinformed (specifically by those with vested interests in the resumption of the 2020 season). Irving was, of course, right. And when he went incommunicado on the Nets early in 2021—coincidentally or not, right after the insurrectionist attack on the US Capitol— there were gasps that he was seriously contemplating retirement. Irving missed a total of seven games.

Obscenely gifted and endearingly flawed, Irving is a high-maintenance partner that every team is willing to put up with—until the moment arrives when they aren't.

ITALIANS

Italians . . . playing basketball? It may sound like that scene from *The Sopranos*, in which lovable scamp Ralph Cifaretto and pudgy Vito Spatafore sweat out the gabagool playing driveway one-on-one, but several of their countrymen have spent time in the NBA. Unlike Spain, whose international cred was carved in stone by the Gasol *hermanos*, Italy has not had a signature basketball import to rival San Marzano tomatoes. In the modern era, two paisanos—guard Vincenzo Esposito and forward Stefano Rusconi—arrived during the 1996 season, though they combined to play in 37 career games. Only five more Italian-born players entered the league over the next quarter-century, and none have been named to an All-Star or All-NBA team.

By most accounts, Andrea Bargnani was supposed to be a spicy meatball. Selected first overall in the 2006 draft by Toronto, he briefly represented one recipe for a modern big man. He was a 7-footer with an outside shot as moist as chicken cacciatore, some mobility, and enough herky-jerkiness to fake an onrushing defender out of his Gucci loafers before charging to the hoop. "He's going to be a match-up nightmare in his prime, once he gets stronger, probably being the player most resembling a young Dirk Nowitzki that you've seen in a while," wrote *DraftExpress* in 2005.

Bargnani wasn't a bust, nor was he good. He posted 21.4 points a game in 2011, but his bag was a greasy sack of Papa John's slices: 44.4 percent of his shots were long 2s and he dished out only 1.8 assists a game. For a big man, he was a lousy defender. The next season, while injured, he moaned to *La Gazzetta dello Sport*, an Italian newspaper, about the Raptors' lack of success. "We are pretty much the worst team in the NBA," he said in his native tongue. Fans and members of the media were already skeptical of perimeter-oriented bigs, and he did not dispel those panettone-soft stereotypes. With awful shot selection, disinterest in passing or rebounding, a leisurely approach to defense, and the basketball IQ of a block of mortadella, he incurred great wrath,

particularly after signing an extension with the Raptors worth many lira.

After general manager Masai Ujiri took over the Raptors in 2013, his first move was dealing Bargnani to the Knicks for a first-round pick, two second-round picks, and several players with unappetizing contracts. He played out his contract in New York, but was clipped in broad daylight by the organization's new capo. "A.B. was and still is a big tease," said Phil Jackson, who inherited Bargnani as team president. "When he was injured, he refused to do simple non-contact activities like dummy our offense in practice. He seemed to be a malingerer."

The town famed for Arthur Avenue's moozadell and rapper Jojo Pellegrino had more luck with Danilo Gallinari, an Italian forward selected by the Knicks in the 2008 NBA Draft. The young EuroLeague MVP had an ally in New York coach Mike D'Antoni, who played professionally for Olimpia Milano, spoke Italian, and dreamed of featuring "the best shooter I've ever seen" in his Tuscan brushfire offense.

When the Rooster was healthy, he had sprezzatura. He developed into a sneering, glassy-eyed gunner who used his 6-foot-10 stature and deep shooting range to exploit matchups against smaller or slower foes. Despite the footspeed of a five-hour osso bucco, Gallinari drew copious fouls by entangling himself with defenders on drives toward the bucket, much like a glob of stracciatella. But D'Antoni's Milanese feast was pulled from the oven too soon. Midway through Gallinari's third season, the sniper was traded to Denver as the centerpiece of a deal for Carmelo Anthony.

Capellini brittle, Gallinari has missed unhealthy chunks of every season since leaving New York. In 2013, he was the leading scorer on a rising Denver team before blowing out his ACL, an injury that caused him to miss the entire next season. During his hiatus, he opened Pagani, a restaurant in Manhattan's West Village neighborhood that sold $2.89 mimosas during brunch. Before its closing, the trattoria was praised on Yelp by user Alexandra L. as an "Ultra romantic date spot in the West Village" with "great food that's easy to share," although Danielle M. preferred "omelettes that have the ingredients in the egg as opposed to more like a burrito, and this was pretty much a burrito with the egg as the wrap." The Rooster has yet to respond.

IVERSON, ALLEN

Back in 1970, a column published in Cherokee County, South Carolina's *Gaffney Ledger* juxtaposed Pete Maravich, a rookie shooting guard on the Hawks, to the shiftless ilk of his generation: "While you were out smoking marijuana, Pete was playing basketball like the good, American boy," wrote the essayist. It included this kicker: "Pete is now a millionaire." To today's conservative intellectuals, that prototype of young NBA player—hardworking, drug-free, and deserving of vast wealth—is a thing of the past, an abstraction supplanted by, as they see it, a dangerous variant. Thug, criminal, ball-hog, team cancer, lazy malcontent, fortune squanderer. Or Allen Iverson.

Iverson grew up in the East End of Newport News, Virginia, a place nicknamed Bad News. His father, the leader of a local gang called the Family Connection, bounced in and out of jail before going to prison in 1996 for stabbing a woman. His mother was fifteen at the time of Allen's birth. "When the nurse brought him to me, I looked at his little body and saw those long arms and said, 'Lord, he's gonna be a basketball player,'" Ann Iverson told *Sports Illustrated*. Light bills went unpaid, a broken pipe spewed raw sewage onto the floor, friends were murdered and incarcerated. As a junior at Bethel High School, Iverson was named the Associated Press High School Player of the Year in basketball and football.

On Valentine's Day of 1993, Iverson and three friends were arrested after brawling with a group of white teens at a bowling alley. None of the white participants were arrested, but he was convicted of "maiming by mob" and sentenced to five years in prison. "It's a high-tech lynching without a rope," said Marilyn Strother, an organizer who rallied against the sentencing. Iverson spent four months at Newport News City Farm before Governor Douglas Wilder granted him conditional clemency (later, an appeals court overturned the conviction). By virtue of his supernatural gifts, Iverson was able to escape anonymously tumbling into the American meat-grinder that has devoured Black lives for hundreds of years.

As his mother knew, Allen was the chosen one. Even by the impossible standards of professional athletes, he was peerless—a sinewy, 6-foot outlier among the fieldstone-shouldered caste of generational deities like Jim Thorpe, Jim Brown, Bo Jackson, and LeBron James. On the court, Iverson moved in a spasmodic blur. He seemed to glide on a different plane than everyone else, shifting with precise coordination to hit a third gear, vanishing with a soft sonic burp to magick a 1-on-3 break into a 1-on-0 layup. Despite his size, he was unyielding. Over his first twelve seasons, Iverson averaged a shocking 41.8 minutes a game while leading the league in the ironman category seven times. "He is, indeed, a prodigy," wrote talk show host Tony Kornheiser in 1995, after watching him play for Georgetown University, "with talent so stunning he shimmers on the court like light reflected off a mirror."

Iverson came to kill your idols. As a rookie, he crossed-up Michael Jordan and buried a jumper in the face of His Airness. It was not a transfer of power, exactly, but the moment when it became clear that Jordan's reign was not indefinite (the clip remains just as poignant today, due to Jordan's decision to retire following the Bulls' 1998 championship instead of succumbing to younger wolves like every other superstar). When Iverson went up against Utah's John Stockton, he snarled, "No fucking white boy is going to stop me."

The Answer won Rookie of the Year and four scoring titles, led the league in steals for three consecutive seasons, and was named to eleven All-Star and eight All-NBA teams. In 2001, he was honored as Most Valuable Player and dragged a low voltage Sixers team to the Finals. His postseason career average of 29.7 points per game is the second-highest in NBA history. After Jordan's departure, there was a several-year window in which Iverson was, unquestionably, the nastiest basketball player on the planet (even if big men like Shaquille O'Neal and Tim Duncan may have been more effective). "I wasn't a point guard," Iverson said after being elected to the Hall of Fame. "I was a killer."

Even as Iverson became the NBA's most popular superstar, he remained enmeshed in scandal. He was accused of ejecting his naked wife out of their home and then showing up at a cousin's house with a gun (all charges were eventually dropped). He put out a rap song under the name Jewelz that included lines like "gats in each hand / twin 4-5s in mine." His tattoos were airbrushed away in photos, his rap album was shelved, his voluminous jeans and chest of platinum chains were banished by league dress code decree. Yet as a teammate, he was beloved. "We had a lot of guys who were just kind of journeyman, guys who hadn't really stepped out and came into their own," Theo Ratliff, a former Sixer, told HoopsHype. "He helped push us and elevated our game and our status

as NBA players. He's a tremendous person." When the younger brother of team president Pat Croce rifled through Iverson's baggy pants in the locker room and stole money, he declined to press charges.

In recent years, there has been an irresponsible compulsion to reframe Iverson as a controversial antihero instead of one of the baddest motherfuckers in the history of basketball. He is acknowledged as an important countercultural figure who shifted paradigms in fashion, branding, and attitude—but is increasingly seen as Monta Ellis with a compression sleeve. Part of this inaccurate portrayal is due to the natural leveling effect of time and recency bias. The peak stature of almost every superstar from the past is eroded by crashing waves of new talent. Hal Greer, another player who spent much of his prime on the Sixers, went to ten consecutive All-Star games from 1961 to 1970, and no one under sixty has ever heard of him. But Iverson was too successful and remains too visible to attribute this rewritten storyline entirely to the swirling zephyrs of time. "I don't think people realize how cold he was," said Kobe Bryant, who cited showdowns with Iverson as motivation for improving his defense. "They have no idea how hard it was to guard this guy."

The greatest threat to Iverson's legacy is the fetishization of efficiency. For his career, he shot 42.5 percent from the floor and 31.3 percent from beyond the arc, both numbers that are inky blemishes when compared to contemporary volume scorers like James Harden or Stephen Curry. But it goes unmentioned that Iverson spent his prime in the early 2000s—his unsightly 51.8 true shooting percentage during his 2001 MVP campaign was exactly NBA average.

The game was played between the fluted Corinthian columns of M. J.–inspired architecture: if you had an offensive star, you soaked the floor with defenders and hoped your go-to guy could drag the phalanx to a brutish victory. Over a five-year span, only the Lakers and Spurs won titles, carried by the aforementioned O'Neal and Duncan.

To some, Iverson is a creature of the millennium NBA. It is believed that his dismal field-goal percentages, spotty perimeter shooting, and taste for contested floaters would not be tolerated in today's game. In truth, he played twenty years too early. Offenses built around singular scorer-distributors like Harden and Luka Dončić flourish. Shooting has unclogged lanes. According to stats for pace (the number of possessions a team gets

per game, on average), the slowest tempos in NBA history all fall exactly within Iverson's late-1990s to mid-2000s prime. The idea that one of the fastest and most unguardable players ever would struggle to eat in today's pace-and-space savanna defies reason. "A.I. would be the point guard and you would surround him with shooters and then just have him run a ton of pick-and-rolls," said Clippers coach Tyronn Lue, describing how Iverson would have been used today.

Sadly, Iverson spent his prime under the eye of coach Larry Brown, a micromanager with a mildewed offensive playbook, who bobbed between passive aggression and shoving his players under the bus. On the 2001 team that went to the Finals, Iverson started alongside Eric Snow, George Lynch, Tyrone Hill, and Dikembe Mutombo. Outside of the Answer, the other starters hit a combined average of 0.3 3-pointers a game. "We tried to get defenders and rebounders and unselfish guys with him because I wanted him to shoot the ball," Brown told *Maxim*. "Allen created double-teams wherever he was on the court. If he missed, we became the best rebounding team in the league." How can one compare Iverson's efficiency in that system, under that coach, with those teammates, in that era, to optimized weapons like Steph Curry or Steve Nash?

As divisive as Iverson was during his fourteen-year career, he has been vindicated. He was right about the blurred future of backcourt roles and the value of the hybrid scorer-distributor. He was right about the wear and tear of practice. He was right about pushing the tempo and playing with fluidity. He was right about the simplicity of putting the rock in the hands of your best player as many times as possible. He was right about the NBA's jittery tightrope act of selling a product created by young Black men to an audience that is fearful of them. Iverson separated the old NBA from the new NBA. In return, both his predecessors and his descendants have used him as a cudgel to hammer away at whatever they dislike about the sport.

But unlike other former players who speak with bitterness about today's game, Iverson has shown nothing but love and support for today's generation of stars. He embodies the joy of basketball.

NBA SUBCULTURES

□ Awesome. ◯ Normal. ◖ Scary.

Action figure freaks.
Allen Iverson Reebok nerds.
Ben Simmons truthers.
Big Face Coffee hipsters.
Crypto currency incels.
Encyclopedia authors.
Eye-test evangelists.
Hall of Fame truthers.
Jordan 1 originalists.
Kyrie Irving futurists.

League Pass hackers.
Nu-metal Knicks beatniks.
Podcasting influencers.
QNBA cyberthugs.
Season ticket nihilists.
Shitposting tweeters.
Sneaker zealots.
Tranquil Gen-X extremists.
Vintage jersey casuals.
YMCA health goths.

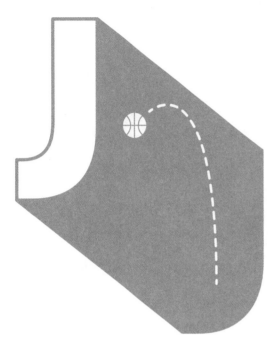

convicted of attacking a man who had scratched his car, and was arrested for domestic abuse. Qyntel Woods, who played only 1,007 minutes as a Blazer, was sentenced to twelve months of probation and eighty hours of community service for participating in dogfighting. Wallace, the team's star power forward and spiritual shaman, was suspended for seven games for threatening an NBA referee outside the Portland arena after a 2003 game—although the ref was Tim Donaghy, who gambled on games that he officiated. Colin Cowherd, then at Portland's KFXX 1080 AM, savaged the team in his autobiography, saying they were among "the most reprehensible group of humans who ever shared a locker room."

Despite the common portrayal of Portland as a twee Xanadu of hipsters patronizing waffle trucks, Oregon was created as a "white utopia" and neo-Nazis squirm comfortably throughout the region. "We can go 40 miles down the road and people are still being hung from trees," Isaiah "J.R." Rider told a writer from the *Oregonian*. And, in retrospect, much of the Jail Blazers' notoriety was steeped in the prejudice that arises when young, famous, and wealthy Black men attempt to lead normal lives in a predominately white city. For example: "We'd be flying somewhere after a game, and they'd be watching 2 Live Crew videos," said Kerry Eggers, who was a flight attendant on owner Paul Allen's private jet. "They were like soft porn—not appropriate for a team plane, in my view." A horrifying platinum-selling album!

Mostly, the Blazers' crime was taking the team name literally. In 2002, Rasheed Wallace and Damon Stoudamire, a AAA-battery of a point guard and a Portland native, were pulled over traveling back from a road game in Seattle. Police smelled marijuana and Wallace admitted that "they had smoked one 'J' but that all the drug was gone," according to the police report. A search of the yellow Hummer yielded a quarter-sized gram of weed, and the duo was cited for misdemeanor possession. A year later, Stoudamire was arrested for trying to sneak an ounce and a half of sticky through a Tucson airport by wrapping it in aluminum foil—and was fined $250,000 and suspended by the Blazers for three months. Later, Stoudamire submitted to (and passed) a drug test by a writer from the *Oregonian*, a creepy violation of personal and professional privacy.

Ironically, the state made marijuana sales legal for recreational purposes in 2015. "Really, what did Damon and Rasheed get in trouble for?" asked Antonio Harvey, their teammate at the time, who

JAIL BLAZERS

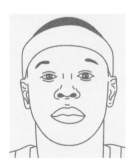

From the late nineties into the early aughts, Portland's core of players—which included Jermaine O'Neal, Rasheed Wallace, and Zach Randolph—was pejoratively nicknamed the Jail Blazers. The phrase was coined in the headline of a *Willamette Weekly* story. "The 12-man crew isn't final yet," read the article, "but it seems clear that when the 1996 Blazers take the floor, the team will boast at least five players . . . who have criminal records and one more who admits dealing drugs as a young teen." In an attempt at edgy humor, the publication created a metric to weigh new players' crimes against their potential contributions to the team.

To be clear, there were nasty characters on the roster. Ruben "Kobe-Stopper" Patterson pleaded guilty to an attempted rape of his child's babysitter (which occurred while he was on the Sonics), was

now owns a marijuana farm in Canby. "They got in trouble for smoking weed. Well, everybody smokes weed in Oregon."

The Jail Blazers' finest season came in 2000, when the team won 59 games and lost to the Lakers in a heartbreaking seven-game Western Conference Finals. Had Portland won a title, the team's reputation for troublemaking might have been viewed as naughty instead of as an affront to community morals. Either way, the team's attitude seemed to reflect its treatment by the public. "We're not really going to worry about what the hell [fans] think about us," Bonzi Wells told *Sports Illustrated*. "They really don't matter to us. They can boo us every day, but they're still going to ask for our autographs if they see us on the street. That's why they're fans and we're NBA players."

JAMES, LEBRON

LeBron James has spent his career chainsawing through objections to a level of greatness that felt preordained. With every box checked, anyone yet unconvinced never will be. Still, it is a time of détente between kingdoms that took up arms against James's reign: Kobestanis, Durantonians, Curryites, the Order of the Rose. Medieval citadels of Jordan worship will never be toppled, but James's two decades of supremacy have created a sprawling empire now overseen by an aging but feared king.

There is no charming bildungsroman here. James was not cut from his high school team. He did not slide in the draft. He did not grow up in the shadow of the Partheon, enter the NBA as an anonymous stick figure, and develop into the Most Valuable Player. We dig the idea of a beggar who shrugs off soiled robes to reveal himself as a god, but no one this athletic, this ingenious, this durable, and this otherworldly could ever sneak up on us. "You ain't ever going to blend in," a fourth-grade football coach told the lanky kid who seemed to change home addresses weekly. "And that can be a good thing."

James was the finest player in Ohio as a freshman at St. Vincent-St. Mary high school. He was on the cover of *Sports Illustrated* as a junior, beside the headline "The Chosen One." As a senior, he played in front of sold-out crowds and pay-per-view audiences. For his 18th birthday, he received a Hummer with three televisions (his mother took out a loan against his future earnings—"LeBron James is collateral

enough," someone anonymously told the *New York Times*). To certain people, an Akron kid who lived in public housing and qualified for free lunches was the bad guy from the beginning.

With James bypassing college, Cleveland unrepentantly tanked by shipping out the team's top three scorers. "The goal was to get LeBron," coach John Lucas told *AOL FanHouse*." When interim coach Keith Smart won two of the last three games, he was reportedly cursed out by the team lawyer for messing up their losing efforts. The Cavs went 17-65 and secured the top pick in the lottery anyway, although not everyone was exuberant. "If he come, he can just hop on our bandwagon," said forward Darius Miles.

Early on, James elicited comparisons to Magic Johnson. Both were big and fast, visionary passers, and triple-double generators—especially in eras before teams guided rebounds to playmakers. James entered the NBA as an unreliable shooter from outside the paint and a mechanical ball-handler, prompting critics to discount his success as a product of linebacker dimensions to this day. "LeBron is more like brute strength," Dennis Rodman told Business Insider in 2019. "And Michael Jordan's more like a racing car."

Not only did James refine those rougher edges—he became an excellent 3-point shooter and post scorer—he earned a reputation as basketball's foremost genius. His ability to sniff out plays, cite tendencies of opposing players, and photographically recall minutiae of in-game sequences is legendary. In a playoff game, Patrick Patterson of Toronto forgot a play until James told him what to do. "We used to joke that he was a computer on learning mode," former Cavs exec David Griffin said on *The Bill Simmons Podcast*. "There's no play you'll run against him he can't name, and then go out there and teach your players how to do it better than anyone else."

Two miracles are required for sainthood, and James's first came in 2007, during Game 5 of the Eastern Conference Finals against Detroit. With the series knotted at 2-2, James reeled off 25 of Cleveland's points in a row and 29 of his team's last 30. There were step-back jumpers, cuts, and 3s, but most impressive were buckets where James barreled into the morals of the NBA's seventh-ranked defense for dunks and layups. "Everybody keeps asking for more, and he keeps giving more," said Cavs coach Mike Brown afterward. "I feel bad that my words don't do justice for what he did."

Despite leading a Cavs team that started Larry Hughes and Sasha Pavlović to the Finals at the age of

BENEFITTED FROM LEBRON JAMES

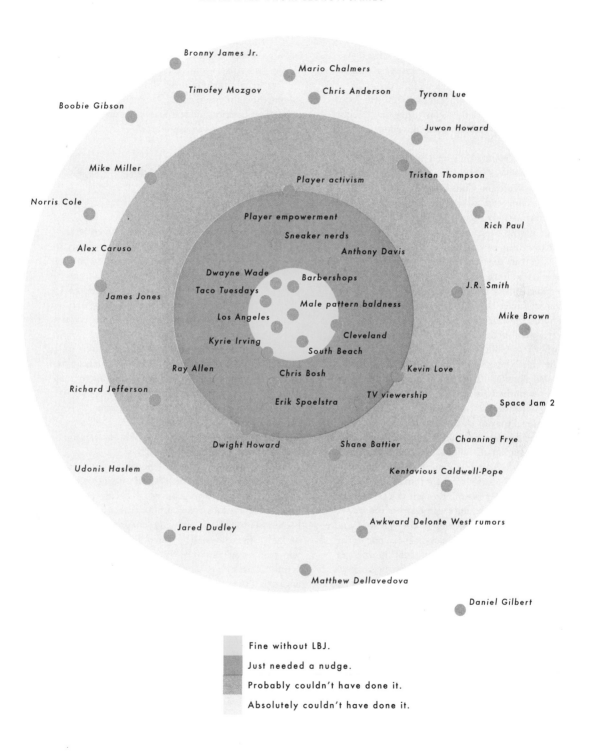

Bronny James Jr.

Mario Chalmers

Timofey Mozgov

Chris Anderson

Tyronn Lue

Boobie Gibson

Juwon Howard

Mike Miller

Player activism

Tristan Thompson

Norris Cole

Player empowerment

Rich Paul

Sneaker nerds

Alex Caruso

Anthony Davis

Dwayne Wade

Barbershops

J.R. Smith

James Jones

Taco Tuesdays

Male pattern baldness

Mike Brown

Los Angeles

Kyrie Irving

Cleveland

South Beach

Ray Allen

Kevin Love

Chris Bosh

Richard Jefferson

TV viewership

Erik Spoelstra

Space Jam 2

Dwight Howard

Shane Battier

Channing Frye

Udonis Haslem

Kentavious Caldwell-Pope

Jared Dudley

Awkward Delonte West rumors

Matthew Dellavedova

Daniel Gilbert

Fine without LBJ.

Just needed a nudge.

Probably couldn't have done it.

Absolutely couldn't have done it.

twenty-two, James did not win a title until his ninth season. The delay gave ammunition to naysayers who dubbed him LeChoke. His dedication to making the right basketball play—especially dishing to open teammates when late-game defenses swarmed like cicadas—offended those indoctrinated by Jordan Originalism. "LeBron has allowed the depth (or lack thereof) of his will to win to become the foundation of all conversations concerning him," wrote ESPN's Scoop Jackson in 2012. "It's about intestinal fortitude."

Ire really bubbled after The Decision, the broadcast where James unveiled that he would join Dwyane Wade and Chris Bosh in Miami. Vectors of mad-making were astounding: free agent superstars aligning instead of warring, a jilted Midwest hometown, players conspiring to create a superteam instead of clever team executives, a death sentence for a Boston team that had gone to a pair of recent Finals.

"It is fair to say that we knew it was going to be terrible, and we tried very hard for it not to happen," commissioner David Stern claimed, according to Ian Thomsen's book *The Soul of Basketball*. In an open letter published in the font of Comic Sans, Cavs owner Dan Gilbert called it "cowardly betrayal." The Heat's loss to the Mavericks in the 2011 Finals healed a broken nation, but James would snag two titles with the Heat.

James was not comfortable as a villain. He has never been edgy or effortlessly cool, primarily because he earnestly cares about his legacy and what people think about him. Despite Cleveland's over-the-top fury at his departure, he made amends—and his second miracle occurred after a return to the Cavs.

With under two minutes left in a tied Game 7 of the 2016 Finals, James warped from the far end of the court to block a layup by the Warriors' Andre Iguodala. It was the crucial moment in one of the greatest upsets ever and a championship win over one of the best teams in history (after being down 3-1 in the series, no less). "Man, that shit was so dope to me, too," Iguodala would tell ESPN about James's signature chase-down swat. "I was a fan. That shit was amazing."

Later in his career, James coined the mantra "more than an athlete." This guiding worldview has compelled him to empower childhood friends who founded the influential player agency Klutch Sports Group, start the SpringHill media company, and open the I Promise School in Akron for at-risk children. He has delved into politics as well, wearing "I Can't Breathe" shirts to protest police brutality, calling Donald Trump "a bum," and launching an advocacy group against voter suppression.

"LeBron James isn't doing what he is doing now because he was taught this playing basketball," wrote former NBA player John Amaechi, in the *Guardian*. "He was taught the opposite: 'Shut up and play.' This is something different: athletes utilising and leveraging their position and status to influence society. That is the way you can use sports."

JOKIĆ, NIKOLA

A 7-footer Serbian who moves as if he ate a pregame shepherd's pie, Nikola Jokić was named Most Valuable Player in 2021—and may be the greatest offensive center in modern basketball history. In a sport that included Shaquille O'Neal and Hakeem Olajuwon—not to mention ancient leviathans like Wilt Chamberlain and Kareem Abdul-Jabbar, who dunked ferociously on part-time cobblers—this claim feels bewildering and offensive.

After all, Jokić has the chiseled musculature of Grimace, was an afterthought in the 2014 draft (going forty-first to the Nuggets), and lacks that superhuman presence that legendary centers are supposed to possess. Rather than making mortals cower as he flattens their shacks, he is a fidgety, googly-eyed schlub whose weight fluctuates as if he is periodically starting and bailing on celery juice diets.

Jokić's wizardry starts with his passing. While most big men distribute the ball as if wearing oven mitts, the Joker has a gorgeous array of delivery techniques: feathery lobs, full-court outlet touchdowns, behind-the-back bouncers, and every variety of no-look assist witnessed by man or beast. He is a seer with panoramic peripheral vision, and his bulbous stature allows him to sling passes from unorthodox angles past the ears of large defenders who are unaccustomed to guarding a playmaking center. "I mean, the guy's just throwing cheeseburgers," said teammate Paul Millsap. "Free cheeseburgers. Just grab as many as you can. Playing with a guy like that, it's unbelievable."

Along with unparalleled dishing, Jokić's offensive toolbox includes respectable 3-point range, dribbling prowess to rumble through the open court like a jumbo point guard, and postups where he fords toward the bucket as if leading a team of horses across a chest-high river. Despite being earthbound,

he is one of the league's better offensive rebounders and adept at batting the ball toward the rim until it nestles home. On defense, Jokić is a lumpy obstacle who knows where to go, but gets tormented by quicker players outside of the paint.

When you stack Jokić's per-possession production up against the most devastating centers ever, comparisons get unsettling quickly. The aforementioned titans may have scored more—although not by as much as one would think, when Jokić's relatively low minute count is factored in—but his efficiency and offensive rebounding keep up with the field. And he has extraordinary advantages in passing and perimeter shooting over *every single one of them*. Part of his edge is due to the evolution of the game, but it is worth considering that our perception of greatness from the center spot is heavily influenced by centers' roles as shot-blockers, rebounders, and defensive guardians of the paint. But offensively, Jokić is that good. "When you see someone like a Nelson Mandela or a Martin Luther King or a Mahatma Gandhi, someone who sees the future before anyone else does, knows how to get to where they need to be, where they want to be, that is Nikola Jokić," said Hall of Fame big man Bill Walton. "Happiness begins when selfishness ends."

In a different offensive highlight, Jokić was fined $25,000 for saying, "No homo, he's longer than you expect," about Wendell Carter of the Bulls in a postgame interview.

JORDAN, MICHAEL

Michael Jordan was yuppie excess in the flesh. He was swordfish at the Four Seasons, the dashboard of a Lamborghini Countach zebra-striped with Bogotan puro, Patrick Bateman with a fadeaway. As the second-best player of all time, he led Chicago to six NBA championships. He racked up six Finals MVP awards, ten scoring titles, and a Defensive Player of the Year award. During the 1990s, the 6-foot-6 shooting guard scored all the buckets and took home all the trophies. "To be successful, you have to be selfish, or else you never achieve," Jordan once said. "And once you get to your highest level, then you have to be unselfish." Coming from a basketball sociopath who was driven by competitive bloodlust, perceived disrespect, and self-mythologization, it had the believability of Gordon Gekko saying, "Greed is good, until it isn't."

Appreciation of Jordan's game never required nuance. It was observable dominance. He overwhelmed opponents with twisting drives, turnaround jumpers, and airborne acrobatics that halted the passage of time. On defense, he hunted ball-handlers like a hyena stalking a limping antelope calf. "All the odds could be in your favor," Sonics star Shawn Kemp told the *Players Tribune*. "And then MJ would score 25 in the first half, stick his tongue out. Just take aim at your entire organization. He lived for that." Jordan defined "clutchness" so thoroughly that it contaminated the sport's groundwater for decades. He was a one-man deus ex machina for the Bulls and, to opponents, a hooded executioner. With the ball in his hands and the clock blinking toward zero, Jordan controlled everyone's fate.

Debuting in the late eighties, Jordan was visibly out of place. The champion Celtics gawped at his ability to dunk as if he was ascending to a UFO in the basket of a bicycle. Bleary videos that show Jordan bewitching flatfooted oafs with waist-high dribbles and effortlessly cruising in for layups do not present a flattering version of pre-nineties basketball. They were playing a different sport. Players drank martinis on the bench and ate well-done tomahawk steaks at halftime. Ronald Reagan decreed that jogging was communist. After Jordan was stonewalled by the brutish Pistons in the Eastern Conference Finals, he did the unthinkable: he started *lifting weights*.

As Jordan's collection of championship trophies grew, he was elevated into Polaris—a supergiant who directed other athletes toward greatness. Due to his exhilarating style of play, marketing heft, and global superstardom, he overshadowed contemporaries and even historical greats like Kareem Abdul-Jabbar and Wilt Chamberlain. Jordan became basketball's moral compass, and one that spun by his own magnetic field.

In a Nike commercial produced by Portland-based ad firm Wieden+Kennedy in 1999, his failures were framed as potholes on the highway to greater glory. "I've missed more than nine thousand shots in my career," he said, over moody guitars and footage of him exiting the arena in a long coat. "I've lost almost three hundred games. Twenty-six times, I've been trusted to take the game-winning shot and missed. I've failed over and over and over again in my life. And that is why I succeed." Winning still remained the only acceptable outcome—and the only result that Jordan would ever acknowledge.

America's most enduring lie is that everything won has been earned. It is, after all, the land of opportunity. Here, the billionaire's son attributes his success to wits and intuition, not to the Dartmouth conservatory with the family name etched on the entrance. Jordan, who grew up in a working-class North Carolina household, was highly susceptible to this orthodoxy—or at least understood its storytelling power. Though he was an incredible athlete with an alleged vertical leap of 48 inches and a wingspan of nearly 7 feet, he cultivated the perception that his accomplishments were feats of hard work, commitment to excellence, and focused desire. It would be unromantic and disappointing if the difference between Jordan and his competitors came down to, say, his ability to release the ball 8 inches higher than everyone else.

During the summer of 1993, Jordan's father was shot to death in a robbery as he slept in a Lexus at a rest stop along North Carolina's Highway 74. "He was my rock," Michael would say later. Following the ghastly crime, Jordan announced his retirement from the NBA, an unrecognized precedent for modern self-care. Instead, he decided to play outfield for the minor league Birmingham Barons. While his .202 batting average was unimpressive for a professional, his work ethic was cited as the reason he ultimately would have been successful had he stuck with baseball. "Two more seasons, he would've been a legitimate extra outfielder for the White Sox, maybe even a starter," said Mike Barnett, his batting coach.

After returning to the Bulls late in the 1995 season, Jordan was defeated by the Magic in the second round of the playoffs. Although more than eight months had passed between his last game with the Barons and the date of his Game 6 elimination, we have collectively decided that the loss did not count because he was tired and had "baseball muscles." It is rarely mentioned that Jordan's stats in the 1995 postseason equaled or topped his combined averages over the next three title-winning seasons in categories such as points, rebounds, assists, steals, blocks, field-goal percentage, and 3-point percentage. The loss presents a snag in the storyline of six consecutive Finals victories: though Jordan was blameless in the Bulls' defeat, he is forced to accept responsibility (he would never let his team lose) while simultaneously shirking it (the Jordan who lost was not the real Jordan).

Jordan retired for the second time after drilling a game-winning shot in the 1998 Finals over Bryon Russell of the Jazz, but even such a scripted, storybook ending could not quell his competitive zeal. He returned to the NBA four seasons later, at the age of thirty-eight to play for the Wizards. Over two seasons in Washington, he averaged 21.2 points on driveway dad post-ups and jab-step jumpers but failed to qualify for the playoffs both years. According to Ray Lewis, the former NFL linebacker, Jordan rued his comeback. "This is the honest goddamn truth," Lewis said, "M. J. said to me, 'The only thing I regret is putting on another uniform.'"

Even in retirement, Jordan has protected his claim with the paranoia of a sun-addled prospector with a shotgun and a gold pan. During the 2020 hiatus, ESPN aired a ten-hour documentary about his unsurpassed trait of wanting it more. *The Last Dance* was more notable for its recitation of Jordan lore than wheedling honesty out of a subject who spent most episodes flanked by a crystal tumbler of Cincoro tequila and snorting at rivals from a quarter century ago. His other middle-age endeavors have included ownership of the Charlotte Hornets, loving distressed denim, and becoming the eponymous face of the "Crying Jordan" meme.

How should younger generations appreciate basketball icons of the past? As ferocious and exhilarating as Jordan was to witness in real time, his legacy has been distilled into the cold perfection of six titles in six Finals appearances. On one hand, it is a feat that is difficult to top, both in excellence and specificity—particularly in a modern era of shorter contracts, player mobility, and superteams that rise and fall like continental empires. But, over time, will that accomplishment be viewed like Bill Russell's eleven titles in thirteen years, as the product of a foreign and cobwebbed era?

The subsummation of Jordan the Athlete into Jordan the Winner was a branding triumph. But what if his domineering persona was detached from claiming those six titles? What if traits like 24-hour competitiveness and alpha dick-swinging were viewed as hindrances, instead of the psychological composition of basketball's greatest champion? What if an NBA superstar does not need to look or play or behave as if cast in plaster from his mold? How might we perceive basketball excellence without it being skewed by the prism of Jordan Originalism?

If there is one Michael Jordan moment that we can all agree upon, it was March 12, 1997: when he got crossed up by Allen Iverson. The torch had been passed to the modern NBA, even if we did not know exactly how it would be carried.

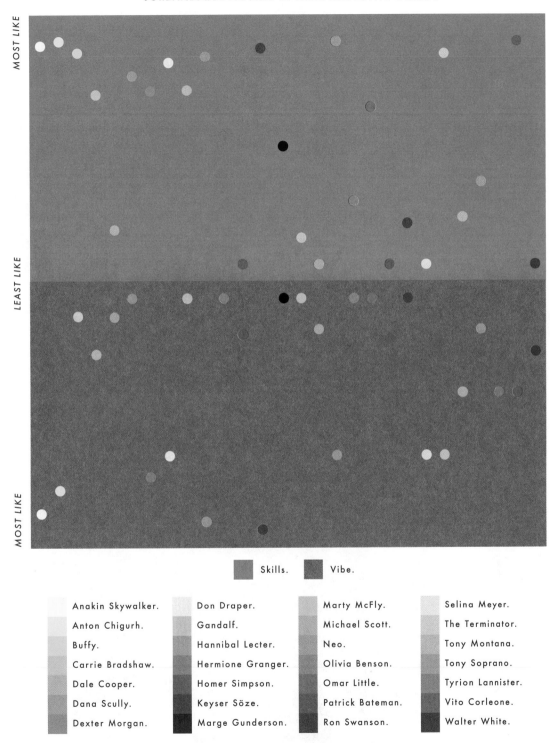

JORDANESQUE FIGURES IN THEIR RESPECTIVE WORLDS

MOST LIKE

LEAST LIKE

MOST LIKE

Skills. Vibe.

Anakin Skywalker.   Don Draper.   Marty McFly.   Selina Meyer.
Anton Chigurh.   Gandalf.   Michael Scott.   The Terminator.
Buffy.   Hannibal Lecter.   Neo.   Tony Montana.
Carrie Bradshaw.   Hermione Granger.   Olivia Benson.   Tony Soprano.
Dale Cooper.   Homer Simpson.   Omar Little.   Tyrion Lannister.
Dana Scully.   Keyser Söze.   Patrick Bateman.   Vito Corleone.
Dexter Morgan.   Marge Gunderson.   Ron Swanson.   Walter White.

KEMP, SHAWN

An intimidator for the ages, Shawn Kemp rose to stardom during the Posterization Era—a mid-nineties confluence of dunk contests, cable television highlights, trash talk, and slow defenders waddling around the lane waiting to be yammed on. Nicknamed the Reign Man, he was a six-time All-Star who never played a second of college basketball before the Sonics scooped him up with the seventeenth pick in the 1989 draft. Along with Vince Carter and Michael Jordan, Kemp is in the highest echelon of history's best in-game dunkers. On the spectrum between elegance and destructiveness, the 6-foot-10 power forward was a *ballerino* wielding a sledgehammer. No dunker has ever been more disrespectful.

Kemp's blend of size, wingspan, mobility, coordination, and coiled python energy was matchless. His windups were spectacular. With the ball palmed behind his head he resembled the silhouette of a javelin thrower on the side of an ancient Greek urn. At times, he seemed to make decisions in midair, whipping across the baseline for a two-handed

reverse or spontaneous windmill. Kemp's post-prandial celebrations included twisting dismounts, dangling nut-grabs, demonstrative pointing, and primal screams. "Un-fucking-believable," said teammate Xavier McDaniel, describing a dunk over Pistons mook Bill Laimbeer, in the *Seattle Times*. "Shawn is just like Dominique Wilkins. When he's on the court, you can expect the unexpected."

Kemp's other secret weapon was less sexy: free throws. Besides him, the only players in the modern era to average more than 18 points a game with proportional trips to the foul line are Shaquille O'Neal and Dwight Howard, both of whom were intentionally hacked because of their ineptitude from the stripe. In 1996, Kemp led all big men in scoring efficiency (63.1 percent true shooting percentage) as he and Gary Payton took the 64-win Sonics to the Finals.

But even as one of the league's most thrilling young stars, Kemp remained a cipher. "He was a loner," said Nate McMillan, his former teammate in Seattle. "He wasn't a guy who partied or hung out in nightclubs." In the middle of the night, Kemp would drive to Regrade Park, a dingy playground on the corner of Third Avenue and Bell Street, to shoot hoops and crack jokes with homeless people.

After he was traded to Cleveland, Kemp's career hit the skids. During the nine-month lockout before the 1999 season, he inflated to a rumored 315 pounds—by some estimates, a 60-pound mushrooming from his listed weight. He had a nutritionist and a recommended diet, but lacked willpower. "We even offered to have a chef go to his house and prepare meals for him," Cleveland general manager Wayne Embry said to the *Plain Dealer*. "I told Shawn the same thing I told Mel Turpin years ago, 'I don't want anyone playing for me that weighs more than me.'"

In 2001, Kemp's season with the Blazers ended prematurely when he entered rehab for drug and alcohol abuse. He had struggled with stardom and craved a sense of normalcy that was foreign to a kid who grew 13 inches between his freshman and junior years of high school. As a teenager in Elkhart, Indiana, he was mocked by opposing crowds for his poor SAT scores. As an adult, it was the lack of postseason success, the weight gain, and the creepy jokes about his numerous children with different mothers. "It doesn't take a genius to figure out this business," he told *Sports Illustrated*. "Once you're done playing ball, people don't remember who you are. You're only as good as your last dunk in this league."

KIDD, JASON

Jason Kidd did not always behave intelligently off the court—like when he was arrested for spousal abuse and drunk driving. But during a nineteen-year NBA career that included being named to ten All-Star teams and appearing in three NBA Finals, the point guard was an incomparable playmaker. There is no rule etched in granite that excludes dickheads from having exquisite talent.

Kidd's medium for artistic expression was the bounce pass. He was a master at manipulating defenders with his eyes to create fissures for behind-the-back assists. He rewarded teammates who sprinted the length of the floor with ricocheting, 30-foot bullets that turned 2-on-4 disadvantages into uncontested dunks. He threaded passes through spaces that were theoretical when the ball left his fingers, but cracked open like an oculus to a parallel universe where scoring was easy. Kidd slung the rock with screwball spins or ankle-high trajectories that would bounce four times before the target collected it for a layup.

Kidd lived to run. The jolt of energy when he grabbed a rebound or received an outlet pass was palpable—it was as if a higher power had thumbed the fast-forward button and sent his legs into Charlie Chaplin double-time. He pushed the ball in the open court with nonnegotiable insistence. Unlike Steve Nash or Chris Paul, both upper-echelon passers on the break, Kidd supplemented speed and vision with 6-foot-4 height and a thick-necked rectangular build. He was an icebreaker crunching through floes. His lack of interest in coy, curvy routes to the basket forced scrambling defenders to flood the paint, and he would wait until the last possible moment to spoon-feed teammates with a twisting pass or lob off the backboard. With the ball out of his mitts, his hurtling frame became an obstacle that walled off foes from getting involved in the play.

Kidd was born in San Francisco and raised in nearby Oakland. He became one of the most hyped teen prospects ever, and crowds flocked to games to witness his preternatural dishes. "People don't know, J was the first LeBron," said Gary Payton, who mentored a high-school-age Kidd by abusing him on the court to the point of tears. "In the Bay Area, that's what all the talk was about." After two years at the University of California, Berkeley, Kidd declared for the 1994 NBA Draft and went second overall to the Mavericks. "There are no doubts about his desire and talent," wrote scout Terence Tek-Leun Lau at the time. "[Kidd is] arguably a better passer than Magic Johnson."

Passing was never the problem. From 1999 to 2004, Kidd led the NBA in assists five out of six seasons and eventually amassed the second-most in history. His sense of timing and quick hands—described by coach Scott Skiles as "suction cups"—made him an opportunistic pickpocket. He would retire second on the all-time list in steals too. He was a magnificent rebounder, racking up boards more than any guard ever. Kidd exited the league third in career triple-doubles, although he has since lost ground to modern players like Russell Westbrook.

But Kidd was rarely a scorer. He came out of college with a reputation for hoisting up bricks from the perimeter and the derogatory nickname of Ason Kidd (because he lacked a J). Over time, he developed a steady 3-ball that eventually became his only real way of scoring during late-career stops in Dallas and New York. Over his last two seasons, 80.4 percent of the field-goal attempts he took were from behind the arc.

While Kidd was selfless on the hardwood, he was not easy to coexist with in a locker room—particularly when it came to coaches. After he was traded from Phoenix, he called coach Skiles a "backstabber" and cursed at him on the court. Whether or not Kidd was responsible, men with clipboards kept dying professional deaths around him: his coach at Cal, Dick Motta during his first stint in Dallas, Avery Johnson the second time around ("They can't blame that one on me," Kidd reputedly told friends. "When I got there, the players all thought he was crazy").

After Kidd's Nets went to consecutive NBA Finals, losing both times, he reportedly prodded management to make a change on the bench—which supposedly contributed to the midseason canning of head coach Byron Scott. "I had nothing to do with this," Kidd claimed at the time. "I'm an employee." Whoever was the triggerman, the mortality rate was consistent enough to earn him the "coach killer" tag.

Years later, when Kidd joined the coaching ranks, Scott reminisced unfondly about their partnership in New Jersey for the *Orange County Register*. "He was kind of known as an asshole," Scott said. "I respect him as a basketball player and now as a coach but, other than that, we're not going to be swapping spit and having dinner and playing golf."

KIRILENKO, ANDREI

A spindly, 6-foot-9 Russian with a krokodil dealer haircut, Andrei Kirilenko emigrated westward to Utah in 2001. AK-47 (47 was his jersey number) bred hardwood mayhem before unconventional stars like Draymond Green or Bam Adebayo. Kirilenko's attributes seemed pulled from a Scrabble bag. He was a passable shooter and a modest scorer, yet efficiently drew fouls and attacked the rim. He was not a distributor, but had a knack for goofy hotdog dimes. In 2005, Kirilenko led the league in blocks per game, despite playing small forward half the time.

Appreciation of Kirilenko's quirkiness requires dorkiness. Since the introduction of the 3-pointer, players who logged at least 1,000 minutes have amassed more than 2.5 steals and more than 4.0 steals per 100 possessions only nine times. Three of those were Hakeem Olajuwon and three were Kirilenko. Similarly, Kirilenko notched three of nine total 5-by-5 games (five points, rebounds, assists, steals, and blocks) since 1997. In 2004, he finished second in the NBA in Value Over Replacement Player, sandwiched between Kevin Garnett and Tim Duncan. The following season, his Box Plus/Minus was second in the NBA, right between Garnett and LeBron James.

Still, Kirilenko was an obscure, one-time All-Star who spent his prime in a dinky market described by guard Vernon Maxwell as "the worst place in the world to play at." His Jazz teams were occasionally strong, but he averaged the fewest points of any starter. Today, he might have been a small-ball center and a social media wonder. Back then, Kirilenko was best known for getting a repulsive, winged tattoo on his back and for receiving permission to cheat on his wife, Masha Lopatova, once a year. "What's forbidden is always desirable," Lopatova told the *Salt Lake Tribune* in 2006. "It's the same way raising children—if I tell my child, 'No pizza, no pizza, no pizza,' what does he want more than anything? Pizza!'"

KNICKS 4 LIFE

In the temple of Madison Square Garden, the Knicks are permitted to win only one way: as they played in the 1990s. The godheads are Pat Riley and Jeff Van Gundy; the war deities are Anthony Mason, Charles Oakley, and Latrell Sprewell; light pours from a stained

glass window depicting John Starks dunking over Michael Jordan and Horace Grant. These hierograms are tributes to an era of violence and intimidation in which defensive-oriented teams took up arms against the Bulls, Pacers, and Heat. "There's a fine line between physical and thug ball, and the Knicks have crossed the line on occasion," said Marv Albert, the team's broadcasting voice for thirty-seven years.

The Knicks reflect the self-identity of the New Yorker—past and present. It is basketball funneled through Fran Lebowitz, wearing Lugz boots and shoveling a bacon, egg, and cheese into her maw while smoking a loosie. As the NBA's losingest franchise from 2000 to 2020, the Knicks have few saints from the modern world. When coach Mike D'Antoni reinvented the team as one that hoisted up 3-pointers and pushed the tempo, fans bellyached about the lack of defensive nastiness until he was elbowed out the subway doors. The code of the streets does not account for pace, son!

There are periodic incidents in which owner James Dolan's thin-skinned sourness causes revolt: kicking Oakley out of a game, kicking a fan out of a game for wearing an insulting shirt, kicking a different fan out of a game for telling him to "sell the team," or kicking a reporter out of a show by his blues band, JD & The Straight Shot. He is a Republican in a Democratic city, and the organization's tepid support of the Black Lives Matter movement reportedly infuriated its employees. "When Knicks acquire players they say 'stay away from media, they're bad,'" tweeted beat writer Frank Isola. "Within 2 months, smart players realize the enemy comes from within."

But expressing fury at Lord Dolan is a futile raindance from playoff-thirsty serfs. Despite being a grouchy meddler, his basketball decisions have been in lockstep with public consensus. His hirings and firings of coaches and executives like D'Antoni, Phil Jackson, David Fizdale, and Tom Thibodeau were popular. He is not frugal. And there is something to be said for Dolan's loyalty—former Knicks like Starks, Allan Houston, Larry Johnson, and John Wallace populate the organization. Most people can't say why, exactly, they want Dolan to sell the team, other than the belief

Very bad. Kinda good.

Relying on hope/faith.
Doubting science/math.
Trading away draft picks.
A thrist for known names.
Chasing enforcer culture.
Phil/Isiah/Mills/Grunwald.
Refusing to extend rookies.

Dealing Ewing for scraps.
Not losing enough games.
Reveling in relegation.
Prioritizing Celebrity Row.
Being too casual with Lin.
Re-committing to Carmelo.
Trading for Starbury.

Hiring Donnie Walsh.
Trading for Sprewell.
Drafting Porzingis.
Staring at candles.
Living the nu metal life.
Raving under bridges.
Practicing the dark arts.

that he sucks. It is a badge of New Yorker–dom, like wearing a Zabar's hat and blurting "This fuckin' guy!"

Dolan's true influence is helming a faith-based organization. He has been sober since the early 1990s—"I was close to killing myself with drugs and alcohol," he told ESPN—and appears to find stability in longtime franchise executives like Houston, Steve Mills, and Isiah Thomas. They switch titles, roles, and Penn Plaza offices, but lurk as a trusted inner circle regardless of who is publicly calling the shots.

Even when the franchise makes changes, they feel as superficial as a car wash. There is a conviction that the Knicks will win because they are an important franchise in an important city. It is assumed that the next superstar free agent (be it LeBron James, Kevin Durant, Kyrie Irving, or Giannis Antetokounmpo) will find the chance to play on basketball's biggest stage irresistible. Face-punching Garden protectors will be prioritized. The team will covet New York natives like Stephon Marbury, Carmelo Anthony, Lance Thomas, Joakim Noah, Taj Gibson, Obi Toppin. Celebrity row will be populated by Spike Lee, Chloë Sevigny, and Pauly D.

While big market teams like the Lakers, Nets, and Clippers have become contenders in recent years, the Knicks remain unshakably convinced of the righteousness of their path. They are true believers in robes of orange and blue.

LEAGUE PASS

As difficult as it is to believe, *Seinfeld* was still on the air when League Pass was introduced during the 1995–96 season. In its larval stage, the package was geared toward out-of-market fans who wanted to watch their favorite teams. But there were viewers who appreciated the deeper cuts, those dreary, meaningless games in late April between two tanking teams that marked the first career start of a second-round pick who would soon be playing for KK Olimpija. Through the umbilical cord of a local cable provider, it was possible to see the Timberwolves' teenaged rookie Kevin Garnett, or, on the other side of the aging curve, Hall of Famer Robert Parish, a forty-two-year-old limestone monolith playing for the Hornets. It was the end of an era in which access was limited to teams that were in local markets or broadcast on cable superstations, such as Atlanta's TBS, New York's MSG, or Chicago's WGN.

In 2006, League Pass began streaming over broadband. For part of the early 2010s, the one-team package was supplemented by a five-team deal that incited the early blogosphere into debates about the merits of watchability by a calculus of team quality, charismatic superstars, and enchanting young losers. The digital service has exploded internationally, with noticeable bumps in the homelands of young foreign stars. According to data released by the NBA in 2019, League Pass subscriptions in Serbia soared by 395 percent—a spike seemingly juiced by the rise of Sombor-born center Nikola Jokić. Similarly, Luka Dončić's relocation from European leagues to Dallas propelled a 186 percent jolt in Slovenian subscribers.

The phrase "League Pass alert" is shorthand for a game careening toward an exciting or notable finish. It could be a player threatening the 50-point plateau or a fourth-quarter seesaw between a pair of 16–60 tanking battalions. The key is that it sits at an enviable nexus point for modern fandom: real-time viewership and social media frenzy. Now every basketball fan across the globe has the chance to call the greatest player ever "LeBitch" on Twitter at the exact same moment.

During the COVID Bubble, the NBA experimented with allowing unaffiliated bloggers and podcasters to "announce" streaming games on League Pass. It was likely a preview of a Patreon-style system where fans pay to hear broadcasts by talking heads of their own choice (with the league taking a slice) instead of simply muting Chris Webber. Around the same time, the league signed a deal with Oculus that made the virtual reality technology company the "presenting partner" for a mobile sideline camera. Considering the exponential growth of League Pass, the opportunity to sell infinite "courtside seats" to a global audience is worth booting Steve Schirripa out of his folding chair at the Garden.

LEONARD, KAWHI

The NBA's greatest supervillain, Kawhi Leonard has left a half-dozen franchises smoldering behind him. He conquered dynasties, salted their farmlands, and scattered their divine relics. He abandoned title-winning organizations. His machinations in free agency coerced rebuilds, sabotaged rivals, and ransomed his own team into emptying their coffer of assets. But even as Leonard's March to the Sea razed sturdy franchises to charred timber, his motivations have been left examined. His Sphinx-like inscrutability conceals a Machiavellian mercenary who won championships in San Antonio and Toronto—while unapologetically seizing everything he ever desired.

Very dastardly.   Kinda dastardly.

Being too boring for boomer critics.

Being too good for grill-master critics.

Breaking apart Lowry & Derozan.

Convincing PG to leave the Thunder.

Gifting Jeremy Lin a championship.

Giving Wingstop free advertizing.

Leaving Toronto holding the bag.

Legitimizing the country of Canada.

Mortgaging the Clippers' future.

Normalizing '97 Chevy Tahoes.

Prioritizing happiness over loyalty.

Providing Drake with another platform.

Refusing to return to the Spurs.

Sabotaging the Lakers' '19 summer.

Taking care of himself over a team.

Throwing Pop under the bus.

A 6-foot-7 forward with a disproportional wingspan and hands like throw pillows, Leonard plays basketball the same way he has orchestrated his career: he takes what he wants. He scores with precision from everywhere, with a robotic affinity for chores like laboring in the post and canning midrange jumpers. He is not sneaky or subtle. Leonard muscles his way to the basket on linear drives and powers home dunks that rank higher in substance than style. A two-time Defensive Player of the Year, he is a light-absorbing presence that brings offensive players to a helpless standstill. He rips the ball out of opponents' hands like a parent taking a plastic pumpkin of Halloween candy away from a toddler.

As a sophomore coming out of San Diego State—where he famously used the phrase "board man gets paid"—Leonard drew comparisons to limber but unskilled wings like Shawn Marion and Gerald Wallace. The Spurs selected him in the 2011 NBA Draft after trading George Hill to the Pacers for the fifteenth pick. According to Mike Budenholzer, then an assistant with San Antonio, the move caused apprehension internally. "It's a great story now, because Kawhi is obviously fucking kicking ass and a hell of a player," he told *Bleacher Report*. "But I will say there were not a lot of people that were real impressed with him in those workouts." (The Phoenix Suns reportedly passed on drafting Leonard with the thirteenth pick because he sweated through his suit during an interview with the team.)

In an organization that emphasized player development and employed Chip Engelland, the renowned shooting coach, Leonard's dedication to self-improvement and physical gifts worked wonders. By his third season, he was named MVP of the 2014 Finals. Leonard's stone-faced grill, work ethic, and achievements within the Spurs' egalitarian system were interpreted as virtuousness. Likewise, pundits used his humble two-bedroom apartment and 1997 Chevy Tahoe ("It runs and it's paid off," he said) to juxtapose his reputed priorities against those of less-thrifty peers.

These ideals assume transparency that he has never allowed. Even when Leonard forced his way out of San Antonio, abandoned a championship team in Toronto to sign with the Clippers, and convinced Paul "PG-13" George to demand a trade out of Oklahoma City to join him, his vacant blankness acted as bulletproofing against criticism. After his team crumbled in the COVID Bubble, it was reported that Leonard had enjoyed objectionable perks of stardom: private warm-up rooms, control over the Clippers' practice schedule, and two-hour commutes from San Diego that delayed road trip flights. "How do you build a strong team with that shit going on?" an unnamed team source said to the *Athletic*. "I thought from the beginning, 'We're doomed.'"

In some ways, Leonard is what people pretend Kobe Bryant was: a cold-eyed killer whose remorseless domination on both sides of the ball grinds fleshy obstacles into red pulp. But while Bryant's human passions were writ large on his sleeve, Leonard has never betrayed any thirst for legacy, public adoration, or even sculpting a storyline into one in which he plays a recognizable character. Whatever he feels, he does not tell us. Contemporaries like LeBron James and Kevin Durant buckled under heavy criticism, but Leonard seems incapable of expressing emotions or even recognizing them. "Umm, didn't make nothing of it," Leonard said after jilted Spurs fans booed him during a return to San Antonio. "Felt like a normal away game." For all we know, the blood-drenched suit of armor is empty beneath its hinged visor.

LILLARD, DAMIAN

A player who has earned more respect than investment from basketball fans, Damian Lillard has spent his career as an indie star in the Pacific Northwest. The slick point guard developed into one of the NBA's most destructive weapons in his late twenties. In an era that has rewarded shooters, he broke ground as one of the first players to attempt ludicrously deep 3-pointers with frequency—a craft he perfected on a court with tape stuck 5 feet behind the NBA line. "The ball can go left or right," Lillard told Kirk Goldsberry of *ESPN* magazine. "You can air-ball. It's far out, so there's more room for error." In 2020, he set a record by draining 45 heaves from between 30 and 40 feet, while scoring 30 points a game.

Despite winning Rookie of the Year and being named to a fistful of All-Star teams, Lillard has never been included in impassioned conversations that surround playmakers Stephen Curry and James Harden. While his peers are jostling on the ladder to basketball's top-10 list, Lillard is a foil. He is used as a yardstick to diminish the subject of a rhetorical attack: "Your guy is not even as good as Damian Lillard."

L

Maybe it was attending Weber State and entering the NBA older than most of his draft classmates. It could be playing in a small and forested market. Or it is the fact that Portland has never carried the menace of a real title contender during his tenure (the team's deepest run ended with a shellacking at the hands of the Hamptons 5 in the 2019 Western Conference Finals). For all of Lillard's late-game, or Dame Time, heroics, he is accepted as a superstar—but not as a threat.

LIMITED-EDITION COLLABS

The term "3-and-D" is suitably unsexy and robotic. Players who specialize at shooting 3-pointers (the "3") and defense (the "D") are not supposed to think, make complex decisions, or be creative. They are not unskilled, but they are limited.

On offense, a 3-and-D guy trots to a spot behind the arc and camps out, waiting to receive the ball. They might do other things, like setting picks or cutting, but the majority of their shots come from long range. If a look is open, it must be launched without hesitation. Otherwise, the rock is immediately shuttled along to a teammate. That is the job. In 2020, 3-and-D kings like Robert Covington of the Rockets and Danny Green of the Lakers held the ball for under two seconds on an average touch, and dribbled it less than once. There is a comforting purity associated with this role. They adhere to "make or miss" minimalism while channeling greater responsibilities into more capable hands. Harsh compartmentalization may feel undemocratic on the basketball court, but the idea of "each one according to his ability" is applicable to the position.

The secret to being a successful 3-and-D player is accepting one's lot in life—as opposed to clinging to childhood daydreams that were inspired by a bedroom poster of Michael Jordan's elongated limbs. "You might be a guy that can be a 20-point scorer, but the team needs you to be a 11- or 12-point scorer and a great defender," said Garrett Temple, a stalwart 3-and-D dude with teams like Washington and Sacramento, to *USA Today* in 2014. "Put your pride away and play your role." Dependable 3-and-D players are members of the NBA's middle class. If these Joe Lunchpails were better at, say, creating their own shot, they might be stars like Kawhi Leonard or Paul George. But they are not. The contemporary player who most fogs the lines between the roles of 3-and-D and star is Klay Thompson of the Warriors.

Bruce Bowen, a wing who won three championships with the Spurs in the aughts, is considered the 3-and-D prototype. He was infamously chippy and made eight All-Defensive teams while wielding pointy elbows, dispatching foes with Mortal Kombat–esque flying kicks, and slipping his feet beneath airborne opponents. Yet Bowen averaged only one made 3-pointer a game over his tenure in San Antonio. "I know I'm not a dirty player," he said on *For the Win*. "I was an aggressive individual."

Another seminal 3-and-D player was Raja Bell of the Suns, who, in 2007, led the league in 3-pointers made and was named to the All-Defensive First Team. He too is an imperfect example, as Bell averaged 14.7 points a game and had the volume of a sharpshooter. His claim to fame was clotheslining Kobe Bryant in retaliation for an elbow to the face. "I don't know how Kobe felt," Bell told HoopsHype (before Bryant's death), "but I genuinely hated the cat at that time." Since retiring from the NBA, Bell has embraced the most noble profession of all: podcasting.

A few early inhabitants of the 3-and-D role include Greg Anthony and Charlie Ward of the Knicks, Greg Buckner of the Nuggets, and Ron Harper of the Bulls (in the odd seasons when he could actually make 3s). The position entered its heyday in the 2010s with players like James Posey, Mario Chalmers, and Thabo Sefolosha acting as key contributors on championship teams and contenders.

Despite how frequently the phrase "3-and-D" is used to describe draft prospects, few players are legitimately good at both. Due to the specificity of the role, some are guys who have slipped through the cracks: snubbed in the draft, crisscrossing the country on G-League buses, balling overseas. Dorian Finney-Smith went undrafted in 2016, inked a dirt-cheap deal with the Mavericks, learned to shoot 3s, and then re-upped with a three-year contract for $4 million a season. "He's been a guy that has fought his way to where he is now," said Dallas coach Rick Carlisle. "He takes nothing for granted."

By the end of the 2010s, the 3-and-D wave lapped up on the beachhead of the center position.

RARITIES

Valuable.   Cheap.

Mike Breen.
League Pass.
Advanced stats.
Trade gossip.

3-and-D wings.
Christmas Day games.
Vintage resellers.
Top Shot.

Virtual reality.
Photoshop.
Instant replay.
A team in Oklahoma.

Kyrie Irving rage.
T-shirt cannons.
Twitter trolls.
All-Star voting.

With post-ups falling out of favor due to the relative inefficiency of those possessions, more teams opted for a pivot player who can lure opposing big men out of the lane. Myles Turner, a braided shot-swatter who was drafted by the Pacers in the 2015 lottery, went from taking under 3 percent of his shots from 3-point distance as a rookie to 42 percent from deep by his fifth season. Even veterans have adapted. By 2020, traditional lugs in their thirties, men with mortgages like Marc Gasol and Brook Lopez, were used as rim protectors who spent much of their time on offense chilling peacefully behind the arc.

LIN, JEREMY

Over the last twenty years, the Knicks have had few feel-good stories. While they were compiling the worst record in the NBA over that stretch, there have been funny stories, disappointing stories, infuriating stories, and stories that left loyalists blaring Papa Roach's "Last Resort" while standing alone in a four-cornered room staring at Julius Randle. Happy moments have been few and far between. The exception was the stunning rise and soft landing of Jeremy Lin.

Until February of 2012, Lin was a seldom-used point guard submerged in the brackish New York depth chart below Toney Douglas, Mike Bibby, and Iman Shumpert. He was undrafted after four years at Harvard University—a loser program that had not produced an NBA player since Ed Smith averaged 2.5 points for the Knicks in 1954—and spent a season riding the pine in Golden State, where he played only 285 minutes. Lin's Taiwanese American ethnicity and Ivy League credentials had curried light attention, but he was an afterthought on a wannabe contender list that starred Carmelo Anthony, Amar'e Stoudemire, and Tyson Chandler. "They have a team to be giddy about," Kelly Dwyer wrote in a *Yahoo* preview.

As the saying goes, Knicks gonna Knick. By early February, the team was 8–15. In a home game against the Nets, coach Mike D'Antoni settled on Lin as a temporary fix for the team's upheaval at point guard. He played more than 35 minutes in the win, posting new career highs with 25 points and 7 assists. After the buzzer, Pearl Jam's "Jeremy" echoed from the Madison Square Garden rafters. Within days, both Anthony and Stoudemire, the

team's two All-Stars and leading scorers, were out of the lineup due to injury. By the whims of fate, the Knicks were Lin's team.

The earliest days of what would mushroom into "Linsanity" were obscured by a Giants win in Super Bowl XLVI (and a breathtaking halftime performance by LMFAO with Madonna). The phenomenon sailed under the radar only briefly. New York reeled off seven straight victories, with Lin averaging 24.4 points and 9.1 assists. Despite being a spotty jumper, the sturdy 6-foot-3 ball-handler was a capable steward of D'Antoni's guard-centric offense that transformed Steve Nash from a borderline All-Star into a two-time MVP in Phoenix. Lin aggressively carved his way into the lane, used underappreciated physicality to live at the free-throw stripe, and fed teammates lobs and deft pocket passes. "I had this coach that was empowering me, constantly in my ear telling me 'Go, go, go. Trust your instincts,'" Lin said on a *Ringer* podcast. "A big part of Linsanity was just being in that environment, being in a pick-and-roll system that suited my style."

In a signature performance, Lin outscored Kobe Bryant 38–34. Prior to the game, Bryant had insisted that he did not know who Lin was. "I played against him multiple times in my rookie year," Lin later said on *Inside the Green Room*. "If anything, I stand out when I get onto the court— I don't look like anybody else."

It happens with the frequency of emerging cicadas, but New York is more fun when people care about local basketball. The firestorm of interest aimed at this unlikely hero—an Asian, Harvard-educated benchwarmer turned Mamba-slayer—felt unprecedented. Before each game there was a sense that, tonight, the spectacle would capsize in flames, and yet, for two weeks, it did not. Instead, Linsanity grew stronger. Due to friction between the MSG Network and Time Warner Cable, Knicks fans were forced to watch games in bars, which led to a communal, playoff-like atmosphere.

As the team won 10 of 13 games, throngs of Chinese fans packed the Garden and makeshift shrines to Lin appeared in Lower Manhattan. Lin was featured on back-to-back covers of *Sports Illustrated* and tabloid headlines screamed permutations of his last name, including LINCREDIBLE, THRILLIN, and VALINTINE'S GIFT. In incidents that were, at best, insensitive, ESPN used the phrase "chink in the armor" several times while

L

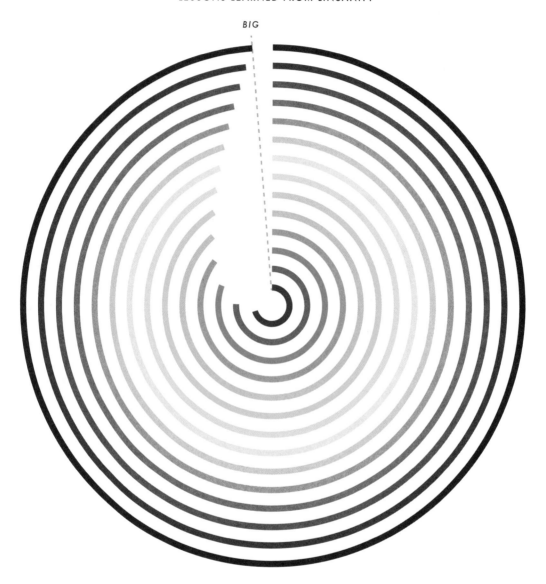

BIG

Delight is watching an improbable success.

Failure is when we give up on the possible.

What we want always changes with our needs.

Sometimes things don't need explanations.

We still haven't recovered from 9/11.

There's no magic, just pretty fun NBA guards.

Obsessing over winning is no way to live.

NYC is less about bullies than about characters.

A full life involves game-winners vs. the Raptors.

Two or so weeks every ten years is good enough.

An uncomplicated story can gas up an entire city.

There's never winning or losing with racists.

They want power and success, we want the Knicks.

Living in the moment is buying a Lin coffee mug.

reporting stories about him. "I don't think it was on purpose," Lin said. "At the same time, they've apologized. I don't care anymore."

As abruptly as it began, it ended. Anthony was a stubborn alpha in his prime, and his preference for operating in isolation at the elbow did not mesh with Lin's free-flowing game. "Everyone wasn't a fan of him being a new star," Stoudemire later told the *New York Daily News*. "So he didn't stay long. Jeremy was a great, great guy, great with teammates, worked hard. A lot of times you got to enjoy somebody else's success. That wasn't the case for us during that stretch." Following a six-game slide and worsening communications between D'Antoni and Anthony, D'Antoni was bullied into resigning. In late March, an MRI revealed that Lin had a partially torn meniscus that required surgery. He did not play for the team again.

During the off-season, Lin signed a so-called poison pill contract with the Rockets as a restricted free agent. The deal was cagily structured to backload the three-year commitment in a way that ballooned the Knicks' salary cap down the line. New York refused to match the offer, reportedly in part because owner James Dolan believed that Lin had worked with Houston to make it economically unpalatable. In subsequent years with the Rockets, Lakers, Hornets, and Nets, Lin proved himself to be an unremarkable but useful point guard—but never recaptured his former glory.

As he bounced around the league, there was often an unsettling tenor to the stream of criticism and mockery funneled in his direction from fans and the media. It was not exactly racist, but it was not exactly not racist, either. After a gnarly knee injury, Lin left the NBA and went to play for the Beijing Ducks. "Out here," he said of China, "this [2020] season has been the closest thing to Linsanity in New York."

LOAD MANAGEMENT

A term appropriate for cargo shipping or a masturbation-free November, load management translates as "precautionary rest." Using a black box of biometric data that include factors like playing time, practice, travel, and sleep, the tactic attempts to lessen the stress inflicted upon an NBA player's body by picking games that he should sit out.

Over the course of an 82-game slog, the goal is making sure that players are healthy for meaningful late-season contests. The specific phrase seems to have been introduced to basketball during the handling of Joel Embiid's post-surgery minutes with the Sixers, but the practice had been used for years. It notably drew attention in 2012, when commissioner David Stern fined the Spurs $250,000 for resting four starters in a marquee showdown against the Heat.

Kawhi Leonard, a prominent subject of load management, played only 60 games for the Raptors in 2019, never appearing in both games of any scheduled back-to-back. A year after missing 73 games and the postseason due to injury, he was named Finals Most Valuable Player and Toronto won the championship. Mark Cuban, owner of the Mavericks, referenced Leonard when praising the strategy. "I think it's the best thing to ever happen to the league," he said. "Worse than missing a player in a game is missing him in the playoffs. If you go back to the days where there were ten guys in the league playing 40-plus minutes, the quality of the game wasn't nearly as good."

By the end of the 2010s, load management was an unexpected frontline for basketball culture skirmishes. It caused grumbles when applied to superstars with troubling injury histories—especially in highly anticipated games—but was more controversial when younger and healthier players had their lean asses glued to the bench. On one side were sterilized sports scientists and teams interested in protecting human investments worth hundreds of millions of dollars; on the other stood fans, pundits, and former athletes who lunged at the chance to boast about how many minutes they played in 2002 (back when men were men and hats were Von Dutch). Even with ticket sales sullied by corporate luxury boxes and StubHub resellers, no one loved the idea of a family piling into a Hyundai Palisade, shucking out $650 for tickets, and watching an understudy instead of a headliner. The NBA threatened $100,000 fines for teams who rested studs in nationally televised games.

Active NBA players were caught in the middle. They attempted to balance medical advice,

THINGS WE REALIZED

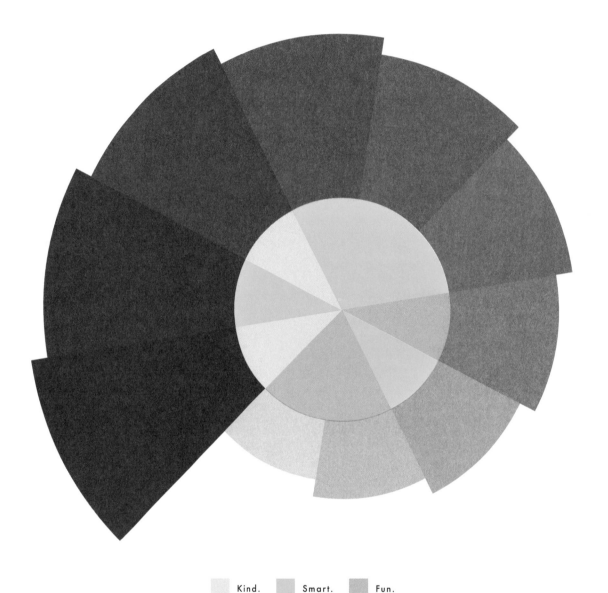

Kind. Smart. Fun.

All teams should be resting players often.

How you score is as important as how much.

Every franchise should employ a therapist.

The most valuable commodity is a draft pick.

The lottery/draft should not reward losing.

There's no winning culture, only good players.

Player empowerment is healthy for the NBA.

Fouls should be erased at the cost of five points.

There should be a multiball period in every game.

A full-court sudden-death shot should be allowed.

professional health, and competitive zeal. "I want to play every game," said Embiid, who was in the minority as a player who publicly objected to the practice. "Load management, that's some BS." Not all teams subscribed to the theory, either. "We've got to get off this load management crap," said soon-to-be-fired Knicks coach David Fizdale, when questioned about rookie RJ Barrett's heavy workload. "Latrell Sprewell averaged 42 minutes for a season. This kid is nineteen. Drop it already."

While players in the 1990s logged more minutes, today's game exceeds in speed, spacing, and prolonged intensity than the game in the era when Americans huddled around their rabbit-eared televisions to watch *Blossom*. With precautionary rest, maybe a player like Allen Iverson, who averaged an outlandish 41.4 minutes over the first 13 years of his career, would not have fizzled out in his early thirties. Considering his workload, the widespread criticism of Iverson's attitude toward practice now sounds like subhuman poop-grunts echoing around a mountain cave.

Besides ethical concerns about teams harvesting biometric information in an industry where the utility of a human body is inextricably linked to salary, the load management debate has clear implications for the NBA's regular season. If teams are signaling that some games—even ones fans circle on the schedule—are unimportant, why should anyone be invested in their outcome? Of course, this is all transpiring in an environment where postseason results have an oversize bearing on everything from individual legacies and coaching jobs to salaries and roster composition. The NBA, as always, wants it both ways.

LOB CITY

From the early to mid-2010s, the Clippers were a windmill-dunking circus that resurrected the spirit of Showtime in Los Angeles. Helmed by Chris Paul, the micromanaging point guard, and featuring the sky-touching frontcourt of Blake Griffin and DeAndre Jordan, the Clippers emasculated foes with the NBA's most pyrotechnic offense. The team posted a 65.8 percent winning percentage over six seasons under coach Doc Rivers, but was famed more for posterizing opponents and carping at referees than for victories.

The name Lob City was coined by Griffin, who excitedly uttered the phrase on a Fox Sports West video after learning about the team's acquisition of Paul. Within a month, the team was already sick of it. "We understand it, but that's not what we're about," Griffin told ESPN. "Before the game, we're not going out thinking, 'All right, it's Lob City tonight.' . . . If anybody says it in [the locker room], it's just a joke, making fun of the whole thing."

Despite showing earmarks of a potential champion—like finishing within the NBA's top four in net rating for four seasons straight—Lob City was undone by ill-timed injuries, a lack of bench depth, and, at times, mediocre defense. In a seven-game first-round series in 2015, Los Angeles defeated a 55-win San Antonio team that had obliterated the Heat in the previous season's Finals. The win had the emotional heft of a championship: "Finally," Chris Paul tearfully repeated after the game, hugging his brother and Billy Crystal, the star of *City Slickers II: The Legend of Curly's Gold*. In the Western Conference Semis, the Clippers blew a 3–1 series lead and were eliminated by the Rockets.

The Clippers' postseason failures robbed us of an epochal matchup against the Warriors, who rose to power during Lob City's prime. Los Angeles ousted Golden State in the first round of the 2014 Playoffs and the two teams did not meet again until 2019, after Lob City was disbanded. It was not just that both teams were electrifying—they hated each other. "We want to take their heads off, and they want to take our heads off," said the Warriors' Draymond Green, after a game rife with technicals and flagrant fouls. "That's just the way it is, so just roll with the punches."

By Lob City's end, a trio that once represented basketball at its most electrifying was detested. They were seen as losers, chokers, and whiners, a collection of arrogant prima donnas who basked in the humiliation of poverty franchises but came up short against legitimate adversaries. "It was the biggest front-running team," said Jared Dudley, who played for the Clippers in 2014. "You're up twenty, everything's good, throwing lobs. Down twenty, people want to fight,

L

bickering." By the 2019 season, Paul was in Houston, Griffin was in Detroit, and Jordan was in Dallas.

LOST ARTS

Back in 1994, several years before the modern NBA took form, a shot doctor named Buzz Braman was dismayed about changes that he believed were perverting basketball. "Shooting has become a lost art," he wrote in an article about 3-point mechanics that ran in *Popular Science*. "Instead of practicing shooting, young players spend their time practicing 'the slam.'" Nearly three decades later, it is clear Braman's concern about the survival of shooting was misplaced.

But even as long-range bombing thrives, that plaintive tone lives on. Recipes are being forgotten. In the eyes of basketball's caretakers, imperiled elements of the sport include midrange jumpers, post play, screen-setting, free throws, defense, interior defense, rebounding, the center position, the traditional role of the big man, toughness, human conversation, passing, scoring, trash talk, taking charges, the bank shot, the way that Paul George and Kawhi Leonard play on both sides of the court, veteran mentorship, moving without the ball, old-school style, the floater, ball rotation, skyhooks, the competitiveness of Paul Pierce and Kobe Bryant, nicknames, and post entry passes. For heaven's sake, will these guys just put down their phones already!

LOST BOYS

In the summer of 1995—a moment owned by Raekwon's *Only Built 4 Cuban Linx*—Kevin Garnett became the first modern player to leapfrog from high school to the NBA ranks. His underage contemporaries trickled in slowly at first, but, by the early 2000s, the league was awash in fake IDs, Bartles & Jaymes wine coolers, requests to borrow mom's Aerostar for a trip to Spencer Gifts, and the stench of teen spirit. In

the 2001 draft, four of the top eight picks were high schoolers, including Tyson Chandler and Eddy Curry. By 2004, eight of the first nineteen players arrived straight from the prom.

While superstars like Garnett, Kobe Bryant, Tracy McGrady, LeBron James, and Dwight Howard did not play a nanosecond of college ball, powerful forces were unhappy about the league's youth movement. The NCAA, for one, was unable to leech profits off the unpaid servitude of the nation's premier schoolboy prospects. NBA commissioner David Stern cited flimsy concerns about the unseemly presence of scouts in high school gyms, but was more interested in mitigating the risks of investing draft picks in unproven talent. In other quarters, the idea of eighteen-year-olds being paid millions of dollars a year caused unarticulated queasiness—especially with the intrinsic dynamics of race and class.

"As a Black guy, you kind of think that's the reason why it's coming up," said Jermaine O'Neal, who was drafted out of high school in the 1996 draft and made six All-Star teams for the Pacers. "You don't hear about it in baseball or hockey. To say you have to be twenty, twenty-one to get in the league, it's unconstitutional. If I can go to the U.S. Army and fight the war at eighteen, why can't you play basketball for 48 minutes?"

Hostility toward the league's acceptance of high-schoolers led to paternalistic focus on players with negative experiences. The message was that these wayward boys should have been coerced into playing in college *for their own good*. Much was made of the doomed adolescent hubris of Rashard Lewis, who slid into the second round of the 1998 draft and wept in the green room (he went on to make a pair of All-Star teams and more than $150 million during his sixteen-year career). Jonathan Bender and Darius Miles were lanky wings with tantalizing abilities and knees that betrayed them in their early twenties. DeSagana Diop, a Senegal-born center, was taken eighth in 2001 but failed to live up to the praise of writer Skip Bayless: "Diop is the only man alive age eighteen or above with the potential to be better than Shaquille O'Neal," he said.

Korleone Young, a 6-foot-7 forward from Wichita who was picked fortieth by the Pistons in 1998, played only 15 minutes in the NBA. "We kept him for a year, really, because we just felt sorry for the kid," coach Alvin Gentry later told *Grantland*. After being cut by Detroit, Young had $300,000 in

HYPED YOUTHS

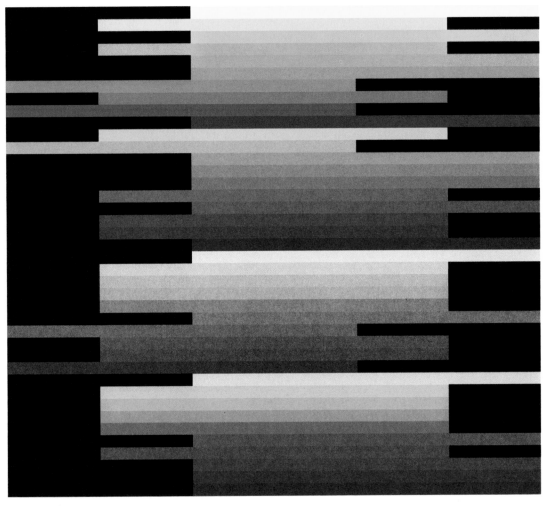

FELL SHORT OF OUR WACKY EXPECTATIONS ←————————→ *100 PERCENT DELIVERED*

Aaliyah.	Eddy Curry.	Kenan Thompson.	Miley Cyrus.
Austin Rivers.	Felipe López.	Kyle Anderson.	Monica.
Billie Eilish.	Foxy Brown.	Lil B.	O. J. Mayo.
Brandon Knight.	Harrison Barnes.	Lil' Bow Wow.	Sebastian Telfair.
Brandy.	Ian MacKaye.	Lil Noo Noo.	Shabazz Muhammad.
Britney Spears.	Jabari Parker.	Lil Wayne.	Soulja Boy.
Cliff Alexander.	Jamal Mashburn.	Lil Xan.	Stanley Johnson.
Dajuan Wagner.	Jared Jeffries.	Lil Yachty.	Taylor Swift.
Darko Miličić.	Jared Sullinger.	Lindsay Lohan.	Trippie Redd.
Earl Sweatshirt.	Justin Bieber.	Lloyd Daniels.	Tyson Chandler.

the bank and spent $120,000 of it on jewelry—and was promptly robbed of it while walking around Philadelphia. It is reassuring to identify Young's missteps, some of which could have been avoided with better guidance, but there is less interest in performing career autopsies on fellow fortieth picks like Denham Brown, Sun Yue, Grant Jerrett, and Diamond Stone, who combined to play a total of 103 NBA minutes. Maybe Young was not very good at basketball.

Kwame Brown, the first high-schooler to be taken with the top overall pick, was selected by the Wizards in 2001 and played unremarkably for seven teams over a dozen seasons. While the 6-foot-11 center is viewed as a blemish on Michael Jordan's résumé as an executive, he was representative of a draft class strewn with high school underachievers. In retrospect, perhaps they were early millennials whose emotional sensitivity was dismissed as a weakness by older generations. Brown is most known for being bullied by Jordan (both as a member of management and as a teammate) over three and a half seasons in Washington. Would Brown have turned out differently with more nurturing surroundings? Probably not. But a teenager who has spent time in a homeless shelter is unlikely to benefit from being held underwater in a pool of boomer masculinity.

Despite a reputation for being soft and unfocused, Brown was a solid defender who averaged 9.0 rebounds and 1.0 blocks per 36 minutes during his career. His issues came on the other side of the ball, where he had granite hands and a klutzy touch. After being traded to Los Angeles, Kwame was insulted by another member of the Bulls dynasty, this time Lakers coach Phil Jackson, who reportedly called him a "pussy" and made "meow" noises as Brown strolled past. While with the Lakers, Brown drew headlines for allegedly snatching a $190 chocolate cake from a stranger outside of a Hermosa Beach nightclub and throwing it at teammate Ronny Turiaf.

In 2006, the NBA instituted a policy requiring draft candidates to be nineteen years old and at least a year removed from high school. The so-called one-and-done rule has led to freshman-heavy drafts—in 2020, the first six players selected all played a single season of college ball, with the exception of LaMelo Ball, who went overseas instead. "There's a bigger reason why the media constantly put a negative spin on things involving me," Brown told HoopsHype

after his retirement. "The league wants to justify the one-and-done rule. I think they've made me the poster child for why players shouldn't go straight to the NBA from high school."

LOVE, KEVIN

A handsome, stubbly paean to the impermanence of all things, Kevin Love went from a superstar who could not make the postseason to the third wheel on a championship team. Over that span, he morphed from the floor-stretching power forward of the future into an undersized, tweener center. But Love stayed the same: he kept swishing 3s, throwing the best outlet passes in the business, drawing bullshit fouls with pump-fakes, inhaling rebounds, and being passable on defense. It was the game that changed.

The nephew of Mike Love of the Beach Boys, Kevin was selected by Memphis with the fifth pick in the 2008 draft and flipped to Minnesota as part of a package for O. J. Mayo. "Thick legs anchor him to the floor," wrote NBADraft.net, of Love's early girthiness. As a rookie, he was portly, knocked down only two 3-pointers, and had a chinstrap beard that made him look like a member of Non Phixion.

Over the next five years, Love developed into an oft-injured All-Star who provided a steep competitive advantage in the early 2010s: he was the rare power forward who was beefy enough to lead the NBA in rebounds but had the perimeter shooting to drag opposing big men 25 feet away from the paint. In 2014, the metric of Box Plus/Minus put Love second in the NBA, wedged glamorously between Kevin Durant and LeBron James. He appeared to be the vanguard of modernity, like a big yellow Hummer H2. Though it is now clear that Love was really a semipermeable membrane between generations, it is also true that the Timberwolves' front office stooges failed to surround him with enough good running mates to make the playoffs even once.

Before the 2015 season, Love was traded to Cleveland for a package that included Andrew Wiggins, the top overall pick in the off-season draft. Love's numbers plunged beside James and Kyrie Irving, and, at times, his role shifted from offensive hub to idle floor-spacer. He was rumored to be

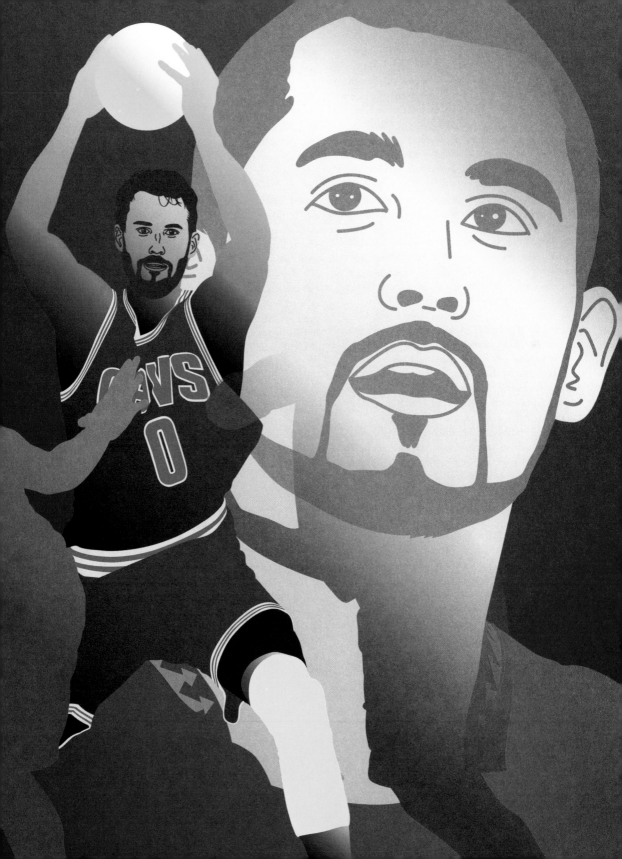

unhappy. "Stop trying to find a way to FIT-OUT and just FIT-IN," James posted, in a subtweet some believed was aimed at Love. "Be a part of something special!" The Cavaliers went to the Finals four consecutive times. In Cleveland's lone series victory, Love defensively put the clamps on the Warriors' Stephen Curry in a climactic Game 7 sequence at the top of the arc. When asked about the play in an ESPN interview, Curry expressed regrets about firing up an off-balance 3-pointer. "I look back and think I could have easily gone around [him]," he said. (Love sarcastically responded on Twitter with one word: "Easily.")

After James and Irving decamped for coastal utopias, Love became the last of the title-winning threesome to remain in Cleveland. He was plagued by injuries and saddled with a leaden contract (from the team's perspective) worth $120 million over four years—making him a difficult piece for a rebuilding franchise to flip. In 2019, the Cavs went 19-63, with only the Knicks winning fewer games.

In response to being marooned in the Rock & Roll capital of the world, Love went full *Office Space*, with zero fucks given on the job. He missed endless games with injuries that kept him lounging in his TriBeCa apartment (which features "Defiance" scripted in neon lighting on one wall), appeared visibly frustrated with young teammates like Collin Sexton, and angrily slapped an inbounds pass on to the court which led to a 3-pointer by Cleveland's opponent. "I just hope that you judge my character, judge me as a man," Love said on a Zoom call with reporters after the inbounding fiasco. "I mean, the basketball stuff, you can crush me, you can kill me by any means. I'll take that on the chin all day."

Later in his career, Love became an advocate for mental health awareness—helping break one of the remaining taboos in a hyper-masculine vocation where admission of vulnerability is unacceptable. In an essay for the *Players' Tribune*, he detailed having a panic attack during a game and undergoing therapy. "No matter what our circumstances, we're all carrying around things that hurt," he wrote. "And they can hurt us if we keep them buried inside."

LOWRY, KYLE

An undersized point guard known for his streaky shooting, flopping, and stupendously thicc wagon, Kyle Lowry has mastered basketball's small but important jobs. He dishes unflashy passes, swerves into big men to draw fouls, boxes out taller opponents, and darts into the lane as a weak-side defender to entice a charge call. Also, Lowry has an outrageous trailer load of ass. "He's the most physical player on the floor, but it doesn't look athletic," coach Billy Lange, who helped recruit Lowry to Villanova University, later told ESPN. "He's waddling around with that body."

Despite Lowry's decade of excellence and the success of teams he helmed in Toronto, he was labeled a postseason choker by practitioners of small sample cleromancy. His bummy playoff performances included going 18 for 57 from the floor against the Wizards in 2015 and, the following year, clanging 36 of 43 shots from beyond the arc against the Pacers. Even in the midst of the 2019 playoff run that culminated with the Raptors claiming their first franchise title, Lowry was frequently trashed. Held scoreless on 0–7 shooting (with 7 rebounds, 8 assists, 2 steals, and a +11 plus/minus) in a first-round loss to Orlando, he asserted that he had impacted the game despite firing blanks. "Oh, hell no," screamed comedian Charles Barkley in response, while emanating the energy of a picnic ham marinated in Seagram's gin. "You're supposed to be an All-Star!" Later, after Lowry shot 2–10 in an Eastern Conference Semifinal loss against Philadelphia, a post on a blog called *12up* scorched him with the headline "Kyle Lowry Quickly Proving He's the Most Disastrous Postseason Player of Our Generation."

In the 2019 Finals, Lowry was redeemed. He posted 16.2 points and 7.2 assists per game, while shooting 36.8 percent from 3-point range. But, more importantly, he demonstrated his knack for quietly altering games in the biggest moments: the Raptors were 11.9 points per 100 possessions better with him on the court during the postseason. After his crunch-time demons were exorcised by a championship ring, Lowry was suddenly (and justifiably) viewed as an underappreciated winner. The man with a wagon became the man with a bandwagon.

In lieu of a punch-by-punch account, here are things that happened. Artest climbed into the stands and grabbed the wrong fan. Teammate Stephen Jackson and other Pacers followed him, with skirmishes erupting. Fans charged down to the court to confront Indiana players, where Jermaine O'Neal slipped on spilled liquid while throwing a potentially life-changing haymaker. Spit, bottles, and chairs rained down on Pacers players as they entered the tunnel leading to their locker room. "I was raised to be with my brothers through thick and thin," Jackson said on *The Rich Eisen Show*. "When [Artest] went, I just went with him. I didn't think twice. Went in there, laid a couple guys out."

Dubbed the "Malice at the Palace," the incident forced uncomfortable conversations about the fault lines that ran between NBA players and abusive fans. Part of live basketball's appeal—and the price tag of courtside seats—is proximity that sports like football and baseball do not afford. The collapse of the invisible fence separating athletes and screeching mobs proved that a ticket stub did not offer immunity from consequences for ugly behavior. "The fans are not part of the family, the NBA family," Scot Pollard, a big man on the Pacers, told *Grantland*. "Even though you're fighting against these guys on the court, they're still in the other team's jerseys. You're not trying to kill anybody. But the fans don't know that, and you don't know what they're thinking. That changed the whole scenario."

Conservative pundits saw it differently. "I think it's time to get rid of this whole National Basketball Association," said now-dead radio host Rush Limbaugh, in response to the brawl. "Call it the TBA, the Thug Basketball Association, and stop calling them teams. Call 'em gangs." In the manner of a Klansman unfurling a freshly pressed robe, he presented a fantasy in which players carried guns on the court and sold CDs at the concession stand. "If a fight breaks out, hey, it's what happens!" Limbaugh said, as pleased with himself as a toddler inspecting his own glistening turd. "They're going in to watch the Crips and the Bloods out there."

Whether the NBA agreed with its players or Limbaugh, the organization's response revealed a league petrified by the optics of players fighting with fans. Artest was suspended for 73 games and the postseason, Jackson was suspended for 30 games, and O'Neal was suspended 15 games after arbitration. The punishments led to the disintegration of a Pacer team with legitimate championship ambitions. A year

MALICE AT THE PALACE

On November 19, 2004, an early season showdown between the defending champion Pistons and the Pacers team they had bested in the Eastern Conference Finals turned into more than a heartland rivalry. It became a day for retribution. With the Pacers holding an 11-point lead deep in the fourth quarter, Indiana tough guy Ron Artest hacked Ben Wallace on a meaningless layup attempt. Wallace overreacted by shoving Artest—perhaps in part because the center had lost his mother only days before—and the teams faced off in a growling scrum. Artest bizarrely lay down on the scorer's table and toyed with a pair of broadcasting headphones. It might have ended there, but a Detroit fan heaved a plastic cup of beer at Artest, splashing him in the chest and face.

Jeff Van Gundy catching a Marcus Camby punch.

Jeff Van Gundy getting stomped by Alonzo Mourning.

Jermaine O'Neal throwing a big ol' haymaker at a fan.

LeBron James reading a letter set in Comic Sans.

LeBron James seeing his jersey burned in Cleveland.

Masai Ujiri being shoved after Game 6.

Michael Jordan being famous for crying.

Ron Artest going into the stands to fight.

Rudy Gobert being blamed for COVID-19.

Stephen Jackson backing up Ron Artest.

later, the league installed a dress code and penalties for fighting skyrocketed. "The NBA was making an example of me at that point in time," Carmelo Anthony told *The Undefeated*, of being suspended 15 games while playing for Denver. "You have to think about where the NBA was at that point in time. The image of the NBA, Indiana-Detroit and what was going on those days."

MARBURY, STEPHON

Once viewed as the avatar of the spoiled star—overhyped, underachieving, greedy, malignant—Stephon Marbury has been redeemed not only by our updated view on professional athletes but through his own deeds. He was a ball-dominant scorer and distributor. He muscled his way to the league's biggest media market. He sold his own brand of affordable Starbury basketball sneakers for $15. He live-streamed a mental illness meltdown. As a reward for helping cast the mold for contemporary playmaking and empowerment, the prickly Marbury was torn to shreds.

From the beginning, Marbury faced the scrutiny from outsiders that would trail him throughout his career, like bloodhounds on a scent. His adolescence as a basketball phenomenon in Brooklyn's Coney Island projects was immortalized in Darcy Frey's *The Last Shot*, a 1994 book that focused on several neighborhood teens hoping to improve their lives through the sport. The 6-foot-2 point guard was a city legend at Lincoln High and with the AAU Gauchos, played one season at Georgia Tech, and was drafted fourth overall in the 1996 draft (he landed in Minnesota in an immediate trade that involved Ray Allen). "I worry about him mentally," said his college coach, Bobby Cremins. "I would recommend immediately that he go to that city, get acclimated, get an apartment, and do exactly what that team tells him to do."

The Timberwolves franchise was only eight years old, but the core of Marbury, Kevin Garnett, and Tom Gugliotta glinted with promise: the team went to the playoffs for the first time in Marbury's rookie season and, the following year, posted its first winning record. But the budding trio died on the vine. "All Stephon talked about was going home to New York and playing in a major market so he could get the publicity and promotions he feels he's being cheated out of," Gugliotta said later. "Stephon couldn't take being overshadowed by Kevin Garnett."

Though Marbury is blamed for splintering the team by initiating a trade to New Jersey, it is rarely mentioned that Googs abandoned the team first, signing a free agent contract with Phoenix for less money than Minnesota reportedly offered.

Marbury and former members of the T-Wolves pack would howl at each other for years. On one occasion, he said that comparing Amar'e Stoudemire to Garnett was "like Michael Jordan and Mario Elie—it's not even close." Garnett fired back. "Out of all his things, he's got what, three kids, a wife, bills. But I'm on his mind every day. It's kind of flattering. It's like a girl," he said in the *Arizona Republic*.

Marbury would make two All-Star teams, once with the Nets and again with the Suns (where he reunited with a shopworn Gugliotta). He was a wonderful offensive threat, vicious off the dribble and a fullback in the lane, whose cannonball-smooth head, evil eyebrows, and Brooklyn arrogance radiated confrontation. Critics branded him narcissistic, but Marbury finished among the league's top 5 in assists per game five times. "He's a very unselfish player," said Heat coach Pat Riley in 2000. "He kicks the ball to open shooters and uses his quickness to get the ball to other people. I don't see a flaw in his game at all."

Still in his prime, Marbury was traded again—this time to the Knicks, where he was anointed the savior of his hometown cagers. After one excellent season, his game deteriorated. He was enmeshed in the sexual harassment trial of team executive Isiah Thomas and testified that he had hooked up with a Knicks intern in his truck. His sneaker brand stumbled. The coup de grace was a 24-hour livestream where he ranted and wept while shirtless. "I wanted to kill myself some days," Marbury said on HBO's *Real Sports*. "It wasn't about basketball. It started to become about me. Because I was that depressed and I was that sick."

After exiting the NBA in his early thirties, Marbury created a successful second act in China. As a member of the CBA's Beijing Ducks, he won an MVP award, captured three titles, and became a beloved icon with a musical play and a film made about his life. He has "China" tattooed on his arm. During the coronavirus outbreak, he tried to broker a deal to export ten million N95 masks from China to New York City. "When you have so many people writing about you, and what they're saying is negative, people tend to fall right in line with it," Marbury told *The New Yorker*. "They'll depict this little Black kid from Coney Island as this rebellious tyrant. And it was never that."

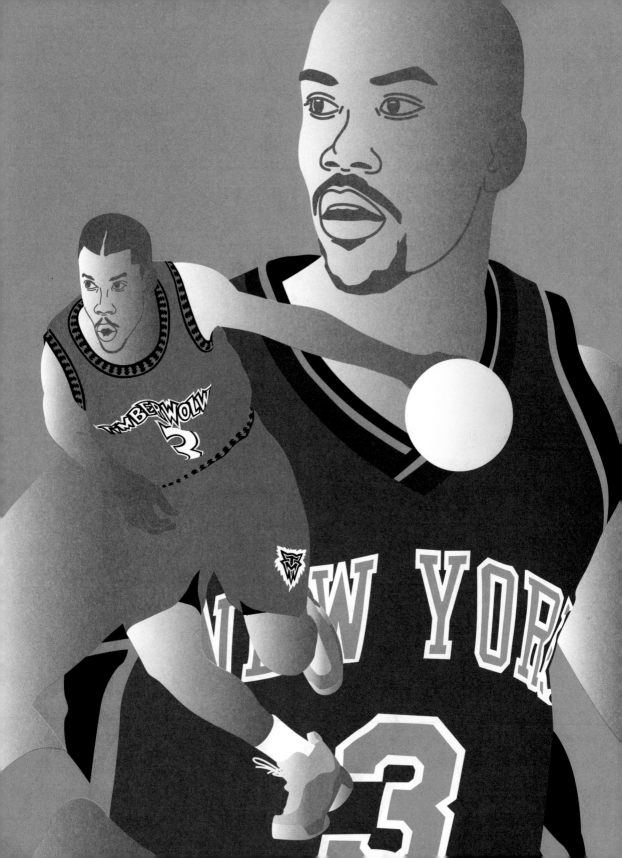

MARION, SHAWN

Like a volleyball star who rules a pick-up run solely off leaping, coordination, and bulbous calves, Shawn Marion failed traditional eye tests for NBA stardom. His dribbling was high and jagged. Though he saw the floor capably, his passes were often two-handed shovels that looked as if he was dousing a campfire with a bucket of water. His jumper was notoriously gruesome: a shotput in which the ball migrated from his waist to in front of his eyes and then was short-armed in the vicinity of the hoop. Despite the ugly-hotness of his game, the Matrix was named to four All-Star teams over a sixteen-year career that included winning a championship with the Mavericks—a feat that tasked him with being LeBron James's primary defender in the 2011 Finals.

Marion was built like a superhero created in an island laboratory by scientists who had only a PDF of James Naismith's rule book—yet needed to liberate the globe from the monochromatic tyranny of the San Antonio Spurs. He was 6-foot-7 with a condor's wingspan, could jump out of the gym, and sped the court as if riding a Ducati. Marion was an electrifying finisher who rammed in lobs while straddling the shoulders of grown men and developed an ungainly jump-hook. Defensively, he bred pandemonium. Among non-centers, the only modern players to mirror his blend of steals and blocks are an elite clique of anarchy enthusiasts that includes Michael Jordan and Andrei Kirilenko.

Despite his poor form, Marion became a passable shooter from deep. From his third season onward, Marion made 33.5 percent of his 3s—not great, but not embarrassing. "He just bumped into a ceiling much lower than it would have been if he ever learned to shoot the ball correctly," shooting coach David Thorpe told the *New York Times*. "People would say, 'Well, it's worked for him.' And I would say, 'Not really.'"

Drafted by Phoenix with the ninth pick in 1999, Marion was a stud by his second season, scoring 17.3 points and gobbling up 10.7 rebounds a game. His role in basketball history changed with the arrival of coach Mike D'Antoni, who turned him into a full-time power forward. Goliaths like Tim Duncan, Pau Gasol, and Dirk Nowitzki still ruled the Pampas at the position, but Marion represented the dawn of the hypermobile, rim-protecting stretch 4. There are echoes of his game today in players like Jerami Grant and Jonathan Isaac. "They say, 'You were born a generation, a decade, too early!'" Marion said in an interview with HoopsHype. "Yeah, but it's okay though. I had a big piece of that last decade and did pretty well."

MCGRADY, TRACY

Due to the reigns of Michael Jordan and LeBron James, the last thirty-five years have provided few opportunities for other men to seize the title of the planet's best player. The window begins in 1999, with Jordan's first real retirement, and ends in 2006, when James lugged the Cavaliers to 50 wins and the second round of the postseason. In that time of uncertainty a legion of strongmen laid honest claim to the throne: Tim Duncan, Shaquille O'Neal, Allen Iverson, Kevin Garnett, Dirk Nowitzki, Kobe Bryant. But for a brief sliver—specifically, the 2003 season—the greatest basketball player on the planet was Tracy McGrady.

McGrady grew up in Auburndale, Florida. His mother was a housecleaner at Disney's Yacht and Beach Resorts in Orlando, which would later be part of the NBA's COVID Bubble. Modeling his game after that of local star Anfernee Hardaway of the Magic, Tracy was a stunning athlete. He stood 6-foot-8, with a 7-foot-1 wingspan and a 40-plus-inch vertical leap. He commanded a plume of airspace around the basket like a center, but ran the floor with a smooth, loping gait and flicked wrap-around passes to teammates like a point guard. McGrady cashed in impossible, twisting finishes around the rim where he hung in midair—just sort of figuring things out—and rained humiliation upon unlucky centers with one-handed baseline dunks.

The only high-schooler taken in the 1997 draft, McGrady was groomed slowly by the Raptors, averaging only 8 points and 20.2 minutes over his first two seasons. He was described as "living like a shut-in," alone in an apartment overlooking Lake Ontario. "In two months, Tracy's gone from 18 years old to around 26," teammate Walt "The Wizard" Williams told *Sports Illustrated*. "He's learned that there are no mommies around here." It was an era when NBA teams did not believe teens were mature enough to handle grown-man playing time (precocious draftees like Kobe Bryant and Jermaine O'Neal had similar experiences at the time).

M

REASONS PEOPLE AREN'T THE GOAT (EXCLUDING INJURY OR DEATH)

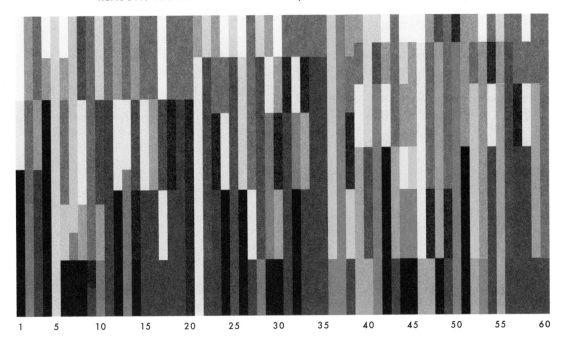

Bad timing.	Humorlessness.	Outside interests.
Caring too much.	Lack of ambition.	Running out of talent.
Dubious teammates.	Lousy luck.	Self-care.
Gen-X tranquility.	Nachos kink (no shaming).	The wrong place.

1. 21 Savage.
2. Adele.
3. André 3000.
4. Anthony Davis.
5. Beyoncé.
6. Carmelo Anthony.
7. Charles Barkley.
8. Chris Webber.
9. Christian Laettner.
10. Common.
11. Dave Chappelle.
12. Dave Grohl.
13. Dirk Nowitzki.
14. DMX.
15. Dwight Howard.

16. Frank Ocean.
17. James Harden.
18. Jeff Mangum.
19. Joe Pesci.
20. Julian Casablancas.
21. Karl-Anthony Towns.
22. Kawhi Leonard.
23. Kendrick Lamar.
24. Kenny Anderson.
25. Kevin Durant.
26. Kevin Garnett.
27. Klay Thompson.
28. Kobe Bryant.
29. Kristaps Porziņģis.
30. Lamar Odom.

31. Larry David.
32. Larry Johnson.
33. Lauryn Hill.
34. Lena Dunham.
35. Lil Uzi Vert.
36. Luka Dončić.
37. Manu Ginóbili.
38. Mase.
39. Method Man.
40. Michael Jordan.
41. Nas.
42. Nicki Minaj.
43. Oprah.
44. Patrick Ewing.
45. Paul Pierce.

46. Penny Hardaway.
47. Rasheed Wallace.
48. Ray Allen.
49. Rick Moranis.
50. Robert Horry.
51. Scottie Pippen.
52. Shaquille O'Neal.
53. Shyne.
54. Stephen Curry.
55. T.I.
56. Thom Yorke.
57. Tim Duncan.
58. Tracy McGrady.
59. Vince Carter.
60. Young Thug.

In a related vein, McGrady's habit of taking naps was mocked as an indicator of apathy, though stars fabled for their work ethic like Bryant and James later made them a focus of pregame preparation. By the end of the 2010s, players and teams viewed sleep deprivation as a serious problem that was inherently tied to the league's travel schedule. "I think in a couple years," Tobias Harris told ESPN, "it will be an issue that's talked about, like the NFL with concussions."

Toronto's cautiousness was a mistake. After spending part of his third season coming off the bench, McGrady became a restricted free agent. Rather than playing for a decade next to his distant cousin Vince Carter in Canada, he headed back to his hometown Magic, where he was joined by marquee free agent Grant Hill. "I didn't know he was that good," said Hill, who would suit up only for forty-seven games over the next four seasons due to injuries. "I don't think he knew he was that good. His basketball mind and his understanding of the game was off the charts. He was forced into becoming a scorer because he didn't have the help around him." McGrady went on to make seven consecutive All-Star appearances, four with Orlando and three with Houston.

In 2003, McGrady was unparalleled. He led the NBA in scoring with 32.1 points per game, along with 6.5 rebounds, 5.5 assists, and 1.7 steals. By more baroque measurements, he led the league in usage rate, Win Shares per 48 minutes, Box Plus/Minus, value over replacement player, and player efficiency rating. He finished fourth in MVP voting because of the Magic's pedestrian 42–40 record.

The bias toward team success—especially in the postseason—haunted McGrady's career. In the seven trips he made to the playoffs during his prime, a span that included three straight Game 7 losses, he never made it out of the first round. It was not due to a lack of excellence on his part: over the period, he averaged 28.5 points, 6.9 rebounds, and 6.2 assists. Nevertheless, it became a pox on the House of McGrady, and his sleepy eyes and decaffeinated personality hung with the heaviness of disappointment. In 2017, he was inducted into the Basketball Hall of Fame. "Anybody can be a champion," McGrady said. "But everybody can't be in the Hall of Fame. This is it. This is my championship."

MENTAL HEALTH

In a profession that interprets wins and losses as a referendum on one's character, any admission of mental weakness has been taboo. Players with psychological issues have been seen as colorful, troubled oddballs—not people in need of help—and more than a few have slipped through the cracks.

Delonte West, for example, was a combo guard who spent most of his career on the Celtics and Cavaliers. He was arrested for riding a three-wheeler with an arsenal of guns, worked at a furniture chain during the 2011 lockout, and was photographed shoeless outside a Houston-area Jack in the Box. While he was diagnosed as bipolar and spent time in the hospital as a child for addiction and self-harm, West remains best known as the punchline for a crude joke about LeBron James's mother.

An even sadder case was Eddie Griffin, a forward who was taken seventh overall in the 2001 draft. Battling addiction and alcoholism, he played only 303 career games and was waived by Minnesota in 2007. Several months later, he drove his SUV into a moving freight train and died in the fiery collision. "Eddie struggled with some issues, but when you got to know him as a kid and as a player, he was genuine and he was a good kid," said Nate Blackwell, a Philadelphia-area coach who had been attempting to resuscitate Griffin's basketball career. "Unfortunately, we didn't get a chance to see the real Eddie come back."

Discussion of mental health has become more acceptable. In 2018, DeMar DeRozan, an acrobatic All-Star wing who excels at drawing fouls, tweeted, "This depression get the best of me." It was not millennial meme-craft, but an acknowledgment of lifelong pain. "It's one of them things that no matter how indestructible we look like we are, we're all human at the end of the day," he told the *Toronto Star*. "We all got feelings." In part due to the honesty of players like Kyrie Irving, Kevin Love, and Paul George, the NBA's de-stigmatization of mental health issues has kept pace with that of the larger society.

But conversations about the impact of mental health on performance are murkier. Admitting you have bad nights is different from broadcasting a vulnerability that could damage your earning potential in an industry that insists athletes possess the stoicism of General MacArthur, gnawing on a corncob pipe and staring at the gray horizon.

Mental aspects of basketball can blur lines between psychology and performance. Andris Biedriņš was a 6-foot-11 defensive specialist for the Warriors who led the league in fouls in 2007, field-goal percentage in 2008, and averaged a double-double in 2009. The following season, the Latvian lost the ability to make free throws. A lifetime 53.2 percent shooter from the stripe until then, he saw his success rate plung to 16 percent by 2010. The slump consumed the rest of his game like fire leaping from the eaves of a neighbor's house, and he was soon out of the league.

Players such as Andre Iguodala and Joakim Noah also suffered dramatic declines in their respective free-throw percentages, years into their careers, without explanation.

Another mystery involved Markelle Fultz, the point guard selected by Philadelphia with the top overall pick in the 2017 draft. The University of Washington freshman was a toolsy prospect who possessed the ability to score or pass, navigated the lane with stick-shift changes of direction, and chauffeured the ball to the rack in the manner of a waiter carrying a champagne bottle through a crowded discotheque. Bryan Colangelo, the Sixers' general manager, acquired the first pick from the Celtics by packaging the third overall pick and a future first rounder (the selections became Jayson Tatum and Romeo Langford). Fultz was viewed as the final piece of Philadelphia's league-mandated rebuilding strategy known as Process 2 Progress.

Over the next two years, Fultz played in only 33 games for Philadelphia, sitting out extended stretches due to an unknown shoulder ailment. Eventually categorized as thoracic outlet syndrome by a doctor who insisted the problem was physical, the condition manifested in inconsistent ways: on free throws but not pull-up jumpers, on 3s but not long 2-pointers. Rumors speculated about motorcycle crashes, unorthodox workouts with his personal coach that altered his form, and undiagnosed anxiety.

Maybe it was just the yips. During Burnergate, one of the anonymous Twitter accounts claimed by Colangelo's wife (@s_bonhams, also known as Still Balling) wrote, "The so-called mentor tried to force him to change the shot. Tapes have surfaced of the guy making Markelle shoot while sitting on a chair, while on his back on the floor etc. The guy denies it as doesn't want to say Y was forced out of kid's life. Y nobody reports this."

Fultz never revealed the cause of his issues and responded to reporters' queries about the condition of his shoulder with silence. He added to the X-Files–like intrigue on his own Twitter feed, posting, "You really can't trust NO ONE!!" without specifying which Cigarette Smoking Man had betrayed him. At the 2019 trade deadline, Fultz was traded to Orlando. He went on to provide solid minutes for the Magic, but has yet to regain his touch from behind the arc.

MIDRANGE JUMPERS

Shots that originate in the purgatorial crescent that separates the restricted area near the basket and the 3-point arc are called midrange jumpers. They could be pull-ups, turnarounds, catch-and-shoots, stepbacks, or any other delivery method. While midrange jumpers have been part of the sport since peach baskets were first bolted to walls, these innocuous field-goal attempts have become a touchstone in basketball culture wars. To some, this ribbon of turf acts as Alsace-Lorraine between quants and vibeists fighting for the very soul of the game.

For ages, the midrange jumper was regarded as a vital skill. Little guys used it to avoid challenging sequoias at the rim. Big men used it to complement their post games, squaring up to shoot over foes who preferred to sumo wrestle in the paint. In the early 2000s, it was midrange jumpers—rather than 3-pointers—that were regarded as the primary tool for keeping defenses from jamming up the lane. Frontcourt lugs like Karl Malone, Brian Grant, and Horace Grant took more 2-point shots from beyond 16 feet than from any other zone.

As time went on, teams began paying closer attention to the effect of shot location on the value

OTHER THINGS MIDRANGE FANS LOVE

Loyalty to one city forever.
Being present in the moment.
Getting to the airport early.
Leaving detailed messages.
There being no "I" in "team."

Army-grade flashlights.
Tactical sunglasses.
Tipping the right amount.
Sturdy phone cases.
Classic guitar solos.

Gut-check o'clock.
Pulled-up bootstraps.
Barbecued brisket.
A total team effort.
Playing not to lose.

of field-goal attempts. Even players who excelled at making long 2s were rarely sinking half of their shots, and the average field-goal percentage on jumpers over 10 feet hovered below 40 percent. Michael Jordan, the omnipotent god, made 49.5 percent of them over the 1997 season.

The argument against midrange jumpers is simple: they are less valuable than other shots. Field goals taken at the rim are successful at higher percentages, earn more fouls, and create opportunities for offensive rebounds. Three-pointers are worth 50 percent more. A few years ago, statistician Stephen Shea used data from the 2017 season to make a claim that sounds implausible: a contested 3-pointer was worth 0.94 points per attempt and an open midrange jumper was worth 0.85 points per attempt. Everything we had been taught about the importance of sticking jumpers from the elbow was from an alternative universe.

As usual, the splayed logo of Jordan hangs over the discourse. Besides his memorable dunks and love of denim that survived a hyena attack, Jordan's signature on-court move was contorting into a diagonal, 12-foot fadeaway. Just as the rockist approach to music codifies rock 'n' roll values in stone, reverence for the midrange jumper is inextricably from idolatry of the Chicago superstar. The idea that Jordan's favorite shot should be avoided feels like blasphemy—the rise of an impious new faith that worships spreadsheets full of indecipherable numerology runes. "I grew up being a Michael Jordan, Kobe fan," said Zach LaVine, the Bulls' shooting guard, to the *Chicago Sun-Times*. "I know that some of the greatest scorers in NBA history were midrange, midpost guys. It's sad to see it be pushed to the side. The analytics don't want midrange 2s."

Daryl Morey, the former general manager of the Houston Rockets, was an early advocate of high-value shot selection. "Moreyball" became shorthand for prioritizing layups, free throws, and open 3-pointers. Guided by James Harden, whose style of play dovetailed harmoniously with Morey's outlook, Houston teams virtually eliminated the midrange jumper from their offense. In 2018 film sessions, the Rockets shamed players who attempted those undesirable shots in games by editing red Xs over their faces in the footage. "Why set something up to get the worst shot in basketball?" asked Rockets coach Mike D'Antoni.

The Rockets were data-driven, mooncalf extremists, but the rest of the NBA eventually took

the plunge, nudged toward the cliff's edge after seeing Houston bobbing safely in the water below. Over the final years of the 2010s, league-wide scoring efficiency soared and use of the midrange jumper dwindled. "We practice 3s, attack, and kick out," said former Raptors coach Dwane Casey. "We rarely work on midrange shots, definitely not as a team." In 2004, 50.2 percent of all shots came from midrange turf; by 2018, it was down to 31.4 percent.

For a decade, basketball's elders have been sitting shiva for the midrange game. To protect the narrative that modern athletes are data-optimized automatons instead of soulful craftsmen, it is rarely mentioned that today's NBA players, on average, make those shots at a higher percentage than their predecessors. Still, one can sympathize with traditionalists who recoil at the suggestion that midrange jumpers are useless. It is the first shot a child takes at the age when hoisting a basketball feels like shot-putting a pumpkin. It is a staple of drills from the elbow or short corner at every scholastic level. For chrissakes, it is roughly 80 percent of the space on the court where a player can stand. To skeptics, the sturdy shot that youngsters have practiced in mildewed gyms since the dawn of time has come under siege from dorks who couldn't even brush net with their soft, uncalloused hands.

"I see dudes passing up open shots in the midrange, like wide open, to force passes to the 3-point line or force up bad finishes at the rim," Kevin Durant tweeted before the 2020 season. "The game is going toward 3s and lays only, so why would anyone work on that shot? If it wasn't forbidden, then players would work on it and they would develop that shot."

The coffin is not closed on the midrange jumper. There is some truth to the adage of taking the shots that the defense gives you. While overall shooting percentages show the vulnerability of relying on midrange jumpers, not all of them are created equal: results depend on distance, time left on the shot clock, and, most importantly, which player is taking the shot. Durant, for example, made 52.3 percent of his 2-point attempts over 16 feet from 2017 to 2019. Despite his irritation with abacus-welding dweebs, they support him taking those jumpers. As seen with other midrange enthusiasts like Kawhi Leonard, Chris Paul, and Khris Middleton, there is a competitive advantage to transforming junky shots into decent ones. Like dousing roadkill with hot sauce, gristle becomes more palatable.

In 2019, the Spurs, a franchise that zigs when others zag, built the NBA's third-best half-court offense (and seventh overall) around two veterans, DeMar DeRozan and LaMarcus Aldridge, who gorge like swine at the midrange trough. The pair combined to make only seventeen 3s all season, and San Antonio was last in the league in attempts from deep.

But by leaning into taking shots that defenses were content to sacrifice, the Spurs wormed into pressure points that freed up easier looks elsewhere: San Antonio was second in the NBA in field-goal percentage, scored capably around the basket, and topped the league in 3-point accuracy. Derided as fusty and old-fashioned, the Spurs' embrace of midrange jumpers was sneakily progressive. This is a league of adaptation, a cycle of ideologies that seasonally bloom and wither. Just when you believe the ancient art of the midrange jumper has perished of obsolescence, it remerges like a virus trapped in melted Siberian ice.

MITCHELL, DONOVAN

Just as pet owners start to resemble their border collies, some NBA players absorb characteristics from the franchises signing their checks. Knicks develop bloodlust for flagrant fouls. Lakers crave cameos on *Arli$$*. In Utah, Donovan Mitchell became annoying. He is, by all accounts, an upstanding young man—one who stopped to help when he spotted a car accident on a Salt Lake City street. But there is a nature versus nurture conundrum at play. Was the volume-scoring guard targeted by the Jazz because their scouts detected undeveloped seedlings for aggrieved whining that were ripe for cultivation? Or does aggrieved whining spread through the region's semi-arid air like viral, 125-nanometer droplets?

As an undersized combo guard, Mitchell is a dazzling scorer in the model of Monta Ellis—but with a shot chart updated for the 2020s. He is a decent shooter from deep who uses a wonderful

arsenal of hesitation feints, timely bumps, Euro steps, and a trademark scoop to finish around larger defenders. Mitchell averaged more 20 points a game for each of his first four seasons and was named to two All-Star teams, but his middling efficiency and selfishness have occasionally irked teammates (particularly Rudy Gobert, his Twinfection partner in the COVID-19 shutdown). "Sometimes he'll try to be the hero and take big shots," an anonymous Jazz affiliate told *ESPN* magazine. "I know he wants to be the guy, but sometimes the play is right in front of you and he needs to pass the ball."

MORANT, JA

For many, the darkest part of rooting for a terrible team is not the nightly stompings. It is the lack of certainty—a prolonged stretch with an undefined identity and an impermanent roster—that is disorienting. By the time competitiveness arrives, the team will not play the same way, and its cast of idling veterans, developmental league refugees, and mid-lottery athletes without a jumper will be wearing sweat-wicking mesh with a different logo. That sense of rudderless ennui evaporates when Ja Morant tumbles from the heavens.

After trading away franchise titans Marc Gasol and Mike Conley Jr., the Grizzlies seemed destined to spend time roaming the wilderness in search of respectability. But Morant, a 6-foot-3 twist-tie of a point guard, immediately gave Memphis polarity. He is true north. Following two seasons at Murray State, he was taken second in the 2019 NBA Draft, averaged 17.8 points and 7.3 assists, and was near-unanimously voted Rookie of the Year. He is a magnetic talent who hurls himself at the rim with such ferocity that it endangers everyone in the vicinity. Yet he is surprisingly adept at using feints to create easy buckets and beaming no-look passes to his teammates from unorthodox angles.

With Morant at the controls, the Memphis reboot felt like more of a system update than a motherboard crash. However shrewd the team's front office has been, he arrived by virtue of dumb luck, a fortunate ricochet of ping-pong balls in a year where he was locked in as the number-two pick behind Zion Williamson. Every team would have done the same—but only the Grizzlies found their person.

MOTOR

A player's activity level is known as his motor. The ability to exert maximum effort over an extended period of time is attributed to mental fortitude and desire, both of which result in "wanting it more." Conversely, guys who are unathletic, tortoise-like, and cursed with poor instincts are accused of dogging it on the court. But effort is as much of a physical skill as running or jumping. It requires endurance, mobility, snappy intuition, and the body control to play with physicality in a sport that punishes unnecessary contact with foul calls. Players known for having ripping engines include Bo Outlaw, Russell Westbrook, Dennis Rodman, Corey Brewer, Reggie Evans, and Ronny Turiaf.

Still, motors are tough to quantify. You cannot measure intensity in lumens or by radioactive glow. Is it fast-break scoring or earning trips to the free-throw line? Disruptive stats such as deflections and loose balls recovered? Contested rebound percentages? Chase-down blocks? According to the league's spatial tracking stats, the players who moved at the highest average defensive speed in 2020 were the Spurs' Dejounte Murray, the Kings' Marvin Bagley III, and the Hawks' Cam Reddish. It is a measurement for young guys who dash around like poultry with their heads lopped off.

We are stuck trusting what we see. Patrick Beverley, the obnoxious guard who has played for the Rockets and Clippers, is famed for a motor that hisses and spits instead of purrs. He is an itchy burdock of a defender and the combative incarnation of Chicago's rugged basketball mentality. His winding path to the NBA included being a suspension from the University of Arkansas for cheating on schoolwork, being drafted in the second round and getting cut from the Heat in training camp, and four years playing in Greece and Russia. "I just had so much aggression and so much anger," Beverley told *Bleacher Report*, "especially because many other teams passed up on me. I just wanted to go out there and every single night just make it hard for the opponent to dribble the ball up the court."

Not everyone is convinced that sound and fury amount to anything meaningful. "Pat Bev trick y'all, man, like he play defense," said Westbrook, after a game in which James Harden scored 47 points against Beverley's Clippers. "He don't guard nobody, man. He just running around doing nothing."

MOTORMOUTHS

Since the NBA's infancy, players have used verbal abuse as a tactic for gaining a mental edge over foes. The league's most notoriously sassy lads are also some of the very best: Michael Jordan, Larry Bird, Reggie Miller, Rasheed Wallace, Kevin Garnett, Draymond Green, Jimmy Butler, and Devin Booker. "If you're a bum, you can't talk trash," said James Harden (who claims he doesn't get lippy in games). "We won't respect you—you gotta have a name or be getting buckets."

With a skinny frame and closely cropped dome, Gary Payton is a shit-popping bobblehead doll. His lifetime totals in assists and steals is in the NBA's all-time top 10, and he is uncredited as a prototype for the modern point guard who scores and distributes with equal lethality.

On a nightly basis, he went chest to chest with opponents, batting and jabbing with his skinny arms, and pursuing loose balls like a hyena tearing at a carcass. As a member of the Sonics, Payton was the only point guard in history to win Defensive Player of the Year and, during the 1996 Finals, enveloped Michael Jordan like a Karl Kani sweatshirt. "A lot of people backed down to Mike," he said in the documentary *The Last Dance*. "I kept hitting him and banging him and hitting and banging him."

And Payton would not shut up. Victims of his rhetorical onslaught ranged from journeymen stiffs like Jamie Feick to superstars like Michael Jordan to non-combat personnel like Sidney Lowe ("Sit down, you smurf," Payton told the Timberwolves' coach). In practice, he was known for talking shit to invisible, nonexistent defenders. "If I knew something about a person's mother, his sister, if he had just got a drunk driving charge, I would go at that situation," Payton explained to *NBA Breakdown*. "You can hate me on the basketball court but I would say sorry to you afterwards."

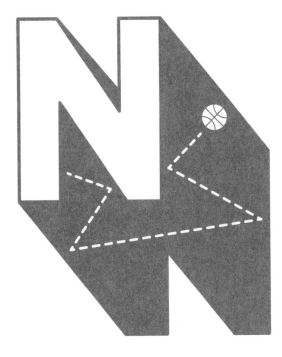

NASH, STEVE

Winner of back-to-back Most Valuable Player awards during the mid-2000s, Steve Nash was a precise shooter, a clairvoyant passer, and the league's greatest beneficiary of progressive offensive philosophy. Blessed with an arsenal of god-bestowed physical gifts—fisheye-lens peripheral vision, balance, core strength, and the hand-eye coordination of a *pâtissier*—the Canadian was shuttled from the womb to be a point guard. In his early thirties, Nash was handed basketball's version of a Nintendo Game Genie, allowing him to orchestrate a multi-season speedrun that earned him personal accolades but fell shy of helping him to beat the final boss.

Born in South Africa to a professional soccer player, Nash was raised as a rare chess nerd/jock in British Columbia. He played four years at Santa Clara University, the only school that offered him a scholarship. He described the experience of balling in obscurity in terms befitting a psychological horror film. "It was like I was trapped in an elevator and I'm screaming, but nobody could hear me," he told *Sports Illustrated* in 1995.

The Suns selected Nash with the fifteenth pick in the stacked 1996 draft. His physical attributes— 6-foot-3, modest wingspan, 31-inch vertical leap— raised skepticism, but his cunning instincts and spatial awareness were obvious. "Like all of the great point guards, Nash has uncanny court vision and a sixth sense for the game," wrote scout Phil Bedard.

Despite his completionist amateur career, Nash spent his first four professional seasons as an anonymous scrub. He was an underused backup in Phoenix, stuck behind star guards Jason Kidd and Kevin Johnson. Nash was dealt to Dallas during the 1998 NBA Draft. It was an eventful, franchise-shifting moment in several ways, as the move was lassoed into the Mavericks' acquisition of Dirk Nowitzki and sent a first-round pick to Phoenix that later became Shawn Marion.

Initially, Nash continued his scrubbish antics in Dallas. During his first season with the Mavs, he played 31.7 minutes a game but posted only 7.9 points per contest, a rate of scoring that ranked beside the rates of the trudging corpses of Charles Oakley and Dan Majerle as the league's least potent. Mavericks coach Don Nelson, a tinkering futurist, begged Nash to play more aggressively, even threatening to fine him for games in which the guard attempted fewer than 10 shots. "It was him imploring me to score," Nash told the *New York Times* in 2018. "My nature is just to pass, pass, pass. Nellie finally got it in my head that that was B.S.— that you're hurting us by doing that. He challenged me, without exactly saying it this way, to realize I was being selfish."

Near the ass-end of the Mavs' mediocre 2000 season, Nash was inserted into the starting lineup and chauffeured the team to a 15–5 record. His stewardship of a spread system was revelatory. Over that short span, the Mavericks posted the league's top offensive rating and evidenced blossoming chemistry between Michael Finley, Nowitzki, and the dainty Canadian. While Nash was never the top dog in Dallas—and, some seasons, may not have been the team's second-best player—he was named to a pair of All-Star teams. He cemented his arriviste creds by dating singer Geri "Ginger Spice" Horner (then Halliwell) of the Spice Girls and actress Elizabeth Hurley, whom he squired around Dallas while she was shooting *Serving Sara*, a romantic comedy with Matthew Perry (the 2002 film was described as "crass and joyless," by the Associated Press). Before the 2005 season, the Suns offered Nash a six-year, $65-million contract to return to Phoenix as a free agent. The Mavs declined to match the deal. "All the advice I got from everybody we had was that he was going to fall apart," Dallas owner Mark Cuban later told the *Fort Worth Star-Telegram*.

As it turned out, Phoenix's faith in a thirty-year-old defensive sieve was insider trading. The league was implementing new rules that would eliminate hand-checking and turn backcourt play into a track meet—and the NBA committee in charge of instituting those changes was headed by the owner of the Suns. "We had a built-in advantage because Jerry Colangelo was the chairman of that board," said executive David Griffin, who worked for the Suns at the time, in an interview with *The Ringer*. "We knew from the very beginning what was likely to come about. We were able to build a team that's pretty ahead of the curve."

There was another gift waiting for Nash in Arizona's urban heart: head coach Mike D'Antoni. The architect of a system that would become known as "seven seconds or less" for its frenzied push for open shots in transition, D'Antoni needed a foreman. While Dallas had used Nash as a conventional table-setter, the Suns' approach was revolutionary for its droning simplicity. Phoenix just put the rock in the hands of the team's best playmaker as many times as possible, every game, over and over.

As the spigot for a flowing offense, Nash went from a borderline All-Star to an MVP candidate. Helmed by the sly Canadian, the Suns were a swirl of no-look passes, transition buckets, pick-and-roll lobs, and mortar barrages of three-balls. He was a low-altitude highwire act who turned bailout passes into open 3s and slipped layups past large defenders with right hand/right leg, off-the-dribble scoops. Phoenix roared to a 31–4 start. In the coming seasons, Nash led the league in categories like assists (five times), free-throw percentage, and true shooting percentage. The Suns dwarfed competitors in points per game, offensive rating, pace, 3-point attempts, and 3-point percentage. Nash was named MVP in 2005 and 2006.

The mid-aughts were a time of societal upheaval that remains inadequately processed. There were shutter shades and faux-hawks, keffiyehs and fedoras, Blogspot-posted photos of Cory Kennedy among dead-eyed partygoers. Grime musician Kano was on the cover of *Fader*. Nash, awash in this chaos, wore billowing pink button-downs, trucker hats, and suits tailored to fit a child. After the racial tension of the Malice at the Palace, an elfin, hipster-adjacent white

superstar was a godsend for a league desperate to appeal to fans who tremble at the sight of men in roomy denim. And, unlike Nowitzki, Pau Gasol, or Manu Ginóbili, Nash was North American and relatively human-size. Fans and the media gobbled it up. The Suns were annually stymied by the Spurs in the Western Conference playoffs, but the team's exhilarating style of play made Nash an icon.

In contrast to other stars, Nash was praised for his craftiness, team-first unselfishness, cerebral approach to the game, and Canadian humility. Through no fault of his own—Nash's own conscientiousness included wearing a shirt that read "No War. Shoot for Peace" to the 2003 All-Star Game—he became a chess piece in the culture wars. "It is simply not fair or ethical to wildly root for Nash, but not challenge the white privilege that he regularly receives by a media that predominantly looks like him, lives vicariously through him, and probably wants to be him," wrote the blog *Cosellout*, after Nash undeservedly won a landslide MVP vote in 2006 over LeBron James.

There has long been a "chicken or the egg" debate about the Suns' offense and Nash's stewardship of the system. His hyper-accurate shooting and breathtaking passing were revelatory, but his years in Dallas provide a comparative baseline. And as Phoenix's principles spread through the NBA like wildfire across the chaparral, Nash looks more like kindling than the lightning strike. Lesser point guards like Jeremy Lin, Steve Blake, and Kendall Marshall also posted career-best numbers on teams coached by D'Antoni. And when James Harden and Russell Westbrook took the reins with the Rockets—even splitting duties—their mass production makes Nash's handiwork look quaint (echoing Nelson, D'Antoni now says that he would have coerced Nash into taking eight 3s a game).

After retiring, Nash spent two years playing for the Los Angeles Lakers, hung out with Vashtie at Santos Party House in Downtown New York, and gave back to the community by mentoring Canadian youth RJ Barrett. In the fall of 2020, Nash was hired to coach the Nets, despite a lack of experience. Again, the subject of race arose. "I'm not saying that my privilege was a factor in this position," he said at his introductory press conference. "We do need more diversity and more opportunities for African American coaches on staff in all capacities."

DYNAMIC DUOS

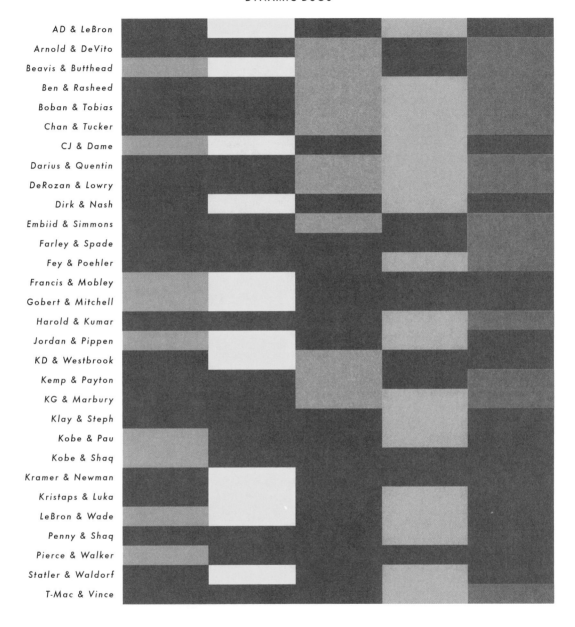

AD & LeBron
Arnold & DeVito
Beavis & Butthead
Ben & Rasheed
Boban & Tobias
Chan & Tucker
CJ & Dame
Darius & Quentin
DeRozan & Lowry
Dirk & Nash
Embiid & Simmons
Farley & Spade
Fey & Poehler
Francis & Mobley
Gobert & Mitchell
Harold & Kumar
Jordan & Pippen
KD & Westbrook
Kemp & Payton
KG & Marbury
Klay & Steph
Kobe & Pau
Kobe & Shaq
Kramer & Newman
Kristaps & Luka
LeBron & Wade
Penny & Shaq
Pierce & Walker
Statler & Waldorf
T-Mac & Vince

Would avoid eye contact with on the street.

Would casually lie to about weekend plans.

Would want to start a streetwear brand with.

Would trust to plan an important pizza party.

Would ask to share magic mushrooms with.

NET ZEROS

In the Association, the tubby midsection of the bell curve is not composed of superstars or bums. It is a meatspace thick with average joes, the guys who spend their short window of professional opportunity minding their own business. Even in this group, however, are a subset of players with an added veil of anonymity—like campers who collect their trash and refrain from building rock cairns for social media clout, they leave no trace.

Basketball's yin-yang symbol, Tobias Harris has bobbed along in a harmonious balance where nothing is lost and nothing is gained. For most of his career, the versatile 6-foot-8 tweener forward was an average scorer, an average rebounder, and an average defender. His effective field-goal percentage and true shooting percentage were about average. An adorably gruff Long Islander and an important voice in the league's Black Lives Matter movement, Harris played on five teams over his first nine seasons, entering and exiting lineups without planting a deep footprint. His game has become more noteworthy in his prime—even borderline All-Star level—but the Duality Tobias inhabited was comforting: in this chaotic simulation, he restores order as if blowing on a giant Nintendo cartridge in the sky.

Other players vanish on the court. They might impact the final score—scoring quietly, for example—but are virtually unnoticeable during the frenzy of a game. Despite the high expectations that accompany being a number-one pick, Andrew Wiggins is one of these invisible men. The bouncy, Canadian-born wing with Plasticine limbs drew international attention as a blue-chip prospect, especially after the virality of a *Hoopmixtape* highlight video that featured many slam dunks from his senior season at West Virginia's Huntington Prep. He captivated fans of the NBA's bottom-scavenging franchises and the phrase "Riggin' for Wiggins" became a clarion call that celebrated intentional losing during the mid-2010s' mythical tanking epidemic. His springiness athleticism, lanky 6-foot-7 frame, corkscrew spin-moves, and moldable jumper conjured comparisons

to Paul George. Yet, as a professional with the Timberwolves and Warriors, Wiggins never figured out how to make an impact in non-scoring categories like rebounding, passing, or defense. "He's so cool, so laid-back," said teammate Jordan Hill. "I feel if he got that Kobe mentality or that Russell Westbrook mentality to go out every night and just be fierceful—ain't nobody gonna stop him."

Lost in the sands of time are forgettable players with bland names, plain mugs, and undistinguished careers who are barely referenced by the sport's legion of nostalgics. They are NPCs, personnel generated to fill out rosters, get crossed over, and receive facial dunks. Bobby Simmons, Kenny Thomas, the Zellers (no one knows exactly how many there are). Did we mention Bobby Simmons?

Blessed with civilian dimensions and a friendly babyface, Devin Harris could gullet a platter of loaded chili fries at any sports bar in the land without being pestered for an autograph. He is also a fifteen-year NBA vet who was a top-5 pick, made the 2009 All-Star team, and has cashed over $76 million in checks from five different teams. The slick, 6-foot-3 point guard was perilously close to stardom. Staying in front of him was like trying to bearhug a draft. Harris had an array of nasty spins, Euro steps, and snatch-back crossovers off the dribble. A *New York Times* article from 2011 that described him as "a terrific player, a fantastic point guard" had the headline "The Invisible Devin Harris."

But forgettable players may be concealing interesting lives. Harris, for one, played NCAA ball for the University of Wisconsin–Madison, where, according to an *ESPN* magazine profile that described him as a "Madison-style metrosexual," his best friends were two women who nicknamed him Bitch. Harris's wife, a former contestant on *Fear Factor* and a *Playboy* Cybergirl of the Month, is the co-owner of a bar in Dallas called Mr. Misster. The Skinny Bitch, a blend of Patrón, Grand Marnier, agave, and lime, costs $8.

NEW WHITES

Basketball was invented by a white guy. Norman Rockwell's "Four Sporting Boys" series includes a painting of four Caucasian kids in shorts and hightops, clustered in argument. The NBA was a segregated league until late 1950—three years after Jackie Robinson broke the color barrier in baseball—when

Earl Lloyd of the Washington Capitols scored six points against the Royals. "Rochester was a sleepy Upstate town where schools were integrated and they were used to seeing Blacks and whites playing together," Lloyd told the *Detroit Free Press* fifty years later. "The game was totally, unequivocally uneventful."

And yet basketball has been inextricably connected to Black culture for a half century. Roughly three-quarters of the league's players are Black, as are an overwhelming number of its superstars—in 2020, the fifteen players selected to All-NBA teams included only two non-Black representatives, both of whom hailed from the beet patches of Eastern Europe. These dynamics have informed league policies for decades, often in disturbing ways, in areas like drug testing, draft eligibility, dress codes, and severe punishments for infractions on the court.

"It's race, pure and simple," an NBA official told Mark Jacobson of *Esquire*, in a 1985 profile of Julius Erving. "No major sport comes up against it the way we do. It's just difficult to get a lot of people to watch huge, intelligent, millionaire Black people on television." Even thirty-five years later, when the NBA's ratings were down during the COVID-19 pandemic—a decline in viewership shared by baseball, football, and hockey—conservative media outlets eagerly pinned the blame on the league's Black Lives Matter sloganeering.

While Michael Jordan's international celebrity coincided with hip-hop growing into the most powerful cultural force of the nineties, the adoration went in only one direction. He has been name-dropped by Golden Era foundationalists like Ice Cube and A Tribe Called Quest and artists young enough to be their kids, like Lil Uzi Vert, Chief Keef, and Lil Baby, but is notorious for disliking the genre. "Jordan is a hater of [hip-hop]," rapper N.O.R.E. said in an interview with *Rap Radar*. He recounted being at a Def Jam Recordings holiday party in which Jordan poohpoohed meeting Method Man and Redman. "He said, 'Fuck Rap'—that shit hurt me," said N.O.R.E.

Jordan's condescending attitude toward hip-hop was not shared by superstars of the late 1990s and early 2000s like Allen Iverson, Shaquille O'Neal, and Kobe Bryant. They all rapped with anklesock-high thresholds of competency and occupied different spaces—collaborating with, respectively, Jadakiss, the Fu-Schnickens, and Tyra Banks. Under pressure from the NBA, Iverson aborted the release of an album with violent lyrics, a decision he is relieved about today. "I thought it was an art form, just like you

see Bruce Willis killing people in movies," he told *Complex*. "Well, he don't do that in real life."

At the time, the counterculture was surging in popularity and tangling with concepts of authenticity and commodification. While hip-hop was shorthand for Black youth culture, its manifestation as edgy music, oversize fashion, ornate haircuts, slang, and a confrontational attitude made it transmittable to people outside of that demographic—and gave racism a flimsy veil of deniability. It also reached millions and millions of white kids, some of whom turned out to be NBA players.

Jason Williams, a flamboyant point guard who entered the league during the 1999 season with the Kings, was a new white. While earlier models included Caucasian jammers Rex Chapman (long before Twitter fame) and Bob Sura, his arrival coincided with Eminem's breakout debut *The Slim Shady LP*, and parallels were obvious. They were alabaster kings who were not only successful in Black art forms but generally respected as peers instead of interlopers.

Williams was from West Virginia, played high school ball with NFL star Randy Moss, sullied his reputation with three marijuana suspensions at the University of Florida, and eventually sported a shaved head and myriad tattoos, including "whiteboy" across his knuckles. "I cherished getting kicked out of school," he said. "It was a great thing. I became a millionaire." Although Williams's affection for ink and weed mirrored that of hippie center Cherokee Parks, it was interpreted very differently.

As a rookie, Williams was dubbed "White Chocolate" by the Sacramento public relations department. "People would ask me all the time if it bothered me," he said later on *House of Highlights*. "No, it doesn't bother me a bit. The word 'racism' is so far from my vocabulary. I don't get into any of that, I just go out and hoop." While that may be true, an Asian fan of the Warriors said that Williams responded to heckling with homophobic slurs and by saying, "I will shoot all you Asian motherfuckers. Do you remember the Vietnam War?" Williams's mesmerizing style of play drew comparisons to Pete Maravich and Jerry West, but was unabashedly grounded in streetball: he bombed deep 3-pointers with questionable accuracy, ricocheted behind-the-back passes off his own elbow, looped 360-degree dribbles around his torso, nutmegged defenders with assists, and was among the league leaders in turnovers. "This dude would do something so creative to embarrass you," Tracy McGrady once said on ESPN. "I didn't like to guard him."

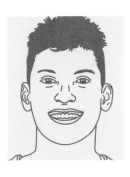

Two decades later, Tyler Herro pasteurized that same Milkbone energy as a rookie on the Heat. The slithery combo-guard wore elevated streetwear brands like Off-White and Heron Preston beneath a tousle of chains, had "NO WORK" and "NO CHECK" tattooed beneath his collarbones, and dated Katya Elise Henry, a curvy Instagram model with more than eight million followers. It is unclear if Herro is very good or sort of good, but his star-making turn in the COVID Bubble postseason included a 37-point outburst in the Eastern Conference Finals and a lip-curling sneer in the Finals that made him look like an insolent weasel. After the Milwaukee native's big game, teammate Jimmy Butler wore Herro's Whitnall High School jersey.

The next off-season, white rapper Jack Harlow recorded a song titled "Tyler Herro" with lyrics like "My homeboy Tyler, he play in South Beach / he told me this summer he gon' fix my jumper." In the video, Herro wore red sunglasses and swished shots on a backyard hoop. Later, on JJ Redick's podcast, he described how he and Harlow had linked up. "Honestly, just both being white, we were just like, 'Yo, wassup, bro,'" he said.

NEW YORK ECCENTRICS

Welcome to New York City, the Mecca of Basketball. Long before pandemic-fleeing inhabitants moved into a farmhouse thirty minutes outside of Binghamton to launch a sourdough-starter Instagram, millions of daily commuters practiced in-and-out dribbles on subway platforms. They barked in guttural tongues about how "Knicks gonna Knick." Each evening, residents were required to lace up their beef-and-broccoli Timberlands, order a chopped cheese from their bodega guy, and, between verses of Nas's *Illmatic*, extoll the greatness of Lew Alcindor, Connie Hawkins, and Bob Cousy. Deadass. The local cagers oozed nativist reverence for Gotham. "Oh yeah, I'm a thief," said Smush Parker, a guard who spent five years in the NBA. "I'm from Brooklyn, aka

Crooklyn. You develop them hands growing up in New York City." But alas, that era is over.

Much has been written about the crumbling of New York as basketball's epicenter. It is evidenced by the lack of current NBA superstars who grew up in the five boroughs, a decline that has been blamed on an array of sociological and generational trends. Theories abound. The scourge of video games has emptied the city's playgrounds of teens, leaving the cracked asphalt trespassed only by tumbleweeds of blunt guts. Gentrification has funneled wealthier transplants from other cities into neighborhoods where basketball was once vital. There is the trickle-down effect of the Knicks, whose two decades of despair have sapped New York of its exuberance for the game and replaced it with cynicism and misery.

It could be the game itself. As the sport has shifted toward perimeter scoring and multi-positional creators, the traditional New York City point guard has gone out of vogue. Modern teams are not looking for flashy dribblers who hoard the ball, aggressively attack the basket, and consider outside shooting effeminate. That style of play, it has been argued, is a product of sloped courts, winter brickness, and notoriously unforgiving "double rims" that were made by blacksmiths on Randall's Island (before they were removed during the first wave of COVID-19). "When you get to the park, since the rims was messed up, the best way and the easiest way to score is to get as close as possible," Sundiata Gaines, a guard from Queens who played in 113 games over three NBA seasons, told Boston's WBUR. Not for nothing, one statistical study claimed that players from New York were slightly worse, on average, at shooting than players from other places.

Just as New York is a refuge for bullied art kids who congregate after midnight in smoky Chinatown banquet halls, the city is a breeding ground for some of basketball's most eccentric characters. There are TV personalities like Kenny Smith and Mark Jackson. Playground legends like Lloyd "Swee' Pea" Daniels, Conrad "McNasty" McRae, and Rafer "Skip 2 My Lou" Alston, all of whom made it to the NBA but were better known for streetball exploits. Then there are the genuine weirdos.

Coney Island, the seaside peninsula at the south end of Brooklyn, has the Cyclone roller coaster, a mermaid-themed parade, and a disproportionate population of NBA oddballs. There is Stephon Marbury, the Vaseline-devouring prodigy. Or his cousin Sebastian Telfair, who flamed out

Proudly wear Timberlands to work and to the club.

Still hear *Illmatic* blasting out of 2010 Escalades.

Understand that "uptown" means anywhere above 14th.

State untrue facts about tap water and pizza dough.

Claim John Starks won a championship on a slam dunk.

Be the most famous player who blew in LeBron's ear.

Know that a folded slice is actually a cheese sandwich.

Get picked right after Frédéric Weis, then win DPOY.

Wonder why there aren't reliable tacos on every corner.

Have Khloé Kardashian rescue you after an OD.

Restart your life and become a national hero in China.

Accept Basquiat as a default mascot for everything.

Be very suspicious of a subway car with no one in it.

Never go to a single Broadway show in twenty years.

Remember when Travis Scott was haunting every party.

Decide that the best era was whenever you were young.

Reminisce about Fashion Week as if it was actually fun.

Declare that all French bistros are Christmas themed.

Eat salads and handheld food items over the sink.

Shut down on showering to research biohacking moves.

Never eat at a diner but be sad they're disappearing.

Go to pick up your cat but it's actually a pile of jeans.

Not rank burgers as if they're not all kinda the same.

Talk about 9/11 as if you've actually recovered from it.

Be drafted by NY and play your whole career as a Knick.

after high school celebrity and ended up enmeshed in a 2006 Manhattan robbery-turned-shooting that left Brooklyn rapper Fabolous with a bullet wound in his leg. And Lance Stephenson, the demonstrative, show-boating wing who tried to bully LeBron James by blowing in his ear during a 2014 playoff game. "I don't regret it," Stephenson later told *The Score*, "but sometimes I look at it like, 'Why did I do that? What made me do that?'"

The neighborhood was also the home of Jesus Shuttlesworth, the fictional schoolboy phenom in Spike Lee's film *He Got Game*, which starred Ray Allen. An examination of the corrupting influences upon amateur sports, the film featured Denzel Washington and Rosario Dawson, as well as NBA players Travis Best, Walter McCarty, and John Wallace. "Even though Stephon, and his father, and his brothers, might think this is the Marbury story, it's not about them," Lee told the *New York Times*. "It happens to a lot of these kids."

Anthony Mason, an early point-forward from Queens, was a perfect totem for New York City basketball. He had knotted shoulders, a nearly bald head, and dead eyes that glowed only with hostility. Not only did he spend his prime playing for the Knicks, Mase embodied the team's intense physicality and fearsome reputation during the franchise's mid-1990s glory years. He was an unsurpassed jostler who courted conflict with chest-bumps and elbows to the solar plexus, but rarely lost his composure (though he hit Dennis Rodman with a throat-chop during a playoff game). "Get the feeling that, in his next life, he's a hitman," said announcer Mike Fratello, during a Knicks broadcast. "One of those guys that just wipes people out and doesn't say a word, just kinda smiles."

But Mason was more than a leering intimidator, he was a leering renaissance man. He was a versatile defender who could stonewall centers, an incredibly efficient scorer due to his ability to draw fouls, and a keen passer who stampeded the open court in an era when big guys were supposed to leave those duties to pipsqueaks. Mason was also ahead of his time as a cultural figure within the expanding hip-hop scene, earning name-checks from rappers like the Beastie Boys and having his barber carve shout-outs like

"Dogg Pound" and phrases like "In God's Hands" into his scalp. "It was just me being myself, with my identity," he said. "And it turned out to be worldly recognized." After Mason's death, rapper Fat Joe claimed the Notorious B.I.G.'s song "I Got a Story to Tell"—in which Biggie recounted boning the girlfriend of a Knick and then robbing the player when he got home—was about Mason.

Ron Artest, another Queens native, had a similarly threatening countenance and bruising defensive chops. He even shared an affinity for etching glyphs into his skull ("Tru Warier," for example, which was his own record label). Artest, who changed his name to Metta World Peace and, in retirement, to Metta Sandiford-Artest, played seventeen seasons, notably for the Pacers and Lakers, and won a Defensive Player of the Year award for his lockdown perimeter defense and quick hands. "I'm going to continue playing hard and out of control," Artest said before one Indiana game, "like a wild animal that needs to be caged in." At every stop, he was a chirpy and pugilistic man who tangled with Kobe Bryant, broke Michael Jordan's ribs in a pick-up game, and earned three suspensions of at least seven games, including once for elbowing James Harden so viciously in the head that he could have died. Artest was the main instigator in the Malice at the Palace brawl and was suspended for the remaining 73 games of the season.

Artest was famed for his absurdist sense of humor and erratic behavior—he once stripped down to his boxers while being interviewed on the *Jimmy Kimmel Show*—but later divulged that he was receiving therapy for anger management. He thanked his psychiatrist after winning a title with the Lakers. "For me, mental health issues were more of an environmental thing," he told *Sports Illustrated*, of a childhood in the Queensbridge housing projects where he was surrounded by the horrors of violence, poverty, incarceration, and drug abuse. "My neighborhood, if you aren't defensive, people will walk all over you." That, for better or worse, is the New York State of Mind.

NINJA HEADBANDS

A short-lived fashion trend during the 2019 NBA season, ninja (alternatively: kung fu or "Karate Kid") headbands were strips of cloth knotted around a player's head. Depending on the length of the headband,

FUN

FUNCTIONAL

STYLISH

SERIOUS

The 6th Man trophy.	Clear masks.	Goggles.	The MVP trophy.
Black masks.	The DPOY trophy.	Headbands.	Ninja headbands.
Championship rings.	Double headbands.	Knee pads.	Supreme sleeves.

the two loose ends could flop behind the wearer like basset hound ears. The taekwondo drip was popularized by De'Aaron Fox of the Kings, Montrezl Harrell of the Clippers, Jrue Holiday of the Pelicans, and Jimmy Butler and Mike Scott of the Sixers.

Before the start of the 2020 season, the league banished ninja headbands. "Teams have raised concerns regarding safety and consistency of size, length and how they are tied," NBA spokesperson Mike Bass said, in a frosty statement to ESPN. The league did not specify what kind of injuries could occur from a poorly cinched judo headband, but the idea of having a limb wrenched off from an on-court bandana mishap is frightening. Following the announcement, Scott posted tweets that blamed the restriction on Nike, which signed an eight-year apparel deal with the NBA in 2015 ("Dem folks in Oregon lol," as he put it). He also wrote that the look was deemed "unprofessional," but did not identify the joyless Poindexter he was quoting.

NOWITZKI, DIRK

Perhaps the best-shooting big man of all time, Dirk Nowitzki was a fourteen-time All-Star whose pristine legacy is evidence of the 15,000-psi cleansing power of victory. Over twenty-one years spent entirely with the Mavericks, he was a prolific scorer whose reputation shifted from finesse big to Most Valuable Player to choke artist to, finally, lionhearted conqueror.

The child of two German athletes who played sports at the national level, Lil' Dirk was raised in Würzburg, a midsize Bavarian city known for minerally white wines. His favorite basketball player was the Bulls' Scottie Pippen, which critics would later interpret as a predisposition toward beta maleness. He was selected by Milwaukee with the ninth pick of the 1998 NBA Draft and traded with Pat Garrity to Dallas in exchange for Robert "Tractor" Traylor.

Early on, Nowitzki ran afoul of traditionalists who were scandalized by a 7-footer who scored only a sliver of his points at the rim. A reluctance to *get his ass in the paint* also dovetailed with stereotypes about European big men. Even when considered as a franchise centerpiece, he had a reputation for coming up short when the game was on the line. In the 2006 Finals, Nowitzki missed a crucial free throw with seconds remaining in Game 3 and went 2–14 in the next game,

as the Mavericks dropped four straight to the Heat. The following postseason, his 67-win Dallas team was upset in the first round of the playoffs by Baron Davis and eighth-seeded Golden State. Nowitzki was harried by smaller, rangier defenders and shot 38.3 percent from the field. After the loss, he spent weeks in the Australian Outback, playing his guitar, being unshaven, and mainlining whiskey. "Why me?" he recalled wondering. "Why is this happening to me?"

Everything changed over two weeks in the spring of 2011. Nowitzki's Mavericks had a Finals rematch with the Heat—but this time, they stood as the lone speed bump between LeBron James and his first title. Your enemy's enemy is your friend, and skepticism about Nowitzki paled in comparison to the white-hot contempt members of the media and the public held for James after his arrival in South Beach. "He was not going to let us lose," pint-sized teammate J. J. Barea said. "The way he prepared the whole year for it. He hated Miami, he hated LeBron, Wade, Bosh."

During the six-game series, Nowitzki averaged 26 points and 9.7 rebounds, while making 45 of 46 free throws. His numbers were excellent if not extraordinary—but he ushered the Heat into the grave with an undertaker's touch. Time and again, he went to his signature move: an awkward jumper in which he thudded his shoulder into the body of a defender before toppling backward. "Probably the most unstoppable shot ever is the sky hook," James told Fort Lauderdale's *Sun-Sentinel*. "I guess you put Dirk second. You have a seven-footer fading away off one leg. There is no one that can block that shot." The tactic has been adopted by guys like James, Kevin Durant, and Joel Embiid.

Nowitzki's Finals win was caustic soda that scrubbed his reputation so thoroughly that all those prior criticisms are barely remembered. But the next nine seasons revealed that his long-term legacy was even more imperiled than we knew at the time. Before his retirement in 2019, Dallas missed the playoffs five times and lost the rest in the first round.

Whenever a lanky European with a jumper lands on American shores, Nowitzki's name is chanted like an ancient Black Forest invocation. It was slapped on Kristaps Porziņģis, the Latvian star. And Lauri Markkanen, the Finnish lottery pick. Isaiah Hartenstein, who grew up in Germany and was selected by Houston in the second round of the 2017 draft. Andrea Bargnani, Darko Miličić, and Nikoloz Tskitishvili—all top-5 picks who badly underperformed and besmirched the name of large European

lads. And even Kelly Olynyk, whose combination of Canadian birthright, tangled hair, and unspellable last name created ambiguous foreignness. "I'm always flattered and shocked by any kind of direct comparisons to Dirk because that's my M. J.," said German center Moe Wagner, who has played for teams like the Lakers and Wizards. "I had his poster on my wall."

Oddly, Nowitzki barely resembled the titan we have mounded together in his image. He did not take that many 3-pointers, at least by modern standards. Per 36 minutes, he averaged 3.7 per game for his career, which is about the same rate that Robin Lopez and Larry Nance Jr. let them fly today. Compared to everyone in the NBA of 2020, it would tie for 354th. During Nowitzki's absolute prime—from age twenty-six to thirty-three, a span in which he averaged 24.6 points a game—only 14.2 percent of his shot attempts came from beyond the arc.

Early in his career, he barely even qualified as the Stretch Big archetype that we associate him with. At times, he started alongside two other large Mavs, the ranks of whom included Shawn Bradley, Eduardo Najera, Christian Laettner, and Raef LaFrentz. Nowitzki played enough at small forward that there was debate over whether he could make the position his full-time home. To be fair, this occurred in the early 2000s, when super-size lineups were as ubiquitous as G-Unit clothing.

Outside of Nowitzki's background, he was less a new paradigm than a better version of a familiar one: the jump-shooting forward. He was not so different, in terms of thriving on long 2s, from big men like twins Harvey and Horace Grant, Tom Gugliotta, or Danny Ferry. His free-throw rate and shot profile were similar to those of Kevin Garnett, just with more 3s tossed in. What made Nowitzki unique was his accuracy. He routinely topped 50 percent on unsexy 2-pointers over 16 feet and was among the annual leaders in that category with the regularity of lunar cycles. He drilled 38 percent of his career 3s and 87.9 percent of his free throws. His touch was as soft as fresh kuchen. Nowitzki may not have been the forerunner of modern basketball that we pretend he is, but he spent his career as a man on fire. "The rules now play perfectly into the hands of skilled Europeans," Nowitzki said.

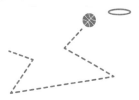

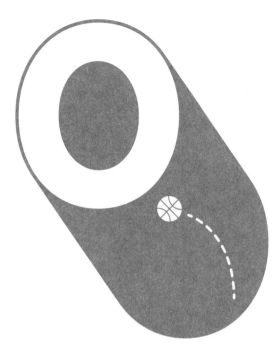

O'NEAL, SHAQUILLE

One of the NBA's last thunder lizards, Shaquille O'Neal stomped through the ferns in a manner that would be impossible today. It is hard to say for sure, however, because players with his 7-foot-1 and 350-pound size, strength, wingspan, coordination, and ballerina feet come around once every Mesozoic era. For those who are accustomed to watching O'Neal mumble witticisms during NBA broadcasts, it is necessary to go down memory lane for a few seconds. Go back, beyond the orb-shape plodder who lingered into his late thirties with Cleveland, Boston, and Phoenix. Even before the ripened Miami version, who won a title, led the league in field-goal percentage, and taunted former teammate Kobe Bryant with the phrase "tell me how my ass tastes."

In a decade spent meting out punishment, the O'Neal we witnessed in Orlando and Los Angeles was peerless. He was an MVP, a three-time Finals MVP, a three-time All-Star Game MVP, and a fifteen-time All-Star who logged the eighth-most points and tenth-most rebounds in NBA history—who is, somehow, underrated.

In a time before League Pass or Basketball Twitter, the spectacle of an O'Neal performance carried the awe of a tornado: you were watching the destruction of property and lives in real time. As a rookie on the Magic, he averaged 23.4 points, 13.9 rebounds, and 3.5 blocks. Bulwark centers such as Robert Parish and Alonzo Mourning—respectable men, men with families—were thrashed like scarecrows. He shattered a backboard on *Inside Stuff*. On multiple occasions, O'Neal's heft brought down the entire basket apparatus during NBA games, once accordioning directly onto his head and, another time, slowly sinking to the floor like an elderly man into a bath. "Shaquille has that quick, unrestrainable explosion," said Bill Walton. "It's a raw power you don't get in the weight room. It comes from somewhere else, deep in the soul."

With O'Neal and young guard Anfernee Hardaway, the Magic had the pillars of a dynasty. The team went to the Finals in the duo's second season together, but was swept by the Rockets. The accepted reading of that series is that O'Neal was badly outfoxed by Hakeem Olajuwon, but examination reveals that Houston's Robert Horry, Mario Elie, and Sam Cassell were human torches (and two games were decided by a single possession). Orlando lowballed O'Neal in salary negotiations and, abruptly, it was over. The gigantor decamped for Los Angeles and a seven-year contract. "This team was burned worse than any team in the history of the league when Shaq left," said Chuck Daly, who was hired as the next Magic coach.

In Los Angeles, Superman became a global icon. He danced, he rapped, he acted. "He's a combination of the Terminator and Bambi," said Leonard Armato, his agent at the time. O'Neal's cinematic appearances included *Good Burger, Steel*, and *Freddy Got Fingered*. In Aaron Carter's short film, titled *That's How I Beat Shaq*, he personified a basketball player named Shaquille O'Neal. In *Kazaam*, he played a genie, and he helped uncork the Mandela effect for a nonexistent movie called *Shazaam* that supposedly starred Sinbad. "Mr. O'Neal should have slam-dunked the script into the nearest wastebasket," wrote the *New York Times*.

Though he became infamous for "playing himself into shape" over the course of the regular season, O'Neal won an MVP award and claimed three titles with the Lakers. "Generally, guys at that size are a little timid and don't want to be tall," said Bryant. "This dude did not care. He was mean. He was nasty. He was competitive. He was vindictive. I wish he was in the gym. I would've had fucking twelve rings."

Despite his dominance, O'Neal was pincushioned with arrows from purists who believed his success was entirely due to enormous size and

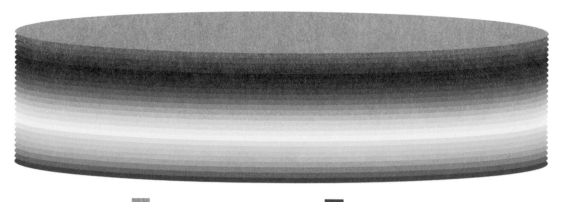

At the very least it's kinda fun.		No kinkshaming!	
Miles Bridges.	Iman.	Kobe Bryant.	Joe Beast.
Shaquille O'Neal.	Dame D.O.L.L.A.	MB3FIVE.	Tony Parker.
C. Webb.	Born Ready.	Metta World Peace.	Charlee Redz.
Dre Drumm.	Jewelz.	Stak5.	Suni Blac.
Dana Barros.	ZO.	Q6.	J-Lunar.
Lou Will.	Kyrie Irving.	Pierre.	T-Hud.

brutalizing strength. His poor free-throw shooting was a tender spot, especially after teams sent him to the line with intentional fouls. The popularity of the "Hack-a-Shaq" strategy among coaches (and deep unpopularity among fans) led to a rule change that discouraged the practice by making it illegal to intentionally foul a player away from the ball during the last two minutes of a game. O'Neal is also credited with inspiring the removal of the NBA's illegal defense rule, which forbade teams from double-teaming a player before he had the ball.

In a tasty bit of irony, the path of his devastation made life in the post much tougher for future behemoths—who he now scolds from his on-air bully pulpit. "They've changed the game because of me," O'Neal once said. "Other organizations whine and cry because of me. Being the best is too easy for me."

ODOM, LAMAR

A two-time NBA champion and the 2011 Sixth Man of the Year, Lamar Odom was an artistic soul who spent his prime painting window frames instead of the masterpieces he was capable of producing. Over his amateur and professional career, the multifaceted forward was confined by the structures of American athletics, narrow roles on great teams, and his own devils. He was also an early beneficiary of the Kardashian blessing, due to his marriage to Khloé.

Odom was not archetypical for any specific era, nor did he own one signature skill. He was the embodiment of what should pop up in your brain when you imagine a basketball player. He had a lean, 6-foot-10 frame with a bald head and hydra arms. He moved with a polished cadence—the bop of muscle memory—familiar to anyone who has watched New York City playground hoops. While a good athlete, Odom was not some moonwalking cosmonaut.

But Odom could do it all. Dribble, pass, and run the floor like a guard; rebound, score in the post, and block shots like a big man; defend everyone from swingmen to centers. Smooth and graceful in transition, he would hunch momentarily in the lane and then extend to finish over defenders with his long left arm. He flicked daring passes and executed Euro steps before they were popular. Odom was better

than almost everyone at *basketball*, even if it was not necessarily reflected by his numbers or the end results of a game.

There is grainy video footage of an Entertainers Basketball Classic game from 2003 that shows Odom playing in the Gauchos' Bronx gym. Seventeen-year-old LeBron James is in attendance with Jay-Z. Odom sizes up an opponent at the top of the arc, then executes a shammgod dribble between the defender's legs before gliding in for an uncontested bucket. He never looked happier.

Born in South Jamaica, Queens, Odom had a troubled home life. His father was addicted to heroin and his mother died of cancer when Lamar was twelve. Tragedy shadowed him: the grandmother who raised him passed away when he was twenty-three, his six-month-old son died of sudden infant death syndrome, a cousin was murdered, his chauffeured car collided with a motorcycle, which struck and killed a pedestrian, two of his best friends died of drug-related causes in a single 2015 week. "Death always seems to be around me," Odom has said. "I've been burying people for a long time."

Though one of the top schoolboy prospects in America, Odom attended three high schools during his senior year. He committed to the University of Nevada–Las Vegas but was released from his letter of intent after his standardized test scores drew scrutiny (while in Vegas, he was arrested in a sting operation for soliciting sex from an undercover police officer). He meandered to the University of Rhode Island, where he was academically ineligible to play as a freshman. As his high school coach Jerry DeGregorio said, "If Lamar says he'll meet you Thursday at 8, he'll be there. The only question is what week."

Despite tantalizing comparisons to Magic Johnson, Odom slid to the fourth pick in the 1999 draft, where he was scooped up by the Clippers. "He's not a bad kid," said Kevin Stacom, a scout for the Mavericks. "There's a lot of lack of discipline. That's the scary part." While Odom initially looked like a key piece of the Clippers' young core, his first run in Los Angeles was plagued by injuries and two brief suspensions for the crime of puffing doobies. "I chose to experiment with marijuana," he tearfully acknowledged.

A few years later, Odom played in the 2004 Athens Olympics, where coach Larry Brown shamed the Free World by bungling his way to a bronze medal. In Odom's autobiography, *Darkness to Light*, he revealed that he had been smoking dope incessantly at the time—but used an inventive vehicle to supply untainted urine. "We started googling 'fake penises' and studied different ways to beat a drug test," he wrote. "After an exhaustive search we ordered a giant, rubber, black cock to arrive the next day."

After signing with the Heat as a free agent, Odom was shipped back to Los Angeles in 2004 as part of a package for Shaquille O'Neal. Despite his versatility, the Lakers were intent on making a frittata out of a Fabergé egg. During back-to-back championship seasons, he averaged only 11 points in 30.6 minutes a game. The team had late-stage capitalistic shot dispersal—it was not unheard of for Bryant to hoist up more attempts than the frontcourt of Odom, Gasol, and Bynum combined. Even more depressing, Odom averaged a hair beneath 3 assists a game. It always felt as if there was an untapped reservoir of talent brewing below the surface.

It is irresistible to wonder how Odom would have been weaponized had he entered the NBA a decade later. At first blush, his lack of a reliable 3-ball might have been an issue. But most modern teams have figured out how to utilize big guys with outlier creative skills, an ability to defend multiple positions, and spotty jumpers. There is no exact comparison for a contemporary version of Odom, but Ben Simmons, Draymond Green, and Bam Adebayo are possible variants. Or he might have been Nicolas Batum—a player whose set of skills adds up to less than what it could.

Odom should not be considered a disappointment, but he has acknowledged some responsibility for failing to maximize his boundless potential. Besides the drugs, he had a taste for Now and Laters, Skittles, and Starburst that earned him the nickname Candy Man. In 2015, he ran up a $79,000 tab over four days at Dennis Hof's Love Ranch, a brothel in remote Nevada. Accompanied by a pair of blondes, he watched *Interstellar* and *Mad Max*. After ingesting a cocktail of drugs that included cocaine—he has insisted that he was poisoned—Odom overdosed and nearly died, suffering a stroke and brain damage in the process. "Virtually every drug imaginable was found in his system," a source from Sunrise Hospital in Las Vegas told *E! News*.

Five years later, Odom compared his opportunity in the NBA to the dynamic of a failed relationship. "That's like having a bitch give you pussy, feed you, give you bread, but you don't keep it all the way 100 with her," he said on the *Drink Champs* podcast with rapper N.O.R.E. "I just took it for granted."

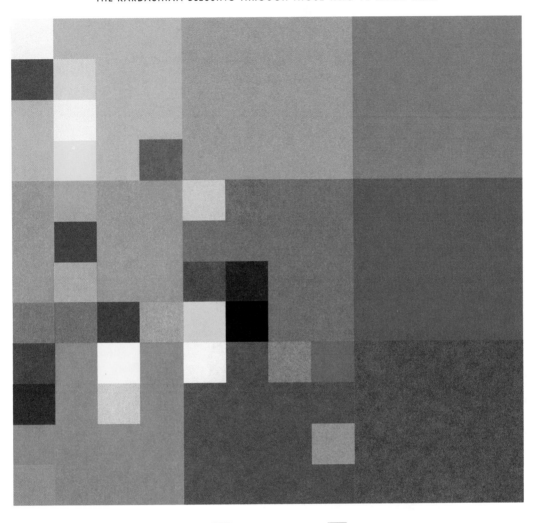

Successful good.

Successful neutral.

Successful bad

Net-zero good.

Net-zero.

Net-zero bad.

Unsuccessful good.

Unsuccessful neutral.

Unsuccessful bad.

A$AP Rocky.

Ben Simmons.

Blac Chyna.

Blake Griffin.

Chris Brown.

Corey Gamble.

Devin Booker.

French Montana.

Harry Styles.

Jaden Smith.

James Harden.

Jordan Clarkson.

Justin Bieber.

Kanye West.

Kris Humphries.

Lamar Odom.

Nick Cannon.

Nick Lachey.

Rashad McCants.

Ray J.

Rick Fox.

Rihanna.

Rita Ora.

Scott Disick.

Travis Barker.

Travis Scott.

Tristan Thompson.

Tyga.

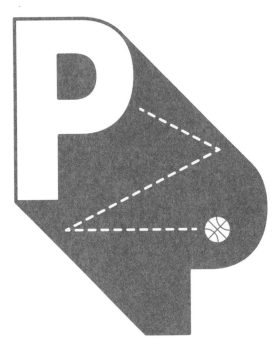

PACE-AND-SPACE ERA

The phrase "pace and space" refers to the two guiding principles of contemporary NBA offense. "Pace," which is measured by possessions per game, is shorthand for playing faster. Transition opportunities, or shots early in the shot-clock, allow teams to attack defenses that are scrambling back in confusion instead of waiting in the half court. Open shots should be taken without hesitation, because there is no guarantee that a better one will be created later in the shot clock. "Space" is shorthand for spreading the floor with capable shooters. Pulling defenders away from the paint clears room for offensive players to operate, whether in one-on-one matchups or multiplayer actions. While putting knock-down shooters at all five positions is ideal in the abstract (see: the 2019 Raptors), having three good ones can do the trick (see: the 2019 Warriors or 2020 Heat).

PAUL, CHRIS

Chris Paul is the greatest point guard to ever play basketball. No, he does not have the hard-won championships of Isiah Thomas. Nor has he amassed bushels of assists and steals to top career leaderboards like John Stockton or Jason Kidd. He has never won Most Valuable Player or led the NBA in scoring like, say, Stephen Curry or James Harden. He is not a power forward like Magic Johnson. But nevertheless, Paul has been deified the "Point God" for a reason. As Kurt Vonnegut might have phrased it, he created the earth and he looked upon it in his cosmic loneliness.

The Chris Paul dilemma is simple and aching: his individual superbness has not coincided with the postseason success one expects from a player of his stature. He played with good teammates on powerhouse squads, yet was consistently been hamstrung by untimely injuries and the cruelties of random results. Paul was a psychotic competitor who tiptoed the line between calculating mastermind and frothing madman—he was as liable to lobby referees to call a technical foul against an opponent on a triviality as he was to punch a foe in the balls—so pablum about "wanting it enough" did not work either.

Paul was born and raised in Winston-Salem, North Carolina. He was a schoolboy star and three-time high school class president—a preview of his grown-ass man role with the National Basketball Players Association. He spent summers working at a gas station owned by his grandfather Nathaniel "Papa Chili" Jones. In 2002, the day after Paul committed to play at Wake Forest University, Jones was beaten, bound, and robbed outside of his home. He died of a heart attack. Five teens were convicted of the murder, though only one of them had a criminal record. "At the time, it made me feel good when I heard they went away for life," Paul told *ESPN* magazine in 2011. "But now that I'm older, when I think of all the things I've seen in my life? No, I don't want it."

After two years at Wake Forest, Paul was taken fourth in the 2005 NBA Draft by the New Orleans Hornets. From his third season onward, Paul was named to nine consecutive All-Star teams, while leading the league in assists per game four times and steals per game six times. A shrug under 6 feet, he became the game's foremost perfectionist. Paul plays like a diamond-cutter and, through his loupe, basketball is a mottled octahedron of rough stone. The way he justifiably sees it, only his steady hand can be trusted to cleave, brute, and polish the gem. He might be good enough to do everything by himself, but we will never know for sure.

Paul is too gifted to be classified as a pass-first caretaker, but his role as a conductor of offensive electricity endears him to traditionalists. The retrograde expression "pure point guard" is applied to his game, though it is intended as a slight to contemporaries who score more aggressively (like, say, Curry or Russell Westbrook). Those biases aside, Paul is a virtuoso at creating good looks for his teammates. He can manifest a competent offense single-handedly. If you do what you're supposed to do, he will reward you with as many dunks and catch-and-shoot 3s as you can shovel down your gullet.

When it comes to his own scoring, Paul is a tidy clinician. He does not specialize in capitalizing off the free money of 3-pointers or free throws (though he is excellent at cashing in on both). He succeeds through mastery of the loathed midrange jumper. More than 50 percent of Paul's career field-goal attempts originate in that nutrient-poor soil, coming in the form of floaters, pull-ups after stomping his anti-lock brakes, and clean 15-footers as centers wilt into drop coverage. There is a resigned sense of doom when a big man finds himself switched onto Paul at the top of the arc—"You're probably wondering how I got here" in agonizing isolation instead of a freeze-frame.

For a little dude, Paul's defense is remarkable. He obnoxiously bedevils opponents, slapping at the ball and flopping from chest bumps. He not only lowers the field-goal percentages of players that he guards, he limits the number of shots they even try to take. According to statistician Kirk Goldberry, who cited numbers from a Sloan Conference presentation with Alexander Franks and Andrew Miller, Paul was the NBA's best defensive perimeter player in the mid-2010s. "They have empirical evidence that the Clippers point guard suppresses and disrupts shot activity as much or more than any other guard in the league," he wrote on *Grantland*. Even when matched up against taller scorers like Kobe Bryant or Kevin Durant, Paul uses core strength and quickness to cause the irritation of a human cold sore.

With apologies to LeBron James, Paul was the best player in the NBA in 2008. Only twenty-two, he posted 21.1 points a night, while leading the league in assists, steals, and Win Shares. Paul's Hornets won 56 games—the highest total for both franchises that have used the handle—but lost against the Lakers in a late-season battle for home-court advantage in the Western Conference. The game was hyped as the battle for MVP, and voters dutifully handed the award to Kobe Bryant as a token of lifetime accomplishment. Paul was robbed. Two years later, he tore his meniscus in a game and never reached the same level of athleticism. "I was so young, and I didn't take my rehab serious enough," Paul said in 2019. "That's the one thing I would change."

In 2011, Paul was involved in a controversial trade that would have air-dropped him in Los Angeles with Bryant. Within forty-five minutes of the three-team deal being agreed upon, it was vetoed by the NBA (who, at the time, owned the Hornets). The cited explanation was "basketball reasons," a phrase that makes Lakers fans apoplectic to this day. More accurately, other team owners were enraged by a swap that potentially draped yet another superstar in purple and gold. "It would be a travesty," Cavaliers owner Dan Gilbert wrote in a letter to the commissioner. "I cannot remember ever seeing a trade where a team got by far the best player in the trade and saved over $40 million in the process. . . . When will we just change the name of 25 of the 30 teams to the Washington Generals?"

Paul arrived in Los Angeles anyway. The Clippers were nominal rivals to the Lakers only because they shared the same arena, but his arrival turned the moribund franchise into a contender. Nicknamed Lob City, the trio of Paul, Blake Griffin, and DeAndre Jordan was stylistically magnificent and the NBA's top-ranked offensive team in 2014 and 2015. After a sequence of playoff disappointments, the trio earned a reputation for being whiny chokers, with Paul's micro-management grating the nerves of his teammates. "You don't realize what you have until it's gone," Paul said on the *All the Smoke* podcast in 2020. "Me and Blake absolutely had our issues here and there and whatnot, but I actually appreciated Blake probably a lot more after I left—especially after he started shooting them 3s. I was like 'Goddamn.'"

Like returning to the city where you spent a honeymoon after a divorce, reminders of Paul's heartbreak are everywhere. The smell of fresh croissants wafting from a bakery, a padlock affixed to a bridge with the key pitched into the green water below, Game 6 of the 2015 Western Conference Semifinals, Game 5 of the 2018 Western Conference Finals, blowing a 2–0 lead in the 2021 Finals. There have always been injuries, freakish episodes of flame-emoji shooting from opponents or frigid bricklaying by teammates, bad bounces in the final seconds.

While Paul's postseason frustrations were once used to question his excellence, his grinding performances in Charlotte, Los Angeles, Houston, Oklahoma City, and Phoenix, even as one of the league's oldest starters, wore the critics down to gravel. And for those who believed in him, there was always a splinter of hope that he could make the most of one last opportunity to win the championship that would put a shiny cap on an impeccable career. The basketball gods have never let it happen.

PLAYER EMPOWERMENT ERA

After years of strong-arming the Players Association for thickers slabs of revenue while crying poverty, NBA billionaires have found themselves in a pickle. To their dismay, a handful of professional athletes remain able to exert a degree of influence over where they want to work. This is normal for almost everyone else—for example, you are not required to live in a Salt Lake City high-rise unless you choose to—but, in the NBA, a sliver of autonomy is called player empowerment. The wobbled power dynamic makes people nauseous for reasons that they struggle to explain without slipping into "the inmates are running the asylum" territory.

The NBA Collective Bargaining Agreement includes layers of architecture designed to limit mobility. It starts with the NBA Draft, in which players have no control over where they touch down. Then there is restricted free agency, where teams can prevent a player from leaving town by matching any open market offer. Even when a player becomes an unrestricted free agent—usually after nine seasons, in the case of an All-Star—rules limit the offers that competing teams can make and incentivize staying put for monetary reasons. Along this career trajectory, a superstar is usually only an untethered free

agent once in his late-twenties prime. Meanwhile, front offices are free to trade or release players at their whim (contracts are guaranteed, however). Life is most precarious for someone like Alonzo Gee, an unheralded wing who was traded three times and waived in the summer before the 2014 season, then signed a contract with the Nuggets—and was traded again at the deadline.

A handful of big names have applied leverage that marginal players like Gee do not possess. LeBron James and Kevin Durant signed deals with opt-outs after one season. Kawhi Leonard silently shut himself down until the Spurs shipped him elsewhere. Anthony Davis's agents made a public trade request while he still had two years left on his contract with the Pelicans. Paul George and James Harden maneuvered to join other big names in high-profile markets. In a queasy twist, unhappy stars can upend the lives of teammates and players on other squads: in the deal that shipped Harden to Brooklyn, six other players changed addresses.

It could be argued that the NBA's ploy to discourage top players from eloping through economic motivations has backfired: not only are small market teams loathe to hand out "supermax" deals to keep stars like Kemba Walker or DeMarcus Cousins, the artificial rigidity of max deals has made factors such as lifestyle, state taxes, weather, endorsement opportunities, and the chance to win titles more important than salary in free agency. If Minnesota and Miami are offering the same contract, not many people are choosing the Timberwolves.

Commissioner Adam Silver has described player empowerment as "disheartening." Under pressure from spurned owners, the league has threatened to confiscate phones and levy steep fines for the devious crime of tampering. The reality is that employers despise being treated like employees. "As a player, you're the worst person in the world when you want a different situation," said Draymond Green. "But a team can say they're trading you, and that man is to stay in shape, he is to stay professional, and if not his career is on the line. At some point, this league has to protect the players from embarrassment like that."

The irony is that the NBA collectively benefits from star players elbowing their way out of lousy organizations and joining contemporaries on marquee organizations. The current Nets, Lakers, and Clippers are title contenders in major media markets that were built by player empowerment. Not a single one of the seven combined 2021 All-Stars on those

three teams was acquired through the draft and three arrived by controversial trades. Despite protestations from teams in woebegone cities without an arts district or a discotheque that stays open after 2 a.m., the off-season drama of player movement is a significant source of excitement. When two-time MVP Giannis Antetokounmpo signed a long-term extension to stay in Milwaukee, the basketball world reacted with a shrug.

PORZIŅĢIS, KRISTAPS

When first described as a "unicorn," Kristaps Porziņģis did not understand the nickname given to him by Kevin Durant. "A horse with a ponytail?" he mused on the *Tonight Show*. "What does it mean?" The 7-foot-3 Latvian came to realize it was a compliment. Selected by the Knicks with the fourth pick in the 2015 draft—and showered with boos from a fanbase that has been terrified of tall Europeans since Frédéric Weis—Porziņģis strung together an unprecedented fusion of spindling height, wingspan, and long-range shooting. But fairy tales last only so long and even chimerical ponies must be shod, groomed, and fed.

From the beginning, Porziņģis captured the imagination. In his fourteenth game in New York, he posted 24 points, 14 rebounds, and 7 blocks. Within a month, his put-back dunks were a signature move worthy of *NBA Jam*. He adopted local slang like "dead-ass" and "b," was adored for wearing cornrows as a Liepāja youth, and received prayers as a Christ-like savior in a short film with actor John Leguizamo. "I think he got his entertainment news from *Worldstar*," said *Worldstar*'s late founder, Lee "Q" O'Denat. "I go to Knicks games when I get a chance to, and, yo, this nigga, he's a real star." Porziņģis felt like an alien who had waltzed down a flying saucer's gangplank with the vaccine to cure a franchise that was rasping on its deathbed.

But visions of a lob-catching rim protector who could stretch defenses with photon-beam 3s gave way to a secular, familiar being. After playing with Carmelo Anthony, Porziņģis began playing *like* Carmelo Anthony. He was increasingly used as a gawky, oversized forward, working out of the post or from the elbow, and paired with frontcourt lunks like Joakim Noah and Enes Kanter. Porziņģis blew out his ACL during the 2018 season. A year later, the Knicks'

front office, pissed off that he had questioned the relegated organization's long-term strategy, traded him to Dallas for a pail of fish guts.

By pairing Porziņģis with rising star Luka Dončić, the Mavericks believed they had assembled a borscht-scented pick-and-pop duo for the modern NBA. During his first season in Dallas, Porziņģis returned to form with 20.4 points, 9.5 rebounds, and 2 blocks a game as the team posted the NBA's best offense rating. Yet TNT's on-air grillmasters were unhappy. Why was a humongous man lurking on the perimeter instead of getting his ass in the paint? Then-Dallas coach Rick Carlisle rushed to his player's defense. "Let's get off all this stuff that KP needs to go in the post," he said in a post-game interview. "We've got to treat KP with some respect. He's a historically great player. And quit criticizing him because he's 7-foot-3."

POSITIONLESS BASKETBALL

Today's youngsters might find it hard to believe, but there was a time when adults had arguments about the sanctity of basketball positions. Point guards painstakingly took care of the ball and seldom scored. Shooting guards chucked up shots. Small forwards were tall guys who could run and shoot a bit. Power forwards rebounded, thudded against each other like horny sea lions, and shot midrange jumpers. Centers were sentenced to lifetime confinement in the lane, where they posted up, blocked shots, and shanked each other with sharpened elbows. It was a time of ignorance and pestilence. We wasted irretrievable hours of our lives debating whether Tim Duncan was an all-time great power forward or an all-time great center.

But a torch flared in the darkness, illuminating a future with sharper tools and less obstinate pack animals. The term "positionless basketball" was coined by *FreeDarko*, the seminal blog that, from 2005 to 2011, blended progressive basketball theory with pop culture, history, theology, and references to Re-Up Gang's *We Got It 4 Cheap, Vol. 2.* "What intrigued us was that players were being allowed to play their own game and have that dictate their roles, rather than have roles imposed on them by a traditional (or nontraditional) system," founder Nathaniel Friedman later wrote on *The Cauldron*. "In turn, players being themselves created new systems, one where a team consisted of making the best out of the ingredients on the roster."

Whether predictive or wishful, the concept has taken root in today's NBA. It has not led to lineups with a pentad of interchangeable, 6-foot-7 components who take turns swishing 3s, beating sloths off the dribble, and posting up runts. Instead, there is broad acceptance of the idea that your best offensive player should touch the ball as much as possible, regardless of their nominal position. Hybrid scorer-distributors have become the model for an offensive superstar: Tracy McGrady, Gilbert Arenas, LeBron James, Trae Young, Nikola Jokić. Large men who can shoot from deep, are no longer gimmicky deviants. Positionality has been smoothed, not flattened. "The league has really changed from where you look at guys as one-position players," said Spurs GM Brian Wright, in 2020. "You've got guards, you've got wings, and you've got bigs, and depending on who they're playing with you diversify. And you want guys who are versatile, who can play multiple positions."

As positional responsibilities melted away, new descriptors sprung up to identify and categorize skill sets. Stretch bigs knock down 3s. A combo guard can manage either backcourt slot to complement whoever he is paired with (much like a vegetarian casserole that, in a pinch, can be served as a main). In 2012, a Stanford senior named Muthu Alagappan won an award at the MIT Sloan Sports Analytics Conference after using topographical data to designate thirteen additional "positions" that included 2-Point Rebounder (like Luol Deng), Scoring Paint-Protector (like Kevin Love), and One-of-a-Kind (like Derrick Rose and Dwight Howard). The study showed evidence of league-wide polymorphism.

The trend of "small ball" is associated with offenses that play at faster tempos and emphasize perimeter shooting. An early iteration was Nellie Ball, pioneered by Don Nelson, who coached Milwaukee, Golden State, and Dallas while racking up the third-most career wins in NBA history. His fascination with nontraditional centers and high-speed attacks was born from both necessity—his teams rarely had a dominating center—and aesthetics. "The best basketball players are the smaller

players," Nelson said. "It's more fun to watch them. They can do more things, they can all pass and shoot and run. Big guys just do it differently." Nelson's tactics were laughed at by puritans who believed smaller teams were exposed in the glare of the post-season, when the game slowed to a half-court slog and defense took on more primacy. He achieved a measure of retribution in the first round of the 2007 playoffs, when his eighth-seeded Warriors, led by point guard Baron Davis and a cohort of rangy forwards, upset MVP-winner Dirk Nowitzki and the top-seeded Mavericks.

As the pace-and-space philosophy became a league-wide offensive trend in the 2010s, lineups adapted. The Miami Heat were praised as innovators for shifting 6-foot-9 James to power forward and 6-foot-11 Chris Bosh to center—a tweak that looks quaint today. Only a few years later, the Warriors captured three titles with lineups that featured 6-foot-6 nutsack-destroyer Draymond Green at the pivot. "What we're witnessing here is a change in the way the game's being played," analyst and former All-Star Antonio Davis told the *Golden State of Mind* blog. "The more skill you have, regardless of size and physical attributes, you can win."

In 2020, the Rockets indulged in the purest small-ball experimentation to date. Midway through the season, Houston traded away starting center Clint Capela and, for all purposes, banished traditional big men from the rotation. It was a radical "microball" solution to an issue that would not have registered as a problem in another time and place: in order to accommodate the poor shooting of guard Russell Westbrook within the team's trifecta-happy offense, Houston employed a frontcourt of P. J. Tucker and Robert Covington, a pair of titular small forwards who had unique abilities to defend larger players and protect the paint. While Westbrook thrived and the Houston defense was respectable, the team struggled to rebound and was bounced from the Bubble playoffs by the jumbo-sized Lakers.

The promise of positionless basketball is not uniformity, but the opposite. Though a lineup needs to collectively address an array of tasks—ball-handling, shooting, rim protection, rebounding—duties do not have to be assigned in any particular way. There is increasing recognition of the value provided by players who have out-of-position skills: guards who can defend bigger players, wings who block shots, bigs who handle the ball. If a team can weaponize Tucker, an ornery, 6-foot-5 paperweight with outlier strength,

immovability, and a 7-foot-2 wingspan, it is freed from the obligation of playing a conventional big man. And when that player annually leads the entire NBA in made corner 3s, you are cooking with gas. "I bask in that whole area of the unknown," Tucker said in the *New York Times*. "It's the most beautiful thing ever."

The future of the NBA looks like Bam Adebayo. He is a 6-foot-9 interior player who seems larger than his listed height. The Newark native is long and agile, strong enough to truck Giannis Antetokounmpo into the basket stanchion, and carries the gaunt mien of an executioner. His shot-blocking and switchability earned him a pair of first-place Defensive Player of the Year votes in 2020, but his passing abilities are what make him unique. Adebayo does not have the seer-like qualities of Nikola Jokić, but pushes the ball up the floor after a rebound and snakes dimes through traffic. "Bam, I challenge him daily to take on all the one-through-five responsibilities on both ends of the court, and he just gobbles it up," said Miami coach Erik Spoelstra, who has grown increasingly comfortable running the offense through Adebayo. "He's one of the most dynamic, unique, impactful players in this entire Association." The world will end with a whimper, but basketball continues with a Bam.

PRE-NBA

While the modern NBA began with Allen Iverson, not every player who preceded him was a part-time electrician. We must respect the league's elder statesmen. Players like Wilt Chamberlain, Bill Russell, Kareem Abdul-Jabbar, Dolph Schayes, Oscar Robertson, Elgin Baylor, Bob Pettit, Julius Erving, Pete Maravich, Moses Malone, Wes Unseld, Magic Johnson, Larry Bird, John Stockton, and Isiah Thomas are icons who helped to popularize and modernize the game we love. They just are not in this book.

PRISONERS OF THE MIND

Anyone in the NBA is likely the best basketball player you have ever met. Scrubs at the end of the bench who are three turnovers away from riding a bus for the Grand Rapids Drive were studs at every plateau of the sport since childhood. The

unreasonableness of the league is that athletes who have been gods for their whole lives are reordered into a hierarchy that dictates fame, wealth, opportunity, and even where they raise their family. We can appreciate the NBA as a raw meritocracy where winners eat what they kill—while being grateful that we do not survive the same way. While most players respond to this professional-grade bloodsport with clichés about competitiveness and confidence ("I don't think anyone can guard me, because I need that mentality"), others confront their limitations with honesty.

A hero and a role model for all of us, Corey Brewer never averaged more than 13 points a game. He was a basketball troubadour whose path wended from NCAA champion and lottery pick to a journeyman who chopped it up in the breakroom for more than a quarter of the league's teams. In 2014, Brewer proved that mortals can briefly ascend to a higher plane by scoring 51 points in Minnesota's 2-point victory over Houston. He sank only two buckets away from the rim all game, including a 49-foot heave at the end of the half. (Other unexpected candidates who exploded for more than 50 points in a game include Willie Burton, Terrence Ross, Tony Delk, and Tracy Murray.) Brewer's understanding of our impotent flailing within this cosmic swirl was revealed in an interview with Mike D'Antoni, who coached him during a stint with the Lakers. After Brewer executed a beautiful spin move only to flub a layup, he described the play like this: "Coach, I did my thing—but then I got to the rim and just ran out of talent."

Or consider Australian national Joe Ingles, who earned his first real NBA minutes at the age of twenty-seven. It might be because he looks like a substitute social studies teacher or a foul-mouthed mattress salesman. Or it could be that the skills which make him valuable as a member of the Jazz are trickier to identify. He is a wonderful secondary passer, a grubby defender who enjoys antagonizing players who are considered his superiors, and a long-range shooter who went from average to deadly. "I didn't know Joe was going to be this good," said coach Doc Rivers, whose Clippers team cut Ingles as a cost-saving measure. He recalled thinking that "this is a bad decision,

and that we're going to regret it."

Ingles loves vengeance. One of the NBA's better trash-talkers, he has blown kisses to opposing crowds after drilling a dagger, mixed it up with Paul George, called Blake Griffin a "flipper," and taunted Bosnian goon Josef Nurkić. "Let's be real," Ingles said of critics who insist he looks like a Minnesotan parole officer. "I've got a receding hairline, I'm slow, and I'm probably not the most jacked-up with abs and all that, but I'm still going to beat you one-on-one."

THE PROCESS

The man who may have been the best NBA general manager in history lasted only two-and-a-half years on the job. Sam Hinkie was hired by Philadelphia in the spring of 2013 after spending eight years as an understudy in the Houston front office. He resigned in 2016, four months after being stripped of decision-making powers. In between was a controversial scorched-earth rebuild known as "the Process," a parade of uncomplimentary centers, a dark conspiracy that went to the mustiest corridors of the league office, and a 47–199 record compiled by the Sixers.

Hinkie's path to the City of Brotherly Love was paved by calamity. In 2012, the Sixers acquired Andrew Bynum from the Lakers in a multi-team trade in which Philadelphia gave up Andre Iguodala, future All-Star Nikola Vučević, and a protected first-round pick. The mammoth but brittle center missed the season with a right knee injury, injured his knee while bowling, and played only 516 more professional minutes before exiting the NBA at age twenty-six. Yet, by plunging to rock bottom, desperation led to courage. Sixers ownership, a coterie of

hedge fund royalty and distressed asset plunderers, empowered Hinkie—a thirty-something fluent in the mealy jargon of market inefficiencies from a stint at Bain Capital—to burn what remained of the franchise to white ash.

Despite its ambitiousness, Hinkie's approach was conventional. The concept of building through the NBA Draft was not new, nor were tactics such as trading veterans for picks, absorbing bloated contracts into cap space in exchange for assets, or giving young players an opportunity to bungle around on the job. But the Process—a name gleaned from the phrase "trust the process," reportedly coined by Sixers shooting guard Tony Wroten—was unusual for its econometric purity. Hinkie made no concessions to the campfire yarns of basketball lifers. He did not care about the toxicity of "losing culture" or the merit of incremental wins (as opposed to what he termed "big leaps"). He did not stock the roster with stabilizing veterans to belay the fall. He did not draft based on fit, which led to the acquisition of three centers and a power forward with lottery picks.

In a moment when tanking hysteria was gripping the NBA, Hinkie and the Process became synonymous with intentionally losing. Over three seasons in which he was employed by Philadelphia, the team won, in order, 19 games, 18 games, and 10 games. It was not just that the Sixers were bad, they kept getting worse—while piling up picks at the top of the lottery. To reactionaries, this was tantamount to cheating.

Hinkie was derided as an emotionless dork who pleasured himself to spreadsheets and never felt the joy of slapping a backboard. Local media screamos dubbed him "Scam Hinkie" while national pundits strafed him with accusations of masterminding a basketball Ponzi scheme. *Deadspin* called him "a TED-humping moron." Over time, the Process has expanded in length from three seasons to rivaling the duration of the Hundred Years' War. "I think we got higher expectations on us than the long, hard five, six years of absolute crap like the 76ers put in," Clippers owner Steve Ballmer told a crowd of 2,500 at a 2018 event for season ticket–holders. "How could we look you guys in the eye if we did that to you?"

While the Sixers found two franchise cornerstones at the top of the lottery—Joel Embiid and Ben Simmons were, respectively, selected third and first overall in their draft classes—the Process was less about purposeful suckiness than focusing on the

The Process

THE PROCESS

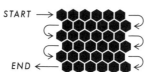

START →

END ←

Not prioritizing winning games as a goal.		Not pushing the "pricey veteran" eject button.	
Finding value where other teams might not.		Enduring purists' slander and math-bashing.	
Ignoring demands for short-term success.		Finding and developing two bona fide stars.	
Being in the position to find one or two stars.		Hoarding cool players but also a few duds.	
Using the NBA's own rules against it.		Aggravating NBA pearl-clutchers forever.	
Sticking to a half-smart, half-hilarious plan.		Seeing hooligans and originalists take over.	
Having to deal with the sports ethics cops.		Being the enemies you made along the way.	

future. Other teams wanted to claw their way up the standings, but Hinkie's disinterest in immediate results allowed him to win trades by default. Over his tenure, the Sixers amassed a marauder's trove of draft picks while sacrificing little in the way of meaningful basketball talent.

Meanwhile, he found dirt-cheap contributors like Robert Covington, Jerami Grant, Christian Wood, Richaun Holmes, and T. J. McConnell by dedicating Philadelphia's roster spots to second-round picks, D-Leaguers, and basketball hobos destined to work at Chrysler dealerships. He drafted two players with career-threatening leg injuries and an overseas prospect, Dario Šarić, who was contractually bound in Europe. Under coach Brett Brown, the Sixers played hard, pushed the tempo, and took high-value shots. This was, in Hinkie's own vernacular, "the longest view in the room."

Even with criticism from the media, agents, and other teams, Hinkie's undoing was sealed with the selection of Jahlil Okafor with the third pick in the 2015 draft. A schoolboy sensation who attended Duke, Okafor was an old-fashioned center who boasted a gorgeous collection of post moves but defended as if his feet were entombed in vats of Nutella.

The team began the next season with 17 straight losses. Even worse, Okafor was seen on *TMZ* heroically assaulting Bostonians following a defeat in Beantown. "Me being drunk, I wasn't in my right state of mind," he said later, revealing that he had stayed inside for two weeks after the incident. The NBA used the cascade of bad press to shunt Jerry Colangelo, the former owner of the Suns and a Joe Arpaio crony, into the Sixers organization as chairman of Basketball Operations. The Process was over, even if few knew it at the time.

In April 2016, Hinkie resigned from the Sixers after learning that he was being demoted. Colangelo's adult son, Bryan, would head the organization, and Hinkie would be assigned a desk in a mildewed basement where he could harmlessly plink away at his Texas Instruments adding machine. In a thirteen-page letter to the team's equity partners, Hinkie referenced extinct flightless birds, quoted Elon Musk, and mentioned the 10,000 Year Clock. "It's clear now that I won't see the harvest of the seeds we planted," he wrote. "That's OK. Life's like that."

PROM KINGS

You know the type: handsome, charismatic, dates the social media influencer, puts up 22 points on 8–21 from the floor against the crosstown rivals, drives his own Jetta. Prom kings are born winners. In movies from the 1980s, they are sweater-vested villains who wind up with liquid heat in their jockstraps. In the NBA, they can be earnest and wholesome, thoughtful scholars or selfless activists who unionize the cafeteria staff.

In the NBA and at every other level of play, scorers are popular. It is the premise of the sport. Even if we appreciate the efforts of an unselfish grinder, the role of scorer is inseparable from stardom. The phrase "hero ball" does not apply to valiant box-outs. Accordingly, prom kings get their corsage flowers without doing much weeding. They are not necessarily *good* at scoring, but fling up enough shots to pile up points. Contemporary prom kings include Andrew Wiggins, Collin Sexton, Michael Beasley, and Bojan Bogdanović.

Back in the 1990s and early 2000s, the role of volume chucker was distinct. Reggie Miller, Allan Houston, and Michael Redd were avatars for their respective franchises. Jim Jackson, a shooting guard who went fourth overall in the 1992 NBA Draft, averaged 20.4 points a game over four seasons in Dallas—and then muddled around inconspicuously for eleven teams over the next ten years.

Another archetypical prom king was Mitch Richmond, a shooting guard who enjoyed mild attention as part of the Warriors' up-tempo RUN TMC era. He vanished into the ether after being traded to Sacramento in 1992. During Richmond's seven-year tenure, the small-market squad was rarely on television, never had a winning record, and made the playoffs once. While no player has scored more career points for the troubled franchise since it arrived in Northern California, there is no concrete evidence that any of it happened.

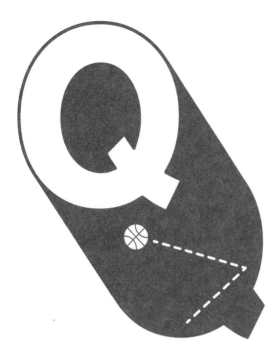

QNBA

Back in 1985, Patrick Ewing was the top collegiate prospect. According to legend, the lottery was rigged to send the Georgetown center to New York, a 24–58 team wallowing in the league's largest market. Some say the envelope holding the Knicks placard was doctored with bent edges or cooled in a freezer to make it identifiable. At any rate, Commissioner David Stern reached into the plastic ball sitting on a makeshift stage at the Waldorf Astoria and the rest is history.

From that moment onward, people have believed that a hidden hand puppeteers the NBA. There are ugly undertones that weave into anti-Semitic tropes ranging from *The Protocols of the Elders of Zion* to the demonization of George Soros. Stern and his more recent successor, Adam Silver, are both Jewish and represent a collective of organizations valued at an average of nearly $2 billion a pop. The league's

machinations are always viewed as financially based, and whispers claim that underhanded measures have benefited superstars and coastal elites.

Several conspiracies have seeped into the game's marrow. The most wild and meritless is that Michael Jordan's habit for high-stakes gambling led to the murder of his father. Some are more plausible, like claims that his habit for high-stakes gambling led to a two-year suspension from the league and his dalliance with baseball.

Others are true, like the NBA's shelving of a trade that would have sent Chris Paul from the Hornets to the Lakers in 2011. At the time, the league owned and controlled the New Orleans franchise. "It was one of the few times I decided to just go radio silent and let it play out, and I got killed," Stern said of the outcry, on *Sports Business Radio Road Show*. "There was never a trade. It was never approved by me as the owner rep." The pieces hinged together when Paul was traded to the Clippers.

In 2007, the veil of secrecy was yanked back by a scandal that appeared to confirm the most sinister plots. Tim Donaghy, an NBA referee for more than a decade, was accused by the FBI of betting on games that he had officiated and making calls to finesse the point spread. After pleading guilty to charges that landed him in federal prison, the seedy ref became an unreliable truth-spiller of the league's secrets. Among his most incendiary allegations was that NBA officials had manipulated postseason games—which he had not worked—in 2002 and 2006 in order to extend the respective series. He admitted betting against the Nuggets in a game where Allen Iverson received harsh treatment from the referees as payback for public criticism. "In the pregame meetings we came to the conclusion that we were not gonna give Allen Iverson any marginal plays for the basket," Donaghy said on *60 Minutes*.

Every fanbase is convinced that basketball's Illuminati conspire against their team. Lottery ping-pong balls are anything but random. Star players in small markets are urged to leave in free agency for cities with philharmonics or a decent Vietnamese restaurant. Sneaker companies lean on the levers to sell more $150 kicks. Agents shepherd players to expand or consolidate industry clout. In recent years, players themselves have been increasingly viewed as tampering schemers who create super-teams via iMessage and finsta DM. The fun part is that they are sometimes right.

THE ACCEPTANCE OF CERTAIN THEORIES

The lottery is fixed to punish the Knicks.

Players are good or bad based on effort.

'90s referees were paid to boost the Bulls.

Adam Silver plotted against the Sixers.

The Celtics won the '14 trade with the Nets.

Our teams are only here to make us miserable.

Kyrie retired in '17 and this is a hologram.

Buddy Hield was actually born in the '60s.

The Heat were actors paid to take an L in '20.

The NBA bosses are all reptilian humanoids.

in areas that require finesse—he leveled up from a spotty shooter to a high-level perimeter scorer from almost every region.

Since the start of the 2010s, power forward has been the league's most chaotic position. With guards and wings monopolizing creative duties and centers diminished to rim protecting stooges, the four slot has become the duct tape that binds the rest together. It is the only safe habitat for non-shooting oddities like Giannis Antetokounmpo, Ben Simmons, and Zion Williamson, and the menagerie includes trifecta-chucking unitaskers, reedy slashers, centers with imposter syndrome, and towering men who do not play enough defense to barricade the paint. On Doctor Moreau's island of power forwards, Draymond Green and Dāvis Bertāns blissfully coexist.

But in the NBA, there are not many like Randle. His taste for midrange junk and double-double statlines make him seem like a traditionalist, but he shoots lots of 3s and operates as the Knicks' defacto point guard in the halfcourt. Unlike heliotropic scorer-distributors who attack with surgical chill, he is a sloppy but endearing maximalist who runs hot, always teetering on the brink of appearing slightly out of control. In a city that romanticizes hustle, Randle's dogged willingness to accept responsibility for his team's fate has turned him from the player New York never wanted to the star New York always needed.

RANDLE, JULIUS

A testament to the importance of finding someone who appreciates you, Julius Randle went from a top prospect to a discarded afterthought to an unloved ball-hog to a folk hero. He has already lived many basketball lives. Following inconsequential gigs with the Lakers and Pelicans, the Dallas native signed with the Knicks as an unimpressive consolation prize after free agents Kyrie Irving and Kevin Durant joined the Nets. As most suspected, New York really cares about only one of those teams—and, by extension, only one of those players.

With box braids, the unwelcoming musculature of a bouncer, and an aggrieved state on the court, Randle was primed to capture the hearts of Knicks fans. It is easy to imagine him draining a turn-around jumper as Gang Starr's "Work" plays in the background, or beefing with referees like someone stridently explaining the merits of cinnamon bagels with lox. Randle overwhelms defenders when shouldering into the high post and wriggles through the lane like a local angling through a pack of tourists in front of Raoul's. Yet his real improvement has been

RELEGATION

Most NBA teams are in the NBA. A few dwell in basketball's shadow realm. Outcomes of their games are meaningless. They are not clawing for the playoffs. They do not bow to the tyranny of wins and losses. Their arenas are silent and dusty, but on moonless nights, some say the sound of squeaking sneakers can still be heard. These teams are relegated. Unlike in overseas professional soccer, NBA relegation does not mean demotion to a minor league. It means exiting the mortal coil.

SELF-CARE ←——————————————————————————————→ *SELF-SABOTAGE*

Being free from the trappings of pleasure.

Ignoring what other people think is failure.

Understanding that darkness is a construct.

Protecting the rap and metal combo dream.

Raving under bridges with your best friends.

Alone, staring at candles, in full face paint.

Ranking the System of a Down discography.

Signing Amar'e to five years, $100 million.

Letting go of Porziņġis for the ghost of KD.

Drafting Jordan Hill over DeRozan and Jrue.

Trading away Nenê and Camby for McDyess.

Swapping two first-rounders for Bargnani.

Frédéric Weis being your most famous pick.

Sending Chicago two firsts for Eddy Curry.

Most franchises follow a natural trajectory of improvement, contention, stagnation, and decline. The plane of relegation is detached from this life cycle. It is the state of blank irrelevance where a team has thudded to rock bottom through intentional tanking, organizational ineptitude, or miserable luck. But relegation is not shameful or morally repugnant. It is a neutral void.

The gray nothingness of relegation is an opportunity for self-care in which a franchise has time to work on itself. While other teams are fretfully eyeballing the standings, it offers the rare opportunity to smash the reset button by prioritizing longer-term goals: collecting draft assets, identifying young talent who slipped through the cracks elsewhere, freeing up cap space for bold moves in the future. In the late 2010s, teams like Philadelphia and Brooklyn used their relegated hiatus to brick foundations for their rebuilds, shrugging at mounting losses while reconstituting players from the scrap heap like Robert Covington, Joe Harris, and Spencer Dinwiddie or taking on bad contracts from other teams in exchange for picks.

A perilous situation arrives when a team in relegation refuses to acknowledge that it has been relegated. The Knicks routinely make this blunder. Whether seduced by self-serving mythology about the honor of playing in Madison Square Garden or secured by the economic power of television deals and ticket prices, New York always believes that it is a couple of moves away from being a playoff team. Despite winning an average of 25 games per season from 2015 to 2019, the previous year's mortifications are forgotten. Come summer, the Knicks operate as if they are merely $60-million-worth of veteran bruisers away from bringing the eighth-seed back to Pennsylvania Station like a backpack of weed on an Amtrak overhead rack. The delusion of being in the NBA—and a profound need to be taken seriously as an organization—has led New York to make counterproductive decisions that, ironically, keep them entrenched in damnation. It is basketball's version of the most hackneyed plot twist: the Knicks were actually dead the whole time.

RICE, GLEN

When the ball left Glen Rice's hand, it had the airiness of a rotating cream puff. Drafted by the Heat in

the second year of the franchise's existence, he was an incorrigible chucker who owned one of the fleeciest jumpers ever seen. His finest seasons came later, in Charlotte, where he was named to three All-Star teams. Over the three-year span when the 3-point arc was moved inward, Rice shot a nonsensical 44.4 percent from long distance—yet took only 30 percent of his shots behind the arc. The 1990s were insane.

According to *The Rogue*, a book by Joe McGinniss, Rice had a one-night stand with future vice presidential candidate Sarah Palin, who was then a sports reporter for an Anchorage television station, KTUU. The tryst occurred while he was playing for the University of Michigan in the 1987 Great Alaskan Shootout. While one of her friends claimed that she had a "freak out" because she "fucked a Black man," Rice recollects the encounter more tenderly. "I remember it as if it was yesterday," he said in 2011. "It was all done in a respectful way, nothing hurried. She was a well-rounded young lady. I think the utmost of her." Barring any unbroken news about Geraldine Ferraro or Mike Pence, this remains the only known relationship between an NBA player and a vice presidential candidate.

Glen Rice's son, Glen Rice Jr., played sixteen games for the Wizards during the 2014 and 2015 seasons. He is not related to Palin, which is why his name is not Trig or Plank or Cart.

RIM PROTECTION

Since the sepia-toned days when the NBA was populated by Pall Mall–blasting dentists who were bored with calisthenics, denying an opponent easy buckets has been the key to a strong defense. That task is known as rim protection, and players who excel at it—usually big dudes, due to their size, wingspan, and proximity to the basket—are described as rim protectors. As the last man standing against trespassers angling for layups and dunks, an ideal specimen not only swats shots and alters their trajectories into moon-scraping rainbows, he prevents them

from being attempted altogether. For twenty-five years, media members who vote on Defensive Player of the Year awards have fixated their gaze on rim protectors like Alonzo Mourning, Ben Wallace, Marcus Camby, Dwight Howard, Tyson Chandler, Marc Gasol, Joakim Noah, Draymond Green, Rudy Gobert, and Giannis Antetokounmpo.

One of the greatest rim protectors ever, Dikembe Mutombo was a joyful, ebullient man whose gift was causing aggravation. The 7-foot-2 center nicknamed Mt. Mutombo was a Congo native who spoke numerous languages and, as a young man, was accused by fellow villagers of being a monster. "People thought I was sick, there was something wrong with my body," he said in an interview after retiring at the age of forty-two. "Today, they are the same people who beg money from me, praise me, think I'm the son of God."

Mutombo had the power to swallow the sun. The eight-time All-Star led the league in blocks per game three times and rebounds per game twice, while winning Defensive Player of the Year four times (an accomplishment equaled only by Wallace). He posted ten triple-doubles that included ten or more blocks. Mutombo was not springy or graceful, but was armed with length and fearlessness. He had the timing of a pendulum clock, limbs that helped him cover distances with unexpected speed, and a trademark finger-wagging taunt that is recognized as his intellectual property twenty years later. According to lore, the youthful Mutombo would stride into nightclubs and proclaim, "Who wants to sex Mutombo?" Although he denies the veracity of the rumor, his Georgetown teammate Mourning confirmed that it was, in fact, Mutombo's mating call. "And it worked, too," he said.

In the battle for NBA air rights—which rivals the brinkmanship of North Brooklyn waterfront real estate—the 2010s introduced another development. According to the league's rulebook, a defender is permitted to make physical contact with an offensive player if he jumps straight upward and keeps his arms similarly extended. Intended as a way to keep players from picking up cheap fouls while guarding post players or trapping the ball, the technique was weaponized as a powerful surface-to-air deterrent against flying attacks. It was called verticality.

Roy Hibbert, the 7-foot-2 son of Trinidadian and Jamaican parents, was yet another big man bronzed on the Georgetown rotisserie—but unlike Mutombo, Mourning, or Patrick Ewing, he was seen as unlikely to develop into a star. After a forgettable rookie season with the Pacers, Hibbert was watching an NBA Finals game in which Magic center Howard was playing against the Lakers. "A guy drove on him, and he jumped straight up in the air," he told *Sports Illustrated*. "There was contact, but it was a no-call. I thought, 'I've got to learn how to do that.'"

The revelation transformed Hibbert into one of the most tiresome defenders of his generation. Using verticality, he was able to create an impenetrable plane of meat in front of the basket. There were fearsome collisions, but he was rarely whistled for fouls due to his diligence in keeping his frame and arms ramrod-straight. Hibbert was named to a pair of All-Star teams and finished second in 2014 Defensive Player of the Year voting. "He takes a lot of teams out of what they are accustomed to doing because he is so great at the rim," said LeBron James, who unveiled a teardrop shot in the playoffs specifically designed to thwart Hibbert. "And they allow him to use his verticality rule more than anyone in our league."

Hibbert's mastery of verticality was appropriated throughout the NBA, including by centers who were younger and more athletic. At the same time, the pace of the game sped up, perimeter shooting improved, and opponents increasingly victimized him outside of the paint. Four years after being a twenty-seven-year-old All-Star, Hibbert was out of basketball. "It just sucks," his former teammate Paul George told FiveThirtyEight. "I guess that's the direction of the league right now. I don't know if teams will gamble on that sort of big [man] that can't move as well." As Hibbert's career waned and Indiana fell out of contention, everyone collectively sighed with relief and stopped discussing verticality.

During the 2010s, rim protection became a prerequisite for NBA centers. With power forwards yanked out of the lane by perimeter shooters and defenses conceding midrange jumpers, it was virtually impossible to survive without a big man who could prevent pipsqueaks from cruising to the rack for easy scores. Spatial tracking data indicates that centers like Gobert, Joel Embiid, Hassan Whiteside, Brook Lopez, and Myles Turner excel at both contesting

shots and holding opponents to disproportionately low field-goal percentages at the rim. After a decade in which rim protection has been mandatory for centers, big men with that skill are relatively easy to find—a growing target are forwards like Giannis Antetokounmpo, Jerami Grant, and Jonathan Isaac, all guys who have the mobility to cover shooters and scramble back into the paint as added layer of resistance. As usual, scarcity is the real difference-maker.

No matter how accomplished they may be at other aspects of the game, centers who struggle to defend are tricky to build around. Taken first overall in the 2018 draft by the Suns, Deandre Ayton is a 6-foot-11, Bahamas-born center with a Ewing-esque scoring repertoire. He has a toothsome face-up game, jump-hooks, the ability to catch lobs, and twisting spin moves with a dreidel's turn-radius. He runs like an elephant bird. Yet Ayton's stardom is not guaranteed. When he was drafted, Embiid tweeted, "Don't compare Ayton to me either . . . I play DEFENSE." As scouting reports prophesized, the young center was not blessed with a ripping motor, struggled to negotiate pick-and-rolls, and meandered on rotations. Yet by year three, he had developed into an efficient scorer and a component in a top-10 defense. But the most perilous threat to Ayton's reputation is no fault of his own: Phoenix drafted him ahead of Luka Dončić, the Slovenian wunderkind who was taken third. Some things are just indefensible.

ROBINS

When a team has an undisputed king, such as Michael Jordan or LeBron James, a pyramidal structure falls into place like tumbling Tetris blocks. Those guys are entrusted to make decisions that determine the outcome of a game or even a season. No coach will face squeals of criticism for buffing his dry-erase board, handing the rock to the team's best player, and living with the results. Still, every caped crusader needs a loyal helper in compression tights. In homage to Batman's little homie, the term "Robin" describes NBA stars who are not

capable of carrying a team alone, but have distinguished themselves from the larger supporting cast.

The most legendary Batman-Robin dynamic was between Jordan and Scottie Pippen. While the superb wing was a bona fide superstar in his own right, he spent years as an underpaid legacist for His Airness. Jordan never made it out of the first round of the playoffs in the five seasons he spent without Pippen as a teammate, but the separation between the two players—in terms of celebrity, organizational respect, credit, and salary—was a chasm. Pippen was a seven-time All-Star who was simultaneously denied enough social mobility to escape the caste of Jordanaire.

But in 1994, Pippen abruptly became the Bulls' top banana when Jordan quit basketball to follow his lifelong dream of batting 0.202 for the Birmingham Barons. Chicago won 55 games, only two fewer than the prior season, and Pippen led the team in scoring, assists, and steals. He won MVP of the All-Star Game and finished third in MVP voting for the season, behind only Hakeem Olajuwon and David Robinson. "It was the first time for me to be the clear-cut star," Pippen said. "I didn't always have a chance to rise up when Michael was there, especially in my first three years. But by him stepping away a little bit, it gave me a little room to grow. And when he came back, it gave me an opportunity to stand beside him instead of standing below him."

It is unclear if Jordan felt the same way. In footage from in the 2020 documentary *The Last Dance*, he could barely contain a grin after Pippen's Bulls lost to the Knicks in the 1994 Eastern Conference Semifinals.

LeBron James has had a Justice League of Robins. Dwyane Wade, Chris Bosh, Kyrie Irving, Kevin Love, and even Anthony Davis all tied on the yellow cape as his teammate. The first remora who clung to his pectoral fin may have been Mo Williams. He was an undersized guard capable of drilling 3s or helming the offense. "A guy being so good, that can do so many things, it takes a special type of individual to play with him," Williams said of his role. "It could be some of the things that you do well also, but he does everything so much better."

When James left for Miami and Collins Avenue, few took it harder than Williams. He grieved openly on Twitter and contemplated retirement, despite several years remaining on his contract. When James and the Heat lost in the 2011 Finals, he logged back on, tweeting, "Dallas just healed my HEART." Later, he clarified, unconvincingly, that his post was part of a broader spiritual cleansing. "Everybody can move on now," Williams said. "People can stop hating him. Okay, you've got what you wanted. Now let him live."

Entanglements occur when Batman is not the best player on the team—but insists on being the one to wrestle the Cluemaster on a catwalk above a vat of bubbling toxic sludge. It is not surprising that Kobe Bryant, one of the most competitive madmen in basketball history, was involved in imbroglios of this type. After wresting control of the Lakers organization away from Shaquille O'Neal, he was viewed as the team's undisputed alpha. In 2010's championship-winning campaign, Bryant flung up 21.5 shots per game, while All-Star teammate Pau Gasol gnawed on table scraps.

But closer inspection reveals that the 7-foot Spaniard was a more efficient scorer than Bryant and led the Lakers in rebounds, blocks, PER, Win Shares, and Box Plus/Minus. In an egalitarian society, Gasol would have risen to the ranks of the Flash. But in the Lakers' extended universe, he was doomed to serfdom by Bryant's ego. Even when the Black Mamba was a creaking thirty-seven-year-old shell of himself, he refused to slither out of Batman's codpiece.

Successful Batman-Batman pairings are possible. David Robinson and Tim Duncan, for two, were equals on the title-winning 1999 Spurs. But even when it works, personal relationships get tricky. Kevin Durant and Stephen Curry won consecutive titles with the Warriors, but Durant seemed to chafe at the perception that it was a duopoly—especially after he seized the reins to win Finals MVP in 2017.

"In my opinion he got the best of 'Bron, like Kevin was fucking rocking," former teammate Draymond Green said on the *All the Smoke* podcast. "And it's like, you turn on the TV the next day, and the fucking headline is, 'LeBron James, still best player in the world?' And then we came back for the 2017–18 season, and Kevin just wasn't as happy. All of a sudden it was kind of just like, 'Fuck, why's Steph shooting this shot?' or 'Fuck, he ain't pass the ball.'" A year later, Durant split to Gotham. As Batman knows, anger gives you great power—but if you let it, it will destroy you.

RODMAN, DENNIS

"I go out there and get my eyes gouged, my nose busted, my body slammed," said demonic energy guy Dennis Rodman. "I love the pain of the game."

After high school, Rodman was homeless and played for a community college in Gainesville, Texas. From there, he became a second-round pick who rose to stardom as a member of the Detroit Bad Boys, played with Michael Jordan, dated Madonna and Carmen Elektra, befriended North Korean dictator Kim Jong-un, and broke his penis three times during sex. "Your dick still get hard," he told *VICE*. "It don't get straight, it's kinda like a big fucked-up carrot." You know, regular stuff. With dyed hair, facial piercings, a taste for painted nails and women's clothing, tribal tattoos (and a full-back piece of a woman who appears to be eating her own stretched labia), Rodman was one of the NBA's most eccentric players and an accidental style icon for Zoomers.

Despite being the height of a small forward—his listed position early on—Rodman was the greatest rebounder the NBA has ever seen (with all due respect to Andre Drummond, the board-vacuuming schlub who now owns the category). From 1992 to 1998, he led the league in rebounds per game. It was rarely competitive. He made a job for losers and fat kids look cool, accentuating rebounds with Rockette kicks in midair, mad dashes to start a fastbreak, or by cuffing the ball and holding it behind his back as if about to surprise a lover with roses.

How was Rodman so spectacular at rebounding? Physical tools were visible: long arms, a quick second jump, diligent box-outs, and the ability to play with cranked-up intensity for long periods of time. He sought any excuse to dive into folding chairs and spectators. But there was a mystical quality too, as if Rodman saw the game through special backboard-glass lenses. "He knew the rotation of every person that shot on our team," said Pistons teammate Isiah Thomas, in the *Detroit Free Press*. "If it spins sideways, where it would bounce, how often it would bounce left or right. He had rebounding down to a science, and I never heard anyone think or talk about rebounding and defense the way he could break it down."

Or he had different priorities. After leaving Detroit, Rodman all but stopped shooting and became a unitasker extraordinaire. During the first of two seasons in San Antonio, he averaged only 4.7 points in 37.8 minutes. He was traded after the arrival of coach Gregg Popovich: "He hated my guts because I wasn't a Bible guy," Rodman said later. "They looked at me like I was the devil."

Heading into the 1996 season, Rodman joined Jordan's Bulls, who were aching from a semifinals bullying administered by Shaquille O'Neal and

PREDICTABLE PLOT LINES

Very much.   Not really.

LeBron James surpassing Michael Jordan.

Ben Simmons upsetting true grillmasters.

Luka Dončić getting a pass from critics.

Kyrie Irving being the #1 boomer target.

Raf Simons claiming skinny jeans again.

Nikola Jokić as the GOAT offensive big.

Luke Skywalker being the actual bad guy.

Pop Smoke's posthumous album flopping.

The feds officially admitting UFOs exist.

Dennis Rodman as a Kim Jong-un day one.

NICKNAMES

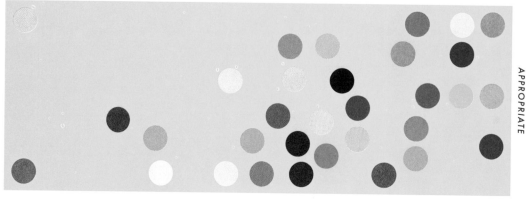

RANDOM

APPROPRIATE

AWKWARD

The Answer.
Baby Jordan.
The Beard.
Beef Stew.
The Big Aristotle.
Big Ticket.
The Blue Arrow.
Board Man.

Boogie.
The Brow.
The French Prince.
The Glove.
The Greek Freak.
The Joker.
King James.
The Mamba.

The Maple Mamba.
The Matrix.
Mr. Big Shot.
PG-13.
The Process.
The Reign Man.
The Slim Reaper.
The Stifle Tower.

Spida.
Three 6 Latvia.
Timelord.
The Truth.
Wave Papi.
White Chocolate.
The Worm.
Zanos.

turncoat Horace Grant of the Magic. With the Worm writhing for boards, Chicago surged to lead the NBA in offensive rebounding and was eighth in defensive rebounding. Control of the glass was the final piece of the puzzle for a team that would be immortalized as the greatest in history up until that point: the Bulls had the league's best offense and best defense, won a record-breaking 72 games, and went 15-3 in the post-season en route to the first of three consecutive titles.

While playing for Chicago, Rodman wore a wedding dress to a Manhattan press event for his autobiography, *Bad As I Wanna Be*, went on a 48-hour midseason vacation to Las Vegas, was suspended for kicking a baseline photographer in the crotch, skipped practice during the Finals to appear on a WCW *Monday Nitro* pro wrestling event, and had sex "all over" the team's practice facility. "Dennis was bizarre," said Bulls teammate Steve Kerr in *The Last Dance*. "But I think what made it work was Phil [Jackson]

and Michael understanding that to get the most out of him on the court, you had to give him some rope—and they gave him a lot of rope."

In 2013, a long-retired Rodman was recruited by *VICE* to headline a basketball diplomacy mission to North Korea. He was accompanied by the Harlem Globetrotters to Pyongyang, where he sat with Kim Jong-un during an exhibition game in a ten-thousand-seat stadium, then joined the dictator for an evening of feasting on sushi, guzzling soju, and watching an 18-piece band of women perform the theme song from *Dallas*. "Next thing I know, we are having dinner and we are drunk as shit," Rodman said on the podcast *Hotboxin' with Mike Tyson*. "He starts singing karaoke and I have no clue what the fuck he's talking about."

SABONIS, ARVYDAS

We know 7-foot humans are rare—you could go a lifetime without seeing one in line for bagels—but their scarcity makes numbers fuzzy. There are supposedly around 2,800 people on the planet who reach that height, and, out of the American men, it was reported by *Sports Illustrated*'s Pablo Torre that 17 percent spend time in the NBA. The math is complicated by basketball's tradition of inflation—for example, Joel Embiid of the Sixers went from a 7-footer to a 6-foot-11 shrew when measured in stocking feet. Whatever the real numbers, virtually every stateside teen who hits a Bunyanesque spurt is funneled by parents, coaches, and peers into experimenting with the one popular sport that rewards being tall as shit. In 2020, there was roughly an average of one 7-footer per NBA team.

Among these extraordinary beings are a tiny number of true giants. Somewhat surprisingly, they are not usually superstars. Perhaps the human body is not designed to grow to enormous sizes through pituitary riot, let alone with enough coordination to catch flying basketballs or sprint down a 94-foot court. Out of players taller than 7-foot-2,

Ralph Sampson, Rik Smits, Yao Ming, Žydrūnas Ilgauskas, and Kristaps Porziņģis have been the best—and all of them were hampered by leg or feet issues. Guys like Mark Eaton, Manute Bol, and Shawn Bradley were healthier, but had limited utility as shot-blocking specialists. And most often, the hugest of the league's titanic men are novelties like Gheorghe Mureşan, Boban Marjanović, Priest Lauderdale, or Tacko Fall.

Leg injuries and international politics prevented us from witnessing basketball's greatest giant in his prime. Arvydas Sabonis was a beer-swilling 7-foot-3 Lithuanian who was selected by Portland in the 1985 draft, but spent the next decade playing in European leagues (despite the organization sending "Free Arvydas" entreaties to Soviet leader Mikhail Gorbachev). "I told everyone, all the time, that if Sabonis was in the NBA, he would be the best player, possibly, ever," said Detlef Schrempf, a three-time All-Star with the Pacers and Sonics, who played against Sabonis as a member of German youth teams. "Guys were like, 'Pffft, come on.'"

In blurry YouTube footage, Sabonis resembles a Cold War wrestling villain. Mulleted and clad in short-shorts, he treats American amateurs such as David Robinson like infants, pinning their shots against the backboard and dunking on rims that look several feet short of regulation in his vicinity. He could run the floor, attack off the dribble, shoot 3s, and pass like a guard. Bill Walton was awed by a nineteen-year old Sabonis. "He probably had a quadruple-double at halftime," he told *Grantland*. "We should have carried out a plan in the early 1980s to kidnap him and bring him back right then."

By the time Sabonis made it to the States at thirty for the 1996 season, his limbs had been ravaged by injuries, including a torn Achilles tendon suffered while running up stairs to answer a telephone. Watching him hobble the court was painful, but he was shockingly good. As an elderly rookie, Sabonis averaged 22.0 points and 12.2 rebounds per 36 minutes, and rate-based composite metrics indicated he had the impact of a superstar. He spent seven seasons in Portland and retired in his late thirties. Arvydas has a tiny, wee, sprite-like, 6-foot-10 son named Domantas, who was named to the 2020 NBA All-Star team as a member of the Pacers.

SECOND-ROUND PICKS

In the 1960s, back when basketball players took one-legged free throws and were part-time night watchmen at sardine-packing factories, the NBA Draft had over twenty rounds. Teams picked up players until they ran out of orthodontists looking to make extra scratch. Over time, the draft shortened from ten rounds to seven rounds, and, since 1989, to the current length of two rounds. Accounting for the league's expansion, second-round picks include selections 31 through 60.

Second-round picks are scratch-off tickets in comparison to lottery selections. In the stacked 1996 draft, for example, only four players taken in the second round went on to play more than 10,000 career minutes—and none of them surpassed averageness. That said, finding talent burrowed deep in the draft is possible. All-Stars like Draymond Green, Khris Middleton, Paul Millsap, Jeff Hornacek, Nikola Jokić, and Gilbert Arenas were all mined in the second round. While studs are a rarity, there are usually a handful of contributors waiting to be plucked out of the litter. Due to the longshot nature of second-round picks, they are tossed around with the frivolousness of chocolate gelt. They are bought and sold, used as trade sweeteners, and offered as bribes to move small contracts for luxury tax relief. If a lottery pick is worth a buck, second-rounders are nickels.

Khris Middleton, a multiple-time All-Star, was selected thirty-ninth in the 2012 draft by the Pistons and dealt to the Bucks a year later as financial lubricant in a transaction that included Brandon Knight and Brandon Jennings. "As a player, it sucks to know you were just thrown into a trade for it to work," the forward told *Sports Illustrated*. While most late draft picks are plucked for having a distinct skill—knockdown shooting, gravity-insulting ups— Middleton's old head arsenal of midrange jumpers and post-play was out of vogue in a league obsessed with 3-balls and assailing the rim.

Even after averaging 20 points a game and being recognized as a valued contributor, Middleton and his oat milk-flavored game are constantly described as being underappreciated (we all get it, he is very good). Though frumpy, Middleton's knack for making tough, contested 16-footers proved a complementary pairing with Milwaukee focal point Giannis Antetokounmpo, a relative non-shooter. During the team's 2021 title run, he drained long 2s

at a 47 percent clip with enough crunchtime buckets to convince some media loudmouths that he, in fact, was Batman of the Bucks. "I told him the day you retire is going to be the toughest day in my career," Antetokounmpo said of Middleton, "It's been an unbelievable journey."

In 2018, Mitchell Robinson was taken thirty-sixth overall by the Knicks. The rubbery 7-foot Pensacolan had speed, athleticism, and leviathan dimensions—but players with that profile rarely slide into the second round without unusual circumstances. Not only had Robinson left Western Kentucky University before playing a game, he did not play overseas or in the G League, and skipped the NBA's draft combine. "Who would willingly choose to just not play organized basketball for a year when trying to make the NBA?" wrote Knicks blog *Posting and Toasting*, following the draft.

In New York, Robinson was often treated with kid gloves or disinterest. As a rookie, he led the NBA in blocks per 36 minutes and field-goal percentage among anyone who played more than 500 total minutes; in his second season, he was the most efficient scorer in the history of the league. And yet, perhaps due to the perception of organizational indifference, Robinson was rarely positioned as an emerging star or a load-bearing beam in the Knicks' two-decade rebuild. It could be that when teams strike gold on a second rounder, there is lingering suspicion that he is a hunk of pyrite.

SHAPE-SHIFTERS

Few players exit the NBA the same way they entered it. But some transform over the course of their careers to the point of unrecognizability. It may naturally occur with roles, as in the case of Andre Iguodala, who went from an All-Star averaging a hair under 20 points a game to a defensive glue guy on championship teams.

But more unusual are changelings such as Larry Johnson, the top pick in the 1991 draft and the first All-Star in Hornets franchise history. A freight train

who was named Rookie of the Year and dressed up in Converse ads as a dunking matriarch named Grandmama, he was a predecessor for undersized interior scorers like Zion Williamson. "He's going to be a superstar, that's without a doubt," said his Charlotte teammate Muggsy Bogues.

But in his mid-twenties, Johnson suffered a series of back injuries that robbed him of his explosiveness. By age twenty-seven, he was traded to New York, where he became a moderately productive jump-shooter who took about a quarter of his shots from deep. Despite being one of the baddest men alive at UNLV, Johnson will forever be remembered for his miraculous 4-point play in the closing seconds of a 1999 Eastern Conference Finals game. "It still sends chills up and down my spine when I see it," said his coach, Jeff Van Gundy.

Another top draft pick (although fourteen years later), Karl-Anthony Towns was accurately projected as the superstar that he turned out to be. But after a few years in the league, he morphed into a prototype that few experts foresaw. "He's a post-first, jump-shot-second kind of player, period" read a scouting report posted on the Celtics' website. While Towns took only 1.1 shots from deep per game as a rookie on the Timberwolves, he was launching 7.9 from beyond the arc at a 41.2 percent clip by 2020—making him perhaps the most lethal big man from long range in history. He has already drilled more 3s than any Minnesota player ever.

Enough 6-foot-11 guys have adapted to the modern game by adding shooting range, but Towns is not some dabbling pick-and-pop dilettante. He hoists off the dribble, after shuffling step-backs, or virtually flat-footed with an opposing center so close that he can smell Nikola Jokić sweating out the slivovitz. When combined with the strength and coordination to get buckets in the paint, Towns entered the 2021 season jostling with Stephen Curry for the unofficial title of the most efficient primary scorer who has ever lived.

On the other hand, Towns's reputation as an excellent defensive prospect has not come to fruition. Despite ranking among the league's top 10 in blocks and defensive rebounds, he does not have snappy intuition or lateral quickness, and reacts a fraction of a second late, as if glued to the hardwood by his size 20 clown shoes. He has never been on a team with a defense that ranked better than 21st and his imperfect fit at both center and power forward deserves some culpability. At times,

composite metrics have slotted Towns as the NBA's worst defender at the pivot and, in 2020, the Wolves surrendered 7.9 more points per 100 possessions with him on the court. He is a complicated superstar.

Just as Towns's game underwent a metamorphosis, so did he. His rounded shoulders and baby fat felt like vestiges of youth, but after a devastating year in which his mother and six other family members died of COVID-19, he carries the leaden heaviness of a man who has suffered. He contracted a bad case of the virus as well. "I felt very guilty about the treatment I got," Towns told *Sports Illustrated*. "And I feel that should be more widely available to Americans, to anyone in the world. I felt very guilty even getting something that could help me more just recover, stay healthy, stay alive."

SHOOTING BIAS

When it comes to shooting the ball, almost every NBA player abides by the acronym of BEEF: balanced stature, elbow tucked instead of flaring to the side, eyes trained on the rim, and follow-through (ideally with a "gooseneck" flick of the wrist). Add muscle memory, concentration, and confidence. *Voilà!* These fundamentals are reinforced at every level, by every summer league coach, half-interested uncle, and tutorial Joel Embiid found on YouTube. "Have you ever seen a normal, thirty-year-old white guy shoot a 3-pointer?," he wrote in the *Players' Tribune*. "You know how in America, there's always an older guy wearing like EVERLAST sweat-shorts at the court? That guy is always a problem. His J is always wet." And yet, despite the same kinesiological checklist, each jumper is as unique as a thumbprint.

Players with beautiful jumpers have quick but unhurried releases, as predictable as a tide table. The ball leaves their hands with an elegant, almost weightless buoyancy on an unerring 45-degree parabola. Their extended arm freezes in place, a tribute to artistry in ice sculpture. Players with

1 2 3 4 5 6 7 8 9 10 11 12 13 14 15 16 17 18 19 20 21 22 23 24 25 26 27 28 29 30

Warning: strobe effects and jumpers.

Offending the sports bar mansplainers.

Laughing at shooting is kinkshaming.

Variety (of shots) is the spice of life.

It's the effort and other skills that count.

They say ball don't lie but eyeball can.

1. Markelle Fultz.

2. Michael Kidd-Gilchrist.

3. Josh Jackson.

4. Chuck Hayes.

5. Josh Childress.

6. Shaquille O'Neal.

7. Marcus Camby.

8. Tony Allen.

9. Tayshaun Prince.

10. Kenyon Martin.

11. Shawn Marion.

12. Lonzo Ball.

13. Joakim Noah.

14. Jason Kidd.

15. Derek Fisher.

16. Kevin Martin.

17. Al Horford.

18. Mike Bibby.

19. Mikal Bridges.

20. Rashard Lewis.

21. Eric Gordon.

22. Michael Redd.

23. Leandro Barbosa.

24. Reggie Miller.

25. Joe Harris.

26. Seth Curry.

27. Joe Ingles.

28. Dirk Nowitzki.

29. Matt Bonner.

30. Stephen Curry.

the prettiest releases are not necessarily the most accurate shooters, but they are usually excellent. In 1994, a story in *Popular Science* about the perfect jumper featured illustrated diagrams of Cavaliers point guard Mark Price, whose textbook form splashed 40.2 percent of his career 3-pointers. The allure of a conventionally attractive jumper helped players like Buddy Hield, Nik Stauskas, and Jimmer Fredette become lottery picks.

Over on the dingy side of the tracks, among broken nips and finger-grasses, are the ugly jump shots. Players with infamously gnarly forms include Shawn Marion, a fibrous wing who shot decently despite chest-passing the ball at the basket, and Michael Kidd-Gilchrist, the defensive stopper whose shot looked as if he was trying to keep the lid on a Crock-Pot filled with hot soup. But "broken" jumpers can sometimes be fixed. Lonzo Ball, the second pick in the 2017 NBA Draft, entered the league with a sideways-slinging motion, but, after retooling it, made 38.3 percent of his 3s in his third season. "Obviously, in the beginning it was a little tough because it just didn't feel right," Ball said on JJ Redick's podcast. "Like, it's not how I shoot."

With the popularity of 3-pointers and the vitality of spacing, life in the NBA has never been harder for a non-shooter. Centrist voices who once decried 3-pointers as a perversion have shifted their timbre, now chanting 3-point field-goal percentages as if scripture. Players like Rajon Rondo, DeMar DeRozan, and Russell Westbrook have been treated with skepticism due to shooting bias. But there is an upside to knowing one's limitations—a mediocre shooter who believes he is a dead-eye marksman is often more detrimental than a self-aware bricklayer who seeks other ways to pitch in.

To some, Ricky Rubio, a teenaged phenom from Spain who was taken fifth overall by the Timberwolves in 2009, qualifies as a disappointment. When his minutes and low field-goal percentage are taken into account, he is one of the worst shooters in NBA history. But due to his playmaking abilities, knack for getting to the line, assist-to-turnover ratio, and apex dreaminess—which causes opponents to get lost in his dark chocolate Iberian eyes—Rubio makes his team better, often significantly. In 2014, Minnesota had an offensive rating of 112.4 with Pretty Ricky on the floor and 100.8 when he was off, the widest split of any Timberwolf. "With regards to Ricky trying to prove to people that he's a shooter, that shouldn't be his role," said former Minnesota general manager Milt

Newton. "His role is to lead our team, hit the open player, and when he has an open shot, have the confidence to knock it down." And, if he misses, so what?

SHOWTIME

The year is 1999. You are concerned about how the Y2K bug will affect the power grid and Napster. As the Southern California sun beats down on your bucket hat, the menacing opening notes of "The Next Episode" begin to play from a nearby Geo Tracker. At the moment, you do not know that the Lakers have just embarked on the first season of a "three-peat" that will return the franchise to rightful glory. The Lake Show has not won a title in an unthinkable dozen years. But you feel it. Because you are a Lakers fan. The world revolves around your team. Every superstar heeds the siren call of tall palms, summertime fires, steaks at BOA, and partying at Tenets of the Trees with Will.i.am. Players who go by one name, as if a Brazilian soccer star or Cher. The Logo, Wilt, Karim, Magic, Worthy, Shaq, Kobe, Bron-Bron. The team is special and so are you.

SIMMONS, BEN

A human Porsche Cayenne who is infamous for the one skill he lacks, Ben Simmons is the most futuristic player in the current NBA. He was selected by Philadelphia with the top selection in the 2016 NBA Draft, won Rookie of the Year, and was twice named to the All-Star team—yet is often regarded as a disappointment, rather than a franchise pillar who is bullet-pointing the résumé of a Hall of Famer. The 6-foot-10 Australia native is a profoundly rarity, both in his collection of on-court attributes that seem randomly generated by a captcha and the hostility he engenders.

Simmons was a schoolboy phenomenon in Melbourne whose American father played professional basketball for the local team, the Tigers. He spent a cursory season at Louisiana State University, where he ditched classes after the team failed to qualify for the NCAA tournament. "Everybody's making money except the players," Simmons said in *One and Done*, a 2016 Showtime documentary about his collegiate fiasco. "They say education, but if I'm there for a year, I can't get much education."

In accordance with Philadelphia rookie tradition, Simmons fractured a bone in his foot before the 2016 season and sat out the entirety of his first year. When he returned, he lived up to his billing in terms of box score production and impact (the rebuilding Sixers finished a surprising 52–30). Despite Simmons's landslide victory in Rookie of the Year voting, a few critics scoffed that he wasn't a "real" rookie because he had missed the prior season. Donovan Mitchell, who finished a distant second, wore a sweatshirt with a dictionary-style definition of the word "rookie" printed on the chest. "How do I feel about it?" Simmons said, when asked about the uninteresting controversy before a road game in Utah. "I don't give a fuck."

As the prototypical scorer-distributor, LeBron James has been a frequent comparison for Simmons—a connection strengthened when Simmons signed with Klutch Sports, an agency run by James's close associates. At times, it has been tough to distinguish Simmons's own silhouette from that shadow. Is he a perimeter player who can't score outside of the paint? A big man who lacks crisp, four-square footwork in the post or the wingspan to snuff out shots at the rim? A leading alpha or a cowardly beta cuck?

At times, Simmons's physical measurements, mobility, ball-handling skills, and vision make his game appear leisurely. His stoic demeanor offers a template that can be read as laziness, apathy, or arrogance. The parade of celebrity girlfriends, closet of Goyard murses, dedication to Twitch streams with his gamer clan, and taste for life in Los Angeles make grimy Philadelphians in State Property jeans uneasy.

And, of course, Simmons doesn't shoot. Over his first three seasons, he made less than 30 percent of his field-goal attempts from beyond 10 feet—and then stopped taking them. Purists are driven to madness by the optics of a professional basketball player declining to take wide-open 12-footers, and frame it as a question of morality and effort. Simmons didn't drain a regular season 3-pointer until November 2019 (against the relegated Knicks, no less), an event that kicked off a week of fireworks along the shores of the Schuylkill River. After he hit another one a few weeks later, Sixers coach Brett Brown laid down the gauntlet. "You can pass this along to his agent, his family, his friends, and to him," he dictated to reporters. "I want a 3-point shot a game, minimum."

Simmons attempted only a handful from that point onward, and Brown was fired following the season.

Even in an era where spacing is crucial, the obsession over Simmons's reluctance to fling up trifectas is odd. Contemporaries such as Giannis Antetokounmpo, Bam Adebayo, and Zion Williamson are functional non-shooters, yet receive a fraction of the vitriol. Footage of Simmons making a few long jumpers during a 2019 summer pick-up run was shared as if a yeti was caught on camera entering a Wawa with Matt Ox. In truth, there is little reason to believe that Simmons's metamorphosis into a middling, low-volume 3-point shooter would help his team. "Just like with Giannis," a Western Conference coach told *ESPN* magazine in 2020, "we're still giving him that shot every single time—and hoping he takes it."

Despite the criticism, Simmons is a two-way superstar. His mulish refusal to be bullied into taking garbage shots is a strength, not a vulnerability. While other players rebel against efficiency-based trends, he icily dumps data into shot-chart spreadsheets with stylized keystrokes: transition dunk, 3-point assist, straight line driving dunk, 3-point assist, dunk off a lob, 3-point assist. He has a handful of tricks that weaponize defenders' instincts to sink into the lane, such as swerving into dribble-handoffs that free up shooters with ribcage-crunching screens. Before being sidelined with a back injury during the 2020 season, Simmons led the NBA in assists on 3-point baskets, was tenth among qualified leaders, and finished fifth in points created off assists per game. Even with his idiosyncrasies, he is the rare player who can sculpt a game to fit his own economy.

On the other side of the ball, Simmons's defense is unholy. His size, discipline, and nimble feet make him a terrible date for volume-scoring wings: they can't shoot over him, can't cook him off the dribble, and can't turn the corner to shoulder-shim their way to the rack. He is not spidery enough to block many shots, but ranks among the leaders in disruptive stats like steals, deflections, and loose balls recovered thanks to a motor that can go from purring to roaring in a blink. Measurements of defensive versatility annually place Simmons at the top of the NBA, and his assignments range from chasing gnats like Trae Young to manning the pivot as a small-ball center.

Over the last twenty-five years, NBA superstardom has been defined by scorers. Michael Jordan, Allen Iverson, Kobe Bryant. Men who yearned for the final shot and vicariously fulfilled the fantasies of every kid who whispered down the final seconds

of an imaginary clock on the playground or family driveway. From that perspective, Simmons's paradigm-shifting excellence is as unrecognizable as an iceberg veiled by fog.

SNITCHING

NBA players describe themselves as being members of a fraternity—and it turns out the Covenant of Ballers frowns on stool pigeons, narcs, and rats. In 2015, D'Angelo Russell, a rookie guard with the kind of creative gifts that makes scouts drool on their bibs, learned about the code of omertà. While on the Lakers, he recorded a video in which teammate Nick Young, a walking bucket nicknamed Swaggy P, discussed hooking up with a nineteen-year-old woman while he was engaged to Australian rapper Iggy Azalea. With Young preoccupied across the locker room, Russell teased out incriminating statements from Young about seeing other women, presumably as a prank.

Young and Iggy lasted another year before breaking up, but, for Russell, the fallout when the video got out was immediate. "I can't really show my face anywhere without people hating me right now," he said, after being shunned in the Los Angeles locker room and forced to eat alone. "I try to handle it the right way and remember why I'm here, which is to play basketball." Despite his talent, Russell played on four teams during his first five seasons.

For all of the tough talk from fellow hoopers (Brandon Jennings, for one, called Russell "a snitch"), players have more lax attitudes about tattling in other circumstances. Most egregiously, Shaquille O'Neal was a reserve police officer. Chris Paul, an elite dime-dropper, has cheesed technical foul points for his team by informing referees about indiscretions like untucked jerseys. In the COVID Bubble, the NBA created a hotline for players to anonymously rat out peers who were violating safety protocols (Dwight Howard claimed someone reported him for not wearing a mask, but also posted maskless videos of himself). And when Giannis Antetokounmpo was

weighing whether to sign an extension, he reportedly showed the Milwaukee brass texts from players on other teams who were trying to recruit him. The NBA is not immune to the rise of narc culture—unless it crosses the most sacred line: the bro code.

SOCIAL MEDIA

As young people with oodles of downtime, NBA players have embraced fucking around on their phones. And like everyone else, they do much of that fucking around on platforms like Twitter, Instagram, Snapchat, and TikTok. Social media has changed conventional methods of communication, friendship, and dating, but for professional athletes, it has truly upended interactions with the public. Where ballers were once separated from fans by a filtration system of televised broadcasts, coverage from beat writers, and magazine profiles, they are now free to engage directly. This runs the gamut from ticket-giveaways and eyeball emojis to players confronting detractors via direct message.

A year before the 2021 Non-Fungible Token frenzy, guard Spencer Dinwiddie—a voluble chap who scored 1,400 on the SAT and was nicknamed Siri by Brooklyn teammates for being a know-it-all—attempted to tokenize part of his $34 million contract. The scheme ran afoul of the NBA, since the final year of his contract was not guaranteed. "Legacy systems generally do fear that type of thing," Dinwiddie told *Forbes*. "And so they kind of drew a hard line and kept talking about termination." The league eventually approved a modified version of the blockchain advocate's plan, but Dinwiddie ran into a non-negotiable obstacle: lack of interest. Only nine of the ninety available $150,000 contract shares were sold.

NBA players are present on Cameo, a platform that allows customers to pay celebrities for personalized messages. For the meager price of $400, one can have 7-foot-5 Tacko Fall congratulate your niece on her quinceañera. If that is out of your price range,

former Hornet and Net star Kendall Gill will do it for twenty bucks. So far, no notable NBA players have been hornswoggled like legendary NFL quarterback Brett Favre, who blithely recited a Cameo message from alt-right trolls that was freighted with anti-Semitic codewords.

One of basketball's oddest rivalries is between Adrian Wojnarowski and Shams Charania, his former apprentice at Yahoo! Sports. Both are reporters who specialize in tweeting out breaking NBA news—trades, draft picks, injuries, suspensions—and one inevitably gets the scoop, even if by seconds. There are fans who delight in this informational horse race, and reply to their tweets with photoshops of the journalists dunking on each other. When Woj sent an email to insurrectionist senator Josh Hawley with the message "Fuck you" during 2019's China imbroglio, Shams allegedly liked (and then unliked) a tweet that called Woj "an NBA bootlicker."

For players, social media is the perfect way to accidentally expose their horniness. Jamal Murray, the polished point guard on the Nuggets, posted a POV Instagram Story during the COVID-19 hiatus that showed his girlfriend performing oral sex on, presumably, him (he claimed he was hacked, which no one believed). Ray Allen similarly insisted that his Twitter account was hacked after *someone* posted an explicit message that read "When u masturbate think about my tongue or your clit and switching back and forth from my dick to my tongue." J. R. Smith offered "the pipe" to a woman attending a game via a private message on Twitter.

Due to the fame of NBA stars, the risk of a reckless holler is magnified by the possibility of screenshots, catfishing attempts, and clout demon culture—or worse. "A girl who hits you up on Twitter knows who you are," center Willie Cauley-Stein told ESPN. "You tell her to come to the hotel, she shows up with three dudes to rob you. This world's crazy."

SOCIAL SECURITY

When their successful careers are winding down, former stars may collect checks from franchises that are hankering for a dose of celebrity. If you cannot acquire an MVP candidate in his prime, just wait until he is in his early thirties, has knees strip-mined of cartilage, and is focused on segueing into real estate or investing in the next predatory food-delivery app.

Players who have benefited from the NBA's version of Social Security include Vin Baker, Steve Francis, Baron Davis, Jason Kidd, Tracy McGrady, Marcus Camby, Kenyon Martin, Rasheed Wallace, Chauncey Billups, Anfernee Hardaway, and Jalen Rose. Pablo Prigioni, a sly Argentinian point guard who joined the league in his mid-thirties, accepted his checks in the form of stolen inbounds passes.

SPACE JAM

In the original *Space Jam* film, Michael Jordan teams up with Looney Tunes characters like Bugs Bunny and Foghorn Leghorn, and with Popeye Jones and Christian Laettner in hopes of leading the Wizards to an NBA championship. Unfortunately, with Jordan's powers sapped by the Monstars and old age, Washington finishes 37-45 in consecutive seasons. In the 2021 remake, *Space Jam: A New Legacy*, LeBron James lures Anthony Davis to play for his Lakers by dangling a salary-cap-circumventing cameo.

SPREWELL, LATRELL

"People say I'm America's worst nightmare," mused Latrell Sprewell, while getting his hair braided to a guitar-lashed version of "The Star-Spangled Banner." "I say I'm the American dream." His patriotic declaration came during an AND1 sneaker commercial that aired during the 1999 postseason. It was an acknowledgment of circumstances that exposed the razor wires undergirding relationships between race and power in the NBA.

Sprewell grew up in a tumultuous Milwaukee household. After joining his high school basketball team as a senior, he did not receive any scholarships to play in college. He starred for Three Rivers Junior College, transferred to Alabama, and was taken by the Warriors with the twenty-fourth pick in the 1992 NBA Draft. "I'm not into having people talking all about what I was like as a kid or what I did way back when," Sprewell said. "I never asked to be famous."

A lean, 6-foot-5 shooting guard, Sprewell was a four-time All-Star who played with fiery desperation. Although he mostly chucked jumpers, his signature sequence was a mad sprint into

BASKETBALL MOVIES

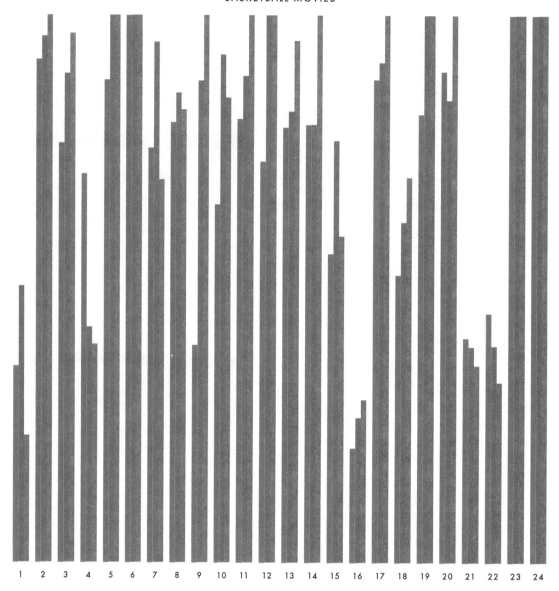

 Educational.   Funny.   Influential.

1. Above the Rim.
2. Air Bud.
3. Blue Chips.
4. Celtic Pride.
5. Double Team.
6. Eddie.
7. Finding Forrester.
8. He Got Game.
9. John Wick 3.
10. Just Wright.
11. Juwanna Mann.
12. Kazaam.
13. Like Mike.
14. Love & Basketball.
15. My Giant.
16. Semi-Pro.
17. Space Jam.
18. Space Jam 2.
19. Steel.
20. Sunset Park.
21. Uncle Drew.
22. Thunderstruck.
23. Uncut Gems.
24. White Men Can't Jump.

a jackknifing two-handed flush where his legs splayed as if riding a unicycle. Sprewell's bristling energy had the sustainability of a grudge: he ranked among the league's top 3 in minutes played for four seasons, and his career average of 38.6 minutes per outing ranks ninth all-time—he was a bright flame that burned half as long. Over six seasons with the Warriors, Sprewell earned a reputation as the league's next shooting guard superstar. "As far as talent, if I could be any other player, I wouldn't be Michael Jordan," said Allen Iverson. "I would take Latrell Sprewell's game."

Sprewell's reputation was forever altered by an incident during a Golden State practice early in the 1998 season. After coach P. J. Carlesimo chided him for not passing the ball hard enough during a drill ("It's embarrassing when a coach does that to you," teammate Bimbo Coles later told ESPN), Sprewell throttled the coach with both hands. Sprewell cooled off in the shower, then returned to scuffle with his coach for a second time. While Carlesimo did not suffer serious injuries—"It's not like he was losing air or anything," Sprewell explained on *60 Minutes*—the episode was a clarion call for reactionary sports fans. In the fallout, the NBA attempted to suspend Sprewell for a full calendar year, the Warriors tried to terminate the remainder of his contract, and Converse stripped him of his shoe deal. Golden State players insisted that Carlesimo had provoked the attack but indignation prevailed. "It was the most outrageous act of insubordination I've ever seen," wept Celtics general manager Chris Wallace.

So Sprewell was traded to the Knicks. In 1999, he came off the bench but led New York in scoring during a surprise playoff run to the Finals. In a city that was bopping to the intoxicating rhythms of the Sporty Thievz' "No Pigeons," Sprewell's rough-hewn edge was cherished. "He fits the perpetrator to a 'T,'" Spike Lee told the *New York Times*, in an interview that has not aged well. "The cornrows. The scowl. Everything. People would think he's another thug the N.Y.P.D. has to protect us from. What's interesting, though, is he's very articulate."

In the twilight of his career, Sprewell aggravated the sensibilities of middle-aged sports journalists again—this time with the lance of hyperbole. After rejecting a contract from the Timberwolves that offered him less money than his existing deal, he said, "I have a family to feed." Unable to fathom the concept of nonliteral phraseology, Rick Reilly of *Sports Illustrated* penned a column citing Department of Agriculture numbers and quoting an unemployed house painter at a Minneapolis soup kitchen. "On the official Ten Most Selfish, Greedy, Spoiled to the Spleen, Multimillionaire Athletes You'd Most Like to See Thrown to a Dieting Lion list, you'd have to rank Latrell Sprewell one through at least eight," Reilly wrote. To date, it remains unclear what other professional athletes he would like to see violently ripped to shreds by giant predators for negotiating their salaries.

STIVIANO, V.

For most of the Clippers' history, Donald Sterling could be found slumped in primo courtside seats, looking like a melting block of maple walnut ice cream in a Sergio Tacchini tracksuit. The man dubbed "slumlord billionaire" bought the San Diego team for $12.5 million in 1981, shamelessly tanked, installed a former model as assistant general manager, and moved the franchise to Los Angeles five years later.

While he was renowned as a buffoonish and greedy owner of the league's worst franchise, his history of bigotry was only slightly more concealed. According to former Clippers GM Elgin Baylor, Sterling brought women into the locker rooms after games and made comments like, "Look at those beautiful Black bodies." During the 2000s, he settled lawsuits alleging that his real estate company discriminated against Black and Latino renters in his Beverly Hills and Koreatown properties.

In 2014, Sterling was broadly exposed as a virulent racist when audiotapes of his demented rants were leaked to *TMZ*. The screeds were recorded by the married real estate mogul's girlfriend and self-described "archivist," who goes by the name V. Stiviano. Among Sterling's repugnant statements were critiques of Stiviano's social media content, where she posed with celebrities like Magic Johnson and Matt Kemp, a baseball star: "You can sleep with [Black people]," Sterling said on the recordings. "The

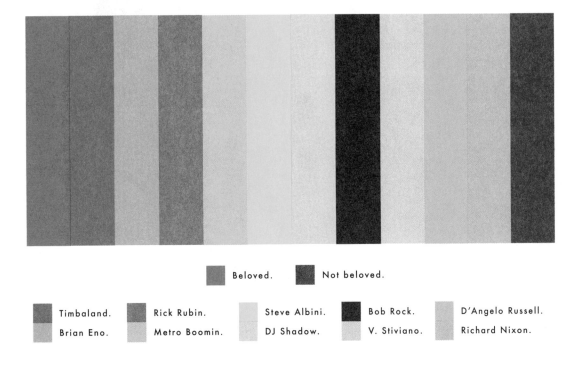

Beloved.   Not beloved.

Timbaland.   Rick Rubin.   Steve Albini.   Bob Rock.   D'Angelo Russell.
Brian Eno.   Metro Boomin.   DJ Shadow.   V. Stiviano.   Richard Nixon.

little I ask you is not to promote it . . . and not to bring them to my games. . . . In your lousy fucking Instagrams, you don't have to have yourself with, walking with Black people."

As fallout from Sterling's ugliness consumed the NBA, Stiviano took to wearing a reflective solar visor over her face in public and basked in her newfound fame. "I'm Mr. Sterling's right-hand-arm-man," she told Barbara Walters, during an interview on ABC News. "I'm Mr. Sterling's everything. I'm his confidante, his best friend, his silly rabbit." Meanwhile, mistress enthusiast Donald Trump called her "despicable" and the "girlfriend from hell."

Following the scandal, which culminated in Sterling being forced to sell the Clippers at an enormous profit, Stiviano was compelled by a judge to return the gifts that her benefactor had lavished upon her. These included a $2.6 million duplex, two Bentleys, a Ferrari, and a Range Rover. When *TMZ* caught up with her on a Los Angeles sidewalk in 2018, she revealed that "inner racism lives in every single one of us."

STRIP CLUBS

Unlike henpecking wives or a houseful of bleating children, strip clubs offer few distractions for the professional basketball player. Athletes are free to redistribute portions of their salary to hard-working entertainers as a healthy way to deal with the stressors of NBA life without being saddled by remembering anniversaries, attending potluck dinners, or reading *Babar to the Rescue* to thankless urchins. Gentlemen's clubs are a form of wellness.

Yet due to puritanical mores, players who use strip clubs as safe spaces are viewed as having a nefarious streak. Overlap is surely possible. Gilbert Arenas, a toxic former Wizards All-Star, used an Instagram post to detail a scam in which he bought $80,000 of ones, snuck out with $40,000 of it, and then claimed his card was stolen. "You kick me out of your strip club, you getting robbed," he boasted. "I'm the reason BIG strip clubs #fingerprint now hahaha."

More often, players are blameless in strip club drama. Patrick Ewing of the Knicks, for example,

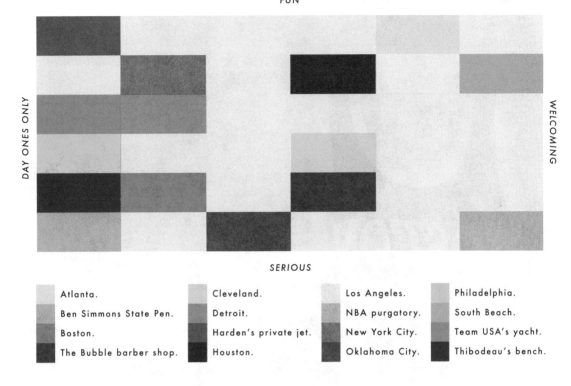

Atlanta.

Ben Simmons State Pen.

Boston.

The Bubble barber shop.

Cleveland.

Detroit.

Harden's private jet.

Houston.

Los Angeles.

NBA purgatory.

New York City.

Oklahoma City.

Philadelphia.

South Beach.

Team USA's yacht.

Thibodeau's bench.

was ensnared in a federal prostitution case in which he testified that he had received complimentary drinks, lapdances, and oral sex at the Gold Club, an establishment in Atlanta ("All they proved was that one of the girls went too far with an athlete in a bar," said a lawyer for the defense). Years later, Cleanthony Early, another Knick, was riding home from a strip club in Queens called CityScapes when his Uber was boxed in by three vehicles and he was robbed by six ski-masked gunmen of his necklace and gold fronts.

Ballers known for creating downpours of legal tender in gentlemen's clubs include James Harden, Dennis Rodman, John Wall, and Will Barton. As usual, Allen Iverson was a rain-making trendsetter. "Allen was the first guy that showed me how NBA players spend money in strip clubs," former teammate Matt Barnes told *Sports Illustrated*. "That guy went hard. He'd throw $30,000, $40,000 every time we went. I'm like, 'You realize what I can do with this money?'"

During the COVID Bubble, Clippers shooting guard Lou Williams left Walt Disney World to attend the funeral of a family friend and mentor in Atlanta. After the ceremony, he went to Magic City, a local institution where he has a flavor of wings named in his honor (Louwill Lemon Pepper BBQ). After being busted—in part due to a post by rapper Jack Harlow, who was also in attendance—Williams was subjected to a ten-day quarantine when he re-entered the NBA Bubble. "I was really going through something," said Williams, who previously received attention for being in a polyamorous relationship with two girlfriends. "I was thrown under the bus. All the attention turned to Magic City because it's a gentlemen's club. I feel like if I was at a steakhouse or Hooters or whatever, it wouldn't be half the story."

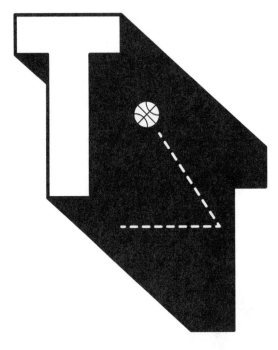

TATUM, JAYSON

A normie king, Jayson Tatum is the layperson's rising superstar. His pedigree includes a higher education at Duke University, being drafted in the lottery's top 3, and, most prestigiously, playing for the Celtics. Tall and proportionately svelte, the forward looks the part. He is a 40 percent shooter from beyond the arc, a disruptive defender, and a volume scorer whose bag includes spinning fadeaways, rehearsed footwork, and a long Euro step that ushers him from the free-throw line to the lip of the rim with a barely noticeable foot drag. Tatum's career trajectory checks off the right boxes: his points per game have increased annually and he has ascended from the role of overachieving rookie to Beantown's primary offensive weapon. He was named to his first All-Star team in 2020.

Tatum came into the NBA young, and there is insistence from the punditry that we have peeped only the tip of an iceberg of talent. He is always making leaps, arriving, making a case for the top 10, leaping again, blossoming into a top-5 player before our very eyes, and making yet another leap. Each off-season he grows a few inches, while remaining nineteen years old. After a sizzling month of shooting in early 2020—which raised his scoring efficiency to league-average—*The Ringer* published a video entitled "How Jayson Tatum Became a Superstar." As a result of media patronage, Tatum is more highly regarded than Pascal Siakam, Brandon Ingram, Luol Deng, and peers with similar talent and equivalent accomplishments. Besides the sin of going to Duke, none of this is his fault. But expectations are dangerous.

While there are legit quibbles with Tatum's game—most worryingly, an inability to draw free throws and a taste for junk-food shots give him a steep path toward being a consistently great scorer—a bigger issue may be the ceiling of a conventional two-way wing. Michael Jordan and his simulacrum Kobe Bryant are archetypes for basketball greatness, but the modern NBA has been lorded over by mutations of the form: LeBron James, Kevin Durant, Kawhi Leonard, Stephen Curry, James Harden, Giannis Antetokounmpo. The chasm between an exceptional mortal and a supernatural being is wide.

TACO TUESDAY

After joining the Lakers in free agency, LeBron James showed reverence for Los Angeles' Latinx culture by declaring that one specific day of the week—in this case, Tuesdays—would be celebrated as "Taco Tuesday." James introduced this obscure foodstuff (tacos) and twenty-four-hour window (Tuesdays) to his millions of social media followers with custom-printed T-shirts and by yelling "Taco Tuesday" into his phone, sometimes with "Mexican" vocal inflections. James drew criticism that included charges of insensitivity, propagating stereotypes, and being hypocritical as a "social justice warrior." He later attempted (and failed) to copyright "Taco Tuesday" but redeemed himself during the COVID-19 hiatus by providing 1,300 meals for families at his I Promise school in Akron.

THOMPSON, KLAY

Is Klay Thompson a real, honest-to-goodness, legitimate superstar? An elite 3-and-D wing who has been named to All-Star teams and an NBA All-Defensive Team, he has benefited—more than anyone in modern history—from a panoply of biases: Winning Bias, Shooting Bias, Crouch Bias, and even from Reverse-Dribble Bias. Any TikTok showing a catatonic Thompson stonily raising a Budweiser draws a chorus from admirers who gush about his effervescent personality as if he was holding court at a Truman Capote soiree.

Thompson is 6-foot-6 and blessed with a jumper of textbook beauty: Vitruvian Man knocks down a 26-footer. After only eight seasons with Golden State, he ranked among the NBA's all-time top 20 in career 3-pointers made. In an era where dangerous shooters receive slivers of opportunity before defenders darken the sky, his jumper has the rapid-but-unrushed clickity-clack of a lifetime's muscle memory. "Ever since he was little, Klay could shoot," his father, Mychal, who was in the NBA for thirteen seasons, told NBC Sports. "At seven or eight years old he could shoot from 20 or 22 feet." In 2015, Thompson scored a record 37 points in a single quarter, a feat that included going 13–13 from the floor with nine 3s.

There is no denying that Thompson has an immensely valuable skill—one that defined the Warriors' quasi-dynasty—and a player who can drain a few open 3s is very different from a specialist who lives to cause a cloudburst. He has true gravity, the kind that hollows out the lane and makes defenders claw around screens in panic. But he does not do much else. After a game in which Thompson rolled up 60 points while dribbling the ball only 11 times, admirers cooed about his "efficiency" and gave birth to the only known case of Anti-Dribble Bias.

Since 1997, there have been sixteen times in which a player averaged more than 20 points, under 4 rebounds, and under 3 assists for a season. Five of those were Thompson (other repeat offenders included Allan Houston, Kevin Martin, and Andrew Wiggins). He is a stout on-ball defender who allows Golden State to hide Stephen Curry, but rarely logs steals, blocks, or deflections either.

Despite Thompson's limitations, the scarcity of supremely magnetic off-ball threats who can play defense is undeniable. It is currently a list of one.

Among shooting specialists like JJ Redick, Davis Bertans, Duncan Robinson, and Seth Curry, only Thompson is invulnerable to being picked on by opposing offenses. He may not be the type of dynamic talent a franchise can build around, but, as a championship component, Thompson might be even more rare and valuable.

THREES

The 3-point line is a 23-foot, 9-inch painted arc that encircles the key area on both sides of the court. It flattens to 22 feet along the sidelines. As one might suspect from the name, shots made behind the 3-point line are worth three points. Before its introduction in the 1980 NBA season, the line was seen as a parlor trick intended to gin up excitement—the migration of *Rock N' Jock*–style tomfoolery from less serious leagues like the ABL, ABA, and the Eastern Basketball Association. "It's a gimmick, but you've got to take advantage of it because other people sure will," Bullets coach Dick Motta told the *Washington Post* before the season started. "A three-point play at the right time can really change the complexion of the game. In our last exhibition against the 76ers, Dr. J hit one from the corner and we weren't ready for it. It turned the game around." The idea that a 3-pointer could be a momentum-changing novelty was about as enthusiastic as anyone got.

Responses were even more tepid from other basketball minds of the day. "It may change our game at the end of the quarters," Suns coach John MacLeod told the *New York Times*. "But I'm not going to set up plays for guys to bomb from 23 feet. I think that's very boring basketball." Over the 3-point shot's debut season, the average NBA team shot 28 percent from deep and sank less than one a night. While a handful of teams embraced the long ball, relatively speaking, the Hawks made only 13 all season. As a ham-handed comparison, Klay Thompson set a new league record by drilling 14 of those suckers in a single 2018 game. Yet, even today, people are still blaming the 3-pointer for boring basketball.

Since the initial splash of the trifecta, its water level has risen by a trickle, a wave, a drought, and, finally, a monsoon. The popularity of the shot inched upward in the 1980s, but, by the end of the decade, specialists like Chris Mullin and Craig Hodges took a only handful each game. Most teams lacked the personnel to knock down 3s at a steady clip and even squads with historically great shooters were as gun-shy as Quakers. The 1990 Cavaliers topped the NBA with a superb 40.7 percent 3-point percentage and attempted more than any other team—yet took only 10.4 attempts a game, despite having Mark Price, Steve Kerr, and Craig Ehlo.

There was an early adopter worth mentioning: over the 1991 season, Michael Adams, a short king on the run-and-gun Nuggets, chucked up 8.5 3-point-ers a night at a laughable 29.6 percent. But, overall, there was a feeling of incuriosity, as if an infectious virus had been inspected under a microscope and it did not seem like a big deal. "We've all but wiped out the 3-pointer where we just come down quickly and launch it," Knicks coach Stu Jackson told the *New York Times* in 1990. "I don't think you'll see us taking 1,100 of them in one season again." As we know, the virus would escape the lab. In 2019, James Harden of the Rockets attempted 1,028 all by himself.

Before the 1995 season, the NBA moved the 3-point line in, making it a uniform 22-feet every-where to match the baseline length (making it shorter than the current collegiate line by almost 2 inches). The change came in response to dipping scores, slower paces, and a Finals matchup between the Knicks and Rockets in which neither defensive-oriented pulverizer broke the 100-point barrier. Over the next three seasons, it produced the desired effect and 3-pointers spiked. On this temporary, child-size court, gunners like Glen Rice enjoyed career-best accuracy. Players with the range to make long 2s became marksmen. One major beneficiary was Chicago. Michael Jordan, a 30.1 percent shooter from deep until that point, was suddenly a 40.4 per-cent sniper; Scottie Pippen, who had made only 26.9 percent of his 3s, overnight, became a 36.4 percent threat from behind the arc. In discussions about the greatest teams of all time, it is rarely mentioned that the Bulls' superstars were incapable of shooting from long distance on an adult court. Before the 1998 season, the league returned to playing on a men's basketball arc.

With apologies to guys like Chris Mullin, Larry Bird, and Dale Ellis, Reggie Miller was the league's first 3-hoisting superstar. He was second in the NBA in total sunk trifectas in 1998, and his accuracy on the redrawn, grown-man arc set him apart from rising gunners like Antoine Walker and, at that point, even Ray Allen. From 1990 until 2004, he finished within the league's top 10 in scoring efficiency each season—in part because he was one of the best free-throw shooters of all time—and headed that column twice.

Through late-game heroics, Miller earned a reputation for being an angel of death as the clock wound to zero. Bony and 6-foot-7, he had the frame and petulance of a runway model. He bore the scratches of catfights with Michael Jordan's Bulls and the beastly Knicks teams of the 1990s. In 1995, Miller famously scored eight points in the final nine seconds to shock New York in an Eastern Conference Semifinals game, punctuating the win by gripping both hands around his own throat. "Other teams fear me so much, just my being out there," he said. "I could even be playing on my deathbed and I'd worry them." Today, Miller is most feared for the tribal sun tattooed around his belly button.

The NBA's 3-point explosion began in the mid-2010s. From 2013 to 2021, the league average jumped from 20 attempts per game to more than 34. There were several factors in the surge of shots from downtown, such as the widespread embrace of pace-and-space principles popularized by coach Mike D'Antoni, the influence of advanced metrics, and the success of Golden State teams who drone-struck opponents from the sky. In decades past, power forwards and centers who took 3s were often specialists—but they have uniformly swapped out 17-footers for attempts from behind the arc. "The big guys that you see now who are coming into the league, the best players, guys like Anthony Davis and Karl-Anthony Towns, they're out there shooting jump shots, because they grew up handling the ball," said Golden State coach Steve Kerr, on a 2016 *Inside Warriors* podcast. "They grew up as guys who wanted to be Kevin Durant and not Charles Oakley."

The rise of the 3-pointer was greeted with dubi-ousness from those who wear tactical sunglasses and own riding lawn mowers. To critics, the league has been homogenized by offenses that spread the floor and ping-pong the ball around the perimeter until chucking up a bomb. Its popularity is seen as con-tributing to the waning of lost arts like turnaround jumpers and post-ups. After a playoff loss by the Warriors in 2015, Phil Jackson tweeted, "NBA ana-lysts give me some diagnostics on how 3pt oriented

THINGS BOOMERS HATE

Small ball.
GPS.
Calculators.
Tanking.
Bad dogs.

Self-care.
Drawing fouls.
The Kardashians.
Online payments.
3-pointers.

Mumble rappers.
Load management.
Low-scoring all-stars.
Player empowerment.
Advanced stats.

Plant-based meat.
College one-and-dones.
Climate change.
Self check-out.
The fire emoji.

teams are faring this playoffs . . . seriously, how's it goink?" Golden State proceeded to win the first of three championships. Few still dispute the utility of long-range scoring, but concerns remain about its aesthetics and the reductionist nature of a shot worth an extra point. "There's no basketball anymore, there's no beauty in it," Spurs coach Gregg Popovich told NBA.com. "Now you look at a stat sheet after a game and the first thing you look at is the 3s. If you made 3s and the other team didn't, you win."

One proposed solution for curbing the alleged overreliance on the 3-ball is moving the arc farther from the hoop. In theory, the change would drop the success rate of marginal shooters enough to return up-and-unders in the paint to their rightful stature. The physical problem with this idea is that it would require widening the court or completely eliminating corner 3s. But the long-term result would probably be increased emphasis on perimeter shooting. Players would acclimate to the new line and defenders would have more ground to cover while scrambling between deep threats and helping out in the paint. Bad news for the Green Egg and Air Monarchs set: the line has been crossed and there is no pushing it back.

TIME BANDITS

The so-called Time-Traveling Hipster was spotted wearing modern clothing and sunglasses in a photo from a Canadian bridge reopening in the 1940s. Snapshots appear to show people using cellphones decades before the devices existed. There is grainy footage from 1996 of Clifford Robinson, a 6-foot-10 big man who would later become an advocate for marijuana legalization, chucking up hundreds of 3-pointers for the Suns. Are they authentic? No one knows.

Most players do not steer league-wide trends—they only ride the bulges and dips of the sport's buckling surface. Futurists, whether or not they moved the game forward in long hurdles or incremental nudges, were suited for a league beyond the one they were part of. Some are easy to identify as prototypes we grew familiar with later on: 3-and-D point guards like Mookie Blaylock or Darrell Armstrong; forwards with outstanding passing skills, like Toni Kukoč or Anthony Mason; early stretch bigs, like Robinson, Sam Perkins, Channing Frye, Terry Mills, Steve Novak, or Matt Bullard. "I always joke that I was born 20 years too soon," Bullard told *SBNation*.

"Big men that can shoot 3s can play a long time in this league."

Others are less obvious. With a generic name and the bulk of his career spent on teams like Miami and Atlanta, Steve Smith has been subsumed into an indistinguishable ratking of perimeter scorers that includes guys like Glen Rice and Joe Johnson. On the other hand, his credentials—All-Star in 1998, Olympic gold medalist in 2000, NBA champion in 2003—do not square with a talent frequency that hummed around third tier. At the handsome and talkative scorer's peak, Smith averaged around 20 points a game. His signature move, uncreatively dubbed the Smitty, was a hesitation tactic off the dribble where he would turn sideways, lightly jump off the ground to fake a spin, then whip back in the other direction. "It was a little bit of a carry," he acknowledged. He hoisted up plenty of 3s with mediocre results—until he bloomed, at age thirty, into a 40 percent shooter from deep (including a scorching 47.2 percent for the Spurs in 2002, which topped the NBA).

Coming out of Michigan State, Smith was projected as a smaller version of fellow Spartan Magic Johnson. "He can play three spots—point guard, big guard and small forward," said Lakers scout Ronnie Lester before the 1991 draft. In a time of role rigidity and obsession with cramming height onto the court, Smith's passing gifts were underused. Today, he would have been a swingman, if not a power forward. Outside of Khris Middleton and Gordon Hayward, few current players of his size share an output of solid scoring, poor rebounding, and respectable assists. With his perimeter shooting and distribution skills, Smith may have been a more potent offensive weapon had he spent his career matched up against slower players instead of quicker ones.

Now that we are armed with better access to stats, some players leap off the spreadsheet in ways that were not apparent twenty-five years ago. To most fans, Brent Barry is notable for being the first white guy to win the NBA Slam Dunk Contest. In the 1996 event—which was immediately buried as the worst ever—he did not bother to remove his Clippers warmup suit and twice rehashed Michael Jordan's famous dunk from the free-throw line. The skinny

6-foot-6 wing reportedly wanted to wear a Kangol hat and dunk to LL Cool J's "I'm Bad," but his plan was ixnayed by the league office. Seven years later, Bones—who was also nicknamed Mango Tree after appearing in a drinkable yogurt commercial—crip-walked during the 3-Point Contest.

When he was not disgracing the sanctity of All-Star Weekend and the Taco Bell Skills Challenge, Barry played with humor and creativity. He was a 3-point specialist, but loved throwing slippery passes and dramatically finishing in traffic. His father was Hall of Famer (and notorious jerk) Rick Barry, and his brothers, Jon and Drew, also played in the NBA. As a teen in a hypercompetitive household that was splintered by divorce, Brent inherited his dad's arrogance. "He was one of the worst kids I've ever been around," his brother Jon told the *New York Times*. "He was cynical, he snarled at people."

But Barry was a subrosa warlock when it came to efficiency. Over a three-year span, he produced seasons in which he led the NBA in categories like 2-point percentage, 3-point percentage, and offensive rating. His career true shooting percentage of 60.7 percent is the sixteenth-best in NBA history—closely trailing Magic Johnson and John Stockton—and is especially absurd considering his best years came during the scoring famine of the early 2000s. The final season of that stretch marked a career-best, as he posted star-level production on the sly: 14.4 points, 5.4 rebounds, and 5.3 assists a game for a 45-win Seattle team. "Statistics are like bikinis," he later said, at the 2010 Sloan Sports Conference. "They're really nice to look at but they don't tell you the whole story."

TRAVEL TRUTHERS

For most viewers, a travel violation is art: you know it when you see it. But to the travel truther, a joyless pedant with fascistic urges, every loping drive to the hoop is a raw-dog obscenity that deflowers the virginal spirit of basketball. Travel truthers are moralists whose identity and self-worth are derived from attempting to bleed the wonderment out of exciting plays by sourly complaining. Common targets of the travel truther include LeBron James, James Harden, and Giannis Antetokounmpo. It is unclear if travel truthers really desire more stoppages in play, take pride in being curmudgeons, or are covertly pushing alternative agendas.

The contemporary travel truther's rage sprouts from an inability to understand or accept the concept of a "gather step," which addresses the kinesiological fluidity of shifting from ball-handling to a shooting motion. According to a change in the NBA rulebook, which was aimed at defanging such criticism, "A player who gathers the ball while dribbling may take two steps in coming to a stop, passing or shooting the ball." With this clarification, even James's infamous "crab dribble"—his mocked description of a drive that was ruled a travel in the closing seconds of a 2009 Cleveland loss to Washington—is a legal play. "'Crab dribble' is when you, uh, travel," said Wizard Caron Butler, following the game. "That's the hottest thing on the market right now."

Travel truthers delight in calling attention to rare incidents in which referees miss blatantly obvious calls. These are brainfarts, like when a player walks several steps without dribbling after catching an inbound pass (in the manner of a casual pick-up game or practice) or forgets to dribble on an uncontested breakaway dunk. To the travel truther, though, such plays are evidence of league-wide conspiracy or the ineptitude of modern officiating. In the same manner that YouTube vloggers who are "just asking questions" open an intestinal tube leading to neo-Nazism, travel truthers are far more susceptible to alt-right basketball ideology than joyful NBA fans. Grouse about Harden's step-back enough times and you may wake up three years from now cheering for Duke University.

TRUE SHOOTING PERCENTAGE

It is impossible to discuss true shooting percentage without sounding like a nerd. While the metric is a combination of field-goal percentage, 3-point percentage, and free-throw percentage that neatly reflects a player's or team's overall scoring efficiency, it has never gone mainstream. As a result, it is viewed as "analytics" and the mathematical witchcraft of dunk-hating wonks who attempt to trick noble games-watchers into respecting Nikola Jokić.

TUNNEL WALK

Instituted in 2005, the NBA dress code required players to wear clothing fit for casual Fridays in accounts receivable. The decree was in response to "image problems"—an allusion to the previous season's Malice at the Palace fracas and Kobe Bryant's sexual assault trial—and outlawed baggy, hip-hop–inspired clothing. Instead of 4XL Mitchell & Ness throwback jerseys, New Era caps, Evisu jeans refurbished from circus tents, Air Force 1s, the finest Vokal garments, and chains that could bang glass tables, players were instructed to wear turtlenecks and presentable shoes. On the hardwood, the league enforced rules demanding that shorts drape no farther than an inch above the knee. If Allen Iverson wore it, it was banned. "The players have been dressing in prison garb the last five or six years," said Lakers coach Phil Jackson, in vocabulary that sounds ripped from an Atomwaffen Division leaflet left on a car windshield. "All the stuff that goes on, it's like gangster, thuggery stuff. It's time."

The adults compelled by the league to wear "dress slacks" were not as enthusiastic. "What's next, we can't wear our hair in cornrows?" Jermaine O'Neal of the Pacers asked in the New York Times. "The message to us is that we're too urban." Jason Richardson, a high-scoring Slam Dunk champ on the Warriors, saw hypocrisy. "You wear a suit, you still could be a crook," he told ESPN. "You see all what happened with Enron and Martha Stewart." Even Tim Duncan, who dressed like a scarecrow, objected: "I think it's basically retarded," he said.

The NBA's ugly behavior went unpunished. Due to shifting fashion trends that Stern and his nanny state never recognized, the billowing clothes that players were forbidden to wear were already falling out of style. Even before the dress code,

Jay-Z, a trendsetter who athletes emulated religiously, mocked the same looks that he had helped popularize. "I don't wear jerseys, I'm thirty plus," he rapped on late-2003's The Black Album. "Give me a crisp pair of jeans, button-ups."

After a few years of rocking six-buttoned Dick Tracy suits with pocket squares, players drip-or-drowned in the fashionable waves of the late 2000s. Slimmer tailoring, dorky cardigans, dumb hats, Mark McNairy shoes, Nick Wooster smoking a bogey at Pitti Uomo dandyism, Kanye interning at Fendi. LeBron James appeared on the cover of Vogue with Gisele Bündchen (albeit in a wildly inappropriate photo inspired by King Kong holding Ann Darrow).

By the time the 2010 draft rolled around, suits that could have been used for parasailing had vanished and the rookies on stage looked like summer hires at Deutsche Bank. As players became more sartorially attuned, the NBA attempted to credit the dress code for the intersection of basketball and fashion that naturally occurred—and always has. "We all wore what was hot in our day, too," Magic Johnson told Esquire. "Unless you came and took a picture of me, no one would've known what I wore."

The pregame "Tunnel Walk" has become a runway for ballers to peacock in their best fits. When players arrive for a game—whether by team bus or matte black Lamborghini Urus—they stroll through a concrete corridor in the bowels of the arena that leads to the locker rooms. Along the way, their outfits are documented by team social media directors, stylists, and flacks who scurry to post the content on Instagram, Twitter, and TikTok. "You look good, you play good," P. J. Tucker, who often carries sneakers culled from a five-thousand-pair collection, told Complex. "It's something that will continue to grow. So many guys are jumping on board and really starting to do that as well, building a sort of personality in their style, in how they're feeling that day."

One notable drip lord is Russell Westbrook, whose tunnel looks include ponchos, Ramones tees, floral shirts open to the navel with shredded jeans, animal prints, Balenciaga sweatshirts, grunge flannels, cuffed overalls, and Coogi sweaters. Kelly

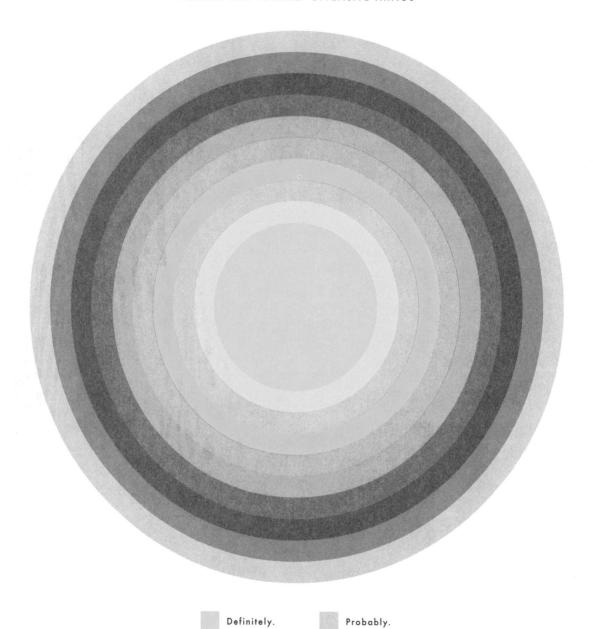

Definitely.   Probably.

The Electoral College.   The NBA lottery and draft.

The NBA revenue split.   The proposed soda tax.

The 2005 NBA dress code.   The 2020 NBA Bubble.

The NBA salary cap.   Restaurant letter grades.

Oubre, a shooting guard nicknamed Wave Papi, has bounced around the league but consistently is dipped in Rick Owens, Chrome Hearts, and Canadian tuxedos (he also played with a Supreme sleeve on his leg in a game). Before postseason games in 2018, James and the entire Cavaliers team wore matching custom shrunken suits from Thom Browne. According to James, the flex represented "camaraderie, solidarity, brotherhood."

Tunnel walks are star-making moments for guys who are better at being basketball players than playing the sport. An unheralded 6-foot-8 forward out of Utah, Kyle Kuzma was selected 27th in the 2017 draft by Los Angeles and stepped right into a star-shaped vacuum. The Flint native was not provably good, but led the Lakers in minutes, points, and shots attempted as a rookie. On the other hand, he dyed his hair Marshall Mathers blonde and sported BAPE flight jackets and pastel suits over mesh tank tops. Kuzma signed a unique deal with GOAT, a middleman for rare sneakers, and has rumored ties with women like Kendall Jenner, Vanessa Hudgens, and Winnie Harlow. "I've got a chance to be really special," Kuzma once said of himself.

TWEENERS

Players who exist in the spongy space between positions are known as tweeners. It has been a pejorative term to imply that a player was not dexterous enough as a ball-handler to be a pure point guard or was too light in the ass to survive bayonet-play in the trenches. "Being a tweener was terrible," P. J. Tucker told the *New York Times*. "You had to be a wing player that could shoot 3s or a back-to-the-basket big—and if you fell in the middle you didn't fit." Guards described as tweeners include Jason Terry, Gilbert Arenas, and Monta Ellis. A few bigs who inspire similar ambivalence are Kenneth Faried, Brandon Bass, Carl Landry, Frank Kaminsky, and Thaddeus Young, winner of the 2021 NBA Hustle award.

Combative and dreaded, Montrezl Harrell measured only 6-foot-7 without shoes at the NBA combine—and slipped into the early second round of the 2015 draft. He did not have the traditional stature of a center, but lacked the perimeter shooting to play forward. After playing sparingly early in his career, he developed into a coiled bundle of wattage and fury in Los Angeles, winning Sixth Man of the Year and the NBA Hustle Award in 2020. "I don't really believe in that 'smaller' stuff, man," he told the *Athletic*. "If you believed in that, the elephant would be the king of the jungle. And that ain't happening."

The tweener of all tweeners, David Lee was caught between not only positions but generations. He was a 6-foot-9 rebounding dervish who spent three consecutive seasons among the NBA's leaders in field-goal percentage—but was a feeble defender who made one 3-pointer in his entire career. Though Lee hailed from a wealthy family in St. Louis (his grandfather sold a company that made hangers for Rubbermaid for $73.5 million in 1992), he was one of several New Whites who came out of the University of Florida: athletic enough to win a dunk contest, cool enough to play at Rucker Park, and able to successfully rap 40 percent of the intro from *The Dynasty: Roc La Familia*. "He wasn't like you'd expect from a rich kid," said Lee's coach, in praise of his work ethic.

Mobile and ambidextrous, Lee split his time between center and power forward. He blossomed as the hub of coach Mike D'Antoni's offensive system during his fourth season with the Knicks—then he signed a princely deal with Golden State. Lee made the All-Star team in 2013 and led the league in double-doubles—but his lack of interior defense and hefty contract were a fault line beneath a young team erected around Stephen Curry and Klay Thompson. "He can't guard anybody," cackled former Golden State coach Don Nelson.

After an injury, Lee lost his starting position to another player who was once described as a tweener: Draymond Green. It was a meaningful spasm in Golden State's timeline, as Green's ability to glide between power forward and center unlocked a Warriors dynasty. Lee, on the other hand, was just the middleman.

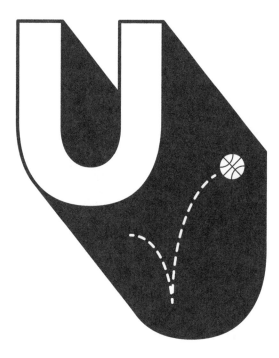

and the fluidity of offensive and defensive responsibilities means an exceptional player has an oversized impact on success. One man's alchemic power can carry a team of chumps to respectability and elevate a squad with a good supporting cast into contention. Just as importantly, maximum salary restrictions mean that a team fortunate enough to have a universe-bending superstar pays him roughly the same amount that a competitor pays a player on the bottom hem of the top 25.

As a result, the same few guys pop up in the Finals repeatedly: Michael Jordan, Hakeem Olajuwon, Shaquille O'Neal, Tim Duncan, Kobe Bryant, LeBron James, Kawhi Leonard. Superstardom is not about catching lightning in a bottle, it's about slogging through season after 82-game season with the hopes of a franchise strapped to your back. Despite measures intended to foster league-wide parity, 80 percent of NBA teams enter the year knowing they have zero chance of winning a title. Without a superstar, you are shit out of luck.

When championships and postseason heroics are stripped away, identifying real superstars is tricky. Is it rainmaking scorers? Distributors who set teammates up for easy buckets? Defensive beasts? Does being able to conjure a basket in the closing seconds of a tight game by Mamba Mentality matter a lot, a little bit, or not at all? Composite metrics provide helpful thumbnails of a player's impact, but are warped on the forge of a statistician's biases. And offensive inflation at the end of the 2010s has cheapened scoring numbers (we are familiar with the concept, since no one takes Wilt Chamberlain's 1962 averages of 50.4 points and 25.7 rebounds per game seriously today). In 2010, sixteen players qualified for the NBA leaderboard while averaging more than 20 points a game. In 2020, there were twenty-seven. We have been trained to regard a 20-point scorer as a star, but nearly every team has one.

In a supply and demand twist, the prototypical star for the current era—a perimeter player who can shoot, dribble, score in isolation, and defend enough to stay on the court—has become common-place to the point of disposability. If you cannot

UNICORNS

Very tall guys who can kinda shoot or dribble are categorized as unicorns. The three players who were first pinpointed as belonging to the phenotype were Joel Embiid, Karl-Anthony Towns, and Kristaps Porziņģis (who adopted Unicorn as his nickname). While initially cute, the term soon became overused. It is now used as a lazy draft-day shorthand for prospects like Mo Bamba, who was drafted by the Magic because he exists at the vector of long arms, very tall, and "can kinda shoot." Pundits who value creativity would be wise to compare players to different cryptids like cockatrices, centaurs, electric eels, and harpies.

But the NBA's true unicorns are superstars. In comparison to sports like baseball or football, the small number of athletes on the court in basketball

MYTHICAL CREATURES

Relatively common.   Make-believe.

A rings counter.   A pleasant tweeter.

An honest politician.   A funny therapist.

A lazy biohacker.   A chill billionaire.

A basketball unicorn.   A sober raver.

An Asian rapper.   Bigfoot.

A troll.   A dragon.

A young deadhead.   A unicorn.

find a Jaylen Brown or Devin Booker, settling for a Dillon Brooks, Terrence Ross, Shake Milton, Patty Mills, or Bogdan Bogdanović might get the job done decently on most nights. On the other hand, there is no substitute for James Harden, Giannis Antetokounmpo, or Nikola Jokić—otherwise known as a blessing of unicorns.

UNITASKERS

A unitasker is a player with one skill. It is the reason they are in the NBA and not cloaked in the lovely pink uniforms of Serbia's KK Mega Bemax. Vague categorical breakdowns are as follows: scorer, ball-handler, shooter, and defensive specialist. If a nation's values are reflected in how it spends its budget, the salaries dedicated to unitaskers indicate the priorities of not only individual teams but the entire league as well.

The nineties were an idyllic period for the unitasker. No one could play basketball and chew gum at the same time. There were guards like Mark Jackson, who acted as a bossy offensive steward in New York, Los Angeles, and Indiana. There were defensive ogres like P. J. Brown of the Heat and Popeye Jones of the Raptors. There were gunners like Reggie Miller, Wesley Person, and Tracy Murray, who simply could not be bothered to do shit besides chuck up shots. To this day, no one understands the role of Hot Rod Williams, who posted 8 points and 8.3 rebounds in a whopping 31.4 minutes a game while starting for the 1997 Suns. Why was he there? What was he doing? Archaeologists have dug up amethyst tablets inscribed with box scores from the Mazatzal Mountains in hopes of deciphering the secrets that Cotton Fitzsimmons carried to his arid tomb, but no one knows.

As time went on, some unitasker positions were folded into other jobs. Scorer and distributor roles that were once independent backcourt slots melded into positionless initiator hybrids. Others vanished from the fossil record like megafauna when humans scraped their canoes ashore upon the beachstones of

a new continent. Perimeter defensive players were required to shoot from deep—thereby turning into 3-and-D instruments—or made obsolete by their coagulative effect on offensive spacing. By the end of the 2010s, only a handful of those endangered critters remained as reserves, like body-snatchers André Roberson and Kris Dunn. The brawny Charles Oakley–style power forward met the same fate. In the modern NBA, every center has to be credible defensively and either a hyper-efficient dunker or enough of a shooter to pull opposing big men out of the paint. There is no featured role left for feral bigs like Enes Kanter, Nikola Peković, or Greg Monroe.

The fetishization of 3-pointers during the late 2010s propped up the market for unitasker shooters. Snipers like Kyle Korver were lethal weapons, but even lower-caliber gunners like Carlos Delfino, Jodie Meeks, and Marcus Thornton managed to stick around. As the modern cliché goes, you can never have too much shooting. JJ Redick, who once claimed to have seen a human caged in the back of a New York car service vehicle, has been a respected modern unitasker. Despite his lack of defense, ball-handling, or ability to thwart rideshare-based child trafficking rings, a career 3-point percentage over 40 percent contorts defenses so effectively that his team can run actions without any threat of Redick's defender leaving him.

But even unitasker shooters are endangered. With bricklayers largely ousted from the league, shooting is no longer a rare commodity. If most power forwards and many centers can shoot, why dedicate minutes to a player who is incapable of bringing the ball up the floor or targeted for attacks? The bar has been raised for young specialists like Davis Bertans, Joe Harris, Duncan Robinson, and Landry "Waluigi" Shamet. In order to thrive, they must either improve at other elements of the game or be such outliers from beyond the arc that their offensive impact cannot be replicated by any ordinary multitasker.

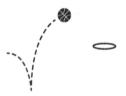

UNITASKERS

TAKES UP VALUABLE SPACE ⟶ *USEFUL*

Reggie Miller.
Pasta machines.
Sushi mats.
Oyster knives.
Corkscrews.

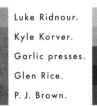

Luke Ridnour.
Kyle Korver.
Garlic presses.
Glen Rice.
P. J. Brown.

JJ Redick.
Mark Jackson.
Pizza cutters.
Ömer Aşık.
Davis Bertans.

Tristan Thompson.
Landry Shamet.
Lemon zesters.
Popeye Jones.
Duncan Robinson.

Greg Monroe.
Pizza wheels.
Robin Lopez.
Salad spinners.
Andre Miller.

Exactly the same. Not the same at all.

Adam Morrison.
Andray Blatche.
Antawn Jamison.
Cole Aldrich.
Eddie Van Halen.
Emeka Okafor.
Evan Turner.
Gus Van Sant.
Hasheem Thabeet.
Jae Crowder.

James Van Der Beek.
Jayson Williams.
Jean-Claude Van Damme.
Joel Pryzbilla.
Jordan Hill.
Kenneth Faried.
Kevin Knox.
Lauri Markkanen.
Ludvig van Beethoven.
Luis Scola.

Martin Van Buren.
Marvin Williams.
Maurice Taylor.
Nenê.
Nick Collison.
Nick Van Exel.
Nikoloz Tskitishvili.
RJ Barrett.
Rui Hachimura.
Serge Ibaka.

Steven Van Zandt.
Tim Thomas.
Townes Van Zandt.
Troy Murphy.
Van Morrison.
Vincent Van Gogh.
Vladimir Radmanović.
Wally Szczerbiak.
Yi Jianlian.
Zach Randolph.

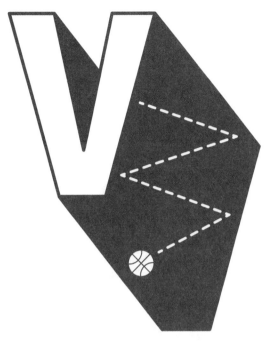

chipped in 8.5 rebounds. He was a stretch power forward before they were socially acceptable, and teams were maniacally driven to use him as a wing (in a few early 2000s, mutant Bucks lineups, Van Horn could have been considered the team's shooting guard). He timed out as a useful role player.

Van Horn was pale, gaunt, and emanated an anxious innocence, in part because he was mistakenly accused of practicing Mormonism after playing at the University of Utah. Bison Dele (then known as Brian Williams) suggested that Van Horn's race earned favorable calls from the officials and the support of Caucasian fans. "If he wasn't the Great White Hope, they would have ejected his butt," Williams said, after a game. He described him as a player "who carries the weight of every guy who plays with four knee guards and glasses on him."

VANVLEET, FRED

Sixty lads are scooped up in the yearly draft, and the statistical probability of guys who will become superstars craters after the first few picks in the lottery. The longest shots are players whose names went uncalled. Notable ballers who entered the league as undrafted free agents include Ben Wallace, John Starks, Wesley Matthews, David Wesley, Christian Wood, Jeremy Lin, and Avery Johnson.

During the 2019 draft, Luguentz Dort, a brolic shooting guard from Arizona State, went neglected in the Barclays Center green room. "I was sad," he told FiveThirtyEight. "It's a dream of every player to walk across, shake the commissioner's hand and put a hat on." The chapeau-less North Montreal native signed with the Thunder on a two-way contract—an arrangement where a fringe player can spend 45 days with an NBA team and the rest of the season in the developmental league—but became a starter midway through his rookie campaign. During the 2020 first round series between Oklahoma City and Houston, Dort covered James Harden like poutine gravy on fries and became the first undrafted rookie to score 30 points in a Game 7.

VAN HORN, KEITH

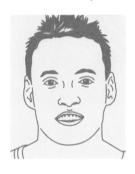

Any player over 6-foot-6 can be compared to Keith Van Horn. He was highly regarded prospect, moderately successful, and has been swept into the dustbin of history. Van Horn was tall (but not huge), active (but not a spring-loaded snake in a box), and could shoot well for a forward (but it was the 1990s). Over a career in which he played for five teams, his field-goal percentage, 3-point percentage, and efficiency were roughly league average. Van Horn is basketball's Everyman.

After four years at the University of Utah, Van Horn was selected by Philadelphia with the second overall pick in the 1997 NBA Draft and quickly shipped to New Jersey in an eight-player deal. A 6-foot-10 shooter, Van Horn had the proper trappings of a future star. In his second season, he finished fifth in the NBA in scoring at 21.8 points per game and

NAPOLEON COMPLEXES

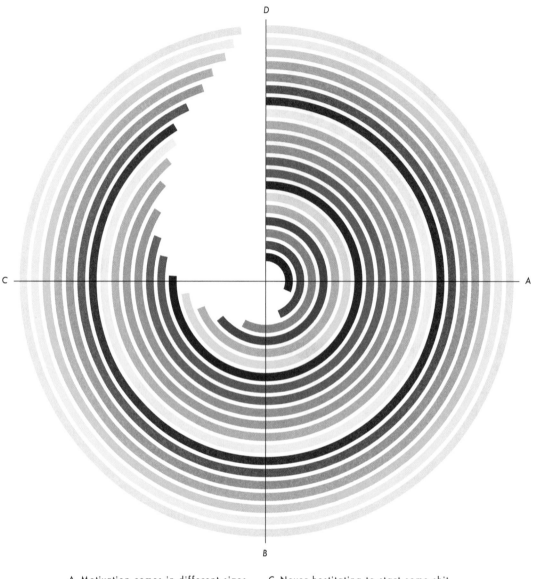

A. Motivation comes in different sizes. C. Never hestitating to start some shit.

B. The most paranoid one in the room. D. Satisfied only with world domination.

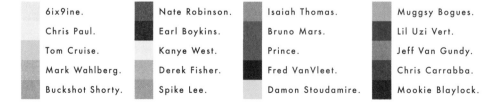

6ix9ine.

Chris Paul.

Tom Cruise.

Mark Wahlberg.

Buckshot Shorty.

Nate Robinson.

Earl Boykins.

Kanye West.

Derek Fisher.

Spike Lee.

Isaiah Thomas.

Bruno Mars.

Prince.

Fred VanVleet.

Damon Stoudamire.

Muggsy Bogues.

Lil Uzi Vert.

Jeff Van Gundy.

Chris Carrabba.

Mookie Blaylock.

The league's finest undrafted specimen at the moment is diminutive noble Fred VanVleet, who "might be 6-2 with the right pair of shoes on," as he phrased it. Stocky, bushy-bearded, and a convincing doppelgänger for Toronto mascot Drake, the combo guard was snubbed coming out of Wichita State. "I had a chance to get drafted but they was talking about putting me in the D-League for two to three years," VanVleet told his friends at a post-draft soiree. "Slaving away for $20,000, $10,000 a year. I turned those down. I bet on myself." Before the 2021 season, his long odds paid off: he inked a deal to stay with the Raptors on a four-year, $85 million contract.

The feisty runt is a knockdown shooter from deep who excels at duties that are invisible in conventional box scores: his assists disproportionately generate 3-pointers, he has oddly strong hands which can pry the ball from the clutches of big men, and he is a thistle of a defender who clings to the bodies of perimeter scorers. In Game 6 of the 2019 Finals, VanVleet scored 22 points—with 12 coming in the fourth quarter—as the Raptors usurped the Warriors as champions. "Freddie's [an] ice-water-in-his-veins type of guy," said coach Nick Nurse of the little royal.

VERTICAL SPACERS

Spacing usually refers to how personnel are spread across the floor to stretch the defense out like saltwater taffy. But some players apply pressure upward instead of outward. Known as vertical spacers, they are frontcourt threats who possess a rare combination of quickness, coordination, and bounciness that allows them to smash home lobs fluttering a dozen feet above sea level.

Despite the scarcity of these traits, such players are viewed as menial jammers because they rely on passes tossed by teammates. The term "vertical spacer" acknowledges the value of their skill and how a dangerous lob-catcher rolling toward the basket collapses defenses. The list of the most efficient scorers in NBA history is clogged by modern centers like Mitchell Robinson, Tyson Chandler, Rudy Gobert,

Clint Capela, and DeAndre Jordan. The alley-oop dunk, once an act of showmanship, has been weaponized as a nerd-approved, high-percentage shot.

One of the first vertical spacers was Theophalus Ratliff. Over sixteen injury-prone seasons, he posted the second-highest block percentage in NBA history, trailing only Shawn Bradley. "Theo's the most graceful, most artistic shot-blocker there is," said Philadelphia teammate Todd MacCulloch. Alongside Allen Iverson on the Finals-bound 2001 Sixers, Ratliff gave the team's constipated offense a pick-and-roll threat who could hammer down the Answer's lobs. The trio of a ball-dominant guard, a vertical spacer, and a stretch power forward in Toni Kukoč appeared to have stepped out of a time machine wearing Yeezys. Lineups with Iverson, Ratliff, and Kukoč outscored opponents by 11.5 points per 100 possession until the Sixers traded the non-cornrowed members to Atlanta for Dikembe Mutumbo.

DeAndre Jordan was a hulking second-round draft pick who rose from obscurity to become the center for the Clippers during the Lob City era. When setting screens for point guard Chris Paul, Jordan would seldom bother making physical contact with the defensive player—a refutation of the traditional purpose of a pick—but would create enough of an obstacle that the opposing center was required to momentarily hedge against a Paul jumper or drive. That window was enough for Jordan, who could take a few steps, leap, and cram in an alley-oop that drifted over the heads of planted defenders. This sequence of events led to one of the most savage dunks of all time: Jordan caught a lob from Paul with one hand, cocked it back, and yammed on Brandon Knight so powerfully that the guard slammed to the floor and lay prone for several seconds.

In 2015, Jordan was involved in a free agency fiasco that included endless social media emojis, a chair barricading a door, and, allegedly, the owner of the Mavericks driving around looking for him. In the incident, the center was allegedly on the cusp of signing with Dallas until a Los Angeles convoy including owner Steve Ballmer, coach Doc Rivers, Blake Griffin, and Paul arrived at Jordan's Houston home and refused to leave until he re-signed with the Clippers at midnight. Finally, appreciation for the vertical spacer.

WADE, DWYANE

Welcome to Miami-Wade County. Your introduction might include a knee to the groin or an elbow to the sternum. For those who visited South Florida, Dwyane Wade's reign as one of history's greatest two-way guards was not a period of joy or enlightenment. It was a place of agony. The twelve-time All-Star (thirteen, if we're counting his "special roster addition" retirement gift) did not have the sparkle of a Steve Nash, the craftsmanship of a Chris Paul, or the peculiarity of a Yao Ming. His most identifiable quality was nastiness.

Wade, the god of war, cast in molten steel. Nicknamed Flash, he was fast and strong, with long arms and pogostick hops that helped him arrive at his destination ahead of schedule and at an unexpected elevation—especially for a 6-foot-4 perimeter player. His posterizing one-handed dunks had the abrupt finality of flash knockdowns from a middleweight: a curling dive into the lane and then he was standing above you, mugging at the crowd and yanking the Heat logo on his jersey. He was named to three NBA All-Defensive teams, regularly among the league leaders in steals, and perhaps the best guard-size shot-blocker ever.

The Chicago native was a lauded prospect after two seasons at Marquette University but overshadowed by LeBron James and Carmelo Anthony. "He had a horrible workout," said Heat president Pat Riley, who selected Wade with the fifth pick in 2003. "We still drafted him." In his second season, Wade blossomed into a star; by his third, he was named Finals MVP after averaging 34.7 points and 16.1 free throws per game in a victory over the Mavericks. He led the league in scoring in 2009 and twice finished within the top 5 in MVP voting. Wade was the definition of a franchise player. And then LeBron arrived.

When Wade was joined in Miami by James and Chris Bosh before the 2011 season, the media huffed the bellows on the Heat's power struggle. Unlike other stars who knelt before the King—like Kevin Love or even Anthony Davis—Wade was the one who had a championship ring. And it was his Will Smith–approved city. Yet he was no fool. "It was probably one of the hardest things I had to do in sports was to, in a sense, take a step back," said Wade, who settled more comfortably into Robin leggings after being slowed by chronic knee injuries. "I felt that it had to come from nobody but me, to say, 'Go ahead, man. You're the best player in the world. We'll follow your lead.' Once I said that, I thought he kind of exhaled a little bit."

After retirement, Wade has remained a public figure, in part due to his marriage to Gabrielle Union, the actress who appeared in films like *Bring It On* and *Bad Boys 2*. The couple has a trans daughter and, despite ignorant sniping from rapper Lil Boosie, Wade has been a vocal ally. "My job as a father is to facilitate their lives and to support them and to be behind them in whatever they want to do," he told *Variety*. For residents, Wade County is a wonderful place.

WALKING BUCKETS

Players who possess a scorer's toolbox are described as walking buckets. While occasionally shortened to simply "a bucket," the "walking" element conveys that the ability to massage balls into the hoop is as effortless as breathing air. Walking buckets include Devin Booker, C J McCollum, Jamal Crawford, Ben Gordon, and Tyler Herro. In a Southern-fried recipe, Jordan Crawford, a shot-happy combo guard for the Pelicans, was nicknamed Instant Grits by teammate DeMarcus Cousins. Similar prototypes are movable

vats, ambulatory basins, self-propelled casks, mobile containment units, wandering bins, roving kettles, and prom kings.

The term "volume scorer" sounds benign, but has cancerous implications for a portable canister. It is a descriptor for gunners who rack up points by taking a shitload of shots, not necessarily by making many of them. Infamous volume scorers have included Jerry Stackhouse, Richard Hamilton, Al Harrington, Michael Beasley, and Jordan Clarkson (although he has shed the label in recent years). Superstars like Allen Iverson, Kobe Bryant, and Russell Westbrook have been dinged with the tag too.

A notorious culprit was Monta Ellis, the mercury-quick shooting guard who led the league in minutes per game for Golden State from 2010 to 2011. While Ellis averaged 24.7 points per game over those two seasons, he posted below-average efficiency in all but one season of his twelve-year career. "To his credit, he's a pretty good player," said his former coach, Don Nelson. "When I had him, all he wanted to do, little selfish bastard, was to shoot every time. And never pass."

When Bradley Beal was a child in St. Louis, the rapper Nelly used to walk him to school. Today, he is one of the current NBA's foremost nomadic urns. As a member of the Wizards, the shooting guard developed from a complementary gunner into a one-man offensive stormfront with the ability to lead the league in scoring. He has a gorgeous jumper, is lethal in the midrange, and creates space with jittering footwork, but has improved at scoring around the hoop, drawing more fouls, and acting as a primary playmaker. Yet walking bucket-hood does not guarantee success, even if it does not come at the expense of it. When Beal was asked if he was frustrated by Washington's lack of winning, he replied, "Is the sky blue?"

WALL, JOHN

Even if John Wall never fully recovers from two Achilles injuries—the second of which was suffered at home while rehabbing from surgery for the first—he has one irrefutable claim: the greatest high school "mixtape" ever. The 2009 video, posted by *Hoopmixtape*, was four minutes of jittery shammgods, look-away passes, tomahawk dunks, and slo-mo blocks in which the guard from Raleigh seemed to hover in midair before spiking shots into gymnasium bleachers.

After a season at Kentucky, Wall was selected by Washington with the top pick in the 2010 draft. He showed the same iridescent talent from the viral reel: trampoline ups, spinning 360-degree layups, slick drop-off passes, and AND1 ball-handling. The 6-foot-4 guard is an undisputed alpha, crouched and growling, with beads of sweat dripping from his thick beard. Wall has been named to five All-Star teams and averaged 19.0 points and 9.2 assists through an injury-marred career with the Wizards and Rockets. He is known as a late-night socializer who has unsubtly broadcast associations with the Bloods by twisting his fingers into gang signs during games and brandishing a red bandana in a video recorded in Brooklyn during the pandemic.

WALLACE, BEN

A four-time Defensive Player of the Year and the ideological mainspring for a Pistons team that won the championship in 2004, Ben Wallace suffers from underappreciation. He stands at the intersection of reputational erosion: a lack of respect for defensive ingenuity, the evolving center position in recent years, and an unspoken agreement to pretend that early- to mid-2000s NBA basketball never happened.

With his shrubby poof of hair corralled by a headband and a physique hewed from marble, Wallace had an oversized intimidation factor for a player once considered too small to play center. Though he is listed at 6-foot-9, most estimates shrink him a few inches. His greatness is attributed to toughness and energy that resembled a one-man melee, but praise for those qualities obscures his craftsmanship. While Wallace was famed for possessing big Tasmanian Devil energy, the cerebral and intuitive elements of his game caused just as much havoc.

Wallace was a master of the game-within-the-game, the tiny battles with parries and thrusts that are almost imperceptible. On one play, he used his tank-like torso to prevent centers from bullying their way to the cup. On the next, he relied on quickness

to front the post. He was adept at shifting his center of gravity to "pull the chair" on aggressive mooks, leaving them stumbling backward into vapor like drunken fools.

Wallace led the NBA in rebounding twice. He racked up both blocks and steals, placing among the league's top 10 in both categories for multiple seasons. Wallace could guard his own man, slide over to snuff out dribble penetration, and recover to devour a rebound. It felt as if he occupied three places at once. "There's never been a player in our era that can impact the game like Ben does defensively," Pistons coach Flip Saunders told the Associated Press. "He can guard five guys on the floor—and sometimes he does it on one play."

Wallace was born in White Hall, a town of fewer than a thousand Alabamans whose claim to fame is coining the name and iconography for what would become the Black Panther Party. He was the youngest of eight boys and has credited his rebounding tenacity to a childhood spent fighting for a chance to touch the ball. "I was under the impression that everybody went out and pursued the basketball like that," he told *Sports Illustrated*. "But I guess not."

After earning enough money as a barber to attend a basketball camp hosted by Charles Oakley, Wallace was challenged to a game of one-on-one by the legendary Knicks enforcer. According to mythology, Oakley battered him bloody but the teen never quit. "I was impressed," Oakley said later. "I could see the fire in him." He became Wallace's guardian angel, helping him get into Cuyahoga Community College and then ushering him over to his own alma mater, Virginia Union University. To date, Wallace and Oakley are the only two notable NBA players who attended the historically Black school.

After earning modest playing time in Washington and Orlando, Wallace found a home in the Motor City. As the Bad Boys 2 put together a wealth of stoppers—Chauncey Billups, Rasheed Wallace, the spindly, calf-like Tayshaun Prince—he became the backbone of a historically stingy defense. His brawny fluidity allowed Detroit to nonchalantly switch high screens, leaving him to cover agile perimeter players without compromising the system. Back then, protecting the paint was how great teams won. To some degree, Wallace deserves the same credit for the Pistons' success that Steph Curry received when the imbalance swung in the other direction in the 2010s.

In the 2004 Finals, the Pistons squared off against a Lakers team that supplemented Shaquille O'Neal and Kobe Bryant with ring-chasing vets Karl Malone and Gary Payton. While O'Neal put up impressive numbers of 26.6 points and 10.8 rebounds on 63 percent shooting, Wallace was tasked with defending the mall cop by himself. "It wasn't never my intention to go out here and I'ma shut Shaq down," Wallace said. "That's impossible. . . . The fact that I was able to play him straight-up and still able to help out the rest of my team—it sent a message to the rest of my guys. Ain't no excuses now."

WALLACE, RASHEED

Blessed with tantalizing abilities, Rasheed Wallace is viewed as a volatile malcontent whose potential was sunk by inconsistent effort and a flinty attitude. While the 6-foot-10 savant made four All-Star teams and won a championship in 2004, his sixteen-year career was peppered by run-ins with the media, law enforcement, coaches, and referees. His volcanic personality may not jibe with our perception of a loafer—but it is familiar to the way most of us regard employment: occasionally inspired, often lazy, more loyal to coworkers than management, preoccupied with daily indignities, there to get paid. "As long as somebody 'CTC' at the end of the day I'm with them," Wallace said. "For all you that don't know what 'CTC' means, that's 'Cut the Check.'"

The best basketball prospect from Philadelphia since Wilt Chamberlain, Wallace was named *USA Today*'s High School Player of the Year in 1993. By the time he reached his prime, he was capable of playing both power forward and center positions, operating from the block, and shooting 3s. Although Wallace never reached arbitrary big man yardsticks of 20 points and 10 rebounds per game, his teams in Portland and Detroit were superior when he stalked the hardwood.

"This guy is a genius," said Chauncey Billups, who was teammates with Wallace on two Pistons teams that went to the Finals. "Sheed will just walk in the door and blow you away," he wrote in the *Players' Tribune*. "He'll literally be predicting, perfectly, where the play is going—every time."

Wallace had a gray ring of hair on the back of his head, a Cossack dancer's footwork, and, reportedly, a 7-foot-4 wingspan. When he got the ball in the post, he would initiate contact with the defender by arching his shoulders as if squeezing into an undersized suit jacket. What he did from there was anyone's guess: unblockable turnaround jumpers in either direction, step-throughs into finger-rolls, lurching shot-puts. His signature finish featured one long arm extending to dunk the ball and his legs spread wide—while spiking a lob on the break, he looked like a flying A-frame house with a prominent tuft of armpit hair.

As his career unfurled, Wallace grew less enamored of shots near the basket. The paint at the far end of the court was, after all, farther for him to jog. He dunked less and trips to the foul line plunged. By the end of his career, he was used as a tubby stretch 5, swapping out long 2s and midrange jumpers in exchange for 3s. It was not an ideal role for a former superstar who shot only 29 percent from deep over two drearily amusing seasons in Boston and New York. "Sheed has an apathy problem," Bill Simmons wrote in a column for ESPN, while Wallace was on the Celtics. "His doughy, nonchalant shadow looms over every game."

Many have wondered what Wallace could have achieved with sustained, annoying, Kobe-like intensity. He played during a peak for power forwards, the transitory period around the swivel of the millennia that bridged the land of earth-stomping centers and today's lanky perimeter players. But even at his lower, rumbling frequency—with zaps of juice when necessary—it is easy to envision him as part of a 2020s powerhouse. Like Wallace, the prototypical modern center is an unselfish big man who protects the rim, rebounds, spaces the floor, and abuses mismatches in the paint. Maybe he was not the one with misplaced priorities.

Wallace had problems with authority. He got dinged with more technical fouls than anyone in the NBA for arguing, cursing, glaring, and heaving towels. "That's just the fire in me," he explained. Wallace's patented bit was bellowing "Ball don't lie!" when an opposing player missed a free throw after a foul call that he disagreed with. A notable incident was recounted in the book *Jail Blazers*. After being hit with a technical by since-tarnished referee Tim Donaghy, Wallace confronted him after the game in the Rose Garden loading dock. "I'm going to kick your ass, you motherfucker," he said, peeling off his jacket. Wallace was suspended for seven games but Joey Crawford, another referee, viewed the confrontation differently. "I wish Rasheed would have beat the hell out of him," he said.

Wallace was cynical about the levers of power, money, and race in professional sports. "I ain't no dumb-ass nigger," he was quoted as saying in the *Oregonian*. "I'm not like a whole bunch of these young boys out here who get caught up and captivated into the league. No. I see behind the lines. . . . I know the commissioner of this league makes more than three-quarters of the players. . . . It's as if we're just going to shut up, sign for the money, and do what they tell us." The interview ignited a firestorm in Portland, with Hall of Fame center Bill Walton describing Wallace as "a disgrace."

In an ominous sign, Wallace wore a shirt that read "FUCK WHAT YOU HEARD" at his introductory press conference in Portland. His relationship soured with the city's porcelain-fleshed beat writers, who carped about his 2002 arrest for misdemeanor marijuana possession and were *aghast* when he was seen laughing in the locker room following a loss.

After a victory in the first round of the 2003 playoffs, Wallace limited his answers at the podium to "both teams played hard" before finishing with "God bless and goodnight." Along with Allen Iverson's "practice" rant, LeBron James scampering out in a Thom Browne short-set, and coach Doc Rivers's heartfelt plea for equality in the COVID Bubble, the moment would enter basketball lore as one of the few postgame pressers anyone ever cared about. "I gave them a bit of Russell Simmons there at the end," Wallace told ESPN after retirement. "There was a lot of things said about us that wasn't true. Both teams did play hard, though—it was the truth!"

WEBBER, CHRIS

Few people have played basketball with the joy of young Chris Webber. At the University of Michigan, he was a huge and coordinated ham whose behind-the-back passes, heart-melting smile, and exaggerated glowers had playful innocence. In an era of authoritarian coaches in sweater vests, the impertinence was electric. His shorts were billowing, he talked trash, he blared EPMD in the locker room. For a generation of early-nineties teens—now rap dads with mortgages and surrendering hairlines—Webber and his Fab Five Wolverine cohort upended college basketball like Wu-Tang Clan kicking over a bootlegger's table of unauthorized tapes. His cultural

impact would eventually include dating supermodel Tyra Banks and producing tracks for Nas.

For all of Webber's sparkle, the sport rarely granted him bright resolutions. Michigan lost twice in the NCAA championship game, and, against the University of North Carolina, he made a crucial late-game blunder by illegally calling a timeout his team did not have. His walk to the locker room was a vision of misery. The mistake seemed to haunt Webber, clabbering his warmth and sensitivity with the bite of shame. He was taken by the Magic with the top pick in the 1994 NBA Draft—birthing visions of a decades-long partnership with Shaquille O'Neal—but was dealt to Golden State for Anfernee Hardaway and three future first-round picks. "I thought it was the greatest trade in history," said Danny Ainge, speaking from the perspective of the Magic.

While Webber won Rookie of the Year, he did not have a harmonious relationship with coach Don Nelson. "He wanted to be Magic Johnson," said Gregg Popovich, who was an assistant coach for the team. "We wanted him to be more like Karl Malone." In a contractual snafu that now looks batshit insane, Webber's fifteen-year deal had an opt-out after only one season. He elected to become a restricted free agent and bullied Golden State into trading him to the Bullets (where he reunited with Michigan teammate Juwan Howard). After four years in Washington, Webber was traded again, this time to Sacramento.

With the Kings, Webber was empowered. The strength and 7-foot-4 wingspan were always there, but his exhilarating talents for showmanship were unlocked in coach Rick Adelman's up-tempo system. His exuberance returned. "Personality that magnetic is hard to find," said teammate Doug Christie. The Kings sprinted at the league's fastest pace and embraced an international sense of flair that was attributable to rotational imports like center Vlade Divac, sharp-shooter Peja Stojaković, and forward Hedo Türkoğlu. "Europeans don't have the close-mindedness Americans have," Webber said. "Plus, they're about having fun, twenty-four hours a day."

Over four consecutive All-Star seasons, he averaged 24.8 points, 10.6 rebounds, 4.7 assists, 1.5 steals, and 1.5 blocks, the type of stat-stuffing associated with toolsy bigs like Hakeem Olajuwon or DeMarcus Cousins. Despite Sacramento's success—and defensive ratings that were annually excellent—neither the Kings nor Webber could shake reputations for overreliance on finesse. "I don't like the playfulness,

the softness about us," he said. "We don't have that swagger. I feel like we're a prep school, and everybody else is a public school." In the second game of the 2003 Western Conference Semifinals, Webber ripped up his knee. He missed a year of action and was never the same.

"I could make the case [that] Webber was the best, overall talented player I ever played with," former teammate Tim Legler told *Bleacher Report* years later. "But he was never the driving force on a championship-caliber team." That may technically be true. But in 2002, the Kings won 61 games and boasted, statistically, the third-best offense and sixth-best defense. Up 3–2 in the Western Conference Finals against the Lakers, Sacramento lost Game 6 in a crushing, controversy-tainted manner: Los Angeles was awarded 27 free throws in the fourth quarter alone, with several coming on dubious calls. "I played one game in which, yes, something definitely smelled weird about the whole situation," Webber has said. "But I didn't think that was the NBA. I didn't think the league was purposely out to get me." Maybe it was, yet again, the unseen hand of fate.

WESTBROOK, RUSSELL

All spasm and crackle, Russell Westbrook is a menace to those who step too close, friend and foe alike. He behaves like a 6-foot-3 snarl of downed power lines. There is no doubting his effort or intentions, but he is the league's most reliable supplier of mayhem. He is a physically astonishing point guard who slashes through defenses, assaults the basket with psychotic zeal, and sprays passes in all directions while moving at a blur. There is a roiling intensity that flows through the South Los Angeles native, and his most common expressions are outraged scorn and celebratory scorn. For an MVP winner and nine-time All-Star, Westbrook has always been divisive—yet there is little debate the Brodie giveth and the Brodie taketh away.

After eleven seasons in Oklahoma City, Westbrook was the last man standing from an exquisite trio that included Kevin Durant and James Harden. He seemed to enjoy being the loyal martyr, and was rewarded with a princely contract and keys to a kingdom of his own. In turn, he led the NBA in points per game twice and total shots attempted three times, but posted a below-average

field-goal percentage every season of his career. He led the league in assists per game twice, but coughed up more total turnovers than any player on three occasions.

Westbrook's passion is undeniable, but sometimes to his own detriment. His eagerness to make amends for ill-advised shots leads to more ill-advised shots, and, in late-game situations, his lack of judiciousness has taken the ball out of the hands of teammates like Durant, Harden, and Paul George. "A lot of people say that I should've put him in his place," Durant said. "He's a player that you can't put in his place. He's a player with a big personality that you can't tame."

In 2017, Westbrook was named MVP after averaging a triple-double with points, rebounds, and assists. Though he was a guard, Oklahoma City funneled defensive rebounds in his direction in order to get jumpstart transition opportunities (the same tactic was later adopted to put Luka Dončić and Giannis Antetokounmpo's board numbers on steroids). He was the first to accomplish the feat since Oscar Robertson stacked up the base-10 qualifications in 1963. Over the next four seasons, Westbrook did it three more times, but, instead of receiving accolades, he was scolded for stat padding—even though the Thunder, Rockets, and Wizards all made the playoffs.

For Westbrook, this has been a career-long theme. He has always played with the same tunnel-vision dementedness, but the critical response seems arbitrary. "There used to be conversations if I was a ball hog," he said. "But now I lead the league in assists for the past three years or whatever it is, that's getting squashed out. So now the conversation is about shooting. Next year I'm going to become a better shooter. After that it'll be probably, fuck, my left foot is bigger than my right one. Who knows?"

WET NOODLES

Like a treasured Marcella Hazan recipe, wet noodles match the right pasta shape with the right type of sauce. They are gangly guys who play with semolina-based stringiness, wriggling into the lane like a twist of rotini or limply flopping in the manner of a band of tagliatelle. Typically guards and wings, wet noodles are more slitherer than slasher. They are

finesse players who are comfortable operating within the steaming marinara of a defense, weaving to the rack for layups or drawing contact like a ribbon of pappardelle adhering to a rusty coat of Bolognese. Meanwhile, lesser wet noodles have the clumpy blandness and undefined texture of an overcooked angel-hair mound. During the 2020 NBA Finals, singer Halsey used the description pejoratively. "Damn is it bringing me unbridled joy to watch Tyler Herro act like human fusilli," the Laker booster tweeted of the squirmy Heat rookie.

Prominent wet noodles include Kevin Martin, Josh Richardson, Mikal Bridges, and Shai Gilgeous-Alexander. In earlier years, Kevin Durant was at home in the bottomless pasta bar, but his increased reliance on long-range shooting, the dwindling effectiveness of scamming "rip-through" foul calls by swinging his linguine arms into defenders, and the authoritativeness of superstardom pulled him from the cloudy waters of the trattoria. Manu Ginóbili, whose Italian heritage has nothing to do with this comparison, was the apex fettuccine of his generation. Like any self-respecting *paisano*, he maneuvered the court with al dente perfection. Bouncy, elastic, and endlessly malleable, Ginóbili was just as tasty in a room temperature tuna salad or flicking off buttery parmesan from a skillet of cacio e pepe eaten over the sink.

Josh Howard was a 6-foot-7 whorl of damp cavatelli. Born in Winston-Salem to a teenage mother, he suffered from curved bones and needed his limbs broken and reset by doctors in order to walk. By the time he reached college, he had developed a reputation for brusque terseness and expressing skepticism toward authority figures (like basketball coaches).

As a member of winning Mavericks teams, Howard filled in negative space around franchise centerpiece Dirk Nowitzki by scoring off the dribble, locking down the perimeter, and volunteering for grimy chores that a German gigantor was unsuited to handle. "Josh is our juice and our engine," said coach Avery Johnson. "If he isn't going full steam ahead—and most of the time he is—we can break down." The Mavs had a full-course menu of talent, but Howard's job was serving up a starchy

WET NOODLES

1 2 3 4 5 6 7 8 9 10 11 12 13 14 15 16 17 18 19 20 21 22 23 24 25 26 27 28 29 30

Premium.   Utilitarian.   Ronzoni.

Acceptable.   Uneventful.   Floppy.

1. Brandon Ingram.	7. De'Aaron Fox.	13. Kevin Garnett.	19. Marcus Camby.	25. Stephen Curry.
2. Bucatini.	8. Fettucine.	14. Kevin Martin.	20. Mitchell Robinson.	26. Stringozzi.
3. Cannelloni.	9. Jamal Crawford.	15. Kristaps Porziņģis.	21. Pappardelle.	27. Tayshaun Prince.
4. Channing Frye.	10. Jaren Jackson Jr.	16. Linguine.	22. Reggie Miller.	28. Tyler Herro.
5. Corey Brewer.	11. Josh Howard.	17. Lonzo Ball..	23. Ricky Rubio.	29. Vermicelli.
6. Darius Miles.	12. Josh Richardson.	18. Manu Ginóbili	24. Scialatielli.	30. Will Barton.

amuse-bouche. "I was the party-starter," Howard told *Grantland*.

Among younger players, Brandon Ingram is the league's foremost rising wet noodle. Drafted by the Lakers and shipped to the Pelicans as part of the return haul for Anthony Davis, he is listed at 6-foot-7 with a 7-foot-3 wingspan. Even after four years in the league, his frame resembles a tube of bucatini and more than 30 percent of his career field-goal attempts have emerged from the thick ragu of the midrange. But Ingram's scoring average and efficiency have ticked annually upward, so far peaking at 23.8 points per game in 2020—a season in which he made the All-Star team and was named the NBA's Most Improved Vermicelli.

WINNING BIAS

When members of the Greatest Generation weren't eating fruit suspended in scalloped Jell-O molds, they were popularizing the phrase "winning isn't everything—it's the only thing." That reductionist perspective is unfortunately true. The all-consuming effects of winning—which grow stronger as levels of competition rise—make it the most tiresome and pernicious of all biases. If history's greatest players and teams are judged solely by titles, nuanced debate splinters into extremes. "Losing is losing," said Kobe Bryant, a sports patriot who wrapped his identity in Staples Center banners. "There aren't different degrees of losing. You either win a championship or you're shit. It's very black and white to me."

From the beginning, basketball has embraced the binaries of wins and losses, along with the absolutism of championships. Take, for example, Stone Age center Wilt Chamberlain, who led the league in scoring seven times, rebounding eleven times, and both field-goal percentage and minutes played nine times. In 1968, he led the NBA in total assists just for giggles. Yet his rival, Bill Russell—a defensive anchor who could accurately be described as Bam Adebayo without the ball-handling, passing, or

free-throw shooting—routinely tops him on lists of all-time greats. ESPN committed this atrocity, calling Russell "the greatest winner in basketball history" because his loaded Boston squad won eleven titles in an era with a single-digit number of teams.

One title can dramatically change the public perception of an athlete. Both Kevin Garnett and Dirk Nowitzki, for example, were viewed as fabulous players who lacked the cojones to win when it counted. The former won a grand total of two playoff series in twelve years with Minnesota. The latter was roasted as a marshmallowy choker after melting into a s'more during several postseason flameouts. But they finally tasted victory in their thirties, and the palate was cleansed. Both are seen as iron-willed victors and leaders of men. Similarly, while Kevin Durant's decision to join the Warriors was criticized, no one can take away his two Finals MVPs and the searing memory of him drilling daggers against LeBron James. Had Durant spent those three years nobly coming up short for the Wizards, he would likely have the same sense of bitterness and discontent—just without the hardware.

An underappreciated benefit to bringing home a title is the opportunity to leave the game with dignity. Players like Bryant, Nowitzki, and Dwyane Wade were allowed pre-retirement victory tours in a decrepit state, as their grateful franchises let them hobble around squinting through bifocals at standing ovations and forgetting the WiFi password on the team bus. We should all be allowed to exit so gracefully.

For players who consistently fail to win, the stain of losing is like an exit wound that grows ever darker and wider. Laypeople view it as a character flaw, indicative of a lack of heart, toughness, or wanting it enough. People with more smarts might suspect it is a basketball problem—the player does not shoot well enough, does not defend well enough, or simply is not good enough to carry a team to victory. While one guy cannot be expected to drag a team to glory without some help, it is worth wondering why certain great players are not predisposed to winning more games.

Karl-Anthony Towns, for example, was part of a winning team only once during his first six seasons

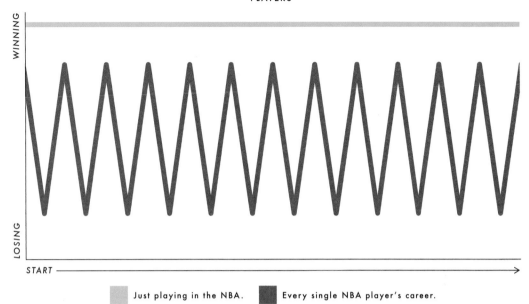

WINNING

LOSING

START

Just playing in the NBA.   Every single NBA player's career.

in Minnesota. Most years, they were wretched. He has posted bloated numbers in categories like points, rebounds, and blocks, but it has rarely corresponded with team success. Is that a Towns issue—or an organizational one? "I think we're still figuring out how to lose," teammate D'Angelo Russell said after the Wolves ate another L. "It sounds crazy, but the way you lose says a lot about the team. And I think, today, how we lost, was a good way to lose."

There are many all-time greats whose lack of a championship is a blemish on their permanent record. Patrick Ewing, Charles Barkley, Karl Malone, John Stockton, Chris Mullin, and Dominique Wilkins were members of the 1992 Dream Team who failed to win a ring. Superstars of the 2000s who never clutched the Larry O'Brien trophy like a champagne-soaked newborn include Allen Iverson, Tracy McGrady, and Chris Webber.

With fans and the media ruminating endlessly about the necessity of taking home a championship, it is natural that today's marquee players prioritize checking that box. In a tasty bit of irony, the player empowerment movement and the league's lack of parity were accelerated to their current states because NBA athletes were browbeaten into believing that winning is more important than money,

fame, or a comfortable lifestyle that does not include playing in June.

WOODSON, MIKE

Mike Woodson coached nine seasons in the NBA, in Atlanta and New York. Known for teams that played deliberately and limited turnovers, Woodson achieved his greatest success in 2013, when he helmed a 54-win Knicks squad and convinced Carmelo Anthony to "buy in." Woodson's Mr. Potato Head nature was exposed in early 2010, when he showed up to a Hawks game without eyebrows. He claimed that a barber had accidentally shorn one of them, so he had the other one shaved off to match.

W

hard," Riley told the *New York Times* of Van Gundy. "He understood the way I thought. He knew the philosophy has to be consistent. He was willing to parrot my voice." Doc Rivers and Mark Jackson, both of whom were Knicks point guards during Riley's tenure, also became head coaches with worldviews that closely mirrored that of *The Godfather*.

Elsewhere, Gregg Popovich's lineage of quiet fascism has marched from San Antonio to the farthest reaches of the league. Mike D'Antoni's up-tempo assault transformed the rhythm of the sport and drove slow-footed big men into the sea. We can even recognize Don Nelson's small-ball muta-tions, Stan Van Gundy's four-shooter lineups, Brad Stevens's inbounds sets, or Erik Spoelstra's and Nick Nurse's trapping zones when they are duplicated.

Coaches are inevitably blamed for a team's failures—and pay the price with their jobs—but as data-driven shot value and lineups have taken hold, the gap between an above-average coach and a below-average coach is more narrow than ever before. As overtly bad coaches are exiled from the bench, the collective quality of the league's 30 brainstems incrementally shudders upward. True innovation is mimicked. Everyone plucks from the same playbook of pick-and-rolls, pindowns, drag screens, dribble handoffs, isolation sets, and Iverson cuts. As much as we invest in categorizing certain coaches as Sun Tzu–esque tacticians and others as bumbling imbeciles, on-court talent prevails.

A subject that doesn't receive enough atten-tion is the NBA's lack of diversity among head coaches. The demographics don't reflect a league where roughly three-quarters of the players are Black. During the 2021 season, for example, only seven teams had Black coaches—with similarly inadequate representation in ownership and exec-utive ranks. With recent emphasis on hiring front office suits with backgrounds in analytics instead of on-court experience, only a handful of organizational decision-makers are Black. "These numbers are just disgraceful," National Basketball Players Association executive director Michele Roberts told *USA Today*. "It's not as if teams aren't uttering the right words. But the players are seeing it. I'm hearing people talk about both publicly and privately that these numbers don't make sense."

Xs AND Os

The NBA is often described as a copycat league, whatever that means. It is true that tactics that work for one team—and the type of personnel that pro-duces those results—are replicated elsewhere. After Golden State won several titles with car-bonated lineups that included a tiny necromancer in Stephen Curry, a deadeye shooter in Klay Thompson, and an undersized center in Draymond Green, Atlanta cribbed the blueprint for a less imposing con-struction of Trae Young, Kevin Huerter, and Omari Spellman. It did not go as swimmingly.

It is not difficult to contact-trace the virality of coaching orthodoxy. For example, Pat Riley's embrace of iron maiden physicality in New York was passed to his assistant Jeff Van Gundy, who in turn bequeathed it to future head coaches Steve Clifford, Tom Thibodeau, and Mike Malone. "He worked

YOKELS

In a sport sometimes referred to as "the city game," country bumpkins are peculiarities. Fishing or being into pickup trucks, though widely popular among all Americans, are deemed personality traits.

Karl Malone, one of the NBA's greatest players and most abrasive people, was a rube. The 1997 MVP, who played eighteen seasons for the Jazz and is the second all-time scorer in league history, owned a 72-foot-long, 34,000-pound eighteen-wheeler painted with a mural that depicted him overlooking a valley of coyotes. He took hunting trips through Idaho on horseback. The media was enamored by the idea that a 6-foot-9 basketball player was into redneck bullshit.

Reporters rarely mentioned that Malone fathered a child with a thirteen-year-old girl when he was a twenty-year-old star at Louisiana Tech University. While he was with the Lakers in the twilight of his career, he caused a rift when he told Kobe Bryant's wife that he was "hunting little Mexican girls." For good measure, Malone once elbowed Pistons star Isiah Thomas in the face so violently that Thomas required forty stitches. "I don't think I've seen anything as vicious and as intentional to a player," Thomas told the *Detroit News*. "When I got home my wife started crying."

Thankfully, not all hayseeds are as awful as Karl Malone. Camouflaged behind his "aw shucks" persona, lipper of tobacco, and Realtree waders he wore while sport-killing animals, Brad Miller was a stealthy offensive mastermind for the Bulls, Pacers, and Kings. At 6-foot-11 and woefully slow, he was one of the league's best midrange shooters, a deft passer, and remarkably efficient. Miller led all centers in assists several times. "I put him up there with Vlade [Divac] and Chris Webber as far as skilled guys, knowing how to play, making their teammates better," said Kings coach Rick Adelman.

A native of Kendallville, Indiana, Miller went undrafted out of Purdue. After he rose to quasi-stardom that included a couple of All-Star appearances, his backwater origins were chum for "fish out of water" profiles that juxtaposed him against his baggy-pantsed contemporaries. "His plan for the day includes no Cristal, zero clubs, and nary an opportunity to get one's freak on," read a *Sports Illustrated* profile. Miller retired to "focus on hunting" and filmed a show called *Country Boy Outdoors* for the Sportsman Channel. He lives in Sacramento and once brought DeMarcus Cousins frozen elk meat.

Chris Kaman, a yokel from Wyoming, Michigan, was what peak male performance looks like: 7 feet tall, red beard, receding hairline. By the end of his thirteen-year tenure, he resembled a craft beer enthusiast who was wraparound shades away from joining the Boogaloo Boys. The center was on the German basketball team in the 2008 Olympics, although his flimsy connection to the Vaterland was his great-grandparents. The Caveman had irresistible genitals that were on the receiving end of a nut punch from Chris Paul and a ballsack grope from Reggie Evans.

As a child, Kaman was misdiagnosed with ADHD, rather than what he later learned was an "anxious brain." In the NBA, he struggled with concentration, forgetting plays after timeouts and spacing on rotations. "He's a pretty bright guy," said Clippers coach Mike Dunleavy. "He can drift, and sometimes he doesn't exactly understand what you're saying." In 2014, Kamen filmed a web series called *Exploring*

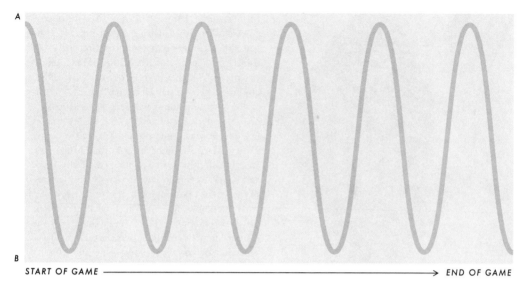

A. There's a fine line between a conscious hip-hop head and a Kid Rock expert.

B. Real men hunt, off-road, crush beers, and deliver pinpoint passes to Stojaković.

Kamen, in which he and his thirty-something friends have misadventures while trying to catch a blue marlin. The trailer shows Kamen picking his nose, putting a fish eyeball in his mouth, and giving his homeboy a titty-twister. In another scene, what appears to be a Roman candle is ignited while wedged in a man's ass crack. Welcome to God's country.

YOUNG, TRAE

Weaving among toenails of giants, Trae Young is an imp. He stands a shade over 6 feet, weighs 180 pounds soaking wet, and has the wingspan of a regular person. His hair is a damp wisp of cotton candy. "I was never the big leaper, the dunker, the long and athletic kid who looked the part of a traditional basketball star," Young said. "Truth be told I wasn't even considered a top guard coming out of my recruiting class."

Yet the point guard from Norman, Oklahoma, who grew up idolizing Steve Nash is a necromancer with the ball. He is at the forefront of a generation of Zoomers who internalized the wiles of Stephen Curry and James Harden: hoisting up shots from the hinterlands, dribbling between opponents' legs, lofting floaters, exaggerating every brush of contact, and powering a perimeter-oriented offense. At twenty-one, Young averaged an ungodly 29.6 points and 9.3 assists per game, while weaponizing his quickness and collapsible frailty to draw the third-most free throws per game. Young's special grift is whipping around a screen at the top of the arc and abruptly pulling up for a jumper that causes a chasing defender to bump him in the back ("That's not basketball," Nash gnashed while coaching against him).

Unlike other electrifying young talents, Young initially failed to deliver a jolt of success to the lowly Hawks. He was not individually to blame, exactly, but it had to be asked: could a notably poor defender sink an entire unit? Since his boyish frame was unlikely to balloon into swoll, Atlanta adapted the surrounding personnel to better conceal his vulnerabilities. With a medley of springy rebounders, shot-blockers, lob-catchers, and wing defenders, the Hawks emerged as a dark horse contender led by an evil gnome who tormented opponents and basked in an emerging role as the league's next shimmying villain.

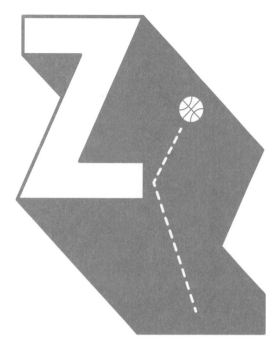

ZEN MASTER

Phil Jackson—known as the Zen Master—spent decades as one of basketball's most appealing figures: the consummate winner who dances to the beat of his own buffalo-hide drum. He was a tough role player on the Knicks' last championship squad in 1973, coach of eleven title-clinching Bulls and Lakers teams, and whisperer to Michael Jordan, Scottie Pippen, Kobe Bryant, and Shaquille O'Neal. He cultivated an image as a New Age seer who infused jock culture with Eastern mysticism, vision quests, and the liberating qualities of LSD. Jackson's methods were ripe for satire, but who could question the results of the coach with the most championships in NBA history? We are all one glug of peyote away from greatness.

Jackson was celebrated for introducing players to spirituality. He gave his charges books intended to convey life lessons. Pau Gasol received *2666*, the novel by Chilean author Roberto Bolaño; Derek Fisher got *Soul on Ice*, the autobiography of Black Panther Eldridge Cleaver; Metta World Peace was blessed with *Sacred Hoops: Spiritual Lessons of a Hardwood Warrior* by Phil Jackson.

Jackson's legacy is inseparable from the Triangle Offense, a system that is named after its base alignment of the center and two perimeter players. It supposedly rewards unselfishness, patience, and rhythm. "There's a mindframe to it, and that mindframe carries off the court," said Allan Houston, while an executive with the Knicks.

Despite the Triangle's success in Chicago and Los Angeles, pushback was inevitable. In the minds of doubters, two of the most stacked teams in NBA history could have won chips with plays scrawled on gin-damp napkins. While the Triangle's principles have been osmosed into contemporary basketball, it is not specifically run by any modern NBA team—in part because of its reliance on post-play and lack of emphasis on outside shooting. "People just have this attitude about the Triangle, like it's this pariah offense," Jackson told *Grantland*. "That's totally wrong. It just takes a little time."

For all of Jackson's charm, he did not age gracefully. He spoke out in favor of Arizona's Senate Bill 1070, legislation that codified racial profiling, and his comments about rap music, baggy clothing, and LeBron James's "posse" now sound, at best, insensitive. When Jackson was asked about his failures as an executive with the Knicks, he compared himself to another blithering truth-teller. "I kind of understand what Trump had to live with probably for his first three and a half years in office with the media," Jackson said, on Coby Karl's podcast, *The Curious Leader*." Truly, a man at peace with the world.

ZION

Three-and-D wings and other ready-mixed components are popular because they require little imagination to deploy. But cookie-cutter players are boring. Tools of the NBA's status quo do not push the sport to metastasize into exciting new forms. Mutants like Zion Williamson do. A dunking sensation who was selected first overall in the

2019 draft, the young forward presents a delicious conundrum that could end in glory or frustration.

The South Carolina schoolboy phenom is an industrial freezer with jet propulsion and a velvety touch around the rim. Though soft-spoken and equipped with a 100-gigawatt smile, Williamson drew comparisons to densely rectangular stars like Charles Barkley and Shaquille O'Neal while sledgehammering dunks at Duke University (a lawsuit alleged that his family took $400,000 before he attended the ivory tower of corruption). As a rookie on the Pelicans, the 6-foot-6, 285-pound brickhouse led the NBA in scoring within the restricted area and shot almost 60 percent from the floor. Grown adults cannot prevent the pushy child from getting to the rim, whether through the blunt trauma of his pottery kiln–shaped torso or by cartoonishly boing-ing a full human head above everyone else.

Despite being a historically unstoppable scorer for his age, Williamson does not gravitate toward any recognizable position. He has an ordinary wingspan and rarely shoots outside of the paint. He is an unremarkable rebounder who logs under one block and one steal a game. On defense, he can be a dawdler who shows up late to the action, like a fireman arriving to inspect the ruins of a warehouse that has already been hosed down. But after some trial and error, a eureka moment occurred when he was deployed as a paint-collapsing distributor like Giannis Antetokounmpo or Ben Simmons, a development that doubled his assists and gave structure to the Pelicans' offense attack.

Williamson came into the league as an unorthodox muffuletta wrapped in a shrimp po'boy. From a normie perspective, the best path seemed clear: he needed to get his ass in the gym, shed some baby fat, practice 3-pointers, and hone areas of coarseness to passable mediocrity. By that reading, he needed to fit our conventional understandings of roles and positionality, however inelegantly. Yet he did the opposite. Discovering new ways to utilize Williamson's singular talents could not only elevate his game, it may liberate other anomalous players in the future from being written off as square pegs in round positional holes. Let Zion embrace his strange greatness and, as if playing God, create a new universe around him.

ZOOMERS

When LeBron James retires—as he presumably will, when the glowing reactor embedded in his torso eventually dims—it will be declared that he is leaving the NBA in good hands. There will be new MVPs and champions. Players will get faster, stronger, and more skilled, as they always do. The sport will continue to grow, with athletes pouring in from around the globe, digital subscriptions surging, and the league contemplating which cities are for expansion franchises. Games will be watched. Sneakers will be sold. Tickets will be bought. Billions will be made. The business model is not in jeopardy.

But a shift has undeniably occurred over the last quarter-century, and those gears are not going to spin in reverse. Players are better than they have ever been, and that trend will continue. The NBA has never been as global or diverse, with increased fluidity in positions and roles. Sports science has improved to the point where few injuries are truly career-threatening and greater attention is being paid to mileage, nutrition, and sleep.

Athletes exert more control over where they spend their careers. They have learned to tap into the economic distributaries that flow from their talent pool, are able to communicate with the public without the filtration system of the media, and have newfound confidence as voices for societal change.

Fans have gotten smarter. Access to streaming video and a treasury of publicly available data has demystified the sport in ways that not everyone is comfortable with, but there is a growing rejection of the idea that success on the basketball court is an indictment of a man's character. Fissures of race and class have not been paved over, but there is less demonization or exotification of players than there used to be.

The future is an open court, with a capable ball-handler pushing the rock and teammates fanning out in front of him. "The older generation, they want to judge," said Allen Iverson. "Older people concentrate on critiquing. And young people, I think they idolize and appreciate the gift that I give them by my survival."

THE WHOLE FUTURE

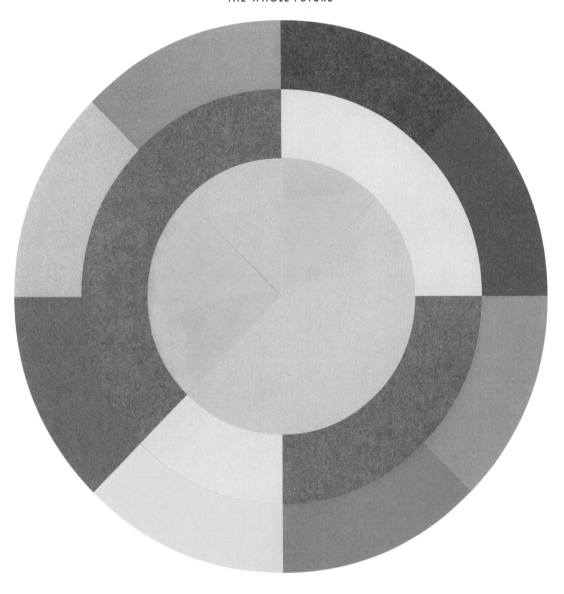

 Kinda sad.    Not mandatory.

Exciting.   Necessary.

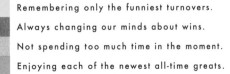

Letting go of the missed game-winners.   Remembering only the funniest turnovers.

Forgiving the picks who did their best.   Always changing our minds about wins.

Finding even better ways to score points.   Not spending too much time in the moment.

Embellishing all the dunks of the past.   Enjoying each of the newest all-time greats.

THANK-YOU

Samantha Weiner
Diane Shaw
Mike Richards
Daniel Kirschen
Desus Nice
Lucian Dickson
Do Kim
Jordan Redaelli
Pablo Torre
Kelefa Sanneh
Pascal Spengemann
Cat Marnell
Adam Abdalla
Mills Moran
David Jacoby

Jason Concepcion
Sarah Buck
Mina Kimes
Sarah Silverman
Joey Rhyu
Mary H.K. Choi
Judnick Mayard
Joe Cole
Hillary Taymour
Jason Nocito
Justin Montag
Bill Simmons
Chris Ryan
Shea Serrano

SPECIAL THANK-YOU

April Swanson
Luka Swanson Kuo
The Detrick family
The Le-Tan Family
Otto & Alpha

Editor: Samantha Weiner
Designer: Diane Shaw
Managing Editor: Mike Richards
Production Manager: Larry Pekarek

Library of Congress Control Number: 2021932531

ISBN: 978-1-4197-5482-1
eISBN: 978-1-64700-300-5

Printed and bound in the United States
10 9 8 7 6 5 4 3 2 1

Abrams Image books are available at special discounts
when purchased in quantity for premiums and
promotions as well as fundraising or educational use.
Special editions can also be created to specification.
For details, contact specialsales@abramsbooks.com
or the address below.

Abrams Image® is a registered trademark of
Harry N. Abrams, Inc.

ABRAMS The Art of Books
195 Broadway, New York, NY 10007
abramsbooks.com

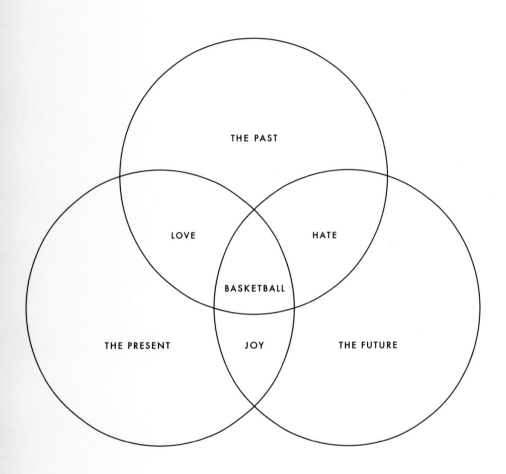